Rural Hours

Harriet Baker has written for the *London Review of Books*, the *Paris Review*, the *New Statesman*, the *TLS*, *Apollo* and *frieze*. She read English at Oxford and holds a PhD from Queen Mary, University of London. In 2018, she was awarded the Biographers' Club Tony Lothian Prize. She lives in Bristol.

Rural Hours

The Country Lives of Virginia Woolf, Sylvia Townsend Warner and Rosamond Lehmann

HARRIET BAKER

ALLEN LANE
an imprint of
PENGUIN BOOKS

ALLEN LANE

UK | USA | Canada | Ireland | Australia
India | New Zealand | South Africa

Penguin Books is part of the Penguin Random House group of companies
whose addresses can be found at global.penguinrandomhouse.com.

First published in Great Britain by Allen Lane 2024

006

Set in 12/14.75pt Dante MT Std
Typeset by Jouve (UK), Milton Keynes
Printed and bound in Great Britain by Clays Ltd, Elcograf S.p.A.

The authorized representative in the EEA is Penguin Random House Ireland,
Morrison Chambers, 32 Nassau Street, Dublin D02 YH68

A CIP catalogue record for this book is available from the British Library

ISBN: 978–0–241–54051–0

www.greenpenguin.co.uk

Penguin Random House is committed to a
sustainable future for our business, our readers
and our planet. This book is made from Forest
Stewardship Council® certified paper.

For Mike, and Manny

Contents

And the country is lovelier & lovelier; & more friendly, still with great empty spaces, where I want to walk, alone, & come to terms with my own head. Another book? What? Merciful to be free . . .

Virginia Woolf, 24 March 1932

In the country

On a hot day in July 1922, Sylvia Townsend Warner visited the cheap section of Whiteleys department store in Bayswater, where she bought a Bartholomew map of Essex. She was drawn, she wrote, to 'the blue creeks, the wide expanses of green for marsh, the extraordinary Essex place names'. A few days later, map in hand and wearing a thin cotton dress, she took a train from Fenchurch Street to Shoeburyness, then a bus to Great Wakering, before continuing towards the River Roach on foot. Her map was soon redundant as she stepped off the dusty elm-lined roads, picking her way between winding, occasionally impassable creeks. Before her, the marsh glowed with luminous, earthy colours, spreading flatly into the distance beneath a veil of mist. Underfoot, it smelled tangy and salty after the night's rain.

Looking out over the marsh, Sylvia was caught between land and sea. A sail glided past; time stilled. 'I stood there for a long time, watching the slow pushing water' and 'letting my mind drift with the tidal water', she wrote. Later, during a thunderstorm, she sought shelter in a cattle-shed, where she was greeted by a group of farm labourers. One of the men took her home to his wife, who undressed her, dried her clothes, and gave her tea. Sylvia returned to London the following day, wearing a pair of rough woollen knickers belonging to the couple's daughter. But her transformation was complete. Passionately, she declared the marsh 'my new landscape'.

The next time Sylvia went to Essex, she stayed for a month, renting a room in a farmer's cottage in St Lawrence, about two hours' walk from Southminster. She returned to London only occasionally – for a bath, a book, clean linen. She spent her days alone, walking over the marsh in 'solemn rapture', or finding sheltered recesses in which to sit and read. With a notebook in her lap, she discovered it was possible to write poetry. Nestled in the tall grass behind banks of shingle and listening to the grasshoppers, she experienced the 'mysterious sensation of being where I wanted to be and as I wanted to be, socketted in the universe, and passionately quiescent'.[1]

Socketted. A space, a hollow into which something naturally fits. A feeling of rightness, and connection.[2] An odd sensation, in an unexpected location, for a young woman living above a furrier's on a clattering street in Bayswater. But Sylvia's life was about to change course. Though she was working as a musicologist and was in a relationship with an older, married man, she would soon begin her first novel, and would leave London for Dorset, where she would meet the woman who would become the great love of her life.

Many years later, Sylvia reflected on her month in rural Essex as one of the most significant, the most life-altering, of her experiences: the instant from which everything followed. 'Isn't it strange,' she wrote to Rosamond Lehmann in 1975, as both writers looked back on their lives, 'that the important, memorable things in one's life came by accident, came on an impulse?'[3]

~

Sylvia Townsend Warner's trip to the country was one of several she took in the 1920s. Leaving London with little more than a map, she made a habit of travelling to Essex, Suffolk or Oxfordshire. Her behaviour was typical for an emancipated young woman between the wars. And yet Sylvia was more adventurous than most: light-footed, independent-minded, she made no bones about travelling alone and spending a week or more in an unfamiliar place among strangers. The people she met intrigued her. Leaning over gate posts, or sitting up late in her hosts' cottages, she could talk nineteen to the dozen. And yet it was the feeling of enchantment which stole over her when she was alone that interested her most. As in Essex, when, on the marsh, she snuffed sea-lavender, bitter southernwood and samphire; expanded her vision across the saltings to the sea. The landscape's strangeness, its flatness and smells, were disorientating and sensual. It set something off inside her: the small, ticking clock of her life's adventures; the flickering, impatient movements of the needle on her private compass.

For Sylvia, Essex turned out to be a fulcrum moment, though the life that took shape afterwards was only ever half intended. It began to materialize in 1930, when she bought a cottage in a small Dorset village, meant as a retreat from London, and a place in which to write. But her heart snagged on the cottage, and the woman she had invited to lodge there, and from that point onwards, she went back to London infrequently, and then hardly at all. Instead, she embraced the creative and radical potential of rural life. What was unfamiliar would become homely. The chalk downs and her new lover were her new coordinates, her resting places; even if, in the end, she wouldn't settle for long at all.

~

For the women in this book, country lives emerged unexpectedly, by accident or impulse. Intervals of convalescence and weekend trips evolved into whole summers, the balance between London and the country tipping one way and then the other. Setting their watches to country time – to the seasons, harvests, the cycles of village news and gossip – they bought rubber boots, thick corduroy coats. Venturing out, they discovered new landscapes, places that might contour the mood of a day, or shape an afternoon's writing – an expanse of downland, a sheltered footpath. Country living – choosing to embrace the daily routines of rural life – changed your perspective, these women discovered; it changed the quality of your attention to the world. It allowed for new experiments in form, and in feeling.

In the summer of 1917, Virginia Woolf was at Asheham in Sussex, in the last phase of her recovery from a long period of illness. She was living cautiously, her days moving according to a quiet rhythm of reading, walking, being. She was finding unexpected happiness in domestic life. Shopping for food at the Monday market in Lewes, or in Newhaven or Brighton, washing bedlinen, storing apples in the loft. There were small household dramas. A puncture to her husband, Leonard's, bicycle, the coal mysteriously missing from the cellar. Though she felt far from London, her Sussex summer was still coloured by war. There were food shortages, airships manoeuvring in the sky, and German prisoners working at the farm. From the tops of the Downs, the gunfire sounded 'like the beating of giant carpets'.[4] And yet, despite the war, Virginia was excited by country life. On her long, solitary walks, she picked mushrooms and counted butterflies, or she stood and watched the fields as the harvest was brought in. She was paying close attention to her surroundings. Emerging from illness, she was discovering a new way of seeing. Finally, after two years' silence following the publication of her difficult first novel, she started writing a diary.

For Sylvia, thirteen years later, the pleasures of rural domesticity were greater because they were experienced outside of conventional sexual norms. At her Dorset cottage, she and her lover, Valentine, went about doing home improvements, installing modest, creaturely comforts: a cold tap, a new hearth, woodwork painted pink. She continued educating herself in country matters. From her doorstep, she observed the material conditions of village life, from the labourers working overtime to the lack of sanitation in tithed houses. During this quiet, domestic period before she committed formally to communism, Sylvia's politics was mostly felt, but in time she began to branch out from novel writing into essays and articles on rural affairs. Planting vegetables, skinning rabbits, and collecting rainwater for bathing, it was a hard and simple life, except for the luxury of Valentine. As they gardened, the women were day-trippers putting down roots. 'A good deal of couch grass remained,' Sylvia wrote. 'So did we.'[5]

Twelve years on, in 1942, Rosamond Lehmann gave up her large marital home for a cottage in a village on the Berkshire border. There, a new life began to emerge, a life of revised proportions and modest pleasures. Each weekend, she awaited the arrival of her lover, the poet Cecil Day Lewis; in the school holidays, she devoted herself to her children. She was an unusual newcomer in the village, softly glamorous, digging potatoes and sowing broad beans in red trousers and an alpaca sweater. But Rosamond's happiness was precarious. Her lover had a wife and children elsewhere, and she battled two wartime winters alone. During a storm, the roof of her cottage fell in, and the pipes froze for weeks. Her daughter was frightened by the sound of bombers taking off from the nearby aerodrome. ' "Do they make special small bombs for children?" '[6] And yet, out of fractured time and emotional uncertainty, Rosamond was writing in snatches. For the first time, she began producing short stories, some of the finest work she had ever written.

These women knew each other, might loosely have been considered friends, but did not form a group or belong to a coterie. Throughout their lives, if only at a distance, they passed writing between them, one to the other, like a baton or a torch. Virginia belonged, if only by a margin, to a previous generation, and her example of how to live a life as a writer, and a life outside of London, was deeply influential to her younger contemporaries. She praised Sylvia's first poems when they appeared in 1925; tapped Rosamond on the shoulder during a dinner party. Rosamond's brother, John Lehmann, was manager at the Woolfs' Hogarth Press, and, through him and others, they remained in each other's orbit. She encouraged Rosamond's writing, the words of an experienced novelist to an aspiring one: 'Are you able to go on with your book?'; 'Are you writing about the same people, or have you come out in an entirely new world, from which you see all the old world, minute, miles & miles away?'[7] Later, Rosamond took up the torch in Virginia's stead. She and Sylvia, outlasting their literary reputations and their friends, encouraged in each other a late blooming of creativity.

In this book, we will meet Virginia, Sylvia and Rosamond at threshold moments, and stay with them for a period of roughly two years each. For all three, country life began with disruption: a set of circumstances – ill health, a lover, a divorce – bringing about a move. What followed was quieter. An interval of self-reckoning, recuperation or making-do; the establishment of domestic routine. For each of them, their time in the country would come to mean something different, and leave its particular mark. Virginia's would become a story of convalescence and recovery; Sylvia's of sexual and political awakening, and eventual disillusionment; and Rosamond's of heart-sickness, motherhood and self-acceptance. Still, the impact on their writerly lives was remarkably consistent. What emerged for each of them was a change of form; a kind of fractured writing, perhaps, that owed much to circumstance. Between house moves, and novels, they turned their attention to elliptical diaries, short stories, essays and poems, besides a range of household texts including notebooks, recipes and lists. There was a growing connection between writing and landscape; the places in which they found themselves merited particular kinds of attention, their different topographies in Sussex, Dorset and Berkshire – and the communities that lived there – shaping both writing and thinking. Emerging from periods of creative uncertainty and private disappointment, these writers were invigorated by place, and the daily trials and small pleasures of making homes. Given the time to observe their surroundings and their solitude, and describe their village neighbours and war, they could each embark on new experiments in writing. They found the courage to live – and to make – differently.

And yet there is danger here. As each of these writers knew, there is a temptation to sentimentalize rural life, to fetishize its hardships; or, simply, to ignore the furrows of class and politics that cut through the English countryside. Virginia Woolf was aware of her tendency to mythologize rural England, for all the close attention she sought to pay it. In Sussex in the years before the First World War, she got about by bicycle. The roads were quiet. As she cycled, her attention lit upon scenes of old-world Sussex, the men scything by hand, the magnificence of a tithe barn, the chalky tracks cut into the hillsides by ancient carts. She was interested, too, in the human life, stopping to watch stool ball (a traditional Sussex game) played late into the evening, or to admire the sight of the village women coming out of their cottages to talk in the street.

Out exploring, she liked coming upon things that set her imagination going – things that conjured a fantasy of old England, romantic and unchanging. It seemed to her that, in the country, the past ran close to the present, was almost touchable, 'close-knit'.[8] When she and Leonard bought a car in 1927, tunnelling through time became swifter. The counties of southern England opened up to them. 'One may go to Bodiam, to Arundel, explore the Chichester downs,' she wrote excitedly in her diary, 'expand that curious thing, the map of the world in ones mind.'[9] In the car, shuttling at relative speed through English villages, she caught sight of 'little scenes', which appeared as if directly out of English history. In August 1927, passing through the lowlands near Ripe, she saw a gentlewoman teaching the daughters of farm labourers to sing. The image was continuous, compacted, 'went on precisely so in Cromwell's time', and 'would have gone on, have always gone on, will go on, unrecorded, save for this chance glimpse'.[10]

But Sussex was not immune to change, and the world lodging itself in Virginia's imagination was seemingly disappearing. In the late summer of 1921, she raged in her diary of the 'spot & rash & pimple & blister' of new bungalow developments along the coast near Newhaven, the motorcars streaming along the road 'like lice'.[11] She had grown protective of her adopted corner of Sussex, particularly the area of the Ouse valley between Asheham and the village of Rodmell, where she owned a house with Leonard from 1919 until her death in 1941. Her feeling for Sussex was not exactly nostalgic; more, it emerged from an acute sense of the landscape's timelessness, an almost spiritual quality, an idea which would interest her throughout her writing life. She was writing in a moment charged with particularly deep feeling about the changes being wrought to rural England. In the post-war years, England witnessed a period of rapid urban expansion: towns and cities swelled with suburbs, villages were engulfed by housing developments, and urban centres unravelled along rural roads. And rural populations were changing. As country-dwellers dispersed to take up white-collar jobs, an increasing number of people wanted to live in the countryside, needing improved transport links, shops, jobs, amenities and schools.

Responses to such rapid changes spanned the political spectrum, with town planners and the Council for the Preservation of Rural England – proposing the genuine need for housing reform – pitched against conservation societies. Out of the clamour, one voice emerged with the clarity of – to borrow a phrase from his 1926 broadcast – the 'tinkle of the hammer on the anvil in the country smithy'.[12] Stanley Baldwin, Conservative prime minister for much of the 1920s and 1930s, became the figurehead for the wave of nostalgia sweeping the discourse about English landscape and identity. In a series of radio addresses to the nation, Baldwin invoked the imagery of rural life – corncrake, woodsmoke, and plough (not unlike the imagery of Virginia's diaries) – to conjure the sights, sounds and smells of Englishness, an Englishness perceived as under threat.

But Virginia refused to be drawn into the current of insular nationalism that characterised the interwar years. 'Baldwin broadcast last night,' she wrote in her diary on 9 May 1926. Hearing the prime minister's voice in her sitting room was a novelty, and yet Baldwin's assertiveness, his reverence for rural England, sounded 'ridiculous [. . .] megalomaniac' coming over the airwaves. 'No I dont trust him,' she wrote emphatically, 'I don't trust any human being, however loud they bellow and roll their rs.'[13] Yet she struggled to distinguish her own feelings for the country from conservative views of old England. Her intervals of rural living, first at Little Talland House in Firle, then at Asheham, and finally at Monk's House, marked a series of attempts at living beyond her usual social circle: she shopped locally, more economically, attempted several times to do without servants (or, at least, to manage with fewer), and appreciated the fallow periods in her social life. And she used her ambivalent status as a newcomer to sharpen her outsider perspective. In a small village, she was able to belong, and also not to belong, to her immediate social class. She lived in the 'lower village world' at Rodmell, she wrote proudly in 1941; remarked, 'the gentry dont call'.[14]

Even so, hers was always to be a version of weekending, her experience of country life in relation to the city. 'Now I must throw my night gown in to a bag,' she wrote to Rosamond in July 1928, as she set about leaving the country once more for London. 'I've just picked all the sweet peas, & our dining room table looks like the whole of Covent Garden at dawn.'[15] In her constant back and forth, there was seepage; one environment transmuting itself onto the other. Between 1911 and 1940, Virginia either rented or owned houses in both London and Sussex. (At one point, owing to impetuosity, she owned three.) She and Leonard were employers in the village; they had a car. What arose in her private writings was an idiosyncratic, often contradictory, and yet deeply personal attitude towards place. She marked her distance from what she took to be the megalomaniacal views propagated by Baldwin about lost England, even – as with the hymn-singing on the flats near Ripe – as she made her own attempts to preserve it.

Unlike Virginia, Sylvia Townsend Warner was unmoved by romantic images of country life. Surveying her surroundings in the Dorset village of East Chaldon, she noticed the damp patches on the houses in which the agricultural workers lived, noted glibly that farmers made poor landlords. Abandoned farm machinery didn't stir her emotions, but led her to think of tractors moving efficiently over farmland as she had read about in the USSR. She hadn't moved to the country to get away from class and poverty; her own background was less important than her chosen affinity with working-class living, a product of her increasingly left-wing politics. She was partly in Chaldon to put theory into practice. In her writing for left-wing magazines, she documented her observations, rural reporting of a rather different flavour. She was pragmatic, and praised ugliness. Her own worker's cottage (left over from a local sale, she assured herself) was plain. It was only bourgeois intellectuals who moved to the country for the best houses; better to take the worst. She thrived on hardship. Despite her literary success, she refused to install a bathroom at Miss Green, the cottage she shared with Valentine. Instead, domesticity was labour-intensive, and a way of practising her politics. 'I am almost a wealthy woman,' she remarked thirty years later from her house in the village of Maiden Newton, a few miles away, 'though I continue to behave as a poor one.'[16]

Sylvia had an intuitive understanding of the country as politicized. Buying her map of Essex in 1922, she knew it was symbolic, a tool of the new leisure class of city-dwellers taking trips from London to the coast. 'For five years I was a complete cockney,' she wrote later. 'If I went into the country it was to disport myself, or to visit.'[17] (Virginia noted the appearance of such day-trippers in Sussex with bewilderment, perhaps a little distaste. 'The younger generation walk across the downs in brown corduroy trousers, blue shirts, grey socks, and no hats on their heads, which are cropped,' she wrote, adding, 'It seems to me quite impossible to wear trousers.')[18] But Sylvia also understood the map as a rulebook, a visual represen-tation of imper-ial masculinity dictating correct behaviour and acceptable ways of being in space. 'I liked maps. I liked place-names, and the picture-making technique of map-reading,' she wrote.[19] But in her first novel, *Lolly Willowes*, her protagonist Laura desecrates her map, marking her own routes and passages with 'little bleeding footsteps of red ink'; eventually, frustrated, she throws it down a well. Then, Laura's movements – like Sylvia's own on the Essex marshes – become those of a truant: errant, wilful, deviant. Laura strays along field margins and into beech woods, walking at night. She makes her own paths, 'wherever she chose to wander'.[20]

Moving to the country, Sylvia's transformation was personal as well as political. With her new lover, she wandered, got lost, explored new territory. In 1934, she sold her London flat. No to-ing and fro-ing, no dividing her time between London and country like Virginia. Instead, she lived in Dorset villages (and occasionally Nor-folk ones) for the rest of her life. She and Valentine always lived a little on the outskirts, at the periphery of the map. Sometimes, Sylvia wondered what her village neighbours made of them: the queer spinsters (one dandified, the other primly dressed) whipping up rumours of witches and communism, walking their dog over the Downs, or lying on their backs among ancient barrows; reserved yet courteous, and rarely apart.

If Sylvia had found a way to opt into social issues in the countryside, Rosamond Lehmann felt compelled to opt out. By 1942, she was fed up with politics. Making a life for herself in a cloistered Berkshire village – landlocked, enclosed on all sides by Downs – she decided if she couldn't escape class, she might as well retreat into it. At Diamond Cottage, she let her conservatisms resurface, in both her writing and her life. She was a product of her upbringing: broadly liberal, wealthy, having spent her childhood in a large house on the banks of the River Thames. She had continued to live in the Thames Valley well into her thirties, in another large house, although by then she was surrounded by her husband's left-wing friends. But she was uncomfortable. The cosmopolitan leftism of the 1930s – her brother, John Lehmann, and the poet Stephen Spender going back and forth in her sitting room of an evening – went 'hideously against the grain'.[21] Instead, she looked for mildness, like the weather the young Olivia Curtis sees from her country bedroom in *Invitation to the Waltz*, 'serene and wan' after the 'huge idiot pangs' of a storm.[22] Her early novels contain much anti-urban feeling, with cities places of lonely bedsits and cheap cinemas; yet their rural locations carry something muffled and closed-minded about them, the apparent indifference of middle-class provincial life.

In fact, out of apathy emerges a quiet practice of resistance. The women in her books are angry, conflicted creatures, drifting between a new world of personal and sexual freedoms, and an older one of disapproval and censure. In these books, country places offer protection, and a gentler sense of belonging and connection. In a later novel, an older woman, Dinah, retreats to a cottage during wartime. She listens for sirens: 'Absurd: this was the heart of Berkshire.' Outside, she thinks of the 'widening rings' of the landscape, the 'village pub, a store, church, vicarage, manor, farm; still farther, torrents of aromatic foam of wild parsley in the banks; and all around, the architectural masses of the Downs.' The outside world, with its hectoring and sexual politics, cannot touch her here. 'She began to hear a steady giant pulse.'[23]

So while Diamond Cottage saw Rosamond settle into a kind of insular conservatism at odds with the fashionable radicalism in which she had engaged in the 1930s, neither her life nor her writing were dogmatic or reactionary. Her best work emerged out of her inconsistency, both of practice (she would write quickly, or not at all) and of sensibility. She was a contradictory character: moving in progressive circles, but intuitively conservative; a knowing lover of a married man, yet wanting nothing more than to settle down; a haunter of literary London, a country wife.

~

These are not the most storied or well-known episodes in these writers' lives, nor do they yield easily to summary. They are episodes not of high drama, but quiet, domestic goings-on, of the kind usually passed over in biographies. They require a different kind of attention, a different sense of scale and orientation. Like a map, life is made up of significant moments, or landmarks; but it also contains untended expanses, lesser-known tracks, surfeits of green. The biographer's prerogative is to find her own way; or perhaps, like Sylvia, to do away with the map altogether. This book takes place on the days on which 'nothing strange or exalted' happened, as Virginia wrote in her diary on 22 August 1929.[24] It settles on the unsettled moments, when these women were between projects, and sometimes between houses; it bypasses already navigated ground. It finds Virginia in her middle thirties, looking for mushrooms; Sylvia, with dirt beneath her fingernails; and Rosamond, with small children in tow, on the cusp of middle age. These interludes were private, lived-in; bookended by war. But they were also generative transitions, in which identities were taking root and ideas were coming into form.

How might such unstoried episodes be told? In piecing together these women's rural lives, I looked to the writing projects they undertook in the country. Some of these were literary, others less clearly so. Rosamond wrote short stories, the only time in her career she experimented with the form; Virginia kept a daily record quite unlike her other diaries, filled with snatches of conversation and microscopic observations of natural life; and Sylvia began to build a private hoard of household texts in the form of inventories, recipe books, gardening notebooks, scrapbooks and lists. These are all forms of life-writing; all make it possible to trace the contours and gradations of their authors' days, to map and sometimes to imagine. I listened for their voices in country lanes, followed their footsteps home over the Downs. When I found them, they were busy, preoccupied with ordinary things, with bedding in, making home, or making do. Virginia, pausing to look at an insect on her windowsill, or stooping to count bedlinen; Rosamond, waiting for a letter, trailed by little dogs; Sylvia, notebook in hand, moving from room to room. This book is an attempt to follow these writers' examples – to reconstruct their rural hours in the same spirit in which they documented them, attending to the everyday and the near at hand so as to find new ways of writing about how we feel, and how we live.

~

Two photographs, taken between 1933 and 1934, reveal the idiosyncratic quality of these women's approaches to country life. The first shows Sylvia at Frankfort Manor in Norfolk, walking Victoria Ambrosia, a decidedly uncooperative goat. (Vicky was a milker, and would be brought back to Dorset later that year.) In the second, Rosamond wrestles with a goat at Ipsden in Oxfordshire, wearing a two-piece woollen suit and indoor shoes. They were practising different styles. And what do I mean by style? Something intuitive, but also considered; a set of aesthetic choices which encourage new ways of living and thinking. Perhaps Virginia summed it up best when she mused, a little ironically and yet with admiration, on the quiet determination of the women she encountered in Sussex (though she might have been talking about Sylvia or Rosamond), their sturdiness, their pastimes and pleasures. 'I got the impression of some large garden flower comfortably shoving its roots about & well planted in the soil – say a stock, or a holly-hock,' she wrote. Shoving her roots about, if only for a time; and yet, 'settled into a corner absolutely fitted for her'.[25] Socketted.

Sylvia walking Vicky the goat

Rosamond wrestling a goat at Ipsden

PART ONE

Experiments

Beetles & the price of eggs

Came to Asheham. Walked out from Lewes. Stopped raining for the first time since Sunday. Men mending the wall & roof at Asheham. Will has dug up the bed in front, leaving only one dahlia. Bees in attic chimney.*

Virginia Woolf's diary entry for 3 August 1917, a Friday, is her first in two years. Since the age of fifteen, when she began her 'record', there have been stops and starts, but none so severe as this.[1] Two years of silence, save a collection of infrequent and often self-consciously light-hearted letters to friends; in the writing of herself to herself, there has been a complete break.

Not, on 3 August, that she begins with writing about herself. In fact, there is no 'I' to speak of. An arrival, a walk; followed by weather, workmen, flowers and bees. *Came to Asheham.* It is an arrival without the act of arriving, but she is there, and that is the most important thing. She has come to her solitary house on the Downs, but she has also arrived at her diary after a long hiatus, ready to begin. She has a format, a method, in mind. How else, after the silence, to start again? Her succinctness reveals her quiet determination, but also her vulnerability. Virginia Woolf is emerging from several years of illness into the relief – weather, workmen, flowers, bees – of ordinary life.

She describes each day of that first weekend with the same economy of style. Heavy rain, a trip to Southease to collect the post, reading the *Daily News*; then, the gift of a hot afternoon, and a walk. On the hillside, she notices butterflies – fritillaries, blues – and

---

* In order to distinguish Virginia Woolf's writing in the Asheham diary from that of her other diaries or letters, and to prevent crowding the text with too many quotation marks, I have italicized the words, passages and entries I quote from this source.

collects mushrooms, *enough for a dish*. By Monday 6 August, her new diary is gaining confidence, and she rounds off the bank holiday in what will settle into an established rhythm.

> *Very fine hot day. (Bank Holiday). Sound of band in Lewes from the Downs. Guns heard at intervals. Walked up the down at the back. Got plenty of mushrooms. Butterflies in quantities. Ladies Bedstraw, Round-headed Rampion, Thyme, Marjoram. Saw a grey looking hawk – not the usual red-brown one. A few plums on the tree. We have begun to cook apples. Eggs 2/9 doz. From Mrs Attfield.*

Still, she is nowhere to be seen. She is the one doing the looking. Over the course of two summers at Asheham, 1917 and 1918, she writes down what she sees in the garden and the fields, or tramping over the Downs. She notices sights others might miss: the first cowslip, a full moon, a rook carrying a walnut in its beak. She looks with the precision of a naturalist. And, in her tightly compressed entries, she describes her domestic life, a routine of walking and foraging, shopping and gardening; each activity a way of thinking about food. The diary is a record of wartime in the country. Eggs and sugar are difficult to come by, and the sound of guns can be heard from France. The aeroplanes flying over Asheham are disquieting, but she likes watching the German prisoners working in the fields, and whistling, *a great brown jug for their tea*.

~

This is the story of a writer's recovery from illness, jealous feelings, and writer's block. From her remote corner of Sussex, Virginia Woolf overcame her silences through the beginning of a practice of attention, shifting her focus to her immediate environment as a way of tethering herself, digging herself in. There, she found sanctity, a state of being which grew out of her feeling for the landscape, with its patina of human history patchworked over the wide, wave-like Downs. Later, Asheham would become merely an interval in her life, a moment before Monk's House and nearby Charleston – where her sister, the painter Vanessa Bell, lived – were marked more squarely on her map. And yet it was at Asheham that she emerged into her identity as a writer, one capable of innovative literary forms, and yet whose eye was trained to the physical, to butterflies and insects, to the living world.

This extraordinary story can be seen by looking at the pages of a small notebook, a diary of a rather different kind. It began as an experiment. In the late summer of 1917, Virginia was well enough to write, to piece together and reclaim the voice of her private writing self. But it would be a cautious, gradual beginning. She turned to what was closest to her. In a notebook roughly the length of her hand, with elegant marbled covers and a strip of claret-coloured leather down its spine, she recorded the weather, her routine, the quiet rhythms of everyday life. Her style was at times elliptical, at times pellucid, but always swift, economical and compact. The notebook dealt in details and tangible things: walking boots, bicycles, eggs. Nothing inward-looking, nothing she couldn't see or hear or touch. She wrote in it almost every day, and, when she had finished each entry, she drew a line across the page.

In the autumn, when she went back to Hogarth House in Richmond, Virginia left her notebook in the country, collecting dust and absorbing damp along with her books and bedlinen and the rest of her things. Soon, she would begin a second, predominantly London, diary, with longer, more descriptive entries of the kind she had written before she became ill. There, the writing 'I' resumed itself. But she hadn't yet finished her experiment at Asheham. Returning to the house in 1918, she documented another spring and another long summer meticulously in the notebook, the only detailed account of her country life. Though its lifespan was short, her Asheham diary altered everything that came after it. Like a rambling plant, it grew outwards, forming a connective tissue with her next experiments in short fiction and her novels of the 1920s. And it re-established her diary as practice, one she would continue for the rest of her life.

At Asheham, during her long recovery, Virginia was in the habit of planting bulbs and forgetting.* Months later, she would watch the emergence of flowers in astonishment, remarking on the strangeness of gardening, on the slow, buried process that takes place underground, unseen, and yet continues to flourish, year after year.

~

One scholar of Virginia Woolf has written that it is impossible to draw a line between her life-writing and her novels; instead, they exist on a continuum, moving freely and engaged in a process of continual exchange.[2] This theory should make room, and find a place, for everything she produced – the letters, diaries, reading notebooks, sketches and fragments which make up both her archive and her published works. And yet, in the context of her life-writing, no one has ever quite decided where her Asheham diary should sit. A slight, single volume containing 143 entries written over a smattering of dates, it details a house, a war, and a corner of rural Sussex which have all been seen as rehearsals for another house, another war, and another corner of Sussex (just around the corner). It doesn't immediately resemble a diary. On the subject of Virginia Woolf, it is evasive, as if, in the writing of her life, she's barely there at all. In the 1970s, when her editor Anne Olivier Bell was compiling the diaries for publication, she decided that the notebook was too different in character, too laconic, to supplement the 'much fuller' diaries that came afterwards and before.[3] The Asheham notebook was only partially published, before being laid aside, and an editorial distinction was drawn.

And yet Virginia *was* writing a diary, of a revealingly self-effacing kind. Hers is a record of humdrum days, a rehearsal for a country life to come. She was finding her voice, writing into the space between her early, earnest journals and the later, longhand diaries for which she has become so well known. And she was writing to satisfy her immediate interests and needs. Sitting on her desk at

---

* 'Plants are very odd things. Bulbs I planted 3 years ago suddenly come up in odd corners.' Virginia Woolf to Violet Dickinson, 24 April 1916, *Letters*, II, 93.

Asheham, the notebook was both pocket diary and field book, a record of rural sightings; it was also a domestic book, a repository for kitchen and garden, for snippets of the servants' lives. Its suppleness was key. In August 1917, when the diary begins, Virginia was voyaging out. She was thirty-five and, for the first time in several years, well enough to write. Her neat entries and obsessive detail represent the writing of recovery, a convalescent mode of engaging with the world. But it was just the beginning. Alongside her diary, she was working on her second novel, and would soon publish under her own name, using a hand-printing press that was set up in the drawing room at Hogarth House.

The roughly two years covered by the Asheham diary precipitated a period of sudden, joyful creativity for Virginia, an explosion of colour after the wan palette of illness. Her excitement, the sense of her readiness, is present across its pages. The diary's economy belies its fullness, its repetitiousness conceals its quiet experimentalism. And Virginia wasn't entirely removing herself. She can be glimpsed out on the Downs, walking with her hands thrust into the pockets of her cardigan, or soaked through after a sudden rain; pushing a bicycle with a puncture along the lane, or retrieving her mackintosh from the hedge. Or she might be out on the terrace, wearing a straw hat in hot weather, or reading late into the evening beneath a lamp or the moon. She was always noticing, counting and collecting, always seeing. As she continued to recover, she was taking solace in routine. In the diary, her days hum with repetition. Turning the pages, she was watching them accumulate, becoming weeks and then months of steadiness and pleasure. Their sameness was accruing texture, and, like the plums on the trees, they were ripening, becoming round and sweet and full.

'Owing to you I've practically got that house,' Virginia Stephen wrote to Leonard Woolf on 21 October 1911, before embarking on a discussion about cesspools. The new house – called Asheham, or

Virginia, voyaging out

Asham – was over a mile from the nearest village, and had no plumbing. Either Mrs Hoper, an elderly local woman, would be asked to clean out an earth closet, or they could construct a private drain. She put the question to Leonard: 'Which would be best?'[4]

In ten months, Virginia would be married. From the first, Asheham occupied a central place in her relationship with Leonard. She was to share its five-year lease with her sister, Vanessa, as part of a plan to establish a place for Bloomsbury outside of London, and yet it was she who grew possessive of the place, and proprietorial of its beauty. It presented a raft of practical problems – its remoteness, the lack of plumbing and the perpetual difficulty of finding servants – and yet it captured her imagination, promising, as she set out with Leonard in 1912, the opportunity for a private space in the country, and an altogether different way of living.

Virginia had first seen it while walking with Leonard on the Downs. In September 1911, she invited him to stay at Little Talland

House, a half-redbrick, half-pebbledash cottage she was renting in the village of Firle. A fly would meet him at Lewes, she told him, before making one request anticipating the informality of all their domestic arrangements to come: 'Please bring no clothes.'[5] During his visit, they climbed up onto the Downs behind Firle. From the top, they could see the sea at Newhaven, and westwards over the Ouse valley towards the villages of Southease and Rodmell. Descending the hillside into Southease, they saw Asheham, lying in a deep basin scooped out of the hillside and bordered by trees.

Asheham was an unusual and romantic-looking house.[6] It was accessible by a single track leading off the Newhaven–Lewes road, the steep banks planted with beech trees giving way to a rough meadow. Built in the nineteenth century by a Lewes solicitor, it was relatively small, its compact size contrasting with the unexpected elaborateness of its appearance. Beneath a slate roof were two rows of double arched 'gothic' windows, while the house was flanked by two whimsical-looking pavilions, with doors opening onto a narrow terrace. With the slope of Itford Hill rising sharply behind, it looked ornamental in the landscape, like a hunting lodge or summer house. Nearby, there was a shepherd's cottage belonging to Itford Farm; otherwise, it was solitary.

Stumbling upon Asheham marked the beginning of the couple's swift courtship. Leonard – a friend of the writer Lytton Strachey and Virginia's late brother, Thoby Stephen, from Cambridge – was in England briefly following seven years with the civil service in British-controlled Ceylon. Meeting Virginia again, he determined not to go back. But when he proposed in January 1912, she hesitated. 'There isn't anything really for me to say,' she wrote to him, 'except that I should like to go on as before; and that you should leave me free, and that I should be honest. As to faults, I expect mine are just as bad – less noble perhaps.'[7] Her first instinct was to protect her writing: she was contributing reviews to the *Times Literary Supplement*, an apprenticeship of sorts, and was working on her first novel, 'Melymbrosia'.

But she was also content to continue their current domestic arrangement. Unusually, Virginia and Leonard already lived together. After deciding to remain in England, Leonard had become a lodger at 38 Brunswick Square where, for several months, Virginia had presided over a communal household along with her brother, Adrian. The economist John Maynard Keynes and his lover, the painter Duncan Grant, were part of the establishment; to the alarm of her friends, Virginia was the only woman. The house, next to the Foundling Hospital, was one of a series of departures from her stuffy Victorian upbringing. Following the death of their father, Leslie Stephen, Virginia, Vanessa and Adrian had left Kensington for Bloomsbury, whose down-at-heel squares and cheap rents were a draw to writers and artists looking for bedsits or studios in the vicinity of the reading room at the British Museum. First, the Stephen siblings had lived at 46 Gordon Square, until Vanessa's marriage to the painter and critic Clive Bell brought about the reorganization of living arrangements. It was decided that Virginia and Adrian would set up in a house of their own, taking in lodgers and so becoming, to Virginia's amusement, 'boarding house keepers'. 'We are going to try all kinds of experiments,' she wrote excitedly to Ottoline Morrell as the Brunswick project got going.[8] She was to notify her cohabiters of mealtimes, and collect the rents. For the rest, she was free to do as she pleased. Taking up her residence on the first floor, she surrounded herself with papers and books. In comparison with her own personal freedoms, the 'extreme safeness and sobriety' of marriage appalled her.[9] Considering Leonard's proposal, she was reluctant to give them up.

But there was another reason Virginia wouldn't agree to marry Leonard. She had begun to experience headaches and sleeplessness, warning signals of the illness which had already stained large parts of her adolescence and early adulthood. (Her first breakdown had come after the death of her mother, when she was thirteen. Beneath the shadow of Leslie Stephen's own grief, she had had little chance to recover. She would always remember the oppressiveness of that time, and the feeling, after Leslie's death in 1902, of release. 'His life would have ended mine. What would have happened? No writing, no books; – inconceivable.'[10]) Now, in February 1912, she was struggling again, the first lap of the year having been busy. As the lease of

Asheham was finalised, and she moved her belongings from Little Talland House in Firle, she and Vanessa hosted housewarming parties. There were two. The first was Virginia's, to which she invited Adrian, Marjorie Strachey and Leonard. Vanessa's was a larger affair, with Clive, Virginia and Leonard, Roger Fry and Duncan Grant. They were only moderately successful: there was no lavatory, the fireplaces malfunctioned and the pipes froze. Afterwards, Virginia began to appear tired. As before, her doctor prescribed rest, and she was sent to Burley Park, a private nursing home in Twickenham. It was, she wrote as off-handedly as she could to her friend Katherine Cox, only a 'touch of my usual disease', easily cured by a fortnight in bed 'among faded old ladies'.[11] Yet privately she was deeply worried about becoming ill again. To Leonard, who sent her books, she promised 'wonderful stories of the lunatics', attempting to distance herself from anyone he might consider mentally ill.[12] She worried what he would think of her, and of the life she would be capable of living. Afterwards, as she recovered, she continued to prevaricate, growing a little defensive in her letters as if the question – at least, in her mind – of her marrying was, in fact, a question about her health. She was 'vehement' on the subject of her personal freedoms, while acknowledging her deepest fear – that she could be 'difficult to live with', and 'so very intemperate and changeable, now thinking one thing and another'.[13]

In May, she wrote Leonard a long letter explaining her feelings. She acknowledged her instability – 'I pass from hot to cold in an instant, without any reason' – and attempted to describe her complicated sexual feelings. 'I feel no physical attraction in you,' she wrote. 'There are moments – when you kissed me the other day was one – when I feel no more than a rock.' If they married, she would need a great deal of solitude and space. And yet she could love him. 'All I can say is that in spite of these feelings which go chasing each other all day long when I am with you, there is some feeling which is permanent, and growing,' she wrote. 'I want everything – love, children, adventure, intimacy, work [. . .] a marriage that is a tremendous living thing, always alive, always hot [. . .] We ask a great deal of life, don't we?'[14]

For Leonard, whatever Virginia felt able to offer him was enough. Soon, she was writing to friends announcing they were engaged, and on Saturday 10 August 1912 they were married in a small ceremony at St Pancras registry office. Afterwards, they caught the train to Sussex, where they spent the first night of their marriage at Asheham.

~

At first, the house belonged more to Vanessa than to Virginia. Perhaps this was the result of a natural hierarchy between the sisters, Vanessa being the eldest and, somehow, the more easily capable. All through the summer of 1912, as Asheham was establishing itself as a place where Bloomsbury could gather outside of London, Vanessa appeared to be at the helm. Following the February housewarming parties, a steady stream of visitors began to arrive: Maynard and Duncan, Lytton Strachey, Roger Fry, and friends including Saxon Sydney-Turner, Ka Cox and Karin Costelloe. Pulling into the station at Lewes, guests were subject to the vagaries of rural living. Depending on the weather, they could either walk the five miles over fields to the house, or hitch rides on farmers' carts or the milk float. At the house, Vanessa presided over a leisurely, unhurried atmosphere. She encouraged the Londoners to take pleasure in country things: walking, or playing badminton on the lawn, or swimming in the sea at Seaford or Peacehaven. In quieter moments, proofs were corrected and chapters finished. When there weren't enough bedrooms, tents were put up in the garden, or less conventional sleeping arrangements found. 'Duncan is easily persuaded to stay on in the bathroom,' she wrote to Roger Fry during a particularly busy weekend.[15]

Of the sisters, Vanessa was the first to exercise her creative freedoms at Asheham. While Leonard and Virginia honeymooned, she decamped from Gordon Square for the winter, bringing her young sons, Quentin and Julian, and the Stephens' old cook, Sophie Farrell, who had been helping Virginia at Brunswick Square and now answered to Vanessa instead. But though she set about sewing curtains and making beds, Vanessa wasn't interested in a conventional domestic life. Changing out of her London clothes, she took to wearing loose-fitting skirts and colourful handkerchiefs wrapped around her head. And she let Julian and Quentin run about naked, taking photographs of their small, vigorous forms.

Unlike her sister, who had yet to publish her first book, Vanessa was emerging into an artistic identity which was increasingly assured. In person, she was sensuous and maternal, and yet she didn't disguise the ambition she held for her work. She was preparing for the second Post-Impressionist exhibition, which would be held, like the first, at the Grafton Galleries, and in which paintings by English artists, including four of her own, would be exhibited alongside those by Picasso, Braque and Cézanne. She was deeply engaged in the debates on 'significant form', which Clive would outline in *Art*, published in 1914. If he and Roger Fry were both present at Asheham, all the talk would be of paint. '[T]he air is teeming with discussion on art,' Vanessa wrote to her sister in February 1913.[16]

Vanessa was approaching a transition in her work. She was shifting away from the semi-pointillist style adopted by Duncan Grant in the wake of the first Post-Impressionist exhibition, and moving towards her own vocabulary of form and colour – larger, more abstract than before. She tried to describe her approach to Roger. 'I am trying to paint as if I were mosaicking, not by painting in spots, but by considering the picture as patches,' she told him. Each patch 'has to be filled by one definite space of colour, as one has to do with mosaic or woolwork, not allowing myself to brush the patches into each other'.[17] In one of the pavilions attached to the side of the house, which had been converted into a studio, she painted several rural scenes, landscapes comprised of solid, structural forms delineated in crude, warm blocks of colour. A haystack at the back of the house became a golden, monolithic form illuminated against strips of greyish sky. A view of Asheham enclosed on either side by woodland reduced the trees to contrasting patches of warmth and dark. Vanessa's interior scenes described the same openness as her landscapes. A double-portrait of the artists Frederick and Jessie Etchells, working in the studio during a visit, shows the windows open to the garden, the boundary between inside and outside porous, as if to paint at Asheham were to paint in the open air. Vanessa continued to explore her new surroundings, taking her watercolours out to barns, or setting up in front of Mrs Funnell's cottage. 'Duncan and I do nothing here but paint,' she wrote to Roger, and to Leonard, who was still honeymooning, 'I envy you very much in Italy now but I doubt if it's more beautiful than this. The trees are amazing colour.'[18]

At Asheham, in the last summer before the war, relationships flourished and thickened. Vanessa grew closer to Duncan, often working on the terrace beside him, or painting from the same arrangement of flowers in a vase. Adrian Stephen met Karin Costelloe, whom he married in 1914; and the painter Dora Carrington, fresh from the Slade, met Lytton, kissing his bearded face before vowing to remain with him for the rest of her life. As the news darkened, inevitably the talk turned to politics. Adrian, David Garnett (known to friends as Bunny), Lytton and Duncan were determined to resist conscription, mistrustful of the militarization of England,

Vanessa Bell, *Asheham House*, 1912

Vanessa Bell, *Landscape with Haystack, Asheham*, 1912

and – led by Clive, who was serving (at the request of Lloyd George, then Minister for War) on a committee to safeguard conscientious objectors – felt the only possible solution for the future of Europe was a negotiated peace. Passionately, the group discussed pacifism on the terrace. And yet, for the time being, Asheham sheltered its occupants from outside cares. Later, during a winter visit, Carrington illustrated her letters with drawings of steaming plum puddings, jellies, and a storybook house wreathed in chimney smoke. 'I love living here so much,' she told Lytton. 'I am in much better health and spirits, who could fail to be in such a place as this?'[19]

~

While Asheham worked its magic on Bloomsbury, the reality of the first years of marriage was as Virginia had feared. Following their honeymoon in France, Spain and Italy, the Woolfs returned to

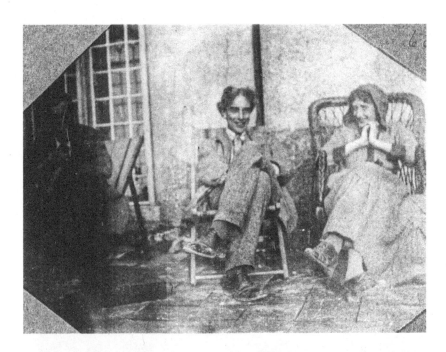

Leonard, Roger, Virginia and Vanessa on the terrace at Asheham, 1912

London – first to Brunswick Square, and then to rooms at Clifford's Inn, off the Strand. (This modest beginning to the couple's marital homes was a measure of prudence on Virginia's part. 'I'm inclined to start with only rooms,' she wrote to a friend, 'until we see how much we've got.'[20]) For a time, she was well, finishing a draft of 'Melymbrosia', and continuing to write reviews. But her health rapidly declined. On 9 September 1913, a year after marrying Leonard, she swallowed a lethal dose of veronal, and her recovery, under the continual supervision of nurses, was slow. In March, she was permitted to go to Asheham, where she could rest. Following the outbreak of war, her friends had scattered, and the weekend parties ended. What followed were quiet, convalescent visits, on which she was accompanied by a single companion – Ka Cox, or Janet Case, or Vanessa. Without the others, the isolation of the house bit. 'Its very like living at the bottom of the sea being here,' she wrote in early April 1914, describing a circumscribed life of routine – 'milk, green fields, early bed'. News of the war reached her intermittently: 'one sometimes hears rumours of what is going on overhead.'[21]

The following year, Virginia seemed better, and returned to Clifford's Inn. She began editing typescripts of her novel, and was making plans to buy a printing press. But Leonard, feeling that living in central London would prove too much for her, moved their possessions to lodgings on The Green at Richmond while he looked for a more permanent home. He was right to be worried; soon, Virginia was slipping again.

'It's a queer winter – the worst I ever knew, & suitable for the war & all the rest of it,' she wrote on 22 January 1915.[22] She was almost thirty-three, and was beginning the diary she would keep, intermittently at first, for the rest of her life. It was a dark beginning, a record of shortened days, in which she voiced her displeasure at suburban living and the dull routine of life half-in and half-out of London. In those first entries, she described the lull between breakdowns, a streak of wintry light before the day's plunge into darkness. She was lethargic and often cruel, her mind jagged and already close to collapse. Sneering at shop-girls in the West End, sickened by vulnerable adults on the Kingston

towpath, or voicing her dislike of Leonard's Jewish family, she was discontented, ill at ease with her fellow human creatures. 'I begin to loathe
my kind, principally from looking at their faces in the tube,' she wrote.[23]
Everywhere, she sensed violence. Walking in Richmond Park, she saw
the Territorial Army flogging carthorses, and her dog, getting into a
fight, badly tore an ear. Three people drowned in the Thames near
Teddington – 'Does the weather prompt suicide?' she wondered – and
a barge crashed into Richmond Bridge during the night.[24] It was bitterly cold, and the river swelled. At her lodgings, the pipes froze and,
when the boiler burst, water dripped through the ceiling into pails. It
was as if her immediate surroundings, half-lit and clogged with winter
mud, were laced with the violence playing out across Europe. Though
only a few months into the war, the news was of refugees and Zeppelin
raids over London. Germany was soon to use poison gas at the Front.
'I shall never find a winter to beat this,' she wrote on 13 February. 'It
seems to have lost all self control.'[25]

And yet there persisted a sensuousness in the weather, in splashes of
winter colour. Kingston, seen from a distance across 'purplish' fields,
had 'a foreign look'; in the park 'the deer exactly match the bracken'.[26]
In her fragile state, there was a porousness between the self and the
world; a sharpness, but also the threat of dissolution.

By the middle of February 1915, Virginia's diary lapsed into the
silence it would keep for another two years. Sleepless and refusing to
eat, she was entering the longest and most severe of her breakdowns.
Soon, she was beyond Leonard's care. Four live-in nurses were summoned to Hogarth House, the Woolfs' new Richmond home. There,
she was kept under almost constant surveillance. At last, in June, she
began to recover, and in September was permitted to go to Asheham, for another long period of convalescence in the quiet house.

'You have been entirely patient with me and incredibly good,' Virginia wrote to Leonard late in her life.[27] She was struggling to

express her gratitude: she owed him her health, and her writing life. The years between 1912 and 1915, when she was so often ill, created a template for the Woolfs' marriage. During that time, as their relationship developed, a dynamic was established, a recurrent pattern of submission and care.

Leonard, recognizing Virginia's desire to write, made her well-being one of the central concerns of his life.* Following her breakdown, he consulted doctors and organized nurses, and presided over a programme of domestic measures at Hogarth House. Virginia was made to rest in bed, drink large quantities of milk and take sedatives. All forms of entertainment were limited. If she became overexcited or tired, or experienced consecutive days of headache, she was sent to bed. If she seemed well enough, she might be permitted to compose a letter (dictated to Leonard), do some typing or go for a walk in Richmond Park. But every activity was strictly rationed, carried out according to a rigid routine. Living under such conditions, it was no wonder she felt, as she had written in 1912, 'like the Tortoise at the zoo'.[28]

Leonard's fastidiousness bordered on control. In 1913, shortly after her suicide attempt, he began to keep a daily record of Virginia's health. In his pocket diary, he noted how she had slept, what medication she had taken and her changeable attitude to food. Often, his notes were written in a private shorthand, encrypted in the Tamil or Sinhalese he had learned in Ceylon, or his own personal code. Or he used abbreviations, such as 'Pʟ' to denote the first day of her period.[29] Rightly, many critics have expressed concern over Leonard's guardianship of Virginia's body, and to the paternalistic aspect of his care. And yet Virginia appeared untroubled by public knowledge of her health. In letters to her sister, and even to friends like Lytton, she often alluded to her menstrual cycle (called her 'affairs'), which could severely affect her mood, and cause her to change plans. It is

* 'For nearly thirty years I had to study Virginia's mind with the greatest intensity,' Leonard Woolf wrote in *Growing: An Autobiography of the Years 1904–1911* (The Hogarth Press, 1961), 53.

possible that, having become used to relying on others, she had long surrendered any privacy regarding her health. But her openness may also have been an extension of Bloomsbury's candour about the body's intimacies; Vanessa, after all, liked to talk about orgasms. Regardless, Leonard's scrupulousness revealed the painstaking efforts it took to keep Virginia well. Over the years, they would speak to numerous doctors, and receive numerous diagnoses – including heart disease, pneumonia and tuberculosis. Later, he would describe Virginia's condition as 'neurasthenia', an outdated and inexact definition which nonetheless accounted for the full range of her symptoms, which could include sleeplessness, a refusal to eat, chattering and visions. They had little else to go on, and no treatment, save sleeping draughts and rest. To live with her, and her illness, was to observe and monitor, or risk losing a foothold. There would always be a double edge to such sustaining and constricting care.

For her part, Vanessa trusted him. 'You're the only person I know whom I can imagine as her husband,' she had written in advance of the wedding.[30] To her, Leonard seemed reliable and sincere. She knew well enough what it took to look after Virginia when she was at her worst. Perhaps, after years of looking after her, she was also grateful to share, and to pass on, the responsibility of Virginia's welfare.

When Virginia was ill, she wrote Leonard short, unhappy letters full of gratitude and regret. 'I got up and dressed last night after you were gone,' she wrote after he visited her at Twickenham in August 1913. 'You do represent all thats best, and I lie here thinking. I think of you in your white nightgown mongoose.'[31] Her affection for Leonard grew sweeter and sadder when they were apart. She tried her best to trust in the future – 'I do love you, little beast, if only I weren't so appallingly stupid a mandril. Can you really love me – yes, I believe it, and we will make a happy life' – though she fretted she was spoiling Leonard's chance at happiness.[32] ('You've been absolutely perfect to me. Its all my fault.'[33]) In the first years of their marriage, they invented nicknames for each other: Leonard was Mongoose to Virginia's adorably ungainly, red-nosed and mistress-like Mandrill. The creatures provided a private language through illness, a means for

Virginia to give voice to the things she couldn't say. But they also paved the way for endearments, creating a space for physical affection and sexual play. Contrary to popular belief, theirs wasn't – at least, at first – a sexless marriage. '[B]e a devoted animal, and never leave the great variegated creature,' Virginia wrote in December 1913. 'She wishes me to inform you delicately that her flanks and rump are now in finest plumage, and invites you to an exhibition.'[34] Yet her sexual feelings were complicated, both by illness and by the painful history of molestation in childhood by her half-brother, Gerald Duckworth. She and Leonard only briefly shared a bed, and then a room; later, it was decided – around the time of her 1915 breakdown – that it would be inadvisable for her to have children. She would often mourn her childlessness. Seeing Vanessa with her lively, growing family, the fact particularly stung.

Yet in the period between 1912 and 1915, despite waves of ill health, Virginia was making other plans. In the letters announcing their engagement, she had made a point of stating that Leonard had no money, repeating to friends, 'He's a penniless Jew.'[35] She took pride in their modest beginning, when they had taken rooms in Clifford's Inn in order to finish their first novels. (Leonard's *The Village in the Jungle* was based on his time in Ceylon.) Virginia had continued to write reviews, while Leonard took a job as secretary to the second Post-Impressionism exhibition, organised by Roger Fry. Their financial future was uncertain, but Virginia hadn't minded: 'It seems idiotic to put Leonard in an office, for the sake of a bigger income.'[36] And: 'We shall, I think, take a small house and try to live cheaply, so as not to have to make money.'[37] Theirs would be a marriage predicated on simplicity for the sake of writing. Neither wished for a lavish life. And Leonard's confidence in Virginia's abilities as a writer had been one of his greatest attractions. 'L. thinks my writing the best part of me,' she had written. 'We're going to work very hard.'[38]

Writing was a way of navigating uncommon ground. Whereas Virginia was born into an intellectual and culturally well-connected family, with deep roots in the 'communicative, literate, letter writing, visiting, articulate, late nineteenth century world', as she would

Leonard and Virginia in 1912

later describe in her memoir, *Sketch of the Past*, Leonard was the fourth of nine children born into a professional, middle-class, assimilated Jewish family who had fallen on hard times.[39] He had begun life in Kensington, but following the sudden death of his father – Sidney Woolf, Q.C. – the large family moved to suburban Putney. Leonard had grown up without financial reserves, and fared badly in his relationship with his emotionally demanding mother. At the time of their marriage, Virginia seemed embarrassed by Leonard's Jewishness. 'You seem so foreign,' she had written to him in her long letter of May 1912, while to friends she quipped about going to tea with 'Jews in Putney'.[40] In fact, she grew fond of the difficult 'Mother Wolf', and of Leonard's brothers.[41] When she later remarked, 'How I hated marrying a Jew' – one of her most controversial statements – it was, in fact, an acknowledgement of her earlier prejudice.[42]

During the first three years of their marriage, she and Leonard were building a partnership which would prove loving, stable and creatively fertile. Leonard – hard-working, rigid, his fanaticism offset by the nervous tremor in his hands – formed the backbone to Virginia's life. Within the parameters of the routine he set for her, she was able to recover and finally to flourish; there were no serious recurrences of her illness after 1915. Though she often railed against him, she was grateful. 'If it were not for the divine goodness of L. how many times I should be thinking of death,' she wrote later.[43] They kept hold of moments of romance and vagary. Leonard would always cherish his first vision of Virginia in Sussex, when he had kissed her on the Downs above Eastbourne; and she held fast to their affectionate animal names. The terrace at Asheham became known privately as 'Mandrill's walk', so-called because they had walked there on the first night of their marriage.

Many years later, in October 1938, Virginia was asked by *Harper's Bazaar* for a story, and began reshaping 'Lappin and Lapinova', a short piece 'written I think at Asheham 20 years ago or more'.[44] In the story, a young couple construct an elaborate imaginary kingdom, in which he is King Rabbit, and she his wide-eyed, diminutive wife. It rescues them in moments of tension, or in social situations: he twitches his nose; she dandles her little paws. Most of all, it is 'secret – that was the point of it; nobody save themselves knew that such a world existed.'[45] The survival of a marriage, the story implies, depends upon hidden happiness, on the creation of little beasts, and of private fantasy worlds.

When Virginia arrived at Asheham in September 1915, she was accompanied by a nurse. She was permitted to write letters – 'only to the end of the page, Mrs Woolf' – and to take short walks 'in a kind of nightgown.'[46] Venturing outside, if only briefly, was the single greatest pleasure of her day. 'It is so lovely that one walk gives me something to see for hours,' she wrote.[47]

Until now, Virginia had experienced Sussex largely as a convalescent. She had taken Little Talland House, in the village of Firle, on the advice of her doctors, who recommended she find a place to recuperate outside of London. The city could become jarring; at intervals, she needed privacy and quiet. The movement between city and country life was recuperative, but it was also an extension of childhood. The Stephen family had spent summers in St Ives, in Cornwall, in a large house from which Little Talland derived its name. Virginia had been brought up to understand this middle-class version of holidaying, or 'weekending'; to enjoy, slightly ironically, excursions into country life. At Little Talland, she decorated the rooms in bright colours, stained the floorboards 'the colours of the Atlantic in a storm' and sewed curtains.[48] There were currant and gooseberry bushes in the garden, and the Downs rose steeply nearby. But she thought the house 'inconceivably ugly', less a cottage than a 'hideous suburban villa', as she warned Leonard by letter.[49] It was a temporary address, an experiment – alongside Brunswick Square – in a new style of living: independent, informal, both in and out of London.

The sense of role-play continued at Asheham. Photographs in Virginia's album show the servants posing in the orchard, pretending to pick apples, or out in the field, recumbent on a bale of hay. Out on the terrace, Virginia – her face full after her seven-month rest cure – sits at an easel, paintbrushes in hand, or in a deckchair, fondling the ears of a dog. (This could have been Shot, who was in the habit of escaping, and once ran into the French windows, shattering the glass.) But for all the pastoral pleasures of weekends in the country, Virginia's relationship with Sussex was beginning to acquire emotional and creative depth. In her 1916 essay, 'Heard on the Downs', she described the rolling forms of the landscape, and a mix of rural sounds: grasshoppers, larks and – unnervingly – the low ripple of gunfire sounding across the Channel from France. But, despite the war, as she continued to recover, walking over the Downs produced states of deep feeling. It was as if the topography of the landscape mirrored her state of mind, at once wide and expansive, and yet marked with hollows and declivities. In the sun, the Downs could shine brilliantly, and yet their surface was continually chased by the shadows of clouds. 'Often down here I have entered into a sanctuary,' she wrote during another September, in 1928, when, recalling those painful summers of recovery at Asheham, she remembered 'seeing to the bottom of the vessel', and yet how the landscape had helped to restore equilibrium and calm.[50] 'How I adore the emptiness, bareness, air & colour of this!' she wrote from the safety of thirteen years' distance, describing 'this ecstasy of mine over the slope of Asheham hill'.[51]

But, in September 1915, she was living according to a strict routine: 'Bed-walk-bed-walk-bed-sleep.'[52] Aside from her nurse, Leonard, and occasional visitors, Asheham was deserted. (Following the outbreak of war, Vanessa moved between several houses in West Sussex, before living for a time in Suffolk.) Yet, as the weeks drew on, Virginia's letters to friends grew more animated, and she played up to her image as an invalid holed up in

Annie and Lily picking apples, and sitting on haystacks at Asheham

the country. 'I have just drunk a large cup of hot cocoa,' she told Margaret Llewelyn Davies; 'my fur cloak is over me, and my feet are wrapped in woollen jackets.'[53] To Lytton, she described feeling 'really all right again' and weighing twelve stone – 'three more than I've ever had, and the consequence is I can hardly toil uphill, but it's evidently good for the health'.[54] (Thinness, to which she was prone, would always fire off the warning signals of her deteriorating health. 'I find that unless I weigh 9½ stones I hear voices and see visions and can neither write nor sleep,' she wrote to Jacques Raverat a few years later.) It wasn't unpleasant, being bigger, but made her feel 'warm and mellow and generous and creative'.[55] Country life, she began to think sleepily, was 'a very pleasant one: swallows, rooks, thistledown, men thatching ricks'.[56] By October, the autumn days were passing quickly, bookended by mist. She helped the servants make blackberry jam, and collected walnuts which were spilling from a tree over the wall and into the garden. In her reports from Asheham, she was beginning to record her observations: 'I have never got so much out of nature before,' she wrote.[57] And yet her participation was minimal: she wasn't yet ready to begin her diary. Still, she felt relieved. She had lost almost three years to illness, and was eager to regain her footing in the world, in her marriage, and to write. 'I am very happy and sanguine,' she reassured Ka Cox, the friend who had superintended her at Asheham following her breakdown in 1913. 'I suppose I am happy merely because it is so pleasant to be well again.'[58] And to Duncan Grant: 'I am to be allowed to write, and gradually return to the world.'[59]

The following year, 1916, was one of continued recovery and routine. Travelling back and forth between Asheham and Hogarth House, Virginia was discovering the rhythm which would define her relationship to the country. It was a process of continual orientation: each place, and each house, established itself as either stimulation or recovery, and the movement between the two a way for her to ready herself for whichever was to come next. She continued to 'dip in' to London, but the city seemed strange, and periods at Asheham had

Virginia, with Shot the dog

their own pleasure, becoming increasingly necessary in preparing her for work.* 'I believe our half in half existence is ideal,' she had written to her friend Molly MacCarthy as the motion first got going. '[A] taste of people, and then a drench of sleep and forgetfulness, and then another look at the world, and back again.'[60] She would maintain this way of dividing her time until the next war; living between places stimulated her thoughts about writing, and kept her country life separate, distinct, as if coloured by its own moods.

She was beginning to write reviews again, and was teaching herself Italian. The publication of her first novel the previous spring

---

* 'London always seems to me rich in romance when I dip into it, which I do about twice a week, but thank God I don't live there,' she wrote to Vanessa on 11 February 1917. 'I find that when I've seen a certain number of people my mind becomes like an old match box – the part one strikes on, I mean. But its pleasant seeing our friends a-hopping in the frying pan.' *Letters*, II, 143.

had passed her by, a note sounded into the silence of illness. Published as *The Voyage Out* after nine years under the working title 'Melymbrosia', the book had been one of the triggers of breakdown. Virginia had laboured over five drafts during that time (and, at one point, had two on the go simultaneously). She worried that the final result was 'long and dull', and 'pure gibberish'.[61] And yet the novel, about a young woman's sexual awakening and death, was quietly radical. Travelling on her father's ship to South America, Rachel Vinrace – young and, like Virginia Stephen, motherless – gradually awakens to her fellow human creatures, to the world and its unreal beauty. Her voyage is one of self-discovery. Standing on a hilltop, she looks out over the lights of human settlements towards an unknown landscape of river and forest, of experience and possibility. But, though Rachel's world is vivid, it is bordered by darkness. She has bad dreams, and later dies of a fever in a state of delirium. In writing the novel, Virginia had been trying, as she told Lytton, to 'give the feeling of a vast tumult of life, as various and disorderly as possible'.[62] Certainly, she had drawn on her own experience, traversing the territory between order and disorder, madness and death. By 1916, though she was yet to find her footing as a writer, Virginia was able to look back on *The Voyage Out* as an experiment – albeit an unfinished one – and a first attempt.

That summer, she began to think more seriously about war. As food became scarcer, she extolled the virtues of semolina – 'We often eat nothing else for weeks. Try it with a spoonful of lard for supper' – and complained that Lytton, who visited, ate all the meat.[63] She was beginning to take an interest in politics and national affairs, and in London – where Zeppelin raids meant evenings on mattresses in the basement with the servants – began to host meetings of the Richmond branch of the Women's Cooperative Guild at Hogarth House. Inspired by her friendship with the Guild's president, the social activist Margaret Llewelyn Davies, Virginia tentatively broached her return to public life. She organised speakers: Ray Strachey on suffrage, Adrian Stephen on pacifism. And yet Margaret's presence revived old feelings of self-doubt. Though she admired her, she was intimidated, reminded, as she wrote in her diary, 'of the incredibly insignificant position I have in this important world'.[64]

Back in the country, she listened to the guns sounding from France. Two of her cousins were killed at the Front. At Asheham, she had missed much of what had been happening before the war, arriving just as everyone was flitting away. 'Bloomsbury is vanished like the morning mist,' she wrote sadly to Ka, who was in Corsica working with refugees.[65] Duncan and Bunny had declared themselves conscientious objectors, and were working in an orchard in Suffolk; Vanessa had gone with them, to paint and breed rabbits. 'I wish you'd leave Wissett,' Virginia wrote to her, with tempting descriptions of a large farmhouse, replete with pond and walled garden, about a mile from the village of Firle. 'You cant think how I miss you.'[66] She followed her friends' exemptions from military service closely: Lytton, declared medically unfit in a lengthy process that culminated in appeal; and Leonard, excused on the grounds of Virginia's health, as well as the tremor in his hand. ('It's a great mercy for us,' she told Ka.[67]) Though she still needed periods of quiet, being in the country sharpened her feeling of separateness, as if she existed on the periphery, an observer of other people's lives. She wrote pleadingly to friends for gossip. She was growing increasingly envious of her sister, both her ease in sexual relationships – by 1916, Vanessa had been married to Clive Bell for nine years, been passionately in love with Roger Fry, and was moving towards Duncan Grant – and her ability to produce and care for children. Virginia would always feel as if she was catching up. While she was holed up, convalescent, in the country, a version of life – raucous, noisy, plugged into the world – was passing her by.

~

She was upset when, during the summer of 1916, Bunny, Carrington and Barbara Hiles (a fellow student of Carringtons from the Slade), broke into the house during a night-time misadventure on the Downs. Scaling a drainpipe to let themselves in at an upstairs window, they ate apples, slept all in the same bed, and stole a book.

Virginia was stonily silent afterwards, and letters of apology followed. (The Woolfs even summoned Carrington to see them at Hogarth House.) But favour was restored by winter, when Carrington wrote to Lytton that she had been tobogganing with Vanessa, Duncan and Maynard on the Downs. She slid happily down Firle Beacon on Maynard's dispatch-case, at a 'terrific rate'.[68]

Why had Virginia been so distressed? As the years of her illness merged into war, her world had contracted, and Asheham, in the absence of Vanessa, was beginning to feel like her own. She cherished her friendships but was ambivalent about entertaining guests. (Later, having Carrington to stay, she wrote that the success of the visit was owing to only meeting her at mealtimes.) In the country, her solitude was best preserved. And, in her solitude, she approached other feelings – most of all, the desire to write. All through the pre-war years, she had been absorbing the vitality of her Bloomsbury friends, witnessing their experiments, sharing their interest in form and colour. She was inspired by her talks with Roger, and by another writer who, after three years of moving in the same literary circles, she was finally able to meet. Katherine Mansfield was to be a deeply influential presence in Virginia's writing life.

In July 1916, after a visit to Wissett, she remarked to Vanessa, 'I am very much interested in your life, which I think of writing another novel about. Its fatal staying with you – you start so many new ideas.'[69] So she began conceiving her second novel, *Night and Day*, in which a young woman casts off her Edwardian upbringing, and her family, in order to live self-sufficiently, as a separate, singular being, according to her own decision-making and ideas. In Katherine Hilbery, we catch a glimpse of how Virginia perceived her sister: courageous, competent, bold. But the observing and comparing went both ways. In a portrait of Virginia, one of four likely painted at Asheham before the war, Vanessa shows her sister in a high-sided armchair, loose brush-strokes emphasizing her relaxed, slouching posture.[70] A mushroom eye-socket and smudge of pink for mouth are all she is given for facial features. She is unknowable, a little obscure, her attention directed to the knitting in her hands. Yet the painting captures all the intimacy of sisters, caught in the middle of a conversation: gossiping, making plans. Virginia leans in, picks up a stitch, is about to look up.

The following year, 1917, was one of new beginnings. Seeing out the winter in London, Virginia was well and, finally, she and Leonard bought a press. Walking in Holborn in March, they noticed a small hand-press with a beginners' manual in a shop window and decided, after two years' talk, to take the plunge. The press was delivered to Hogarth House on 24 April, and was so heavy they needed the help of their servant, Nellie, to unpack it and set it up in the drawing room. One part was broken, so they sent for a replacement. Soon, however, the press was working, and they were hooked.

Vanessa Bell, *Virginia Woolf*, c.1912

As her biographer Hermione Lee describes, Virginia's job was typesetting.[71] Unwrapping each block of type from its brown paper parcel, she first arranged it into the type-case, taking each piece – upper- and lower-case letters, numerals, punctuation, all in Caslon Old Face – and placing it in its correct position. ('The work of ages, especially when you mix the h's with the ns, as I did yesterday,' she told Vanessa.[72]) Then, she began to compose words and sentences, taking the type from the type-case and placing it, face up and upside down, into the composing stick. To fill the stick exactly, lines were filled in with differently sized pieces of spacing. When each line was completed, she covered it with a strip of lead, and started on the next. The tray containing the composing sticks could hold four or five lines of type. When she had filled the tray, pressed tightly together so that none fell out, she carried it to Leonard at the machine, who began to arrange the pages in the right order, level up the type, and ink the disc. It required absolute concentration and precision. Virginia's vision swam with type as she composed each tray, letter by letter, line by line. She worked slowly at first, but would grow quicker.

The Woolfs' first publication was, by their reckoning, a success. Printing first a notice, they began work on a small booklet containing two stories, Leonard's 'Three Jews' and Virginia's 'The Mark on the Wall', illustrated with woodcuts by Carrington. The booklet – called, simply, *Two Stories* by Virginia Woolf and L. S. Woolf – was published in July, and sold all 134 copies. With a beginner's enthusiasm, Virginia began to expand her ideas. '[W]e are now in treaty for a much larger press,' she wrote ebulliently to Violet Dickinson, 'and mean to take it up seriously and produce novels with it. And we are even getting an apprentice!'[73] More quietly, to Margaret, she admitted that the press, bought with the idea that a project would aid her recovery, might be having its desired effect: 'You can't think how exciting, soothing, ennobling and satisfying it is.'[74]

~

And then, in August 1917, Virginia came back to Asheham. By now, Vanessa, Clive and Duncan were settled four miles away at Charleston, and she and Leonard had the house to themselves. Her health was steadily getting stronger, though Leonard insisted it remain a matter of careful domestic management. 'Please dont treat me as an invalid,' she had entreated her friend, Ottoline Morrell, several weeks earlier; '– save for breakfast in bed (which is now a luxury and not a necessity) I do exactly as others do.'[75] But to Leonard, who left Asheham periodically in August to attend Labour Party meetings, she delivered obedient little reports, aware she was still being monitored. 'Here I am, just having had a very good luncheon, ending with an apple,' she wrote knowingly, almost childishly; 'I'm drinking my glass of milk and ovaltine as I write.'[76]

In *Mrs Woolf and the Servants*, Alison Light outlines the domestic apparatus of the house; the Woolfs were not, in fact, alone.[77] They were accompanied to Asheham by their servants, Lottie and Nellie, who had previously worked for Roger Fry. But Lottie and Nellie didn't take to life in the country. Asheham was lonely and isolated. To go shopping, the women had to bicycle four miles to Lewes or Newhaven and, in the absence of plumbing, were made to carry water to the house in buckets. They cooked on an oil stove, and when the coal ran out were sent to look for sticks and branches. Nellie found the house 'too depressing' and tried, several times, to give notice.[78] 'Neither she nor Lotty feel they can face 6 weeks there in the summer,' Virginia had written despairingly to Vanessa, giving little thought to the women's own experience of country living, to the texture of their rural hours.[79] (Eventually, she persuaded Nellie to stay on.) For the rest, the Woolfs relied on local help. When they had first taken the house in 1912, they employed two young women, Annie and Lily, to cook and clean, supervised by Mrs Hoper, whose family owned both Asheham and Itford Farm. But Lily – an unmarried mother Woolf referred to unkindly as 'the prostitute' – was dismissed when she was found with a soldier in the kitchen, and Mrs Hoper was considered rather too old.[80] Mrs Funnell, the wife of the local shepherd, came next. By 1917, the Woolfs had engaged Mr and

Mrs Attfield, who lived at Asheham Cottages, as gardener and house-keeper. It was Mrs Attfield's job to prepare Asheham for their arrival, lighting fires and airing beds. But no one would agree to pump water for the house, or empty the pails ('Who emptied the sewage was a serious issue among the servants since it affected their earnings and their self-respect,' writes Light); eventually, a farm labourer was paid to do both.[81] At first, Virginia was complacent in her role as local employer. In letters, she drew caricatures of her neighbours, relishing the story of Lily's soldier, or Mrs Funnell's discovery of her daughter's pregnancy, the girl giving birth suddenly one night. (Virginia noted, with a mixture of condescension and admiration, how Mrs Funnell took the child in without fuss, as if adhering to an alternative code of country morals.) Later, she showed impatience in her diary when, arriving at Asheham, she *found no fires lit, Mrs Attfield not expecting us so late she said*, or the garden dishevelled, *Will hasn't done anything*. Yet, in time, she and Leonard grew to appreciate their rural community. Out walking, they talked to Mr Funnell, the shepherd, or to Frank Gunn of Itford Farm, or to Mrs Wooler, who, showing Virginia which fruits were for stewing, became a source of local knowledge.

Virginia liked Asheham for the reasons Nellie and Lottie didn't. Besides not having to worry about the more gruelling household jobs, its isolation, and its secluded atmosphere, pleased her. It seemed as if the house resisted human intervention; it had a life of its own.* Insects lived in the walls, and rats could be heard scampering through the attics at night. It was musty. Once, arriving from London, Virginia noticed the walls mottled with mildew, and a veil of steam rising from Leonard's armchair. (Promptly he caught a cold in the head.) Living at Asheham was to live in the natural, rather than the human, world. In spring, the place reverberated

---

* Writing many years later, Leonard remembered the house as having a 'personality of its own', something 'romantic, gentle, melancholy, lovely'. Leonard Woolf, *Beginning Again: An Autobiography of the Years 1911–1918* (The Hogarth Press, 1964), 56–57.

with animal noise, with the sounds of birds, of ewes giving birth in the meadow, or a barking vixen out with her cubs. From within, the rooms had a greenish, watery light, the trees coming up to the windows, filling the panes with shining apples and jostling leaves. Early attempts at dusting – 'It's really rather fun, and makes a wonderful difference, even in the smell of the air,' she evangelised – were soon abandoned.[82] Instead, Leonard would come in from the garden, a dog or two at his heels, and visitors were enjoined not to bring formal clothes. Scruffiness was part of Virginia's experiment in living, in which she was exercising small, domestic freedoms. The house made her feel 'completely natural', she told Saxon Sydney-Turner; inviting Carrington to stay, she boasted of Asheham's 'attractions', both 'animal and spiritual'.[83] Increasingly, she would describe its otherworldliness, the calm it restored to her, its atmosphere of sanctity.

She captured this atmosphere in a story of 1921. In 'A Haunted House', Virginia imagined a ghostly couple returning to the house in which they had once lived, wandering the rooms, and remembering their past lives. They are sensed by the house's new occupants – in the gentle movement of a curtain, the quiet shutting of a door. In daylight, the silence is broken by rural sounds, the 'wood pigeons bubbling with content and the hum of the threshing machine sounding from the farm'. And the atmosphere is sleepy: the shadow of a thrush crosses the carpet, a book slips into the grass. But, at night, the spirits return, persistent, harmless. Once more, they begin 'Wandering through the house, opening the windows, whispering not to wake us, the ghostly couple seek their joy.'[84]

~

Came to Asheham. When Virginia recommenced her diary on 4 August 1917, the men were mending the wall and roof, and Will Attfield had dug up the front bed. It had been raining, and there were bees in the attic chimney. Summer was tipping into autumn. But she liked the look of bare trees – 'as trees ought to be' – and the fading colours.[85] On her walk from Lewes, she passed through fields and dripping lanes, looking for mushrooms and insects, and watching the prisoners of war bringing in the harvest. Arriving in Sussex from London always shifted her mood. She became contemplative, sharpening her eyes for looking. In the hedgerows, she noticed the blackberries ripening.

Later that evening, sitting over a fire, she summarised her day in the small, marble-covered notebook. They were burning logs from the trees which had fallen during the spring storms, and they smelled 'so delicious'.[86] Whether she was tired, or aching, or melancholy, or content, she did not say. Thoughts and moods would not be part of her record, a story she chose not to tell. Instead, over the following weeks, until the Woolfs returned to Hogarth House on 5 October, her record would be of weather and walks, and the daily round of rural domestic life. It was an exercise in compression, each day pulled into a single, rhythmical paragraph. There was safety in containment, satisfaction – without the risk of overexcitement – in assembling each entry, like the tray at the printing press holding four or five lines of type. If she was careful, everything fitted in. It wasn't much, but it was enough to begin.

That August, Will blew up the wasps' nest with gunpowder, and Leonard made bookcases. He had injured his foot, and so Virginia went out walking alone. At Southease, she watched the men restoring the village church, and picnicked with Vanessa and the children on the Downs above Firle. Vanessa's sheepdog followed her home, bit Will, and terrorised the servants. She and Leonard had tea at Booth's in Brighton, and bicycled to Lewes for the market, and later to the cinema and to collect Katherine Mansfield from her train. Bunny, Barbara Hiles, Goldsworthy Lowes Dickinson, Lytton, Barbara and Nick Bagenal visited, and were taken on walks, or left to work on the terrace, or play chess. By 23 August, all the guests had gone. *Glad to be alone.* The weather worsened. The newspaper reported the wettest August on record, but Virginia kept her eyes on what was closest. The garden was *dishevelled*, the butterflies *ragged & washed out*, and rain soaked through her clothes. The harvest, Gunn told her, was ruined.

September began in mist. On the Downs, she watched a dog herding sheep and struggled to distinguish the sound of thunder from guns. She saw an aeroplane come down in a field near Glynde. Leonard spotted a farmworker scraping apples from their trees into a bucket, Will caught a rabbit with his ferrets, and the servants went shopping on the milk float. In Lewes, she bought a new pair of boots, and Leonard had his hair cut. One afternoon, on her way back from Glynde, she bicycled through a herd of Alderney cows; a few days later, on the way back from Charleston, she lay down in order to escape Vanessa's dog. There were more visitors. On 17 September, the clocks changed to winter time. *Spent afternoon indoors, a treat.* She busied herself with inside things: making a chair cover, printing photographs. When Desmond McCarthy visited, they walked to the pub in Rodmell, but were refused whiskey. They talked about the war – '*Whats it for?*' – and greeted German prisoners in the road. The evenings grew colder. *Real winter now.* The dahlia in the front bed came out.

In her small diary, Virginia's entries resembled bulletins; short, swift records of events. She was experimenting with a reporting style. 'We all know the charm of a country newspaper,' she had written in a review the year previously, 'in which columns are devoted to the flower show, or the trial of a poacher, or the wedding of the mayor's daughter, while the speeches of the Prime Minister and the agitations of the Empire are dismissed in very small type in some obscure corner.' The effect, she noted, was a 'delightful change of proportion', as if looking through a magnifying glass. Beyond its edge, the rest of the world has 'no existence at all'.[87] Following the years of her illness, Virginia wasn't yet ready to engage in politics. In her Asheham diary, world events fall away. It was a decision. How does one continue living in the midst of horror but by focusing one's attention on nearer things: the garden, dogs, things noticed in Lewes or Firle? Her news is of a local kind. Ordinary life is reassuring and quietly compelling. She tightened the focus of her looking. The guns were sounding from France, but she reported there was no yeast for baking bread, no sugar for jam.

Quickly, she established a pattern. Each day, she first recorded the weather, *Queer misty day*; her walk, *Went to post at Southease*; and anything she noticed, such as insects, *Saw 3 perfect peacock butterflies, 1 silver washed frit; besides innumerable blues feeding on dung*; or flowers and plants, *Round-headed Rampion, Thyme, Marjoram*; or birds, *Swallows flying in great numbers very low & swift in the field*; or labourers working in the fields, *Men working very late carting the clover*; before noting her route home, *Home by the fields*; and a domestic activity, *Made chair cover after tea*; or a task in the garden, *Planted a red flower with bulb given by Mrs Wooler to Nelly – some sort of lily*. Then she recorded the availability of rationed goods, *The co-op will allow more sugar, so we can now make jam, Gunn charges 4d quart for milk*; who visited, *Duncan over for dinner, Quentin ate till he was nearly sick at tea*; and what she ate, *Eating potatoes from the garden, We have begun to cook apples*. Occasionally, as on 26 August, she gave a glimpse of herself, planting a bulb, or holding her coat, or peering at a small object in her hands. *We meant to have a picnic at Firle, but rain started [. . .] Left my macintosh, so it came down hard, & we were very wet*; and, *The wind has brought down some walnuts, but they are unripe; the wasps eat holes in the plums, so we shall have to pick them. My watch stopped.*

Roughly, three days fitted to a page. She was used to composing in units, both at the press in Richmond and also in her notes for Leonard's research. He had begun work on a new book, *Empire and Commerce in Africa*, commissioned by the Fabian Society and published in 1920, which offered a critical account of international trade and economic imperialism. In its early stages, Virginia helped by compiling notes from consular records and trade documents, copying out quotations and drawing up tables in blue and purple ink (the same she used for her diary) on index cards made of thin paper. In total, by the autumn of 1917, she had compiled over one hundred notecards, nearly seventy of which were handwritten, the rest typed.[88] She tried her best to follow Leonard's instructions to be tidy: 'I copied out the notes, have put them all in order on your table (this is a lie, but I will do so).'[89]

Index cards are at once self-contained and relational; their meaning emerges in serial. The entries in Virginia's Asheham diary are threaded to the previous and the next. As the days go by, certain images and activities are repeated, so that patterns emerge and a more complete picture grows. Almost every day in August, she went looking for mushrooms with Leonard or one of the servants, walking up the down behind Asheham into a hollow scooped out of the hill. She documented each day's find in her diary. Monday 13 August. *Walked back from Glynde. To get mushrooms before dinner; every grass almost had blues asleep on it. Found very few mushrooms, having seen the shepherd bring a bag down in the morning.* Tuesday 14 August. *To get mushrooms & blackberries; the rings of horse mushrooms seem to put an end to the others: we only get a few.* Wednesday 15 August. *Went into hollow without success; but Nelly found more mushrooms on the top.* It was an ordinary, absorbing activity, and a way of marking and measuring time. She was becoming a creature of habit, her diary replaying her daily routine through tautology and repetition, each day gently modulating from one to the next, as in her competitive daily tally, *A certain number, Got plenty, almost a record find.* She was lingering on small deviations, the differences in sameness, by way of getting closer to describing the feel and texture of daily life. 'Almost every day has been lovely for some reason or other – all different,' she had written to Saxon Sydney-Turner in 1916, describing her rural routine.[90] The most mundane activities accrue meaning over time. Occasionally, she looked further afield, or branched out into the next hollow, though she always came back to Asheham, which she referred to as *my patch.* And she absorbed local knowledge. *Shepherd says mushrooms come for a fortnight & go for a fortnight; The servants got huge mushrooms called 'plate' mushrooms; the others 'natives', so the Woolers say.* When Mr Funnell offered her a bag, she could proudly identify its contents, but was *too timid to try.*

As autumn approached, the mushroom crops began thinning. On 14 September, she found *none*, though she *Cut up a great fungus like cheese.* Yet, in her diary, other patterns were emerging: the recurring dramas of rain storms and wasps' nests; getting her watch mended or buying a new pair of boots in Lewes. She continued to record each day, a meditation on ordinary things. The following year, looking back on her record, she noticed parallels: 'this week we went to buy an overcoat for L.; last year we bought boots.' Odd and pleasing, she thought, to realize 'how exactly one repeats one's doings'.[91]

Thinking in units – a paragraph, an index card, a tray containing a handful of lines of text – is to think in terms of forms which can be filled, completed, held. At Asheham, Virginia was staking out her boundaries, moving within her orbit of house, garden and Downs, while in her diary, she strove to find a form which could mirror her need for containment, keeping her a little shut off and protected from the world. Her entry for 10 September, a Monday, reads:

> *To post at Southease, but my boots hurt, from being too big, so we sat down, & L. went on. A perfect rather misty but cloudless day, still & very hot. Odd to find no flowers in the hedges, all brown & dead, because of the storm. Often a sound like rain, which turns out to be leaves falling. German prisoners stacking corn at the back of the house. They whistle a great deal, much more complete tunes than our work men. A great brown jug for their tea.*

Boots too big, complete songs, a great brown jug filled to the brim. There is safety in the feeling of fitting snugly into an allotted space. Mist envelops; Asheham is hedged about. In the wake of her illness, she was forming a protective shell around herself, a way of regulating what came in, and what could get out. Her desire for control found its way into her diary, revealed in her terse phrases, her abbreviative shorthand. It was a method of organizing, of taking the world and shaping it into a manageable thing, an inventory, or a list. She scraped back her language, rarely used the unruly, capacious 'I'. To find her, we need to follow her looking. The quality of her attention says most of all about who she is. For who else looks closely enough, pauses long enough, is precise enough, other than a novelist, a typesetter, a researcher, someone coming back to life, having been ill?

Was Virginia describing shifting skies, or interior states? Her diary was a record of natural phenomena and physical sensations, yet it was also a study in atmosphere in the lyric sense. Each daily entry is a prose poem of sorts. She was writing in a lyric mode, albeit a minor one, tuning deep feeling to a lower key. On 10 September, when she sat by the roadside and waited for Leonard, her scene is directly from English folk: a woman sitting by the roadside and contemplating the weather and her aching feet, listening to harvest songs and waiting for her lover. It's an emotional life in miniature, a cycle of subdued longing and ecstasy. Virginia was, in fact, creating a record of her interior life, in the many instances when pleasure, triumph, or melancholy seep out from within her neat paragraphs, as if such feelings cannot be wholly contained within the text. Waiting for Leonard, as she often did by roadside or field edge, had a special texture of feeling. Several years later, when he failed to appear from a late train, she bicycled frantically to the station, determined to find him. 'What an intensity of feeling was pressed into those hours!' she wrote. She would always feel lonely, an outsider, the 'old devil' of her illness chasing her in the dark.[92] At Asheham, such events were quieter. Her diary was stripped back, but not bare. *I walked back & waited for him in a barn where they had cut mangolds which smelt very strong. A hen ate them. L. came back & we walked back, very wet.* Her skies had their own intensity, chasing feelings of gloom and contemplation, desire and reverie.

~

If Virginia was using her Asheham diary as a way of regulating the world around her, she was also, in a more practical sense, using it to organize her domestic life. Wartime housekeeping was certainly more enjoyable in the country than in London. 'I bought my fish & meat in the High Street – a degrading but rather amusing business,' she had written in her unhappy diary of 1915. 'I dislike the sight of women shopping. They take it so seriously.'[93] Her aversion to shopping in Richmond was partly snobbish: she disliked, though she doesn't quite go so far as to say it, the sight of suburban housewives, with their shabby overcoats and string bags. Going shopping herself was a wartime necessity: she may have prided herself on living differently since childhood – doing with fewer servants, and learning to bake bread – but she wasn't content to stand in a queue at the butcher's shop.

Not a whiff of suburbia at Asheham. Shopping in the country had a very different flavour, made colourful with lively characters. Throughout August 1917, Virginia made a habit of going to the Monday market in Lewes, first bicycling to Glynde and then catching the train. She recorded her journeys in her diary, noticing *Calves wrapped in sacking lying on platform*, and *a drunk man being driven into Lewes on his fruit cart by a policeman*. She bought cigarettes and stamps, a pair of boots (before finding her old ones tucked away in a cupboard), and had her watch mended. Mostly, however, foodstuffs were bought closer to home. She cycled to Killicks or Bottens, local dairy farmers, for milk, and negotiated eggs with Mrs Attfield. She logged the fluctuating prices in her diary, *Eggs 2/9 doz. from Mrs Attfield, Gunn charges 4d quart for milk, Great question about Mrs Wooler's chicken; offers it for 2/6. Eggs now gone up to 3/- the dozen. Sausages here come in.* Rationing was becoming more severe. She noted its effects on the larder, *No yeast, so had to eat Bakers bread, wh. is very dull & dry.* As often as possible, meals at Asheham were supplemented with foraging. *We dined off blackberries last night.* And, *Servants got enough blackberries to make 4 lbs. jam, as well as pudding. Mrs Wooler calls them bilberrys, & says the jam won't keep.* She had a particularly sweet tooth for jam. And she recorded their spoils from the garden, *Eating our own broad beans – delicious*, and *A few plums on the tree. We have begun to cook apples.*

For if Virginia was recording domestic activities, she was also making a record of human life. Already, she was positioning herself as a local historian of a sort, writing down her impressions of country towns, and documenting manners and customs in her diary. On 8 August, she watched the pews of Rodmell Church being put into a tractor by *a man without a hand, a hook instead*, and met Mrs

Attfield carrying a *dead chicken in a parcel, found dead in the nettles, head wrung off, perhaps by a person.* Two days later, she gathered mushrooms *called 'plate' mushrooms; the others 'natives' so the Woolers say.* We might imagine all these conversations happening, Virginia out walking or in the kitchen, amused by and yet respectful of others' knowledge, their local speech. She was interested in her rural neighbours. Further afield, the church restoration at South-ease intrigued her, and on 25 August she went back, noting the *Wood from the church so rotten that it left sawdust on the grass where it stood,* and *A notice to say that restoration will cost £227. The church there in 966 AD.* And she watched the agricultural labourers closely. Though her diary evidences little grasp of the consequences of a ruined harvest on the local community, she was aware of the *Corn being cut by hand,* and the *Men still working & women too at 9.* Otherwise, she simply marvelled at the work being done. *Two mowing machines, with 3 horses each!*

As the war drew on, she became more methodical in her audit of local and domestic life. Her diary was evolving into a stock-taking exercise, a daily inventorying of food and household supplies. On 18 September, on the left-hand page of her diary, facing the entries for 17 and 18 September, she made a note:

Wed. 19: have had 6 eggs from Mrs W.
     3   „   „   Will.
    there are 2 over (Wed. A.M.)
Thur: 6 eggs fr. Mrs. Att:
    There are 5 at Thu. A.M.

And the following summer, similarly on the verso, she began comparing prices to the previous year's record. Pages in her diary were beginning to resemble a grocer's bill. Given wartime restrictions, domestic calculations were necessary, and yet Virginia's commitment to her diary – marking up the pages, day after day – was also a matter of style. She was practising her role as housekeeper, continuing the experiment with domesticity begun with Vanessa in Bloomsbury and continued with Leonard. It was from him she learned the practice of bookkeeping. From early in their marriage, Leonard logged every household expenditure in a large notebook, 'Accounts' handwritten in crude lettering across its front, its covers held together with a metal clasp. The book begins on 23 October 1914, in Virginia's hand. She records weekly totals for servants' wages, parcels, tea, the Co-op bill and the laundry, and notes any additions such as chocolate, sultanas or flowers. Already, there is a distinction between necessities and small extravagances, such as a trip to Somerset House, for which she notes refreshments and their fare. During Christmas 1914, she records a postal order for honey, and buys apples; on New Year's Eve they eat fish, pigeon and bacon; and on 4 January 1915, they buy a frying pan. But Virginia is slapdash in her bookkeeping, her handwriting untidy, often skipping over a double page. Her last entry in the account book tallies with the last in her diary: Monday 15 February 1915. During her breakdown, Leonard took over, quickly devising a table – dates by week along the top, categorised expenditures down the left-hand side of the page – in his tiny, spidery hand. Each week, he calculated the household balance, whether credit or deficit, until the notebook ran out of pages in 1953.

Writing to him from Asheham in October 1917, Virginia called him 'that generous old gentleman Mr Household'.[94] The nickname was partly affectionate, partly deferential: she was letting him know she had bought a first class railway ticket, rather than her usual cheap fare. Leonard's preference for systemization – for daily expenditures, notes about Virginia's health, for index cards put all in order on his desk – imposed itself on the Woolfs' household, which was run scrupulously. Begun during the early years of their marriage as a response to uncertain finances, Leonard's project of domestic economy nonetheless extended to every part of their lives. Virginia's Asheham diary is in keeping with the household accounts; whether food prices or natural phenomena, she was practising another kind of stock-taking. And yet, crucially, she was also practising her own domestic style. After Christmas, she conducted her own household reckoning – no tables, and taking in the weather.

Christmas. 1917. No milk to be had either from Gunn or Killicks. We got a certain amount from Bottens. 7ᵈ quart. had to make up with Nestle & Ideal Milk. Eggs 5ᵈ each. Had to buy dried eggs. Turkey 2/6 lb: so did not buy one. Bought a chicken which cost 6/- from Mʳˢ Attfield. Able to get 4lbs. sugar weekly from Coops. Christmas itself was wonderfully fine – frosty, but still. It took 5 hours to come down, owing to fog & frost. Liz & her 2 children here for Christmas & til new year. Ka came for the week end. Julian & Quentin. Two very bad days, but now (Jan. 3ʳᵈ) it is quite still, heavy frost on the grass, unclouded blue sky. Trees of course quite bare, with an occasional patch of soft bloom on them. Prisoners at work in the ditches. Threshing machine at on the road to Firle. Read Augo; Othello; received 2 books. Clive, Maynard over. Spent a night at Charleston. Rum honey 1/a lb: in Lewes.

The domestic mood was taking her. In early January 1918, she wrote another list. On the flyleaf of her notebook, she inventoried the household linen – the numbers of pillow cases, bath towels, table napkins, tablecloths – and what was left, after the Christmas guests had gone, to be washed. 'In' and 'out'. A list is both intimate and terribly ordinary. It is a condensed form, an accumulation of material details, a history in miniature. It produces a still life, an image of a house when no one is there, the beds stripped, the dining table glossy and bare, a notebook left in a drawer. Or a tableau, a moving image, of Virginia sorting and sifting, thinking about guests and the washing, planning her next visit to Asheham. Was she impatient with such tasks? Making a list, making a record; she was letting the details pile up. A list is lyric, compressed. And a list is testimony. To herself, that she was keeping hold of things by writing them down. And to others, to Leonard and Vanessa, that she was managing as keeper of her own house, and was content, and well.

Virginia's laundry list

~

But a list can also be constrictive. Occasionally, in her attempts at housekeeping, Virginia's old failures nipped at her. She continued to compare herself to Vanessa, who was living four miles away at Charleston, 'like an old hen wife among ducks, chickens and children'.[95] Virginia wrote another exaggerated description, this time in a letter to Violet Dickinson, barely disguising her jealousy: 'Nessa seems to have slipped civilisation off her back, and splashes about entirely nude, without shame, and enormous spirit.'[96] The shame, in fact, was entirely hers. She resented the restrictions of her own life, her retreat into Leonard's fastidiousness, and her routines, while knowing that she relied upon them all. Since her illness and marriage, the sisters' lives, and their styles of living, had continued to diverge. Vanessa could be chaotic, unmethodical – asked questions by her children, 'she invents all sorts of answers, never having known very accurately about facts', Virginia scoffed – and yet she was freely sensuous; even the birdsong at Charleston sounded sweeter, more voluptuous, Virginia thought, when she stayed the night.* She was desperately sensitive to comparisons of the two houses, which seemed to represent something different to each of the sisters. To Vanessa, Charleston was a place of experimentation and creativity, while for Virginia, Asheham meant privacy and recovery. 'I see you're going to say that Charleston is better than Asheham,' she wrote defensively to Vanessa. 'It cuts me to the heart.'[97] She made no secret of thinking Asheham the more beautiful, though her protestations could sound sticky and false. 'I don't think Charleston can hold a candle to it,' she wrote to Saxon Sidney-Turner, lapping up his praise of Asheham, and, by extension, her way of life.[98]

To her friends, Virginia was far from the brittle, frigid creature she felt herself to be. Bunny Garnett remembered her differently: walking to Charleston to visit Vanessa, bringing with her a light-hearted, roaming spirit, and the freshness of the wind off the Downs. She was practising her own vagaries, establishing her own freedoms from constraint. On 18 August, when she went into Lewes where they *bought several things*, she left it to Leonard to take up the account book and itemize their expenditure in the shops. Instead, her diary began to document small departures from efficiency and timeliness – walks and picnics scuppered by rain, a shortcut on her bicycle which took double the time. The garden continually surprised her, bulbs flowering late, anemones emerging from dormancy, nasturtiums surging over the wall. She was losing punctuality. Is that why she wrote the year 1907 on the title page of her diary, before crossing it out, and rewriting 1917? *My watch stopped. We forgot the change to summer time on Sunday, so didn't*

---

* Virginia Woolf to Lady Robert Cecil, 14 April 1917, *Letters*, II, 149; and, 'Last night at Charleston I lay with my window open listening to a nightingale, which beginning in the distance came very near to the garden. Fishes splashed in the pond. May in England is all they say – so teeming, amorous, & creative.' Woolf, 28 May 1918, *Diary*, I, 151.

have breakfast til 10. She was adjusting to country life, to rural hours, which were measured in mushroom crops and corn stacks, in journeys home across the fields or over the Downs.

Over the years, as she spent more time at Asheham, Virginia began to look for precedents of country living, and for other experiments in diary-keeping to measure against her own. In the spring of 1917, she had read *Walden*, Henry David Thoreau's account of living in semi-isolation near Walden Pond in Concord, Massachusetts. In the essay which followed, Virginia described Thoreau's circumscribed life: a life of walking, camping, staying at home, and keeping a diary – the habit of ' "settling accounts" with his own mind'. And yet, in Thoreau's diaries, it is the 'common things' – weather, daily routines – which are rendered astonishing and strange. 'When we read [. . .] the record of his two years in the woods, we have a sense of beholding life through a very powerful magnifying glass,' she wrote, recalling her essay about the country newspaper. 'To walk, to eat, to cut up logs, to read a little, to watch the bird on the bough, to cook one's dinner – all these occupations when scraped clean and felt afresh prove wonderfully large and bright.' She liked Thoreau's 'method of intensification', his manner of closely observing his surroundings.[99]

Virginia's essay was published in the *Times Literary Supplement* on 12 July to mark the centenary of Thoreau's birth; her own two years' record of rural living began three weeks later. She was beginning to write her way into an English literary tradition of naturalism, taking her place alongside figures such as Gilbert White, the eighteenth-century clergyman who meticulously documented the flora and fauna around his home in the Hampshire village of Selborne. And yet she had long been wary of a genre which could appear quaint. Holidaying in Warboys in Cambridgeshire in the summer of 1899, she had written in her diary, 'I am, at the present moment [. . .] in love with a country life. I think that a year or two of such gardens &

green fields would infallibly sweeten one & soothe one & simplify one into the kind of Gilbert White old gentleman or Miss Matty old lady that only grew till now for me inside the covers of books. I shd. be writing notes upon the weather, & I shd. turn to my diaries of past years to compare their records.'[100] Such projects were better suited to clergymen and spinsters than young women. Later, however, reading Dorothy Wordsworth, she found a model of nature writing closer to her own. In 1929, she began notes for a series of four essays about eighteenth-century figures, for which she read Dorothy's journals – both the diary she kept at Alfoxden in Somerset, and the four rough notebooks written between 1800 and 1803 at Dove Cottage above Grasmere, in the Lake District, where she lived with her brother, William. Virginia liked the 'homely narrative' of the journals, which described, as Dorothy's biographer Frances Wilson puts it, 'a routine of mutton and moonscapes, walking and head-aches, watching and waiting, pie-baking and poem-making'.[101] It was their style which caught Virginia's attention. The terse, method-ical entries left little room for Dorothy and her moods of melancholy and desire. The passionate, searching 'I' of the Grasmere journals – like the 'I' at Asheham – was 'ruthlessly subordinated', Virginia noted in her essay, to water, trees and sky. And yet the plainest state-ments could be unexpectedly evocative. Dorothy's descriptions were unadorned and direct: moonlight on mountains, light catching on a sheep's fleece, ripples like herrings on water. To read them, Virginia wrote, was to follow her line of vision, to witness the landscape opening up by degrees, to 'see precisely what she saw'.[102]

She was thinking about Dorothy's diaries in the light of her own. 'It is strange how vividly all this is brought before us,' she wrote in the essay, which she revised for her second *Common Reader* in 1932, 'con-sidering that the diary is made up of brief notes such as any quiet woman might make of her garden's changes and her brother's moods and the progress of the seasons.'[103] Their compressed style, so like the one she had cultivated in her notebook at Asheham, pleased her to the point of frustration. '[I]f the written word could cure rheuma-tism, I think her's might,' she wrote to Vita Sackville-West. 'Have you ever read her diaries, the early ones, with the nightingale singing at Alfoxden, and Coleridge coming in swollen eyed – to eat a mutton chop? [. . .] I like them very much; but can't say I enjoy writing about them, nine pages close pressed. How can one get it all in?'[104]

To write about the natural world was to contain it, requiring a style, she noted to Vita, 'pressed as tight as hay in a stack'.[105] But if it was a literary style, it was also a scientific one, with roots reaching far back into Virginia's life. As a child, she had been schooled in the Victorian tradition of the natural sciences, with its emphasis on species collection, taxonomy and classification. Walking with her father in Kensington Gardens, the young Virginia Stephen had learned to botanize, and there were outings to the Natural History Museum, where she went with her siblings – members of the family Entomological Society, of which Leslie Stephen was president – in search of some 'mythical underground collection of bugs'.[106] At home, they carried out their own natural history pursuits. Virginia's letters to her brother, Thoby, were filled with snippets of news about insects left in her care – 'the chrysalises are still in their maiden state', 'No bugs are out [. . .] I am afraid they must have overslept' – and, in her diary, she recounted their twilight business of catching moths.[107] One summer evening at Warboys, the siblings set off into the woods, where pieces of flannel dipped in rum and sugar had earlier been pinned to trees. Excitement swelled as the lantern illuminated a large moth, a red underwing, 'his wings open, as though in ecstasy, so that the splendid crimson of the underwing could be seen – his eyes burning red, his proboscis plunged into a glowing stream of treacle. We gazed one moment on his splendour, & then uncorked the bottle.'[108]

The Stephen children felt 'some unprofessional regret' at the death of the moth.[109] The large, delicate creature would resurface in Virginia's essays, a reminder of her ambivalent feelings towards the practice of specimen collection. A review of 1916 opens with a recollection of a trip to the Natural History Museum, where, peering into display cases, she had examined rows of 'insects so small that they have to be gummed to the cardboard with the lightest of fingers, but each of them, [. . .] has its fine Latin name spreading far to the right and left of the miniature body. We have often speculated upon the capture of these insects and the christening of them, and marvelled at the labours of the humble, indefatigable men who thus extend our knowledge.'[110] The case was impressive: there was reassurance in knowledge, in organizing the natural world into groupings, and pleasure in nomenclature. But she was also aware of its limits. Museum collections were histories of empire in miniature. And they implied other boundaries and exclusions, not just between species, but also between those who study them and those who do not, differentiating between the educated and the uneducated – namely, women. Virginia took up the idea. Throughout her life, she would refer to the study of natural history to sharpen her outsider politics, particularly in her writing of women's lives. In essays of the 1920s, she celebrated unschooled, adventurous and complex Victorian women of science: the entomologist Eleanor Ormerod, whose investigations into 'pests' led her to advocate for the – extremely toxic – insecticide 'Paris green'; the biologist and botanical artist Marianne North (a model for Clarissa's Aunt Helena in *Mrs Dalloway*), who erected a gallery to house her life's work at Kew Gardens; and Mary Kingsley, whose discovery of fish species in West Africa, despite her lack of formal education, would become a model for the untold scope of women's achievements in *Three Guineas*.

By 1919, when she returned to the Warboys expedition in her essay, 'Reading', Virginia had long put away her butterfly net. In her retelling, the greater pleasure of catching moths lay not in the killing, but in the ritualistic sugaring of the trees, the sight of the quivering forms in torchlight. In the essay, the evening is darker than in her diary, the beam of the torch contracting her vision, so that – to echo her earlier imagery – 'the little circle of forest where we stood became as if we saw it through the lens of a very powerful magnifying glass'. She becomes aware of the presence of a multitude of insects – 'here a grasshopper, there a beetle, and here again a daddy longlegs' – besides the 'soft brown lumps' of the moths on the trees.[111] It is a heightened, sensuous moment – the moths drinking, the grass crackling, the whirring of innumerable wings. Virginia, now in adulthood, pauses, less a huntress than an observer of the scene. Her stance reflects broader currents in the life sciences in the early twentieth century, when the natural history tradition – with its practices of species collection, preservation and taxonomy – was giving way to new disciplines of ethology and ecology. The scientific study of the natural world was shifting from museums and gentlemen's collections towards the observation of living things in the field. Mischievously, in an article for *The Times* in 1916, Virginia suggested the skills for the new biology were, in fact, those acquired in a late Victorian childhood. Trawling the air with a butterfly net, or lying in wait on a hillside, she had developed her capacity for looking. 'Are there as many butterflies now as when we were children?' she asked. 'Where are the Small Coppers, the Wood Arguses, the Clouded Yellows which were then so frequent?' The truth, she wrote, is 'that having ceased to collect, we have also ceased to notice'. She urges her reader to sit for an hour, training their eyes so that they might see 'some brown insect on a swift, curved flight' or 'attached to each grass stem near the top'.[112] The net is redundant, the pin and canvas to be put away, and yet to find insects, and to observe them, requires a return to a simpler set of practices – waiting, watching, looking.

At Asheham, she was conducting her own enquiry into the natural world.* Her small diary was both a kind of private, neurotic writing, but also an experiment within a broadening discourse of curiosity and discovery. Taxonomy was useful. The notebook reads as a topographical record of her long walks, during which she observed insects and birds. She noticed butterfly species, both common varieties, *A few brown heath butterflies*, and rarer ones, *Saw a fritillary on the downs. Moderate size with silver on the back of the*

---

* Partly, it was a return to childhood adventures. 'Wouldn't bugs be a good thing to start?' she wrote to Vanessa on 26 April 1917, telling her she had bought a book by the nineteenth-century naturalist Francis Buckland at Bumpus on Oxford Street. '[W]hat fun to sugar the trees again. When Moore was with us last summer he discovered several varieties of Blue on the downs.' *Letters*, II, 149.

wings; plants appearing in unexpected places, or as signifiers of seasonal change, *Heather growing on the top, making it look purple; never seen it there before, Saw the first chestnut leaves out on the avenue*; and she watched the flights of birds, *A great white owl, looking like a sea gull, Swallows flying in great numbers very low & swift in the field*. She didn't flinch from gruesome sights, but described them plainly and without flourish, *We walked, startled hawk in the hollow, & found the feathers of a pigeon, he having carried away the bird, Then to get milk at cottage, & round into hollow, where we found 3 mushrooms; & the spine & red legs of a bird, just devoured by a hawk – either pigeon or partridge*. She was immersed in fieldwork, and was assiduously writing up her notes. 'My record must be solely of beetles & butterflies,' she mused the following August in the longhand diary she was by then keeping, alongside her smaller Asheham one.[113] And later, 'Asheham diary drains off my meticulous observations of flowers, clouds, beetles & the price of eggs; &, being alone, there is no other event to record.'[114]

As her diary developed, Virginia was writing both within and against the scientific tradition in which she had grown, was creating her own living taxonomy. She was becoming expert in the still, slow practice of observation, studying insects, animals and birds according to their behaviour, and in their natural environment. Sitting or lying for long periods in the hollow above Asheham, she began to recognize the relationship between living things and the surrounding landscape, noticing the hillside *swarming with little black beetles* in unusually hot spring weather, butterflies with *red spots on their necks – some parasite*, or *ragged & washed out* after rain. Her vision swam with insects as it had swum with the blocks of type at Hogarth House. She monitored the flight patterns of birds, the *Rooks beginning to fly over the trees, both morning and evening, sometimes with starlings*. She was concerned with accuracy. *I heard what I thought the first half of cuckoo*, she wrote in March, *but the book says it's too early*. And she found new ways of studying insects. There was a small episode involving a pupating caterpillar, recounted in the style of her childhood letters, a series of entomological bulletins: *Saw a large green caterpillar in hollow, with 3 purple spots on each side by the head,* she wrote on 12 August; a few days later, she noted its progress, *Sat in the hollow; & found the caterpillar, now becoming a Chrysalis, wh. I saw the other day. A horrid sight: head turning from side to side, tail paralysed; brown colour, purple spots just visible; like a snake in movement.* The following August, in the same spot, she found another, *Into the hollow after tea & found the same caterpillar – dark brown with 3 purple spots on either side of the head – that we found last year. We took him home*; then, on Tuesday 6 August, *The caterpillar has disappeared. There is a purple smudge on the window sill, which makes it likely that he was crushed.* Finally, a week later, *Found another caterpillar*; and, on 6 October, *Our caterpillar has turned into a chrysalis.*

'How does she rewrite that major figure in her own upbringing, her own "development", Charles Darwin?' asked the scholar Gillian Beer in 1996. 'Darwin's early writing elated Virginia Woolf, I think.'[115] There was a strong family connection. The Stephen and Darwin families knew each other, and Leslie Stephen owned inscribed copies of *On the Origin of Species* and Darwin's journals of his voyage on the *Beagle* (to which Virginia owed her descriptions of Rachel Vinrace's journey to South America in *The Voyage Out*). These books re-emerged many years later when, collecting belongings from her bombed house on Mecklenburgh Square in October 1940, Virginia wrote in her diary: 'A wind blowing through. I began to hunt out diaries. What cd we salvage in this little car? Darwin & the Silver, & some glass & china.'[116] Darwin was her inheritance, and what she absorbed from reading his work she reflected upon creatively and appraised throughout her writing life. When, at Asheham, she sat in the long grass watching for butterflies and insects, she was engaged in her own contemplation of an entangled bank, relaying the fullness and variety of nature, its complexly woven, interdependent systems, in her diary.[117] In her other writing, the image of the magnifying glass recurs; later, in her short fiction, she would adopt it as narrative method. In 'Kew Gardens', one of a series of bright, rapid literary experiments she produced between 1917 and 1920, scale is reversed. Set over the course of a hot July afternoon, the story moves from an oval-shaped flowerbed to the groups of people walking by, and the conversations passing airily between them. In the descriptions of the bed, vision narrows to focus on the 'vast green spaces' among stalks, where a snail 'now appeared to be moving very slightly in its shell, and next began to labour over the crumbs of loose earth'. The pebbles obstructing its way are like 'round boulders of grey stone', and the grass appears massive, as 'flat bladelike trees'. In the story, human life takes place off-centre, in the murmur of conversation floating over and past the flowerbed. Hierarchies, boundaries between species, have been unsettled and disturbed. The people walking in the gardens are 'not unlike' the insects in the beds, moving with 'curiously irregular' movements, zig-zagging like butterflies.[118]

Like the chrysalis, Virginia was emerging into her identity as a nature writer, developing a style by turns creative and scientific, poetic and precise. She used her Asheham notebook as a storehouse, filling it with images and incidents to be drawn upon later in her novels: Julian and Quentin each carrying home a skull with antlers, like those in the attic nursey in *To The Lighthouse*; *A snake, grass, about 2 feet twisted across the path in front of us* – and another, this time eating a toad – like the one Giles Oliver crushes with his tennis shoes in *Between the Acts*. A continuous stream of butterflies and moths. Always, she was practising. ' "Whats the phrase for that?" ' she would ask her diary in 1928 when, sitting in the garden at Charleston, she attempted to describe rooks in flight. The birds had fitted so neatly into her phrases at Asheham – *Rooks building in the evenings, Rooks stealing walnuts in great numbers* – when she had fixed them in her notebook, like insects secured by a pin. Then, her project had partly been one of containment, of organizing the natural world into a manageable form. In 1928, she was reaching for something fuller, more open-ended, trying to 'make more & more vivid' the sight of the rooks rising and falling, moving through the air 'like swimmers in rough water'.* But to try to fix living things

---

* Here is the remarkable description in full: '[W]hy did my eye catch the trees? The look of things has a great power over me. Even now, I have to watch the

in language was to attempt the paradoxical; words make specimens of creatures. 'The look of things has a great power over me,' she reflected; 'what little I can get down with my pen'.[119]

~

And if Virginia was becoming a nature writer, she was also developing her own philosophy of the living world, one conceived around a metaphysics of connection. In her article for *The Times* in 1916, she recalled the appearance of a death's-head hawkmoth at Asheham, an insect as 'large and soft as a mouse', its wings the texture of velvet.[120] She described it drowsing, and hearing it squeak; in the evening, it took its flight. Moths would become one of the most potent images in her writing, a complex symbol for the emergence of human creativity, but also for something inexplicable, some undercurrent or spirit: what she described as, 'All the romance of life'.[121] She liked their splendour. (In a letter of March 1917, she compared Duncan Grant to 'a beautiful but rather faded moth' after a night's 'debauch' among 'the red hot pokers and passion flowers of Hampstead'.[122]) Looking at the span of her work, moths trace a wavering yet determined path, taking off from her Warboys journal to flit through *Jacob's Room* – in which the young Jacob Flanders, an incarnation of her brother, Thoby, describes their markings in his notebook – and 'The Moths', her working title for *The Waves*, before settling finally on the windowsill in one of her final essays, 'The Death of the Moth'.

At Asheham, moths provided a key to her developing ideas. She was thinking about connection between organisms, but also

---

rooks beating up against the wind, which is high. & still I say to myself instinctively, "Whats the phrase for that?" & try to make more & more vivid the roughness of the air current & the tremor of the rooks wing <deep breasting it> slicing – as if the air were full of ridges & ripples & roughnesses; they rise & sink, up & down, as if the exercise <pleased them> rubbed & braced them like swimmers in rough water. But what a little I can get down with my pen of what is so vivid to my eyes, & not only to my eyes: also to some nervous fibre or fan like a membrane in my spine.' Woolf, 12 August 1928, *Diary*, III, 191.

between human and animal life. Was there some greater force, or spirit, within which the earth revolved entire? She seemed to feel it in Sussex, where, walking or reading in the garden, she sensed a life-force moving through the landscape, joining human, insect and animal life with the timeless, undulating Downs. After all, it was in the country, as she wrote in her diary in March 1918, that one 'develops the spiritual side of life'.[123]

Yet, while moths symbolised connection, they were also creatures of the underworld, living remnants of an enduring, primeval darkness. She had visited the dark in the wood at Warboys, where the effect of the torch beam, like the magnifying glass, was to concentrate, to create a microcosm. Beyond it was the sound of deep sighing, of innumerable 'unseen lives'. To capture the moth had, in that moment, 'proved our skill against the hostile and alien force'. She had visited the dark in her illness, a darkness to which she hoped never to return. Now, in her convalescence, she was emerging, like the garden from nightfall, into 'morning sounds, trees, apples, human voices'; an 'order [. . .] imposed upon tumult; form upon chaos', perpetual as day.[124]

At Asheham, as she continued to recover, Virginia was finding a new way of being in nature. She was practising a convalescent quality of attention, through which she reached an understanding of the natural world. There were no hierarchies, and proportions could be reversed. All was threaded together. A day spent outdoors in the late summer of 1918 clarified her emerging, unifying philosophy. Lying in the hollow, waiting for Leonard to come out mushrooming, she watched a hare moving close by, unaware of her presence. 'I seemed to see how earthy it all was,' she wrote afterwards in her diary, imagining the sight of herself from above, miniscule, 'as if a moon-visitor saw me', and 'thinking suddenly, "This is Earth life"'.[125]

When Virginia sat down to write at Asheham, she did so at a table in front of the window, looking out over the meadow which stretched down to a line of trees, their shapes pared back, their colours bright, like one of Vanessa's paintings. She was interested in the differences between working in London and the country. At Asheham, it seemed as if something unusual took place in her brain, so that the texture of her attention shifted. Reading *Othello* in the garden, she described a kind of ecstasy, her thoughts becoming 'clearer & more concentrated, & reading print as if through a magnifying glass'.*

It was a relief to be away from the manuscript for her second novel, *Night and Day*, at which she was continuing to struggle. The form felt complicated, burdensome, its mode historical. In the country, however, she could enjoy different processes of thinking and feeling. On her walks, new ideas took shape swiftly, colours were deeper, as if her senses were more acute. Throughout the summer of 1917, she had been thinking about naturalism, but also about painting; now, ideas and images began to cross-pollinate and connect. Could there be an entirely new way of approaching her work? The vision she had been practising at Asheham – both microscopic, and abstract – could, Virginia realized, be applied to her own writing, and to printing books.

Following the publication of *Two Stories* in July, she and Leonard had moved swiftly onto new projects. Virginia was anxious to catch up, to squeeze the time lost to illness into the next two years. Earlier that summer, she had agreed to printing Katherine Mansfield's long short story *Prelude* (though it wouldn't come out until the following year), and now conceived an idea for a book of woodcuts produced by Vanessa and Duncan. What had begun as an idea for simple, decorative elements to the stories – 'they make the book much more interesting than it would have been without', she had written to Carrington about the four small woodcuts commissioned for *Two Stories*, including two domestic scenes and a snail – was quickly evolving into a preoccupation with the medium itself.[126] Virginia liked the handmade quality of woodcuts, their jagged

---

* Woolf, 9 June 1919, *Diary*, I, 278. Later, she remembered reading *Othello* at Asheham, 'sitting in the garden there, so sublime'. 28 March 1937, *Diary*, V, 72.

edges and not-quite-straight lines. Images could be cropped, or expanded into focus; an artform in miniature. Interest in woodcuts among the Bloomsbury painters was largely due to Roger Fry who – following William Morris's example at the Kelmscott Press, along with experiments among European painters – began commissioning pieces from the Omega Workshops, the decorative artistic project he was running out of 33 Fitzroy Square. Christmas cards by Fry, Duncan Grant and Winifred Gill had circulated since 1911, followed by bookplates, and by 1917, when they were commissioned by the Hogarth Press, both Carrington and Vanessa had made their first forays into the medium. The painters relished such an intuitive process. Carving directly into soft wood, the markings of tools and the tremors of hands were as much a part of the final pieces as form and composition. And they were a democratic medium, relatively easy and cheap to reproduce. The final product, Virginia observed to her sister, 'could easily be framed, or pinned up'.[127]

In London in the autumn of 1917, on her return from Asheham, Virginia shopped excitedly for brightly coloured papers, considering at length their weight and finish. And yet her hand-press, assembled in the drawing room at Hogarth House, was small. One day, struggling to fit a woodcut of Carrington's to the page, she took a chisel and began hewing at the block herself. Working directly, and in a visual medium, pleased her immensely, and she was in a flush of ideas. It was as if she had brought all the energy of her looking at Asheham back to London, and to the Press. '[W]e must make a practice of always having pictures,' she wrote to Carrington, outlining her plan for a better way of printing reproductions; and, to Roger Fry, 'Its most fascinating work'.[128]

The following summer, in July 1918, she wrote to Vanessa requesting illustrations for 'Kew Gardens', her burbling, murmuring story of voices drifting above the flowerbed. Sending her the manuscript was significant: at last, Virginia was moving away from the apparatus of novels like *Night and Day*, and was revealing work in a new style. '[Y]ou will see that it's a case of atmosphere, and I don't think I've got it quite,' she wrote of the story, adding, 'Don't you think you might design a title page?'[129] Vanessa responded quickly with a design for a frontispiece depicting two hatted women walking side by side against a leafy background with flowers, and a tailpiece of a butterfly and a caterpillar. 'It's a relief to turn to your story,' she wrote, 'though some of the conversation [. . .] I know too well!'[130] The conversation to which Vanessa was referring – 'My Bert, Sis, Bill, Grandad, the old man, sugar, sugar, flour, kippers, greens, sugar, sugar, sugar' – is a queasy aspect of the story: Virginia's portrayal of working-class women, like her depictions of her neighbours at Asheham, is cartoonish and imitative, though the women's voices contribute to the general, wavering tissue of sound.[131] It put Vanessa in mind of a painting she had begun for the Omega in 1913, and worked on for several years. *A Conversation* was one of her major achievements, hailing the revolutionary pre-war period in which she had shifted towards simplified forms and patches of colour. In the painting, three women hunch together by a window, engaged in serious, secretive talk; behind their heads, a flowerbed is visible. It is interesting that Vanessa thought about this painting in response to Virginia's story. Reading one onto the other, visual and atmospheric affinities emerge. There is the curved line of the flower-bed, the bright blooms, and the conversation itself – intimate, conspiratorial – just out of earshot. But there is also a feeling of collapsing scales. The three women at the window might be large insects, with their monolithic, rounded forms, painted beetle-black, or the striated colours of soil; their small faces craning inward, drawing to a point of three sets of narrowing and expanding eyes.

'Kew Gardens' was published on 12 May 1919. It was a wonderfully homespun production. The cover, cut by hand from commercial wallpaper, was marbled with daubs of black, indigo and earth-coloured paint, the patterns of the wallpaper – one chintz, another peach-coloured art deco (each copy being different) – visible overleaf. It seems Virginia and Leonard couldn't decide how to print their names, and so a small slip of paper – typed 'V and L S Woolf', impersonal, professional – was pasted over what was originally beneath. The story was bookended by Vanessa's woodcuts. Bold,

Vanessa Bell, *A Conversation*, 1913–16

simple, they pick up on the sensations in Virginia's story, of looking closely, of training one's vision to the natural world, of seeing with a botanist's eye.

The sisters' collaboration was important to Virginia. Since her illness, and given the mixture of admiration and jealousy she felt towards Vanessa, she craved closeness. She was gratified that, in responding to her work, Vanessa had produced something 'just in the mood I wanted'.[132] She wrote gratefully: 'I think the book will be a great success – owing to you; and my vision comes out much as I had it, so I suppose, in spite of everything, God made our brains upon the same lines, only leaving out 2 or 3 pieces in mine.'[133]

But Vanessa wasn't so sure. The woodcuts had bothered her, and she was displeased with the appearance of the book, telling Virginia she wouldn't illustrate any more stories 'under those conditions'; that is, the feeling that they were making it up as they went along. 'Nessa & I quarrelled,' Virginia wrote in her diary on 9 June; 'she [. . .] went so far as to doubt the value of the Hogarth Press altogether [. . .] This both stung & chilled me.'[134] And yet, for Virginia, 'Kew Gardens' marked a turning point, heralding her independence as a writer. Though set in London, the story bore the imprint of the solitude and clarity of vision she had experienced at Asheham, when, having recovered from illness, she answered to no one but herself. And in London, too, publishing her own work freed her. For the first time, she realised, she was 'able to do what one likes – no editors, or publishers, and only people to read who more or less like that sort of thing'.* As she had done with her small, elliptical diary, she now lingered over the pleasures of writing 'short things', 'all in one flight', with none of the weighty clumsiness, the responsibility and apparatus of a novel. She was approaching a breakthrough in her work: 'I daresay one ought to invent a completely new form.'[135]

Virginia's unfolding experimentalism owed much to Vanessa's own. Just as she observed, not without jealousy, the freedoms of her sister's life at Charleston from the safety of her station at Asheham, so Virginia monitored developments in Vanessa's work. She was, perhaps, learning to channel her rivalry into something fruitful, by connecting deeply, artistically, with the sister who had, she felt, overshadowed her for years, A little competitively, she began her own interrogations into her 'aesthetic emotions', what she described, hesitatingly, as 'my plastic sense'.[136] She was practising with ideas that had emerged earlier in the decade, when the Bloomsbury artists, following the French painters, engaged in debates on 'significant form'; the idea, as Roger Fry asserted in his introductory essay to the Second Post-Impressionist Exhibition, that the artists did not 'seek to imitate form, but to create form; not to imitate life,

---

* Virginia Woolf to David Garnett, 26 July 1917, *Letters*, II, 167. And, 'Its tremendous fun,' she remarked to Vanessa, 'and it makes all the difference writing anything one likes, and not for an Editor.' 26 July 1917, *Letters*, II, 169.

but to find an equivalent for life'.[137] Now, Virginia was determined
to absorb some of Fry's thinking into her own work, to experiment
with the idea that form could take precedence over content, and to
determine whether words could behave as paint.

During the course of their long conversations, Virginia listened
attentively to Fry's ideas, measuring them against her awakening
visual sense. In April 1918, following a visit to see Clive and Vanessa
at 46 Gordon Square, she recorded as much as she could of their
talk about a small Cézanne – 'about the size of a large slab of chocolate' – which had recently been acquired by John Maynard Keynes in
Paris.[138] 'There are 6 apples in the Cézanne picture,' Virginia wrote
in her diary,

> What can 6 apples *not* be? I began to wonder. Theres their relation-
> ship to each other, & their colour, & their solidity. To Roger & Nessa,
> moreover, it was a far more intricate question than this. It was a
> question of pure paint or mixed; if pure which colour: emerald or
> veridian; & then the laying on of the paint; & the time he'd spent, &
> how he'd altered it, & why, & when he'd painted it—

Though she was amused by the painters' enthusiasm – 'Roger
very nearly lost his senses,' she wrote to her friend, Nicholas Bagenal, 'I've never seen such a sight of intoxication. He was like a bee
on a sunflower' – she was also excited.[139] Recounting the scene, she
had, in fact, written a kind of checklist in her diary, the conversation
between the painters furnishing her with a new critical approach.
A new vocabulary was becoming available to her: form, colour, *texture*. When, occasionally, Roger swivelled his attention to books,
Virginia was eager to apply the ideas to her own work. 'I said one
could, & certainly did, write with phrases, not only words,' she
scribbled in her diary. 'Roger asked me if I founded my writing upon
texture or structure; I connected structure with plot, & therefore
said "texture". Then we discussed the meaning of structure & texture in painting & writing. Then we discussed Shakespeare, & Roger
said Giotto excited him just as much.'[140]

But in her mind, the two mediums continued to war with each other. Often, she was sceptical of the painters' approach. (She felt vindicated, as if she had uncovered the flimsiness of painting, when Roger admitted 'pictures only do "to look at about 4 times"'.[141]) And yet, as ever, her defensiveness had much to do with the lack of confidence she felt in her work. In 1912, while Vanessa's paintings were being shown alongside Picasso and Braque, Virginia hadn't yet published *The Voyage Out*; and later, peering over her sister's shoulder at Cézanne's luminous apples, she was still stuck in old forms, labouring over the final stages of *Night and Day*. During those intervening years, too often it had seemed as if painting was the principal medium, the single dominating discussion among her friends. She wanted her part in it, and yet was appalled when her own vocabulary failed her, becoming 'rather random & desperate' when discussing a picture, or faltering in her letters, her language 'tainted'.[142] 'Its a question of half developed aesthetic emotions,' she admitted to Vanessa, as she sent her 'Kew Gardens', 'constantly checked by others of a literary nature – in fact its all very interesting and intense.'[143] Doggedly, she continued to experiment with aesthetic ideas; at the very least, she desired to achieve in her writing the freedom Vanessa was experiencing in paint. Describing her response to one of Vanessa's paintings in contrast to her feelings about an Omega chair (whose yellow cover had sent her into a rage), she asked: '[D]o you think that this semi-conscious process of coming to dislike one colour very much and liking a picture better and better points to some sort of live instinct trying to come to existence? I humbly hope so.'[144]

In fact, her instinct had come into existence at Asheham, where she had studied the colours and textures of the natural world, considered forms in relation to their surroundings, and trained her vision to microscopic things. This private practice, combined with her responses to art and the making of her own books, paved the way for a new method in her fiction; all three were predicated on a kind of independence of mind that Asheham afforded her, and deepened. She approached her work impatiently, writing to Vanessa:

'I mean to write a good many short things at Asheham.'[145] Back in the country, she started to produce a series of rapid, experimental pieces – not stories in the conventional sense, but agile studies in colour, association and consciousness, works that would eventually make up her 1921 collection, *Monday or Tuesday*. In 'The String Quartet', a woman's thoughts accelerate in response to music; in 'Blue and Green' – two sketches, each a single paragraph in length – colour sets off a sequence of images and associations in the mind of the observer; and in 'The Mark on the Wall', a woman fixes her gaze on a small, round mark hovering above a mantlepiece, and tries to identify it without getting up from her chair.

Critics have tended to focus on these stories as depictions of consciousness, rapid flights of the mind. 'How readily our thoughts swarm upon a new object,' the narrator says in 'The Mark on the Wall', before letting her thoughts wander, lighting spontaneously upon on houses, objects, Shakespeare. In fact, the stories begin with looking at or listening to something, a practice of attention and observation Virginia had cultivated at Asheham. In each, there is a fixed point of beginning, a stimulus – a snail on the wall, an ornament on a mantlepiece, a piece of music – from which thoughts ray out, languid, associative, 'all so casual, all so haphazard'.[146] From being in the country, Virginia was eager to explore visual states, and different ways of bringing attention to bear: murmuring and atmospheric, as in 'Kew Gardens'; gliding, as in 'The Mark on the Wall'; or associative, in order to convey the potency of pure colour, as in 'Blue and Green'.

And in these nimble, questioning short pieces, she was edging towards a new kind of voice for her fiction, shifting from the intimacy of interior monologue towards something disembodied, and not quite human. It owed much to her writing practice at Asheham, where, in her small diary, she had described daily life as if she were all but absent from it. In 'Monday or Tuesday', the narrator swoops down on a provincial street scene, snatching at conversations, before sailing out again as night falls, continuing its quest for 'truth'.[147] Who, or what, is the narratorial presence in these stories? In many of her sketches, vision seeps through cracks, penetrating where eyes cannot. Then, a different world becomes visible: the recesses of a flowerbed, the bustle of feet on a pavement, a room filled with collected objects, glinting. Virginia was practising the techniques she would use in her most experimental fiction: human absence as presence in *Jacob's Room*, the searching airs of the 'Time Passes' section of *To The Lighthouse*. And she was developing her authorial character, one that was liminal and yet totally receptive; or – as she described in her 1934 essay on Walter Sickert, describing visitors in a gallery looking at paintings – like some intuitive creature, an insect, 'all eye'.[148]

~

Though she requested woodcuts for 'Kew Gardens' in July 1918, Virginia had, in fact, been working on the story the previous summer at Asheham. 'Yes, your Flower Bed is very good,' Katherine Mansfield wrote to her on 23 August 1917, having just been to stay. It was the most concentrated time the two writers would spend together; though their friendship was thorny, it would prove one of the most generative of Virginia's writing life. Records of Katherine's visit are slight, but the talk was almost certainly of work. Afterwards, Katherine thanked Virginia, and encouraged her, before conceding – as if to appeal to her host – the magic of Asheham: 'It is very wonderful & I feel that it will flash upon one corner of my inward eye for ever.'[149]

Virginia recorded the visit sparingly in her diary. On Saturday 18 August, Katherine's train was late, and so, with time to spare in Lewes, she went to the cinema, and bought lilies, which she later put into the big bed. Once they arrived back at Asheham, Leonard had to leave for a conference in London, and so the women walked undisturbed on the terrace, an airship on its way towards Brighton passing overhead. It was hot and windy, the *thistledown beginning to blow*. That evening, Lytton, Bunny, and Bunny's father, Edward Garnett, walked over from Charleston for dinner, after which the group read a play. Finally, on Wednesday 22 August, Katherine was loaded into the fly outside the Ram Inn in Firle, along with Lytton's suit-case, to begin her journey back to London. All details. Virginia recorded nothing of their talk, save a note for Maryland cigarettes from a stall at South Kensington station, near to where Katherine was living. (On his return, Leonard brought with him ten packets from London.)

Yet the Asheham diary belies Virginia's intense preoccupation with the New Zealand writer. 'I'm always on the point of meeting her, or of reading her stories, and I have never managed to do either,' she had written to Lytton the previous summer.[150] Katherine, six years Virginia's junior, had been published widely, and lived with the critic John Middleton Murray. Lytton met her at a party of Otto-line Morrell's at Garsington House in Oxfordshire, where she had praised *The Voyage Out*, and said she wanted to meet its author. Vir-ginia was wary. 'I am going to see Katherine Mansfield, to get a story from her, perhaps,' she had written to Vanessa in April 1917, as the Hogarth Press got going.[151] She found Katherine 'an odd char-acter', well-travelled (in contrast to her increasingly country life) and experienced, and yet her story, 'Prelude', seemed 'a good deal better than most'.[152]

The relationship which emerged between the two writers was rivalrous. Virginia found Katherine clever but disagreeable, and arrogant about her writing. (She was snobbish about Katherine's foreignness, and didn't like her musky perfume.) There was fault-finding, gossip, umbrage over unanswered letters. Briefly, in September 1917, she got into trouble for repeating unflattering remarks about Katherine, which reached one of Ottoline Morrell's parties at Garsington.[153] She decided to remain silent on the matter, except to tell Vanessa, after reporting their rapprochement, that she found Katherine to be 'forcible and utterly unscrupulous'.[154] Typic-ally, Virginia was acting defensively, Katherine's talent – and her mounting successes – exacerbating the insecurities she felt about her own writing. On reading Katherine's story 'Bliss' in 1918, Vir-ginia's response was difficult, double-edged: she found the story 'brilliant – so hard, so shallow, and so sentimental'.[155] She wrote to

Katherine to say she was 'glad and indeed proud' of its publication – by no means the only 'insincere-sincere' letter, as she described it in her diary, she would produce by way of congratulation.[156] She couldn't bring herself to read 'The Garden Party', another story, when it was published in 1922. Katherine 'takes in all the reviewers', she wrote bitterly to Janet Case, 'swims from triumph to triumph'.[157] And yet her jealousy – an 'awful' affliction, she admitted to Roger Fry – couldn't conceal her admiration. 'Have you at all come round to her stories?' she asked him. 'I suppose I'm too jealous to wish you to, yet I'm sure they have merit all the same.'[158] Later, hearing Katherine criticised publicly, she conceded, 'in my heart I must think her good, since I'm glad to hear her abused'.[159]

And yet, just as with Vanessa, Virginia found a sense of shared craft in competition, a mutual energy; there was no one from whom she would rather win respect. At Asheham in August 1917, though Virginia's diary remained silent on the texture of Katherine's visit, the women pooled and discussed their work. 'It was good to have time to talk to you,' Katherine wrote afterwards, indicating that the women did more than simply wander up and down the terrace. Katherine had said previously that she wanted to discuss 'The Mark on the Wall', Virginia had recently read *Prelude* – the longest story Katherine would publish, written ambitiously in twelve vignettes, like hours, and drawn from her own country childhood in New Zealand – and at one stage, the manuscript of 'Kew Gardens' was brought out.

The story, as we have seen, was a fulcrum in the evolution in Virginia's style. Yet some critics have argued that Katherine Mansfield influenced her at this point in her writing life. The week before her August visit to Asheham, Katherine had written two letters describing the garden at Garsington, one to Ottoline Morrell, and one to Virginia. To Ottoline, Katherine distilled the feeling of the place:

Your glimpse of the garden – all flying green and gold made me wonder again *who* is going to write about that flower garden. It might be so wonderful – do you see *how* I mean? There would be people walking in the garden – several *pairs* of people – their conversation their slow pacing – their glances as they pass one another [. . .] A kind of, musically speaking – conversation *set* to flowers. Do you like the idea? [. . .] Its full of possibilities. I must have a fling at it as soon as I have time.[160]

Katherine's letter to Virginia hasn't survived, but we can guess that its contents were similar. Virginia reported it back to Ottoline, paraphrasing Katherine's descriptions of 'the rose leaves dying in the sun, the pool and long conversation between people wandering up and down in the moonlight'.[161] Had Katherine planted a seed in Virginia's mind? Katherine's passage shares remarkable affinity with 'Kew Gardens': its haziness and spots of colour, the low music of conversation, the flowerbed quietly thrumming with insect life. But if she was irritated that Virginia pursued her idea, Katherine didn't show it, instead praising the 'still, quivering, changing light over it all and a sense of those couples dissolving in the bright air which fascinates me'.[162] She recognised, as Virginia would later write, the story as 'a turning point' in her work, 'the right gesture', just as *Prelude* was in Katherine's own. Like 'Kew Gardens', Katherine's story was an attempt at a new method: episodic, an exploration of atmosphere and sensation; 'a coloured postcard', as Virginia remarked. Katherine, too, was beginning to write in a 'new manner', Virginia noted; had 'mastered something'.[163]

And yet Virginia found talking to Katherine difficult. Their meetings, which usually began with an air of 'discomposing formality & coldness', unsettled her. She tried to describe the 'queer effect' Katherine produced, 'of someone apart, entirely self-centred; altogether concentrated upon her "art": almost fierce to me about it, I pretending I couldn't write'. She envied the way Katherine presented herself as a writer – and particularly, the way she held her own as a woman writer – while Virginia's own tendency was to minimize her seriousness, and to self-deprecate; to try and dismantle the 'I'. And yet speaking to Katherine – hours of 'priceless talk' – was to experience the uncanniness of hearing her own ideas spoken back to her, of feeling 'a common certain understanding between us – a queer sense of being "like" – not only about literature'.[164] (Such affinity had been lacking in all Virginia's conversations with the painters.) For both women, the most important thing was writing. 'I find with Katherine what I don't find with the other clever women,' Virginia reflected in her diary; 'a sense of ease & interest, which is, I suppose, due to her caring so genuinely [. . .] about our precious art.'[165] And: 'To no one else can I talk in the same disembodied way about writing; without altering my thought more than I alter it in writing here.'[166] For Katherine, too, their paths were aligned. '[W]e have got the same job, Virginia & it is really very curious & thrilling that we should both, quite apart from each other, be after so very nearly the same thing,' she wrote to her, not without a glint of competition, soon after leaving Asheham. 'We are you know; there's no denying it.'[167]

When Katherine died suddenly of a haemorrhage in January 1923, a result of her five-year battle with tuberculosis, Virginia grieved the place she had occupied in her life. Now, it seemed, she was writing 'into emptiness': 'Katherine wont read it. Katherine's my rival no longer.'[168] For many years, she would reflect on their barbed, stimulating friendship, which seemed so closely connected with Asheham, and to that uncertain, emergent period in her own life. In 1917, she, too, had been ill; was on the brink, in her work, of stepping into new forms. Katherine – unscrupulous, arrogant, perhaps, and yet genuinely talented – had provided Virginia with an example of one stepping up, fearlessly (striding along the terrace), to meet her identity as a writer. Katherine had demonstrated the power of vocation, and it was through knowing her (as much as it was other things, she understood) that Virginia had crystallised, with the emergence of 'Kew Gardens', a writerly style of her own.

~

Almost a year after Katherine's visit, in July 1918, Virginia folded and stapled 300 copies of *Prelude*. It had taken nearly nine months to print, due to the length of the story and the fact of the press

being too small. Once she had set the type – letter by letter, string-
ing Katherine's sentences together in the holding tray – Leonard
took the story to a larger press in Richmond, which he operated
himself. Their small publishing scheme was beginning to grow
beyond itself. When 'Kew Gardens' was published the following
summer, the Woolfs returned from Asheham to find Hogarth
House flooded with orders, rushing the short book into a second
imprint, fulfilled with the help of a commercial publisher. In the
1920s, they printed T.S. Eliot and Hope Mirrlees, and the first English translation of Freud (though they turned down Joyce's *Ulysses*,
Virginia sceptical about the book's merit and fearing it would be
too much work). And, into the 1930s, both creatively and politically, the Press remained at the vanguard of British publishing.
Hiring an ambitious Cambridge graduate, John Lehmann – a
friend of Virginia's nephew, Julian Bell – as manager in 1931, they
championed experimental, left-wing and, to a certain extent,
working-class writers. (Eventually, in 1938, Lehmann bought Virginia's share of the Press, running it as a joint venture with
Leonard until 1946.) In Virginia's lifetime, the Press would always
retain its domestic, rather chaotic atmosphere. John Lehmann
recalled entering the basement of 52 Tavistock Square, where the
Press moved in 1924, to find typists working in what was once a
Victorian kitchen, the printing press set up in a former scullery,
and his own office in the butler's pantry. In a studio at the back,
which was also used as a stockroom, was a temporary office for
Virginia where, at a scrubbed table, she would snatch an hour's
writing surrounded by boxes and parcels of books.[169]

Five months after 'Kew Gardens', in October 1919, *Night and Day*
was published. It was the last of Virginia's novels to come out under
her half-brother Gerald Duckworth's imprint; from then on, she
would publish exclusively with the Hogarth Press. In 1921, she began
to collect her short stories together for publication as *Monday or
Tuesday* – 'the little book', wrote John Lehmann, 'which announced
her new style'.[170] Those not-quite stories, fleeting impressions,
marked the transition from her first two novels, closer to Edwardian

realism, to those she was yet to write. They had 'showed me how I could embody all my deposit of experience in a shape that fitted it', she reflected later to her friend, Ethel Smythe. 'I saw, branching out of the tunnel I made, when I discovered that method of approach, Jacobs Room, Mrs Dalloway etc – How I trembled with excitement.'[171] Seeing them 'taking hands & dancing in unity', those 'little pieces' – written mostly at Asheham – had lighted her path.[172]

The following year, 1918, and Virginia was finally emerging out of convalescence. She was stronger, and her attention was shifting away from the country, towards other things. (There was briefly a plan, mooted in the last months of the war, for the Woolfs to move to Asheham full time, and set up the press in one of the studios adjoining the house. Virginia was tired of sitting through raids in London, night after night; it wasn't the noise she minded, she told Ka Cox, so much as the 'infernal boredom' of the servants' domestic talk.)[173] In the end, Asheham wasn't the answer. There was too much happening in London: printing, writing, seeing friends. Still, she reflected, a week alone there with Leonard was 'the greatest & most unmixed pleasure this world affords'.[174]

In her small diary, she documented one more year at the house, one last litany of country events: her visits in the spring, the long summer, a final Christmas reckoning. She was following the pattern of the previous year, but also deviating; everything was familiar, and yet nothing was quite the same. There were still small, domestic incidents. The coal went missing, which was blamed on Saxon Sidney-Turner's charwoman, a Mrs Mason, who accompanied him from London during a visit. By late summer, the cottagers and the Gealls – the Woolfs' new housekeepers – were going without, and *there is not eno' to cook dinner.* They foraged for fuel, buying a two-handled saw in Lewes, and picking up sticks in the woods, *At first tried the left hand plantation. Mrs Geall won't go there because of snakes.*

Found plenty of wood blown down. Gunn has given us a tree. We saw wood every day with the new saw. L. splits it with a chopper. Food shortages persisted, *Eggs are 4d from Mrs. Wooler. She has had a record year, makes 16/a week lately; To Coops; no jam. Could get no sausages.* At one point, something from the butcher's in Lewes made them ill, *We have both been poisoned – I slightly, L. considerably, by bad meat, or flies lately. Marsh insists upon sending large joints though we are alone. Which go bad.*

In the spring, a disease killed off the lambs – *Gunn very angry about the lambs. They & the ewes have died in large numbers; makes a loss on them; Gunn has lost £100 by the sheep here* – and there was little milk to be had, *Killick will give us a goat. Otherwise we have to fetch it from Gunns – 3½ miles.* Virginia continued to watch the fields, noticing a *Threshing machine on the road to Firle, Fields full of clover, Corn being cut by hand.* Compared to the previous year's storms, the summer of 1918 was faultless, *Another fortnight like this, Mr. Killick says, will mean a perfect harvest.* It was *got in at a great rate – said to be the best for 50 years,* the men working *in spite of Sunday.* Gunn's fields were still being worked by German prisoners. On her way to Southease, Virginia watched them, met them in the lane on her way back. *When alone, I smile at the tall German.*

She and Leonard were making great leaps in the garden, which she recorded with greater attention than before. They planted seeds and wallflowers in the newly dug round bed, and she noted the flowers with pleasure as they appeared – daffodils, primroses, nasturtiums, columbines, Japanese anemones, dahlias. Often, she sat by while Leonard worked. *Afternoon in the garden. L. planted vegetables. I sewed.*

Towards the end of the summer, the war was edging towards its conclusion. For the first time, newspaper reports crept into her diary, glimpses of a world beyond Asheham. *No guns heard, save in the Channel apparently, though the fighting is so heavy, & the news this (Monday) morning very bad. News of the battle rather better today. L. heard guns yesterday morning.* In August, she reported, *Good news from France these last days,* and in September, *News that Bulgaria makes peace.* The ambit of her attention was widening. In her letters, she dared to imagine a future beyond war, was 'keeping up a lively discussion with Leonard about life in general. Is he happy? Are we successful? Do people like us? What shall we do when the war's over?'[175] Coming back from a shopping trip in Brighton, she found the house 'lovelier than ever', and the sight 'of an English gentleman walking the stubble after partridges' a 'foretaste of better days'.[176]

And yet her vision, once so inexhaustible, was waning. *We came down in Feb. after influenza for 10 days; but I made no notes*, she reported in her Asheham diary by way of summarizing an undocumented visit. *Nothing particular to be seen* became the new refrain of her walks, the natural world seeming to offer little to catch her eye, or spark her attention. *Nothing new*; *A fine day, but nothing particular to be noticed*; *Nothing to notice*. All through the previous summer, she had walked as if with a magnifying glass, looking for the purpose of noticing, aware of the project in hand. Now, her attention was shifting away from her notebook and from Asheham, and towards other things. She made notes until December 1918, as methodically as before, but her rapture was gone.

'Shall I say "nothing happened today" as we used to do in our diaries, when they were beginning to die?' she had written in January 1915, before illness caused her diary to lapse for two and a half years.[177] She had broken the silence on 8 October 1917 when, four days after returning to Hogarth House from her first long summer at Asheham, she opened a new notebook, and began documenting her life again. Quickly, her Hogarth diary – as inscribed on the title-page – fell into step with London: street scenes, sketches of friends, books, printing. But when she took it to Asheham, its style became self-conscious, as if she couldn't yet describe country life in longhand form. Attempts produced disjointed, clunky phrases – 'Yesterday was as wet a day as England often produces. Almost always the afternoon is dry in England' – as if there was a lingering desire for the safety of her smaller diary's neat paragraphs, its staccato phrases.[178] And yet, 'To recapitulate the events of Asheham is no longer in my power,' she wrote tellingly in May 1918, where the things that happened were now 'mainly of a spiritual nature'.[179] She was caught between forms. In her

Asheham diary, what had begun as a record of concrete things –
walking boots, bicycles, eggs – now struggled to be contained. The
tangible was becoming intangible; the microscopic abstract. Virginia's needs had changed. As she grew stronger, she was yielding
more easily to atmosphere, to states of feeling.

The transition from her Asheham to her Hogarth diary was staggered, producing a period of interplay between the two notebooks.
Sometimes, one picks up where the other leaves off. 'L. is cutting
our beans for dinner,' she writes in her Hogarth diary on 31 July
1918; and, two days later, in Asheham, *Eating our own broad beans –
delicious*.[180] There are seventeen occasions, scattered between July
and October 1918, on which Virginia writes in both her diaries at
once. Which comes first? For a time, her Asheham notebook retains
the impetus of its original purpose, a repository for things noticed,
dashed down before they are forgotten. On 3 August, Asheham
records, *All butterflies clinging to grass*; and in Hogarth, 'There's nothing but rustic news to record.'[181] On 9 August, in Asheham, *A fine
hot afternoon; corn being cut by hand on the slope over Glynde*; and Hogarth, 'In the absence of human interest, which makes us peaceful
and content, one may as well go on with Byron.'[182] At times, the
purpose of each diary becomes distinct: Asheham for weather and
walks, Hogarth for reflections on work. As on 5 August, in Asheham, *Mist all day, sometimes pouring wet. A few bank holiday people up
the drive*; and in Hogarth, 'my impressions first of Christina
Rossetti'.[183]

As the summer progressed, the energy between the two notebooks began to shift. It was a question of one diary diverting
attention from the other, the need to assimilate the notebooks into
a single volume. Gradually, Virginia's Hogarth diary became the
place in which she recorded her impressions. On 24 August, she
described the 'beautiful very worn carpets' spread over the Downs,
their 'semi-transparent look'.[184] (Asheham: *A plague of bees, wasps &
flies*). And on 27 August, she reflected on the strangeness of seeing
the German prisoners at work in the fields, or in the lanes, the leanness of their bodies, and the unknowability of their lives. (Asheham:

Fine & windy. Nothing new.) Irony crept in. 'Our tragedy has been the squashing of a caterpillar,' she wrote in her Hogarth book, having recorded every stage of the drama in her Asheham dairy, as if she was raising an eyebrow at her own amateurish, Miss Matty experiment.[185]

Her small diary persisted, a series of increasingly short, bulletin-like entries. No rhythm, little rapture, compared with the previous summer at Asheham. It revived slightly in October, just as it was drawing to a close. Finally, on 6 October:

> *A fine but windy day. L. busy packing all day as we go at 10.15 tomorrow. We are taking in jack of apples, & leaving a good many here. We took the cat out but it ran away & has not been seen since. Too windy for M's walk, though very sunny. It is a very late autumn. The tree at the end of the field still too thick to see the postman through. We are going via East Grinstead to avoid crush.*

~

Her Asheham diary, like her short stories, set Virginia on her way, a prelude to a practice of diary-keeping she would maintain throughout her life. From then on, her diary would remain central to her writing practice, a place in which, alongside her fiction, she could experiment with narrative technique and style. 'It strikes me that in this book I *practise* my writing; do my scales; yes & work at certain effects,' she would write in 1924. Her Asheham diary, then, was a warm-up exercise, a feeling into the form after silence; ultimately too rigid, with not enough room. For what she would come to desire in her diary was something 'loose knit, & yet not slovenly, so elastic that it will embrace any thing'.[186]

Where should we situate the Asheham diary, in Virginia's personal papers, or with her writing? And how should we read this short interval of time, of rural hours, within her life entire? It would be easy to skip over the years between 1912 and 1919 – the years covering the lease of Asheham – in Virginia's life, to see them as years diminished by illness and war. Looking to her small notebook,

I would like to reclaim this period. The diary bridges the gap between illness and health, convalescence and work. It is coterminous with her other work of the period, occupying the same kind of adjacent space as editing and printing to her writing. Both were forms of putting things in their proper order and place, of containment and possibility; forms of not-quite authorship, in which Virginia's hand is felt, though she's barely there.

The two years documented in her notebook belong, of course, to a longer sequence of experience, but they also mark something distinct from what came afterwards and before. Asheham was the connecting tissue. Virginia acknowledged the emergence of one diary from the other when she wrote, in May 1918, that 'to take up the pen' directly upon coming back from Asheham was to show that Hogarth was 'a natural growth', 'a rather dishevelled, rambling plant' with its roots in her smaller diary, once more placed in a drawer.[187]

Asheham represents an interval in Virginia's life. Though she would continue to divide her time between London and country, the years between 1915 and 1919 grew to have their own particular meaning. It was then that she emerged out of illness, separated her jealousies from Vanessa, and rose up to meet her writing life. Her feeling, as war had broken out, that she had been left behind in Sussex, and was isolated, had evolved into a greater sense of self-possession. She could be content by herself, tramping over the Downs, or working, knowing that Leonard was nearby. Their marriage had traversed its own ground while she had been at Asheham. Now, she looked upon the house and landscape as part of her transition, from silence to writing, illness to recovery. A few years later, she would declare herself 'astonishingly happy in the country' – 'a state of mind which, if I did not dislike hyphens, I should hyphen, to show that it is a state by itself' – but in 1915, Asheham had been just her beginning.[188] In her small, rhythmical diary, she had meditated with increasing gratitude on her daily pleasures, the slow turn of days. Those were the days which mattered, and which would be counted, among the happiest of my life – I mean among the happy undistinguished days, ripe & sweet & sound; the daily bread; for nothing strange or exalted has happened; only the day has gone rightly and harmoniously; a pattern of the best part of life which is in the country like this; & makes me wish to command more of them – months of them.[189]

~

On 13 January 1919, Leonard received a letter from John Hoper, a solicitor in Lewes, notifying him that Asheham was needed to accommodate Frank Gunn, the bailiff of Itford Farm. On 10 March, he gave the Woolfs until 29 September to leave. It was an 'appalling prospect', Virginia wrote, as she began casting around for somewhere else to live.[190] In May, she and Leonard, without seeing them, took three cottages on the Cornish coast, and in June, on an impulse, she bought the Round House in Lewes, an odd dwelling converted from a windmill, for £300. To Virginia's embarrassment, Leonard decreed it cramped and unsuitable. She was becoming unhappy, but a week or so later, they saw an auctioneer's notice for Monk's House, a quiet, weather-boarded place next to the church in the village of Rodmell, across the Ouse valley from Asheham. Virginia liked it immediately. Monk's House was long and low, with many doors, its garden – which she knew Leonard would love – giving on to water-meadows and views of the Downs. On 1 July, she and Leonard bid for the house at auction in Lewes, buying it for £700. (The Cornish cottages were annulled, and the Round House sold two weeks later.) Monk's House, Virginia wrote passionately to Ka Cox, was going to be 'our address for ever and ever'. Indeed, 'I've already marked out our graves in the yard which joins our meadow.'[191]

They left Asheham on 1 September, their furniture and belongings rumbling over the bridge at Southease in waggons borrowed from Itford Farm. The journey to their new home across the valley was significant. Earlier in the year, Virginia had reflected on the period of her life since 1911, formulating the changes as a series of departures, or passages: 'an Omega, a Post Impressionist movement, [. . .] a country cottage, a Brunswick Square [. . .] a printing press'. [192] To this, she might have added an Asheham, a collection of stories, a new diary. She was moving from one period of her life – quiet, convalescent, awakening – into the next.

Eating our own broad beans – delicious

Miss Green

On Easter Monday in 1930, Sylvia Townsend Warner was walking along a lane in the Dorset village of East Chaldon when she passed a small house. It was a plain building with a dirty stucco exterior, but she liked its neat proportions, slate roof and narrow porch. Looking towards the back, she could see a thicket of overgrown garden. She had heard from friends in the village that the cottage was for sale, and now, on an impulse, she decided to go in. Crossing the road briskly, she went into the pub opposite to borrow the keys.

After the bright April sunlight, the cottage was stuffy and dark. Sylvia looked over the rooms: the sitting room and compact kitchen, which was tucked beneath the sloping roof; the two upstairs bedrooms, one large, one small, with an adjoining door. Its unloveliness pleased her. There was no electricity or running water, but after the death of its previous owner, an elderly Miss Green, it was available freehold. 'It is very nice inside,' she wrote in her diary later that day, 'sizable rooms, a good back-kitchen and stairs. No water, but a water-butt. The garden is charming – snow on the mountains, clove carnations, lavender, apple and cherry trees.'[1] Several weeks later, she received the surveyor's report. 'This is a small undesirable property, situated in an out of the way place and with no attractions whatever,' it began unenthusiastically, before conceding that the cottage was sound and dry.[2] By then, Sylvia had returned to London with plans of redecorating, and on 19 June, the sale of the cottage went through, costing her £90.

~

The prospect of a country life appealed to Sylvia. She liked the village of Chaldon and, after a dreary winter in London, craved a different setting for her work. At thirty-six, she was already a successful writer, with two poetry collections, three novels and a book of stories to her name. In 1925, when her first book of poems was published, Virginia Woolf hailed her as 'the new Chatto & Windus poetess', remarking in her diary that, 'indeed she has some merit – enough to make me spend 2/6 on her, I think'.[3] But it was Sylvia's first novel, published a year later in 1926, which established her reputation. The story of a spinster who moves to the country and becomes a witch, *Lolly Willowes* was an unexpectedly nonconformist tale of a woman's search for freedom. Sylvia had revelled in its success. At a party in Bloomsbury, Virginia asked how she knew so much about witches. 'Because I am one,' Sylvia mischievously replied.[4]

Sylvia in 1930

But by 1929, Sylvia was reaching an unsettled feeling. She was jittery in her work, abandoning a biography of her friend, the writer T. F. Powys, and suffering over mixed reviews for her third novel, *The*

True Heart. After her first success, it seemed her books had become odd and difficult, her landscapes unfamiliar, her characters unruly. Her experiments with myth and folklore no longer possessed the lightness of touch for which she had become famous, but felt old-fashioned and moved heavily. Her first readers were disappointed. She considered her predicament dryly: 'If I am to be my own raven I must recapture the Lolly manner, and be light and satirical and talk of gentlemen and ladies.'[5]

In her personal life, too, she was beginning to feel gloomy. She was bored by a long-term relationship with a married man and felt herself getting older, worrying that soon she would be 'too sad and middle-aged for whistling'.[6] Two years previously, she had given up a promising career in musicology to devote herself to writing, though it suggested a future of financial uncertainty, and one she feared would be lonely. 'I am quiet, I might almost think myself resigned,' she wrote sadly in her diary, a week after offering to buy the Chaldon cottage. 'I have lost initiative to be happy, my instincts, my roots into life, decay.'[7]

Her instincts were only numbed. Buying the Chaldon cottage, Sylvia knew herself to be on the threshold, the cusp of something new. 'I could still be saved at any moment,' she wrote in her diary, intimating the great change that was to come. And yet she was weary, and easily defeated: '– but I shan't be, and I can do nothing about it myself'.[8]

~

Sylvia had known the village of Chaldon for several years. When she first visited in 1921, it was to meet the reclusive Theodore Powys, whose friendship would prove deeply influential to her writing life. Powys was an unlikely lynchpin of a small, bohemian community that had gathered in the village, though otherwise it was an out-of-the-way place, lying in an isolated valley, and enclosed on all sides by a rising swell of chalk downland. Though the sea was only two miles distant, it had the feeling of an inland village, self-contained and watertight. To the south were the white cliffs at Bat's Head, with views of Durdle Door; to the north lay the great stretch of Winfrith Heath. At the village's northernmost edge rose a steep ridge on which stood a series of ancient barrows, known locally as the Five Marys. The Marys marked the boundary of the village and a branch of the Southern Ridgeway, a network of pre-Roman roads covering the downs from Poxwell to Winfrith. At dusk, their rounded bells would become silhouetted against the skyline, silent and watchful. When she visited, Sylvia often walked along the ridge with William, her black chow-dog, sitting 'a cigarette's while' on one of the mounds and looking out over the landscape, at the low thatched cottages strung out along the lane into the village, at the farm buildings, and out over the Downs, pockmarked with chalk-pits and lime-kilns, towards the sea.[9]

In the early summer of 1930, as the sale of the cottage went through, Sylvia turned her attention back to the country. She would, for the time being, keep her flat on Inverness Terrace in Bayswater, and catch the train to Dorset for long weekends. The rhythm of moving between places would, she hoped, invigorate her. At Miss Green, as she christened the cottage, she would shrug off her disappointments, dispel her gloominess and settle into a working frame of mind.

The question of leaving the cottage unattended while she was in London was settled when she asked a young poet to move in. Valentine Ackland, an acquaintance of Powys's, had found herself homeless in the village when, earlier that spring, she had offered Sylvia her cottage as a place to stay when she visited Chaldon. Hearing of the offer, Valentine's landlord assumed she would be sub-letting the cottage for profit, and abruptly turned her out. Sylvia, who barely knew the younger woman, was nonetheless touched by her generosity, as well as feeling responsible for her living situation. She made her an offer. Would Valentine consent to being her tenant and the steward of Miss Green, as she began calling the cottage, on the condition she could visit at weekends? Valentine, who had a flat in London but spent the greater part of her time in Dorset, agreed. Their paths would cross infrequently; it was an arrangement that suited them both. Sylvia was delighted. 'You do understand, don't you, that I want you to feel a coheiress of the late Miss Green?' she wrote encouragingly from London, where she had begun to make arrangements for the house. '[Y]ou should know how pleased I am too.'[10]

Any scruples about buying the cottage were dealt with quickly. Following the success of *Lolly Willowes*, Sylvia was fairly well off, and able to imagine living comfortably between London and the country. Even so, she was anxious about owning a house in the village. Miss Green was a labourer's cottage, originally built for workers on the Lulworth Estate, a twenty-mile stretch of south Dorset downland which had belonged to the Weld family since the seventeenth century. Yet, for Sylvia, it was an extravagance, satisfying, as she later admitted, a 'bourgeois craving' for home-ownership.[11] In June, she wrote to Valentine describing a 'sharp fit of conscience about robbing the poor of their dwellings', but was reassured when Powys, to whom she went for advice, explained that 'they have tried in vain to let it, and that anyone who wanted to buy a house and could afford to do so, did so during the Weld sale. So we need not worry on that score.'[12]

Unusually for a writer of her class, neither was Sylvia concerned with the prospect of doing without running water or electricity. At Miss Green, she would have to collect water in a water butt, heat it over a fire, and spend her evenings by candlelight. She could afford to live without such hardships, and yet she chose not to. Sylvia wasn't easily daunted; she was practical, and took pride in domestic work. But she also intended to live simply, an intimation of the politics which would take root at Miss Green. She was well aware of capers of her kind: intellectuals moving to the countryside and doing up the best cottages. As far as she was able, hers was to be a whole-hearted attempt at rural living.

That said, in her excitement, Sylvia did launch into home improvements – though of a relatively modest nature. Her foremost desire was to make the cottage, which had been inhabited by an elderly woman for many years, 'comfortable and shipshape'.[13]

With Valentine in Dorset to superintend the work, she was soon writing almost every day. From London, she directed Mr Miller, a local builder, to mend the roof and gutters, and paint Miss Green's grubby stucco exterior. 'Don't you think she had better be lime-washed?' she asked Valentine. 'Nothing can make her picturesque, nor do I desire it, but I think limewash might make her look clean, when at the moment she don't.'[14] Then she addressed Miss Green's waterworks. 'I will have one indoor tap,' she decided, 'because the moment water is carried in and poured or scooped with other vessels, there are slops on the floor, wet feet and misery. Whereas with a tap and a sink all is gas and gaiters.' Soon, a water butt was attached to the cottage – 'like a very large procreant martin's nest hanging from our eaves' – supplying a small tank installed indoors, and draining into a sump in the garden. The system, though far from luxurious, was sophisticated for a labourer's cottage, and Sylvia was pleased. With her tap, oil stove, and a copper for heating water, the kitchen was transformed into 'a paradise of dainty devices'.[15]

Miss Green's cottage, East Chaldon

In the small garden at the back of the cottage, Sylvia set Valentine to hoeing – 'a very Virgilian occupation' – though not out of 'a wonton wish to sunburn you', she teased, 'but because hot weather hoeing is supposed to kill the weeds from sunstroke, poor lambs'.[16] As well as raking and digging, there was a garden wall to build, which would replace a temporary fence of posts and chains. Foundations were expensive, but 'I cannot have roaming cattle, as Mr Miller said, or roaming hens, as I added, walking at pleasure all over the garden.'[17] She hoped that the garden would mature into 'a moderate wildness of things', with hydrangeas and fuchsias grown from her mother's Dartmoor cuttings, and valerian and St John's wort spreading along the stony paths.[18] She chose plants that would tolerate the salty air – small, hardy shrubs and a Burnet rose, which 'grows wild in some places, and won't grow anyhow away from the sea'.[19] 'I find the contemplation of this garden very encouraging,' she wrote to Valentine. 'My mind is still dazzled with that prospect of newly dug territory, with the respected montbretias blooming in the midst of it.'[20]

In July 1930, Sylvia took an early train to Dorchester and a taxi to Chaldon to check on the progress of Miss Green. She found the garden 'like the sluggard's, so wildly met – grown, but full of flowers and fruits. Calico pink shoe-rose poppies, corn-cockles, pretty Fannies, red and pink roses, the garnet rose under the window, red-currant, sweet-currant and raspberry bushes, strawberries, very smooth and sweet, plums and apple-trees.'[21] Already, the plenteousness of her new environment – like Virginia's at Asheham – was finding its way into her writing in the form of lists. To Valentine, who was in London for a few days, she wrote of her pleasure at the place: 'Doesn't the late Miss Green look charming with a wreath of flowers in her dishevelled hair? Have you found the strawberries? They are up at the back, delicious!'[22]

Next, Sylvia began thinking about the cottage's interior. In the sitting room, which was dingy even in daylight, she set about redesigning the fireplace, instructing a mason to lower the chimney breast and remove the grate to expose an oak beam – the agent 'implied that if I wanted to let Miss Green mention might be made of Queen Elizabeth' – and to build a hearth out of bricks. Afterwards, Mr Miller put up shelves, and painted the woodwork pink. Sylvia was pleased with the effect: 'Brick, timber, and pink paint: a queer mixture but I think it should look well enough.'[23]

As she set about designing the rooms, Sylvia was embarking upon an imaginative process of adaptation and improvement. She had a taste for old and unusual things, for second-hand furniture and objects recalling no specific historical period but which, arranged together, achieved playful juxtaposition. For the sitting room, she bought 'a very romantic and rococo gilt mirror with sconces' to hang near the doorway, its elaborate design striking a note of unexpected refinement against the cottage walls. 'No woman who bought that mirror for a cottage could conceivably be thought efficient,' she remarked to Valentine after buying it. 'It is completely inappropriate, and will effectively destroy any cottage feeling: which is what I desire.'[24] In refusing to fill Miss Green with objects that matched their rustic setting, Sylvia was rejecting old-world cottage quaintness for a more subversive aesthetic, one that was charismatic and a little irreverent, and reflected her own sensibility. She liked the mirror – 'partly to give more light, partly to gall our visitors' – and so she bought things to go alongside it: a rosewood card-table, 'large enough to feed two, and shutting up to half its span when not in use', a Chippendale wash stand, and a cross-stitch picture of a horse.[25] From her mother's house, Sylvia had her eye on several things, including 'a long narrow table wearing slender brass boots which would be fine to write poetry on', a kitchen cupboard fashioned from an old bar counter, a standing mirror, and a small grandfather clock.[26] 'This place is overflowing with oddments in the way of furniture and crockery,' she told Valentine, 'so quite a lot could come from here and never be missed.'[27] The cottage was filling up nicely, and she was pleased: 'Now except for the kitchen, I have got practically all the furniture, and all of it is rather comely.'[28]

Queer and comely. At Miss Green, Sylvia was engaged in an aesthetic parody of heterosexual domestic life. Her efforts at home improvement, and her taste for interiors, would prove increasingly unconventional as she continued to build a home with a woman, rather than a husband. And yet, in the summer of 1930, it wasn't yet clear where her sexual life would fit. Instead, the cottage began to reflect the different roles Sylvia would inhabit there: the writer, the homebody, but also a character – like Sukey Bond in *The True Heart*, perhaps – more light-hearted and childlike. In a letter, she described the two interconnecting bedrooms, the curtains in cotton lawns with crisp calico linings, the beds strewn with coverlets of Turkey chintz. The general effect, she told her new companion, was to remind them of waking in a nursery.[29] Was she disguising the feelings for Valentine which were emerging? Certainly, she was being mischievous. The cottage, she felt, was to host a new and updated version of spinsterhood. As if detecting a trace left by its previous owner, she sensed it had a character of its own which appealed to her, a solitary female spirit, grown untidy and a little wild. She envisioned Miss Green as a place of total creative and domestic freedom. There, she and Valentine would break from their previous lives, joining the cottage's female lineage, to live undisturbed and as they pleased.

In London, Sylvia succumbed to her new, acquisitive delight. For things of daily use and household gear, she went shopping, and was surprised at how much she enjoyed herself. 'It is unexpected,' she wrote in her diary, 'but the Devil has but to bait his traps with an enamel sink-drainer and I walk in.'[30] She kept lists of everything she bought, including six pounds of soap, six stainless steel cheese-knives, and two enamel jugs. Valentine was charged with sourcing candlesticks – 'old-fashioned brass ones, with large trays to catch the wax, and handles, like frying-pans,' Sylvia stipulated – and a chopping block. 'These are the sort of thing we can buy better in the country,' she wrote. 'May I leave them to you?'[31]

~

As their plans for the cottage knitted together, the letters between the two women became homely and flirtatious. Sylvia teased Valentine about her moods – 'I feel you need a nice weatherproof shed, tarred black, to be in keeping with your frame of mind' – and admired her appearance, a jacket fitting 'tighter than a moleskin', and her 'beautiful narrow hands'.[32] When Valentine wrote to describe a satinwood bureau from the Ackland family's home in Norfolk, Sylvia approved it for the smaller of the two bedrooms. 'I should like to think you had something from Winterton,' she told her, 'just in case you wanted kind company one night when the fog blows in from the sea.'[33] She continued to visit Chaldon regularly, meeting Valentine at the cottage or at Powys's house, a red-brick dwelling near High Chaldon, called Beth Car; and on the occasions Valentine was in London, she lamented her absence. Once, leaving the village hurriedly, Sylvia realised she had 'never said goodbye' to her new friend, 'which was painful'.[34]

A few weeks before she went down to Dorset with her things, Sylvia gave Valentine a snuffbox – 'a much needed talisman', Valentine wrote to thank her – and the first of many gifts.[35] In return, Valentine sent her a teacloth embroidered with sea creatures, which Sylvia added to her packing list.[36] These were domestic tokens and acknowledgements of the home they were building, but they were also indications of an increasing tenderness, the nudging of friendship into deeper affection. Both women were restless. For Valentine, Miss Green would provide a stable home after a period of tumult and confusion; for Sylvia, their living arrangement would bring an end to the solitude into which she had slipped for so long.

~

On 23 September 1930, Sylvia left London. Valentine, who owned a car, picked her up from Inverness Terrace, and together they began the long drive to Dorset, the car made lively by 'dog William' and rattling with Sylvia's possessions.[37] They went via Guildford, lunching on cold chicken and pears in a copse. It was evening before they reached Chaldon, the clouds breaking into 'a blue and yellow curd sky' and Miss Green 'in her pink and white, a geranium on her doorstep and Mrs Moxon clattering a pail'.[38] They were given gifts to celebrate their arrival: a marrow from Mrs Moxon, who lived opposite, and a bedspread from Mrs Way, who lived in the village and was newly employed as charwoman. On their first evening, they dined on fish and chips with Powys and his wife Violet at Beth Car, before going off separately to sleep – Sylvia at Mrs Way's and Valentine at Florrie Legg's, an arrangement that would last a week while they put the finishing touches to Miss Green. Over the next few days, they received deliveries of oil and coal and assembled the cooker, though Sylvia, while out walking William, was bitten on the wrist by a Great Dane from the vicarage. With her hand bandaged, she relied on Valentine to unpack boxes and light her cigarettes. 'I lean more and more on her trousers,' she wrote.[39]

Finally, they moved in. 'My first act was to have a bath,' Sylvia wrote, before making up the beds, putting out soap, washing the crockery, and arranging the larder.[40] In the evening, she and Valentine returned from a walk to find Mrs Moxon lighting the first fire, 'with a gin-fuelled incantation of good-will upon us'. Miss Green was coming to life. 'It burned merrily,' Sylvia wrote in her diary, 'the room began to live, like a ship getting under way.'[41]

But the next morning, Sylvia was confronted with the reality of sharing her home with another person. After living alone, she realised she must adjust to Valentine's habits. Greeting her with a kiss, she felt Valentine's body stiffen with embarrassment, and she was put out by her abstemious breakfast of a glass of water. She sensed Valentine's reserve, and the extent to which she could pull away from the world. In their first days at Miss Green, they lived according to what she remembered later as a kind of 'unintimate intimacy', mitigating the suddenness of their proximity by preserving the decorum of near strangers. Ceremoniously, they established the routines which would provide the framework for their everyday lives. 'From the first morning when Valentine in silk dressing-gown and green slippers laid and lit the fire, our parts were established, and we never contested them,' Sylvia remembered later.[42] From then on, Valentine cut firewood, shot rabbits with her rifle and drove the car, while Sylvia cooked and gardened. Mrs Way would occasionally 'keep house' (cleaning the cottage and laying out breakfast), and took away their laundry. But Sylvia and Valentine did most of the work themselves. Housekeeping, cleaning and tidying were domestic rituals; they had a performative, role-playing quality, but were also ways of feeling at home.

The cottage quickly became the women's shared privacy from the world. They desired few visitors, installing a partition in the sitting room that allowed one person to escape upstairs unobserved while the other answered the door. Sylvia's ownership of the cottage, her affectionately officious letters, and her growing desire to protect Valentine established an enduring habit of seniority in their relationship. Sylvia was older and better off, and Valentine, inclined to dependency, yielded to her assurance. Often in those first months, as Sylvia decorated and furnished the house, Valentine was too eagerly grateful. 'I am very happy here,' she wrote to Sylvia in August, two months after the sale went through. 'I thank you very much more than I can manage to.'[43] 'This habit of being the Royal Family seems to fasten upon me,' Sylvia grumbled in her diary. 'Alas, it is my means, not me. [. . .] It's not that people are mercenary; only that they are human beings, and must butter their parsnips.'[44] To her, money meant little: 'I like spending it, I like disposing of it – in between I never give it a thought.'[45] But for all her umbrage, she enjoyed the dynamic of their new relationship. 'Love is impossible between equals,' she later wrote. 'One must have a little condescension or a little awe.'[46] She was proud and philanthropic, and Valentine flattered her.

News of the cottage and its contents spread quickly through Chaldon: rumours of pink paint sent from London and 'the grandeur of saucepans and not a single upholstered chair'.[47] Sylvia – already known in the village as the owner of the fluffy black dog who gambolled on the village green – had no qualms about baffling people. The cottage expressed her playfulness and she revelled in its deviation from convention. On a chest in the sitting room, beneath the rococo mirror, she placed a 1646 Bible and a 1787 edition of the Book of Common Prayer, which became known as 'Mrs Johnson', the first of her private jokes with Valentine. Every evening, she would pick a passage at random and read aloud, much to their amusement and the bewilderment of their guests.

In the country, Sylvia was beginning to feel at home. She was pleased with the view of High Chaldon from her bed, the look of the candles in the mirror sconces, and her possessions placed carefully about. With Valentine, she had created a household that reflected her character. It was rustic but refined, coupling Chippendale with cross-stitch, Regency furniture with patchwork quilts. Her domestic aesthetic replicated the bric-a-brac atmosphere of her books, but it was also a statement of purpose, a style for living. Later, she remembered 'conversing, not talking' with Valentine during their first days at Miss Green, for the 'formality of "conversing" matched the tall candlesticks, her Regency coffee-spoons, my egg-shell porcelain coffee cups, white outside, lined with sugar almond-pink. With these and the mirror we declared against the grated carrot, folk-pottery way of life.'[48]

Unlike Virginia Woolf, Sylvia wasn't finding her footing as a writer through country living; rather, it was the other way around. As if following in the footsteps of one of her wilful, wayward characters, Sylvia had arrived at country life. Chaldon suited her. The village answered her need for lightness and acceptance. Among its incongruous community, its mixture of newcomers and locals, she could more easily be herself. Her arrival was unexpected, and right. As one scholar has written, the common thread of her books is her characters' capacity for momentous decisions, for sudden changes of course.[49] Sylvia's move to Miss Green had, imaginatively at least, already taken place. In her first novel, *Lolly Willowes*, her protagonist also exchanges London for the freedoms of country life. Laura Willowes, twenty-eight and unmarried, having cared for her elderly father until his death, is dispatched to live with her brother and his family in London, as if she were 'a piece of family property forgotten in the will'.[50] There, Laura is stripped of autonomy and becomes simply Aunt Lolly: affable, companionable, indispensable at Christmas and during the household sewing. But Laura is quickly bored by her new situation and begins to lead a secret life: licking marrons glacés from her fingers in teashops, roaming Bunhill Fields in the dark. Looking for escape, she finds the village of Great Mop in a guidebook. Once there, Laura is reinvigorated by her new solitariness. She rambles in the beech-woods and sits up long into the night, and finally realises the vocation her previous life had denied her – she becomes a witch. Attending her first Sabbath in the village, she meets Satan, disguised as a gamekeeper, with whom she makes her pact: she accepts Satan as overlord in exchange for her privacy. Finally, she will live as she pleases, unobstructed and undisturbed. It's an odd bargain, perhaps, but it befits the novel's heroine, a reclusive woman who, preferring Satan's ownership to that of her urban, bourgeois family, sets out on her own unorthodox path.

Sylvia had begun the novel by accident in 1923 when, inspired by reading accounts of witch trials in sixteenth-century Scotland, she imagined a lively story of a witch set in contemporary rural England. Unlike Virginia, she wrote her first book without difficulty: 'One line led to another, one smooth page to the next. It was as easy as whistling. [. . .] I told nobody. I barely told myself. I felt no obligation to go on, let alone finish.'[51] Two years later, when her first book of poems, *The Espalier*, was accepted for publication, Charles Prentice, her editor at Chatto & Windus, asked if he could read something else and so she sent him 'my story about a witch', adding, '[i]f you like it well enough to think it worth publishing I shall be extremely pleased. If you don't, I shan't be much surprised.'[52] The novel came out the following year and was an instant success: reprinted twice in one week a month after publication, it was nominated for the Prix Femina and was selected as the inaugural Book of the Month for the new American book club, securing Sylvia a loyal and enduring American readership.

At first glance, *Lolly Willowes* is a whimsical story, a mild-mannered tale of post-war spinsterhood that shifts from family saga into fantasy of the kind in vogue in the 1920s, in novels of supernatural transformation such as David Garnett's 1922 *Lady into Fox*. But in

the future she imagined for her heroine, Sylvia had outlined a sur-
prisingly far-reaching feminist vision. She was attempting to
reimagine spinsterhood through the metaphor of witchcraft,
thereby proposing an alternative to the dreary and marginalized
fate of legions of women following the First World War. Unloosing
Laura from the obligations of family, tradition and duty, and grant-
ing her a life of rural seclusion, Sylvia was calling for female privacy
rather than power, and proposed that women would prefer simply
to be left alone. After the witches' Sabbath, Laura delivers a speech
to Satan in which she laments the fate of women as dependents
and dogsbodies, 'living and growing old, as common as blackberries, and as unregarded':

> I see them, wives and sisters of respectable men, chapel members, and
> blacksmiths, and small farmers, and Puritans. In places like Bedford-
> shire, the sort of country one sees from the train. [. . .] Well, there
> they were, there they are, child-rearing, house-keeping, hanging
> washing from the currant bushes; and for diversion each other's silly
> conversation, and listening to men talking together in the way that
> men talk and women listen. [. . .] And all the time being thrust further
> down into dullness when the one thing all women hate is to be
> thought dull. [. . .] If they could be passive and unnoticed, it wouldn't
> matter. But they must be active, and still not noticed. Doing, doing,
> doing, till mere habit scolds at them like a housewife, and rouses them
> up – when they might sit in their doorways and think – to be doing
> still![53]

What Laura desires is 'to escape all that – to have a life of one's
own, not an existence doled out to you by others'.[54] Though it's a
cry for freedom as striking as Virginia Woolf's in *A Room of One's
Own*, published three years later, Sylvia was articulating a complex
and not easily optimistic version of independence. After her speech,
Laura goes off in search of a nest of dry leaves or a haystack in
which to sleep. She knows that Satan, going about his rounds, will
not disturb her. His 'profoundly indifferent ownership' guarantees

what she most needs for herself: the freedom to do nothing.[55] She wishes to be passive, to go unnoticed, to join herself with the earth. In London, when she dreamed of her escape, she pictured a solitary old woman picking fruit in a dusky orchard, 'standing with upstretched arms among her fruit trees as though she were a tree herself, growing out of the long grass, with arms stretched up like branches'.[56] With no orchard of her own, Laura is content to harvest what she finds, 'common herbs and berries [. . .], growing wherever she chose to wander'. She decides: 'It is best as one grows older to strip oneself of possessions, to shed oneself downwards like a tree, to be wholly earth before one dies.'[57] Her quest for independence is subversive, not only because she rejects her family and the drudgeries of domestic life, but because she casts herself off entirely from the material world. For Laura, freedom means the right to total indifference and unsociability; she has unhooked herself.

Laura's was a more extreme version of independence than the one Sylvia was settling into at Miss Green, where she took pleasure in *doing, doing, doing*, and enamel sink-drainers. Yet at the time of writing, Sylvia was thirty and unpublished, and her vision for Laura's freedom matched her desire for her own. The problem, it seemed, was that the novel was too subtle. 'Other people that have seen *Lolly* have told me that it was charming, that is was distinguished, and my mother said it was almost as good as Galsworthy. And my heart sank lower and lower,' Sylvia had written to her friend David Garnett (who was known in Woolf's circle as Bunny), exasperated that her readers were missing the novel's political core. 'I felt as though I had tried to make a sword only to be told what a pretty pattern there was on the blade. But you have sent me a drop of blood.'[58] Setting the novel in 1921, Sylvia placed Laura among the last generation of women for whom not being married meant futures as serviceable daughters in the households of their ageing relatives. As a single or 'surplus' woman, Laura has negligible social status and even less claim to a sexual identity. But, rather than being a deprivation, her singleness becomes a source of power. She is roaming and unattached, and finds her satisfactions elsewhere,

stroking her hand over the garnet-coloured mop-headed chrysanthe-
mums in the London greengrocer's, or in her wanderings of the city's
dark burial grounds, which rouse in her 'a kind of ungodly hal-
lowedness'.[59] At Great Mop, she finds a community of women like
her – gentle and dowdy to the eye, and yet bristling with private passions. These women make ordinary, workaday witches and yet, like
sticks of dynamite, they 'know in their hearts how dangerous, how
incalculable, how extraordinary they are'.[60] Sylvia had read Margaret
Murray's *The Witch-Cult in Western Europe* when it was published in
1921, but her housewifely vision of black magic owed more to Robert
Pitcairn's *Criminal Trials of Scotland*, in which the verbatim confessions
of real women 'impressed on me that these witches were witches
for love, that witchcraft was more than Miss Murray's Dianic cult; it
was the romance of their hard lives, their release from dull futures.'[61]
The novel celebrated such women, women living in obscurity, but
with lively hearts. They made mild witches, village widows and
spinsters – women, as Laura puts it, 'a little odd in [their] ways'.[62]

~

By 1930, Sylvia, like Laura, had begun to feel solitary and spinster-
ish. She felt past her prime, and was wary of settling into odd habits.
She felt most alive during the changes in the seasons or when walking in the dark, as she often did with William. Her decision to buy a
cottage in Chaldon reflected something of Laura's escape. In rural
Dorset, she hoped to find the quiet necessary for work, and to be
accepted by a small circle of friends. In Valentine, she recognised a
twin desire to live an untethered, individualistic life. During their
first evenings at the cottage, as they sat by the fire and listened to
music on Valentine's gramophone, their familiarity grew. Theirs
was not unlike the contentment Sylvia had imagined for Laura at
Great Mop, where she discovers the pleasures of female companionship. With her landlady, Mrs Leak, Laura enjoys long evenings of
conversation, learning the recipes for homemade wines – dandelion,
cowslip, elderberry, ash key, and mangold – and the lives of her
neighbours. The scene is of an 'indoor pleasantness', the two

women 'tilting their glasses and drinking in small peaceful sips'.[63]
By now, Laura is no longer the mild-mannered spinster her family
once housed, but is independent, on the brink of learning her own
wildness, and free. For Sylvia, Miss Green made a life like Laura's
possible. Sitting with Valentine as the wind blew in gusts from the
sea, she felt herself in such a 'cocoon of warmth' that 'it seemed
odd that we had not been living there for years'.[64]

Setting up at Miss Green was not her first attempt at escape. As for
Virginia, freedom had first revealed itself to Sylvia in the aftermath
of her father's death. In 1917, in the final months of the First World
War, George Townsend Warner, a respected housemaster and the
head of modern history at Harrow School, died suddenly, opening
up a chasm in Sylvia's life. Father and daughter had been close.
Sylvia had grown up at the school in lodgings adjacent to the boarding house, where the education she received from George was
musical and scholarly if not conventional. By the age of seventeen,
she had been dubbed the 'best boy at Harrow'.[65] Following George's
death, she was, as she described later, 'mutilated': 'He was fifty-one,
and we were making plans of what we would do together when he
retired. It was as though I had been crippled and at the same
moment realised I must make my journey alone.'[66] Suddenly, her
future narrowed. Her mother, Nora, planned to leave Harrow for
the family's villa on Dartmoor. Sylvia was to live with her there.

Her luck changed when, shortly afterwards, she was accepted
onto the editorial committee for *Tudor Church Music*, the Carnegie
UK Trust's project to catalogue and publish a vast collection of
English sacred music from the Tudor and Jacobean periods. She was
put forward for the position by Percy Buck, a fellow editor on the
committee, and her lover. The pair had met at Harrow, where Buck
was a music master; when their affair began, Sylvia was nineteen
and he was forty-one, married, and a father of five. Offered the job,

Sylvia didn't hesitate. Using her first wages to put down the rent for a flat in London, she broke free.

At twenty-five, Sylvia was the youngest member of the five-strong editorial committee, and the only woman. Buck's sponsorship would certainly have helped, though the position arose at a moment when, in the immediate aftermath of war, greater opportunities for work arose for women, and the possibility of their economic independence glimmered. Yet Sylvia was also an excellent musician, proficient in several instruments including the piano, and a composer of her own work. In 1916, under the direction of Richard Terry, the music master at Westminster Cathedral, she joined the Bach Choir and lectured on the nuances of sixteenth-century notation. Working on *Tudor Church Music* suited her scholarly inclinations, and her developing archival sense, and for several years she was engrossed in the project. It also opened her up to a particular kind of rural experience. Catching the train into the country, she visited university towns to rummage through archives, or arrived at remote rural churches where she was met by a warden, or the woman who cleaned, and shown around vestry and belfry by taper. Occasionally, she played the organ. Back in London, she settled in her flat or in the warmer comforts of the manuscript room at the British Museum to begin the painstaking process of transcribing and editing. The manuscripts she worked from were old and incredibly rare – sheets of choral church music, largely in Latin, by Taverner, Gibbons, Byrd and Tallis. It was an ambitious project and the work was highly technical, taking the committee twelve years to complete, but, by 1929, all ten volumes of *Tudor Church Music* had appeared, published by Oxford University Press.[67]

Sylvia's first flat was on Queen's Road in Bayswater, above a furriers, where she became 'absorbed by the fascinating discipline of living alone'.[68] She existed with 'economic trimness' on a salary of £60 per year from the Carnegie UK Trust along with £100 in annuities from her father's estate. Her rent was £90 per year. It was little to go on, but like many young women who were drawn to London after the First World War as a host of new professions opened up to them, Sylvia's independence was imperative: 'If I couldn't live within my £160 I should have to leave my stately solitude and doss down in some dreary receptacle for working girls.'[69]

She relished the challenges of living frugally. An account book, quickly abandoned, shows an early attempt at budgeting, itemizing the weekly shop: bread rolls, butter, winkles, watercress and a bunch of violets (a treat). Eggs were a shilling each. Once, finding she'd bought a bad one, Sylvia returned to the shop carrying the offending egg in a teacup, and demanded a replacement from the grocer. Dining out meant 'a sixpenny fish tea', and the feeling that '[c]heap low-class meals are such a pleasure, I wonder I don't take to chewing-gum', as she recorded gleefully in her diary.[70] (Like Virginia, Sylvia was embracing aspects of working-class living; there was a degree of role-play.) But frugality was also flouted. On seeing crisp, white bedlinen arranged in a shop window, she ignored prudence's remonstrances that 'thrift was not only for fun – that freedom depended on it', and, reasoning that they would do for a shroud, went in and bought them. It was a great occasion, and for many years her linen sheets remained a source of triumph and pride. There were simpler, everyday luxuries, too: 'I never debased myself by giving up smoking.'

By day, she worked in the British Museum, 'smirking at the thought that for hours and hours I would be kept warm by public expenditure'. Days off were spent contriving activities for free, such as visiting the Chinese markets at Penny Fields or 'ennobling' her-self with public statuary and the Wren Orangery. She loved London and enjoyed thriftiness: 'Every little advantage I filched from cir-cumstance, every penny I stretched into three halfpence, every profitable abstention, every exercise of forethought, [. . .] made me feel gay as Macheath.' She lived cheerfully: 'From time to time I felt hungry, and in winter I often felt cold. But I never felt poor.'[71]

Sylvia continued to keep her relationship with Buck a secret. Their longest sojourns were in the country, driving out to cathedral towns on committee business and staying in small hotels. In London, their arrangement suited Sylvia, giving her companionship as well as independence. With a family of his own, Buck stayed with her once a week, outside of which she was able to enjoy the pleasures of living alone. But she treasured her evenings with 'Teague', as she called him, during which they played duets on the piano and talked into the night. Their affection depended upon distance; later, she remembered that he 'couldn't, and said he couldn't, endure more than three days on end of my company', which seemed to her very wise.[72]

In 1923, Sylvia moved into a new flat on Inverness Terrace, and took a housemate – William, the black chow. It was there that she wrote *Lolly Willowes* and her second novel, *Mr Fortune's Maggot*. Now, with some money to spare, she invested in her surroundings. Her taste was sophisticated, splashed with cultured good humour. She painted the walls of the flat bright, glowing colours and sewed patchwork cushions for the sofa. On each of the large, plain curtains, she appliquéd the forms of a man and a woman, their arms aloft, which became known teasingly as 'Duncan and Vanessa', after the Bloomsbury painters, and drew together at night. But it was the bathroom that caught her imagination. In her flat on Queen's Road, the bathroom had been across a shared hallway, and she often forgot her latchkey, forcing her to make her way back via the window and a glass skylight, 'a feasible route, but so smutty that I then had to have another bath'. But at 121 Inverness Terrace the bathroom was private. Converted from a Victorian conservatory, it had glass walls and a glass roof and 'clung to the outside of the back wall like a snail'. It was decorated with fading arabesques, presumably designed for decency, but Sylvia dismissed them, unconcerned with modesty. '[A]t that time,' she remembered, 'there really wasn't enough of me to make a fuss about. Besides, there would be steam; and in summer trees.' And so, on the long summer evenings she bathed in the shade of the sycamores, 'watching cats and sparrows, looking into those gently moving recesses of green; while [. . .] the garden beneath exhaled breathings of lilies and violets whenever a surge of bath water went down the overflow'.[73]

London's pleasures were plentiful, and, in 1927, Sylvia began to keep a record of her full and busy life. Her diary recorded afternoons spent lying with William under the plane trees in Kensington Gardens and evenings dining with friends. Charles Prentice took her

Sylvia, with William the black chow (inscribed on reverse, 'MINE – V. Ackland')

to supper at Marcel Boulestin's newly-opened restaurant in Covent Garden, where she ate 'Oysters, red mullet grilled with a slip of banana laid along it like a medieval wife on a tomb' and 'the best peach I have ever eaten'.[74] She went to concerts and recitals – Mahler at the Courtauld, Stravinsky at the BBC – and, in her diary, described what she had heard. She possessed an amazing language for music. A performance of Thomas Tallis' forty-voiced motet, *Spem in alium*, was 'like the Milky Way, a glimmering unaccountable tissue' and left her unable to sleep, 'my head still ringing with the shining stir of the motet, and the choirs tossing Creator to one another'.[75] (On her expeditions into the country, she was already tuning her ear to a different music. At Long Melford in Suffolk, listening to church bells, she described the B♭ bell, which 'clanged, swelled, grew out-ward on the air, trembled and then settled on the third', like 'a wave breaking everyway outwards, thinning, ebbing back again'.[76])

As with music, Sylvia's best pleasures were solitary. Her social circle brushed Bloomsbury, yet she disliked parties. At Edith Sitwell's house, appalled by the sight of Nina Hamnett in a tight-fitting dress, she retreated to the cloakroom to read. She played up to her role as the voguish writer of witchcraft, but treated her success warily. 'I have felt what it is to be famous,' she remarked dryly when, wrapping plates to help a friend move house, she had the disconcerting experience of seeing newspapers printed with her name.[77]

~

It was during this initial flurry of celebrity that Sylvia met Valentine for the first time. Late in 1927, while visiting Chaldon for the weekend, she went to one of the Powys's tea parties at Beth Car. As she talked animatedly to the other guests, a tall figure slipped quietly into the room. Immediately, Sylvia felt herself being watched. She had heard of the poet in the village from Powys's letters, but was surprised by the stylishly dressed young woman. Valentine was reserved and polite, with short hair and a slender, six-foot figure emphasized by men's clothes. Often, she was mistaken for one of Powys's sons.[78] To Sylvia, she appeared like 'a willow-wand, sweet scented as a spray of Cape Jessamine, almost silent, too'.[79] Valentine, in turn, noticed Sylvia's quickness and her intelligence, which expressed itself in her 'tensely beautiful' face.[80] Their first conversation, conducted publicly in the stuffy room, embarrassed them both. Their differences – in age, appearance and sensibility – stood out immediately: Sylvia's jangling earrings, and her loud, high voice; Valentine's urbane coolness.[81] Sylvia dismissed the young woman, but knew herself unsettled, 'disconcerted by feeling myself so gravely and dispassionately observed by someone I was making a poor impression on'.[82] For the next few months, Valentine avoided Sylvia during her visits from London. She was a solitary figure, glimpsed in the village or walking over the downs, or sliding out of Beth Car by the back door as Sylvia came in through the front.

What Sylvia knew of Valentine she gleaned from letters from Chaldon friends. She had been told that Valentine was living in Chaldon in the wake of an annulled marriage, but little more. In truth, Valentine had arrived in the village in a wretched state. In 1925, she had married a man called Richard Turpin after meeting him at a dinner party, and left him soon afterwards. At their wedding service in Westminster Cathedral, Molly – as she was then known – wore a nun-like coif beneath which she was hiding her newly cropped hair. Her craving for conventionality jostled with her desire to shock: removing her cap at the reception, she was delighted by the gasps from the scandalized guests. She was not attracted to Turpin, but hoped the marriage would please her watchful and disapproving family. It had been an impetuous decision, an attempt to escape her mother and what she supposed would be her fate as a spinster, 'one of those miserable, dowdy daughters', she wrote later in her autobiography, 'travelling from place to place, unhappy, cheated, oppressed'.[83]

In fact, Molly was in love with a woman, Bo Foster, and Turpin, too, was gay. Both looked to marriage to hide their sexualities; for Molly, though being a lesbian wasn't a criminal offence – the bill had been shelved by parliament in 1921 on the basis that it might provoke deviance among women – female sexuality still, as Valentine reflected, 'aroused loathing and vituperation' from society at large.[84] As a teenager, she had borne the consequences of discovery. Her father, reading Molly's love-letters from a schoolfriend, had rejected his daughter so swiftly and severely that they had remained unreconciled until his death. Now, honeymooning at her family's house in Norfolk, she quailed at her husband's physical proximity. Turpin's reluctant sexual attempts confused and sickened her. 'As he lay very close to me I felt the hairs on his arms and loathed him,' she wrote later. '[H]is hands seemed too large and curiously insensitive. I was thinking about [Bo] all the time.'[85] On returning to London, Turpin took Molly to see a doctor, who, concerned that Turpin was not able to enjoy his conjugal rights, instructed she have an operation to remove her hymen.

Afterwards, Molly convalesced in a nursing home, where she endured considerable pain and dreaded the twice-daily humiliation of having dressings.* She decided that she could never return to her husband. She was invited by a friend of Bo to go to Dorset, where she could rest, free of Turpin, in the village of East Chaldon. She accepted. The day before her departure, still dizzy from the anaesthetic, she took a cab to the Army & Navy Stores and bought a pair of men's flannel trousers, taking a celebratory turn around St James's Park. She travelled to Chaldon the following day, arriving to a supper of biscuits and Bovril by the fire in Mrs Wallis's cottage. Unpacking her belongings in the small bedroom upstairs and blowing out her candle as she climbed into bed, she felt the 'extraordinary pleasure' of being alone again, lying on her back and listening to the owls as she fell asleep.[86]

Molly found solace in the country. After several weeks, she moved from Mrs Wallis's into a rented cottage. By day, she sunbathed naked on the beach below Bat's Head and roamed freely over the downs; in the evening, she settled at Beth Car and typed for Powys or read aloud to Violet, his wife. She enjoyed scrambling over gates in trousers and began to dress entirely in men's clothing, striding through the village like a dandyish country squire.[87] Finally, in a gesture towards her newfound individuality, she changed her name to Valentine. It was an androgynous, elegant choice, a nod to her sexual pleasures and her masculine–feminine persona. At the age of nineteen, and in the country, she had emerged into a new identity.

But, as she divided her time between Dorset and a rented flat on Mecklenburgh Square, Valentine's life continued to be hectic. Meeting Bo's friends, she was surprised to hear their frank discussions about sex with women, and for the first time saw her sexuality as not unusual. With Bo, who was 'considerate and gentle' in bed, she was released from self-doubt into a new sexual confidence. 'I found deep

---

* This is the narrative set out by Valentine in her memoir, *For Sylvia*. It is perhaps more likely, given her sexual activity during this period, and the need for a general anaesthetic, that Valentine entered the nursing home for an altogether different gynaecological procedure, about which she wished to remain private. But this is speculation.

pleasure, true pleasure and complete satisfaction from making love with women,' she wrote later. '[W]ith women I was released and happy.'[88] She met artists and writers connected with Bloomsbury, going to parties with Clive Bell, Nina Hamnett and Beatrix Lehmann, and was sketched by Eric Gill. She flitted between passionate relationships with women – with Anna May Wong, Nancy Cunard, and Dorothy Warren, who owned a gallery on Maddox Street – and was writing poems feverishly: 'They were always very bad, but I was confident that I was a poet.'[89] There were male lovers, too, and in 1926 Valentine discovered she was pregnant. Happy at this unexpected turn of events, she began to imagine a daughter she would raise in the country with Bo. But in the spring of 1927, while out walking in Chaldon, she slipped down a bank and within minutes began miscarrying. She sought help from Violet and haemorrhaged for several days before travelling to see a gynaecologist in London. She was devastated: 'my whole thought and my whole love were concentrated on that unborn child. And now it was gone?'[90]

Valentine in trousers

By the time Sylvia met her, Valentine had learned to contain her traumas beneath good clothes and impeccable manners. Sylvia sensed her shyness, but was yet to realize the depths of vulnerability that lurked beneath the tailored swagger. Yet she found Valentine's youthfulness and the display of her sexual identity compelling. In London, their worlds brushed – once, Valentine saw Sylvia walking down Queen's Terrace, her expression fixed and downcast – but, after the disastrous tea at Beth Car, they rarely met.

~

Sylvia, like Valentine, was to find acceptance in Chaldon. It was an unlikely setting for a creative community, but, since Powys had settled there, the village had become home to a coterie of artists and writers. Several of Powys's siblings lived nearby. His sisters – Gertrude, a painter, and Phillipa, a poet and novelist – settled at Chydyok, a farmhouse just outside the village, and his brother Llewelyn rented one of the coastguard's cottages on the cliffs at White Nothe. Llewelyn had recently returned from New York where he had married the writer and editor Alyse Gregory. Alyse had given up her position as an editor of the prominent literary magazine *The Dial* in order to live in Dorset with Llewelyn. In her journals, she recorded the tenor of their daily lives in the cottage on the headland, where they were cut off from the village by a mile of muddy track. They ventured into Chaldon for the post office or the pub, but preferred to walk on the cliffs where they watched the cormorants nesting on the rocks and the black-backed gulls circling over the sea.

When Sylvia had first arrived in Chaldon in 1921, she was holidaying with Stephen Tomlin, known as Tommy, the Bloomsbury sculptor who had been a pupil of her father, and her friends George and Bea Howe. Staying at the Weld Arms in Lulworth, she walked on the downs every day, admiring the sweeping, chalky coastline. At Arish Mell, a small cove east of Lulworth, she undressed and, to the surprise of her companions, waded naked into the sea.* When the week was over, she travelled back to London with George and Bea, leaving Tommy to explore Dorset by himself. He walked to Chaldon and soon met the reclusive Powys, writing excitedly to Sylvia of 'a most remarkable man living just beyond the village. He is a sort of hermit [. . .] [and] I believe he writes'.[91] A few months later, Tommy invited Sylvia to meet Powys. Their first conversation, over tea at Beth Car, was a success. Sylvia found Powys warm and courteous; he admired her 'biting mind'.[92] The following Sunday, as he read the lesson in St Nicholas Church, he gave thanks for the arrival of the visitor, and from then on, Sylvia visited as often as she could. When she was in Chaldon, they discussed each other's work and walked together over the downs, to Holworth, or the stone circle at Poxwell, or to the Marys. 'How strange to look back at a time when I knew not you, nor Chaldon,' she wrote to him in 1925, the year Valentine arrived in the village, 'and now writer and landscape are both well-known and dear.'[93]

Sylvia was Powys's first real audience. After he settled in Chaldon, the writer had received little recognition and struggled to make ends meet. The scratched Dorset landscape provided the backdrop for his grim, rustic fables of English rural life: he described the 'poor low lived countryside bare and bleached like a worn garment' and set his stories in dreary villages inhabited by small, bickering communities.[94] Early in their friendship, Sylvia had written asking to see his work, and received the manuscript for *Mr Tasker's Gods*, a novel about a deceitful churchwarden who keeps murderous pigs. She admired the cadences of Powys's writing, which owed much to his reading of the Bible, his unsentimental natural imagery, and his depiction of scandalously behaved local clergy. 'I feel battered and excited, as if I had come in from fighting a high wind,' she wrote to him on finishing the manuscript. 'You

---

* Later, Sylvia remembered travelling in a 'waggonette' along the Wool to Lulworth road, 'my first journey in Dorset', with George and Bea Howe. Warner, 25 July 1931, *Diaries*, 86.

know the feeling one has after *Wuthering Heights*? I feel rather like that.'[95] But, though she connected deeply with Powys's writing, she was disturbed by the novel. As a young man, Powys had farmed in Norfolk, where he had become disillusioned by his observations of the rural poor. 'Their quaint clothes and rustic speech made them seem to me like pictures,' he had written, 'and I ought to have left them as pictures, but I was foolish enough to look into their lives. I found that their lives were marked, scarred, and torn; greed and jealousy and hatred lived in them.' His memories of East Anglia included long rambles on which he encountered tramps on the dusty roads and an 'old hag' stealing sticks from farmers' fields.[96] He reduced rural life to a litany of bleak events, from the suicides of working men to the unhappy marriages that produced unwanted children. Of the natural world, he recorded only failed crops and the gruesome deaths of animals.

Sylvia saw life in the country differently. She shared Powys's preference for realism, but she was more sympathetic towards the people she encountered, a respect that was returned when she began living in Chaldon with Valentine. Powys's treatment of his neighbours made her queasy and she wrote to him in their defence, outlining her belief in the 'steadfast virtue' of country people and the dignity of their often difficult lives. 'I found it hard to stomach the ruthless hatred with which he pursued the peasant characters,' she admitted. *Mr Tasker's Gods* 'has left me with a feeling of perturbed melancholy'.[97] Nevertheless, she was determined to help him, and took the novel to Tomlin's friend David Garnett, then running a bookshop in Bloomsbury. Together, they approached Charles Prentice at Chatto & Windus, where the novel was accepted. It was published in 1925, ten years after he had begun writing it. Powys recognised his friends' help and devotion: his next book, a collection of stories called *The Left Leg*, was dedicated to Sylvia, David and Tommy.

They were not alone in their admiration for Powys. As Sylvia's evangelism about his work grew, visitors to Beth Car multiplied. Valentine arrived, and Naomi Mitchison visited along with Liam

O'Flaherty and T. E. Lawrence, and the painters Dora Carrington and Augustus John. (The village was to feature in several novels of the period, including David Garnett's *The Sailor's Return*, published in 1925, and Naomi Mitchison's *The Corn King and the Spring Queen*, which came out in 1931.) Hearing of the secluded literary genius, the Bloomsbury socialite Ottoline Morrell foisted herself upon Beth Car after he refused to go to her at Garsington, near Oxford. But, for much of the time, Chaldon was a quiet place where work could flourish. Tommy packed up his London studio and rented a half-cottage in the village; not long after, the sculptor Elizabeth Muntz followed. She remained in Dorset for the rest of her life, drawing Valentine as she bathed in the sea, and carving a bust of Powys from Purbeck stone. Despite his visitors, Powys remained reclusive, which served only to increase his charm. 'Mr Powys seems without a fault. He was so beautiful good and gracious,' wrote Carrington after visiting with Tommy.[98] He was obscure and grandfatherly, an unlikely and generous patron in so secluded a place.

~

As she continued to visit Dorset regularly throughout the 1920s, Sylvia began to lose heart with London. By 1929, more than a decade had passed since her father's death, and her relationship with Buck was solid and cool. Often, there were long absences, though she was surprised on his return to discover 'how massively intimacy can just sweep on as before'.[99] *Tudor Church Music* was published and she finished her third novel, *The True Heart*. ('Goodbye, my dear Sukey; first child of my middle-age,' she wrote in her diary.)[100] It seemed as if time had stilled, and the past washed around her. In November, listening to a concert at the Courtauld, Sylvia had a 'curiously strong illusion' that she was looking at her younger self – a melancholy creature, an apparition both distant and familiar.

She was sitting in the upper circle, very white-faced and black-haired. She wore horn-rimmed spectacles and a slightly odd severe grey dress, her hands were red and chillblainy: each time I looked up it was a shock to see her still there. She was not good-looking, but she had a kind of disdainful corpse-like vitality which was impressing; and I suppose I was like that au temps que j'étais belle.[101]

It was then Sylvia decided to give up musicology for writing. After finishing *Tudor Church Music*, she had edited several manuscripts and could be certain of work, but it was time consuming and poorly paid, and would demand a frugality to which, after the success of *Lolly Willowes*, she was reluctant to return. Increasingly, it seemed as if editing and composing was to dwell in past forms, and to find herself, alone, in concert halls. There was little of the freedom she was discovering in writing – a freedom which had much to do with the new perspectives, and the sense of community, afforded by the country. Her first three novels had left her with 'nothing except a wish to go on'; it was in writing, rather than music, that she could express herself: 'I never had a doubt as to what I meant to say.'[102] Meeting Herbert Howells after a concert, she was asked – as she was often asked by those who knew her as a musicologist – if she was working on 'music or t'other thing' and was saddened but relieved to admit that she had given music up. 'Perhaps you will be composing again when you are eighty-five?' Howells teased, to which Sylvia replied with her customary mischievousness that 'at 85 I should be taking up monumental sculpture'.[103] Soon, music began to feel as if it belonged to a previous life, like London: a 'secret past' which was 'inalienably mine by renunciation'.[104]

~

By the summer of 1930, Sylvia was caught between remembering past pleasures and discovering new ones. Imaginatively, it was as if she was living between places: conjuring the sights and feelings of her London years, while working with Valentine on the cottage. She was grieving music. And yet, out of this melancholy state, she began, after a long hiatus, to write poetry again, 'odd to be shot into that feeling again, that deliberate trance, without a word of warning'.[105] Stimulated by her visits to Chaldon, she started a long

narrative poem about an old countrywoman who turns her flowerbed into a commercial success in order to finance her thirst for gin.
Odd and ironic, the poem was a take on traditional pastoral forms,
and yet it was also, like Sylvia's first novel, an elaboration of a
woman's quest for freedom.

Opus 7 tells of Rebecca Random, who, like Laura Willowes, is
solitary and green-fingered, a kind of witch. She plants flowers in
the dead of night, waking each morning to a magical profusion in
her cottage garden. She is a 'sorceress', with a touch that 'pros-
pered all she set, as though there were a chemical affinity 'twixt
her/stuff and the stuff of plants'.[106] Gradually, Rebecca converts
her patch into a thriving marketplace, drawing customers from afar
and selling to tourists, passers-by and the local gentry. But, though
she makes good money from her garden, she devotes her earnings
entirely to her own pleasure: 'Rebecca lived on bread, and lived for
gin.' At the end of each day, she returns from the village pub and
retreats indoors where, with the 'order, solemnity, and ritual' of a
high priestess, she lights the lamp, combs her hair and drinks, the
cool liquid running like 'a shout of Alleluias all along her blood'.[107]
She finds in gin what Laura finds in witchcraft: intensity of experience and a wild, secret joy.

The poem contains an arresting image of Rebecca at work during
the night: 'moving with her lantern to and fro', she 'pulled darkness
after her'.[108] There is ceremony in her planting, creativity and sensuality, just as in her drinking. The terms of Rebecca's freedom, like
Laura's, are unusual: she wishes simply to be left to do as she pleases.
Later, Sylvia remembered living next to an elderly woman who
drank herself 'tidily' to death, just as Rebecca does at the end of the
poem. She praised the woman's 'recklessness', for what was so haz-
ardous to her health was also a display of autonomy: 'she knew
what she wanted (not many women do)'.[109] Sylvia admired such
flouting of respectability, and – perhaps more seriously – believed
firmly that individuals should be left to their own choices, without
accommodation or consequence. In all her writing, she would elaborate versions of freedom predicated not on selfishness, but rather

a kind of tolerance. In Sylvia's mind, every person should have the right to decide how to live, and be whoever they wished to be, however reckless or imprudent their decisions might appear to others. Self-determination, non-conformity: those were her terms. And so the woman's ending, like Rebecca's, is strangely triumphant. 'If there is a heaven,' Sylvia wrote of her neighbour, 'I am sure she went there like a cork from a champagne bottle.'[110]

The poem was also an early exploration of Sylvia's emerging rural politics. *Opus 7* is plush with the imagery of rural England and yet subverts any illusions of idyll by drawing attention to decline both human and social. Sylvia was following in the footsteps of eighteenth-century poets – 'I bethought me that it was about time to try to do for this date what Crabbe had done for his: write a truthful pastoral in the jog-trot English couplet' – by writing against the grain of a tradition which celebrated rural life.[111] Though Rebecca lives in a thatched cottage in a 'silly, soppy landscape', Love Green is a melancholy place. The labourers ache from work, doomed 'lifelong the same sour clods to grub forlorn', and the drinkers complain about taxation on their drink. The villagers are the last to benefit from Rebecca's entrepreneurial success. Her deference to her patrons – 'Mrs. Hawley of The Bungalow, who worshipped flowers, but couldn't make them grow' – and her inflated prices come at the expense of her poorer neighbours.[112] They can't afford her flowers, nor does she pay for them in the pub, where she used to drink alongside them. Sylvia was tempering the poem's fantasy – the imagery of Rebecca's miraculous midnight garden – with materialist and social concerns. She was edging towards a contemporary pastoral, using a traditional poetic form to respond to the conditions of everyday life. In *Opus 7*, thatched cottages and wallflowers exist alongside hardship and poverty. Black magic is possible. The country could be a place of enchantment, of wildness and possibility, but it could also be tedious and cruel. It owed much to Sylvia's impressions of Chaldon, both Powys's grim realism and her own eclectic tastes. She was drawn to local stories, and to unusual characters – like

Annie Moxon, who lived opposite Miss Green, and was busy plying Valentine with 'strange sly plants' for the garden.[113]

~

House and poem were nearly finished. 'I have been gently acquiring things like lamps and meat-safes, in the intervals of nearing the end of op. 7,' Sylvia wrote to Valentine in July. 'I find poetry and house property go very kindly together.'[114] Her writing was often characterized by this miscellaneous quality, the lively juxtaposition of registers, genres and forms. She was interested in history, fantasy, folklore and ballad, and moved easily between them. She also adapted old stories into new. In *The True Heart*, a utopian fantasy of rural living in which the young orphan Sukey Bond strikes out on her own to live on an Essex marsh, she had rewritten the myth of Cupid and Psyche, but, as she wrote in her preface to the book, 'in the terms of late nineteenth-century rural England'.[115] And, alongside *Opus 7*, she had resumed *Elinor Barley*, a story of a woman who murders her no-good husband according to the English folk song. Both stories had historical settings and yet were contemporary in tone, with rustic, determined heroines who switch between town and country, their stories weaving and unravelling like the sewing they repeatedly take in hand. Along with the imagery of rural landscapes, Sylvia often used needlework as a weatherglass for her characters' emotions. Elinor Barley stitches a quilt throughout her unhappy marriage, while Sukey Bond darns dreamily beneath a pear tree. The imagery of needlework acts as a reminder of the narrative's puncture and pull. Yet sewing could also be subversive. 'Womanly qualities: nice calculation, neat stitches, industry,' Sylvia wrote ironically in her diary later, calling to mind the thread that rasps against Laura Willowes's roughened and rebellious fingers.[116]

In London, in the late summer heat, Sylvia could sense her life was changing course. The resilience she had built around herself – the work of years – was slackening, her boundaries dissolving. She was unusually perceptive and alert, her awareness of the natural world sharpening to a point. In her diary, she described the night-sounds of London outside her window, the 'chatter' of dry leaves along the pavement, as if she was readying her musical ear for rural sounds.[117] Often, she walked William as it was getting dark, drinking in the 'scented unmoving voluptuous dusk' and listening to the trees jostling thickly overhead.[118] She was continuing to sew a patchwork quilt begun earlier that summer. One evening, sitting outside with Buck beside her, she was contented and companionable, cutting hexagons out of his *Evening Standard*, both of them marvelling at the 'New England matrons' who 'worked out how to construct them with one snip'. The quilt was to be made the English way, using hexagonal pieces of fabric, each carefully tacked onto paper before being sewn, back-to-back, in a honeycomb pattern. In her dressing-gown in the warm air, stitching, unpicking, and stitching again, she was like Sukey or Elinor, contemplating an unknown future with languid thoughts and busy hands.

Sylvia sitting up in bed at Miss Green

Later that night, as Buck slept, Sylvia went out into the dawn where she lay down on the grass, the dew 'so thick and cold that for the first minute it was like going into the sea'.[119] She listened to a blackbird and a cuckoo, and bees humming among the snapdragons. In the late summer of 1930, she was suspended between tenses. As she neared the end of her long poem, she started to think about Chaldon. Her friendship with Valentine was warm but remote, their living together an occasional arrangement, while life in London would carry on calmly as before. She would write. Looking up at the trees silhouetted against the pale, pewter-coloured clouds, she began to shiver. The days on her 'blossoming isle of solitude' were drawing in.[120]

By October 1930, Sylvia's home in the country was finished and she was settling into life at Miss Green. The pleasures of her new cottage were great, as was Valentine's chaperonage. Her wrist was healing, and she was enjoying her daily walks to the Marys, where in high weather she watched as the wind moved over the heath in 'a cloud of sea-spray and earth dust'. Her afternoons were spent cooking with William at her feet, or making a sackcloth rug – 'like a fallen woman'.[121] She was discovering a peaceful vision of domesticity; unlike Laura Willowes's sewing for her brother's family, these tasks were in the service of no one but herself.

Meanwhile, the village was becoming restless. All summer, rumours had been circulating about the vicarage, where its tenant, an elderly Miss Stevenson, ran a domestic training college for vulnerable young women going into service. The villagers reported seeing the women labouring in the garden, and hearing screams from within the house. On 10 October, one of them escaped, only to be returned to Miss Stevenson by a police officer. Sylvia and Valentine, hearing of the woman's bid for freedom and her subsequent imprisonment, were indignant. Who, from the village, was prepared to recriminate Miss Stevenson for the abuses she was inflicting on her charges? They would set her to rights. So, later that evening, they set off for the vicarage, arriving to find Miss Stevenson out, and the Great Dane – which had bitten Sylvia – barking inside. Returning to Miss Green, they ate a 'rapid dinner, cooked with fury', before venturing out once more. This time, they were let in, and a hostile interview followed. Miss Stevenson, according to Sylvia's diary, 'shook like a blancmange, and kept trying to ingratiate herself into our assistance by laughter and uneasy cryings', though Sylvia remained resolute, and chided her. Valentine, with a pistol in her pocket, 'sat white and motionless like Justice'.

Sylvia's reporting of the evening at the vicarage betrays the significance of what follows. In her diary, she dallies over details: the 'strange stilled light' over the landscape, an admiring glance at Valentine's legs. Walking away from the house, she marvelled as Valentine 'shook her stick in the air like a squire', and continued to observe her once they were back at the cottage. 'Righteous indignation is a beautiful thing,' she wrote, 'and lying exhausted on the rug I watched it flame in her with severe geometrical flames.'[122] That night, as they lay in bed, the women began to talk through the thin wall that separated their rooms. When Valentine cried out suddenly for loneliness, Sylvia rushed in to comfort her, and was soon clambering into bed beside her.

The following morning, Sylvia woke in Valentine's bed knowing she had found 'an irrefutable happiness'.[123] She hailed the new day as 'our first', 'a bridal of earth and sky'. She and Valentine spent the morning outside, behaving like lovers, 'lying in the hollowed tump of the Five Maries, listening to the wind blowing over our happiness, and talking about torpedoes, and starting up at footsteps'.[124] Finally, they could reveal their true feelings for one another, the gentle tide which had been gathering during the weeks of their courteous house-sharing, the painful pretence of formality. For Sylvia, the transformation was instant, and complete.

~

Her relationships – with places and people – were changing. As she settled her vision on Valentine, so, too, her emerging political awareness shifted to the country. In London, during the war, she had written about the young women working in a munitions factory; now, she took up the plight of Miss Stevenson's charges as her test case, her first errand of social justice.* Like Virginia with her microscope at Asheham, she was focusing her attention on what was nearest, on what was local. And yet she needed Valentine beside her. In the long and private history of their relationship, the evening at the vicarage marked the beginning, a starting point from which the fires of romantic and political feeling burned equally bright.

A few days later, Sylvia returned reluctantly to London to work, but for the short time she and Valentine were separated, they wrote to each other. She began to receive gifts from Chaldon: a ring ('My hands are not beautiful, my dear. They were once, but now they are spoiled, like most of the rest of me'); a rosebud from the garden, which opened and bloomed on her desk; and two snail-shells, 'one orange, one lemon-yellow', which Valentine had scented with her perfume, Fougère Royale.[125] The smell overwhelmed Sylvia and so she 'shut them firmly into a box with a lid, for one has no defence, no possible counter-sallies against the inanimate'.[126]

London seemed unreal and 'full of simulacra'.[127] She wrote to Valentine of her encounters with the 'bleached shadows' of friends and acquaintances and her walks with William in Kensington Gardens, 'visiting the trees that have been kind to my old distress and bewilderment'. 'I have so little strength left, except to love you,' she told her.[128] Four days passed slowly. '[H]ow shall I live out the muffle of time still between us?' she wrote on the dawdling eve of Valentine's return. 'Tomorrow. My love, my tremblings, my hurrying heart's blood.'[129]

Before long, Valentine joined her, and routines reversed themselves. The day began in the evening when Sylvia walked to

---

* Sylvia's earliest journalism was an article titled ' "Behind the Firing Line", by a Lady Worker' published in *Blackwood's Magazine* in February 1916, in which she described her experience working the night shift at a munitions factory in southeast London, the conditions of the place, and her interactions with her coltish, working-class female colleagues.

Valentine's new flat at Queensborough Studios, a short distance from Inverness Terrace. She had been desolate with longing; now, her diary lost track of itself. As it got dark, Valentine drove her to Whitechapel and on to Greenwich through the Blackwall Tunnel, before returning to Bayswater for a picnic of caviar and champagne on the floor of her flat. Afterwards, in bed, they 'packed a month's impatience and curiosity'.[130] Sylvia described nights 'so ample that there was even time to fall briefly asleep in them' and the loveliness of Valentine's embrace, 'her arms and neck pour[ing] from those narrow shoulders, like a smooth torrent of water limbed as it falls over a rock'.[131] 'I had not believed it possible to give such pleasure,' she remembered later, 'to satisfy such a variety of moods, to feel so demanded and so secure, to be loved by anyone so beautiful and to see that beauty enhanced by loving me.'[132]

One evening in late October, she told Buck that she had fallen in love with a woman. 'It was not an easy thing to say,' she wrote, saddened at losing the man who had been both lover and friend for so long. But Buck was magnanimous, accepting the news quietly: 'I can scarcely believe it is done; nothing more became it than its ending. [. . .] It was most perfectly taken, the blow I dealt.'[133] Afterwards, they ate Stilton and talked about Donne.

Returning to Dorset with Valentine in November, the world appeared transfigured. The couple woke to the winter's first frost, walking out into a 'silver-green world' in their dressing-gowns before going back to bed.[134] The afternoons were still mild and beneath the Five Marys they picnicked and talked, Sylvia writing a poem in 'the new kitchen memorandum book' and describing her 'amazing happiness to be writing there, full of cold snipe and beer, with my love lying beside me, her lappet of hair trailing into the winter grass'.[135] Valentine thrilled her. She was like 'a very young, fastidious, urbane pirate', and Sylvia watched her reverently. She had a 'lovely gait', her walk 'slender, erect, determined', and 'the footsteps [. . .] exactly aligned on a narrow track, regular as machine-stitching'.[136] Often, they were silly with each other, spending the morning 'rollicking in bed' and the afternoon 'rollicking on bed (nice distinction)', and fooling around out of doors.[137] They delighted in small indiscretions: walking in view of the Powyses at Beth Car, 'shamelessly embracing' in the porch (where they were caught by the oil man, who bolted 'as though I were a vampire bat'), or lying in the gorse beneath the footpath leading to the Marys.[138] In time, they would become accepted in the village as outsiders, and a couple. They benefited, perhaps, from seeming an extension of Powys's bohemian circle of friends. But, for now, at Miss Green, their coupledom was accepted with little comment. Mrs Way, finding them sitting up in Sylvia's bed one morning, cried simply, 'twins!'[139]

At thirty-six, Sylvia had come late to love. She could feel herself ageing and fretted that she wouldn't be able to keep up with Valentine's moods, and her frequent capriciousness. Valentine could be prickly, was liable to gloom, and believed whatever anyone said about her, good and bad. She was sensitive about her poetry – which Sylvia, in an effort to encourage her, praised perhaps too much – and was often unwell as a result of her secret drinking. What had begun in camaraderie with Bo in Bloomsbury had now taken a firmer hold over her life. Supplied by Florrie Legg at The Sailor's Return, she drank steadily and on her own. She had always been ill at ease in company and, fettered by shyness, had learned to cope 'by being a little drunk all the time'.[140] Marking each day in her diary as 'DD' or 'TMD' ('Devoid of Drink' or 'Too Much Drink') she attempted to manage her consumption, mostly unsuccessfully. Like poetry, drinking had become a tool for self-punishment, locking her into patterns of shame that repeated throughout her life. It was her guiltiest secret, and one she kept from Sylvia, though the many references to Valentine's faints and migraine attacks in Sylvia's diaries suggest she knew more than she let on.*

---

* For example, Sylvia's diary entry for 15 July 1931: 'Valentine, indulging in one veramon too many, was taken sick – stalking about the house white and grim. I lay awake alone, remembering too well the first migraine attack. In spite of the example of The Ladies [of Llangollen] I was bundled out of the way.' Warner, *Diaries*, 84.

But Sylvia had her own demons. For too long, she had been the chillblainy, angular girl in chilly concert halls, Buck's contented and quiet mistress, and an affable and auntly figure to her male friends. Her independence had hardened into solitariness, into 'this death I have sat so snugly in for so long, sheltering myself against joy, respectable in my mourning, harrowed and dulled and insincere to myself in a pretext of troth'.[141] Valentine was the first woman she had loved and, though for Valentine there would be others, Sylvia remained faithful. Years later, she would say that Valentine was 'the best lover I ever had'; she never needed another.[142] She had found fulfilment, and in her Valentine found safety. As it developed, their relationship became an exchange of wants and needs. It ran according to its own logic, finding success in inversion – in the differences between age, culture and temperament. 'They each had something to give the other, which they alone could give,' remembered Sylvia's friend, Bea Howe. '– and isn't this the base, the keystone, for all enduring human relationships?'[143] Identity, relationships, a marriage, history: 'all are works in progress,' writes Alison Light, 'always in the making, never made'.[144] Most of all, Sylvia wished to protect Valentine, and vowed never to change her. Walking alone up the Drove one evening, she wondered, 'How to house, and not to tame, this wild solitary heart, so fierce even in its diffidence. And I, lumbering, so I seem to myself after, clogged with all this cargo of years and tolerance and mind's dust.'[145]

On their first morning as lovers, as she looked at Valentine's body silhouetted against the first light and listened to the autumnal silence, Sylvia felt loosened from her past life. The cottage, and the freedoms of Chaldon, had given her Valentine, and a new sense of herself. It couldn't have happened in London, or anywhere else. In the wake of her gloomiest years, she felt relieved. Together with Valentine, she 'laughed as people do who have escaped, by a miracle, from some deadly peril and find themselves safe and secure'.[146] Not long afterwards, in the new year, the women committed themselves to each other fully. On 11 January 1931, while out driving, Sylvia told Valentine that she wanted nobody else, and that evening at the cottage they exchanged vows. The next day, Sylvia wrote: 'It was our most completed night, and after our love I slept unstirring in her arms, still covered with her love, till we woke and ate whatever meal it is lovers eat at five in the morning.'[147] Later, she recalled the seriousness of her oath: 'For my part, why not? I loved, I increasingly honoured, and if being bewitched into compliance is obedience, I obeyed.'[148] From that point on, they were rarely separated; it was as though, Valentine described later, their 'lives joined up, imperceptibly, all along their lengths'.[149]

~

From 1931 onwards, Sylvia would return to Inverness Terrace for only short visits and remained in Dorset with Valentine. Besides the pleasures of living together, country life was beginning to suit her increasingly left-wing ideals. After the events at the vicarage, she and Valentine came to recognize their shared views, which began to find expression in their everyday lives. The cottage became a place where love, work and politics entwined (perhaps best evidenced in the writing on cookery Sylvia would produce for left-wing magazines), and from which a radicalism emerged, shaped by the realities of rural life. By 1935, when they joined the Communist Party of Great Britain, they had, in fact, been practising living politically for years.

Sylvia had long been interested in rural ways. In her essay 'The Way By Which I Have Come', published in *The Countryman* in 1939, she described her political awakening by way of country life. As a child in Harrow (which in the early 1900s was still a landscape of clay fields and slouching farmhouses), she had watched the tramps coming in for hay harvest, and marvelled at the belongings they abandoned in the ditches. Holidays were spent with her grandmother on the Surrey–Sussex border. Flora Townsend Warner regaled her granddaughter with appalling tales of the village: of her neighbours' violence and hypocrisy; of incest; and the many other 'patiently-wrought vices that develop under thatch, the violent dramas that explode among green pastures'.[150] But, though she enjoyed these visits – rambling on her own and learning folk songs – Sylvia's brushes with the country were brief. Meadows 'meant buttercups and white violets' and fresh cow's milk made her sick.[151] Hers was, for thirty years, a town life.

It wasn't until 1922 that her observations of the country shifted into political awareness. Sylvia went to Essex, staying for a month in a farmer's cottage at Drinkwater St Lawrence near Southminster, occasionally sending to London for clothes and books. She spent her days alone, walking over the marsh in 'solemn rapture' and finding hollows in which to sit and read. It was there, sheltered in the tall grass behind banks of shingle, that her mind stilled and she found a new kind of clarity, the feeling of being 'passionately quiescent'.[152] The marsh would later inspire the landscapes of her 1929 novel, *The True Heart*, in which Sukey's delight at the strangeness of the place, and of its quietly transformative effects, mirrored her own.

In the evenings, Sylvia sat with the farmer and his wife in their cottage, pleased by its green walls and the 'deliciously cold smooth oil-cloth' floor.[153] For supper, they gave her bread and cheese, runner beans and herb beer. Mrs May, the farmer's wife, was 'an admirable talker, with the usual country-long memory for local stories and local characters', but she also impressed Sylvia with 'the less usual gift of being able to talk clearly and illuminatingly about agriculture and the problems of the small farmer'.[154] In 1922, Britain was in the midst of an agricultural depression. The repeal of the Agriculture Act the year before had ended all wartime price guarantees for cereal crops, while the abolition of the Wages Board saw labourers' wages fall by nearly half between 1921 and 1923. Many farming households were plunged into poverty. For the first time, Sylvia learned of the difficulties of agricultural work directly from the people whose lives depended upon it.

When she returned to London, she continued her education with books. She read the Hammonds' *Village Labourer*, *Piers Plowman*, and Cobbett's *Rural Rides*; and she wrote to Powys – whom she would soon meet in Dorset – for the manuscript of *Mr. Tasker's Gods*. 'I was much impressed by it, and, further, I believed in it,' she wrote of Powys's bleak tale, which joined 'Cobbett and the Hammonds and Mrs May and my grandmother' to form 'a cloud of witnesses towards the likelihood that the English Pastoral was a grim and melancholy thing'.[155]

She was also reading a series of articles in *The Nation* which condemned the decline of English villages and exposed the plight of rural labourers. Written by J. W. Robertson Scott, a liberal journalist turned social reformer, the articles observed the conditions of rural England 'from the life'.[156] Scott was calling for 'radical change' in the country, and was trying to reform his own village, Idbury in Oxfordshire, through practical, albeit paternalistic, philanthropy.[157] During the 1920s, he purchased the land for council houses and rehomed villagers – sometimes reluctantly – from their centuries-old, run-down cottages; and he campaigned for the telegraph, extolling the benefits of the radio as a source of cultural enrichment in rural areas. His ideas appealed to Sylvia. In 1924, when she saw an advert in *The Nation* for the tenancy of a half-cottage 'with privacy and electricity' at the bottom of his garden, she saw not only the chance to finish *Lolly Willowes* in relative quiet, but the chance to meet reformers after her own heart. She stayed in Idbury for a month, invigorated by Scott and Elspet, his wife: 'We met, so to speak, round the same cauldron.'[158]

The village's revival was in full swing. Sylvia was invited to lecture at the school house, where on Sunday afternoons a programme of events had been organized to entertain and educate the villagers. A recital of Socrates and a string quartet had been extremely popular, Elspet told her; an upholstery demonstration less so. During her stay, Sylvia saw the evidence of Idbury's transformation. What had once been 'a melancholy little hamlet, full of picturesque houses that had gone bad' was now a lively place, rich in fellow-feeling among its growing population. Other writers and artists came to observe such a fine example of English country life. In Scott's visitors' book, opposite a line of music in Sylvia's hand, E. M. Forster wrote his mantra 'Only connect', while later signatures included the novelist May Sinclair and the potter Bernard Leach. When Scott founded *The Countryman* in 1927 – the monthly magazine about rural affairs described by Sylvia as one that would 'treat of the country not only as a place to grow corn and rear cattle in, and hunt and shoot in, but as a place where people lived' – she was one of its earliest contributors.[159]

Her trips to Essex and Oxfordshire formed the early part of Sylvia's rural education. When she arrived to live in Dorset in 1930, she observed Chaldon as she had Idbury, finding it poor, lacking in community and dependent upon a decaying agricultural industry. Many of the farms had been turned over to cereals, their land put down to grass, and what labour was left included hedging, ditching, or working as a cowman or shepherd. In her essay 'Love Green', published in *The Countryman* in 1932, Sylvia described the cottages dominated by stone-built barns and the surrounding landscape gone to waste, the 'large squares and oblongs of arable [. . .] like carpets tightly stretched upon the contours of the downs', bristling with sorrel and flint. For the labourer, 'a-field for eight hours', the village is simply the place where he 'breakfasts, sups, keeps his wife and children, and visits the inn', returning home each evening to a 'small and inconvenient' cottage which is 'barely weatherproof, and infested with vermin'. Entertainment is sparse. At the pub, the labourer 'meets other such tired animals as himself, and treats them with [. . .] the comradeship of a team of cart-horses'. The women are excluded, driven to making their own wines – carrot, mangold, and elderberry – and to home-drinking, which only 'increases the suspicions and narrow-mindedness which are cankers of village life'. At the fortnightly whist drive, the players fight over cheap prizes from Woolworths – a set of tea knives, a biscuit barrel, a cigarette case – where in past years they preferred 'something solid' like 'a marble-topped washstand or a set of grand fire-irons'. Local characters are colourful but small-minded: Mrs Taddy, wife of the village communist, who competes with Mrs Trey in new clothes and household gear; and Will Francis, who will drink eleven pints at the pub if someone puts up the money for a dare. In short, Love Green is,

> so little a true community, so increasingly a fortuitous collection of dwelling-houses, that perhaps it is idle and epimythean to look for saving virtue in anything out of the past. With the decay of farming the labouring class is becoming migratory – people come to the village, stay for a year or two, and then move off in search of something better; motor transport brings town commodities and town novelties to the cottage door, education and the newspaper direct attention away from the village to the advantages of genteel professions or what is being worn on the Lido; and if any commendation of rusticity reaches Love Green it is of the folk-dancing, rustic pottery, sun-bonnet-rural kind – so many hand-made nails in the coffin of rural life.[160]

Like many of her contemporaries concerned with the state of English villages in the 1930s, Sylvia mourned the loss of rural culture. Community and craftsmanship – including West Country skills such as basket weaving, which she liked – were rapidly declining. But, unlike the conservative discourse that idealized the traditions of life on the land, she refrained from nostalgia. Rural communities were changing and it was useless to try to return to the past. Instead, Sylvia voiced a practical concern for living standards, equality and welfare, and often returned to the issue of rural housing. The cottages in Chaldon appalled her. '[H]ouses that have gone bad weigh heavily on those who live in them,' she wrote.[161] With Valentine, who was collecting evidence for her 'Country Dealings' column for *Left Review*, she visited the homes of working men and their families, taking note of the numbers of sleepers per bedroom, the unsanitary privies, the walls streaming with damp. The system of tithed cottages, which yoked labourers to their jobs because their homes depended upon it, was a broken one. Farmers didn't make good landlords. Like Scott, Sylvia had little time for sentimental attitudes towards cottages. There could be no opposition, she argued, to proposals to 'pull down a vermin-ridden, sixteenth century nuisance and build a sound dwelling in its place'.[162]

Buying a cottage in the village, Sylvia would have been aware, as her thinking developed, that she had become complicit in the structures of ownership she meant to critique. Yet her own 'little stocky grey house' was justifiably ugly.[163] Visiting Chaldon, her friend Jean Starr Untermeyer was dismayed to find that Miss Green had 'no thatch, [. . .] no climbing roses, no leaded casements, none of the country endearments associated in the literary mind with rural England'.[164] But its plainness quieted Sylvia's conscience. Unlike other urban intellectuals in search of the good life – those who, as Valentine wrote in 'Country Dealings', took the best houses, and did them up – Sylvia had chosen the worst. In dedicating herself to its upkeep, she hoped it might become an example of an efficient village dwelling. In her essays, she described the challenges of daily life at Miss Green, offering advice on collecting water, disposing of rubbish or growing food, as if to demonstrate the sincerity of her attempt at rural living. In time, she became proud of her cottage, with its rudimentary plumbing and unattractive front. Inviting friends to stay at 'my little workman's cottage', she approved its humble heritage which chimed with the political one of her own.[165]

By 1933, both she and Valentine were contributing regularly to the left-wing press on rural matters. They were positioning themselves as local historians of a kind, recording their observations of Chaldon with journalistic realism, and sharpening their essays with anecdotes gathered from their neighbours. It was a style – factual, with an eye on the historical – Sylvia would absorb into her fiction, in her politicized books of the 1930s, eventually leading to one of her finest wartime novels. Enabled by their class, both women moved easily in the village; they were brisk and always extremely polite.* Valentine, in particular, earned her neighbours' trust, and was welcomed into the cottages in order to write about the

---

* Sylvia's friend Susannah Pinney remembers how polite Sylvia was. Courteousness, both in herself and others, was extremely important to her; and in

conditions in which they lived. In her 'Country Dealings' series for *Left Review* – published in 1936 as *Country Conditions* – she set out the disadvantages of the agricultural worker, quoting the evidence she had collected on wages, landlord–tenant relationships, and the role of women in rural domestic life. And yet where Valentine could be earnest and hectoring in her appeals to good sense and social justice, Sylvia tended toward lightness and sardonicism. Her own essays, though serious in subject matter, were witty, and she was as ready to satirize the villagers for triviality and pretension as to uphold their dignity in the face of poverty. Of all her neighbours, the women interested her the most. She admired their wisdom and their racy speech, their friendships, and the quiet unfolding of their daily lives. A few elderly villagers, like Annie Moxon (believed by local children to be a witch), lived alone. Leaning over their gates, Sylvia listened for the quality of incantation in their speech and watched their gardens for the flowers which seemed to grow as if by magic from their rough fingers.

But rural life wasn't only to be observed, appreciated from a distance. As 1931 drew on, Sylvia and Valentine threw themselves into the daily routines and physical demands of country living. Spring was showing itself in the garden. 'We woke very early, just after dawn, and heard all the birds singing,' Sylvia wrote in her diary on 4 April. 'That day everything came out: the Winterton wallflowers and rosemary, the yellow jasmine, and the new ribes.'[166] She and Valentine worked in the garden almost daily, taking breaks from writing to weed beds and prune fruit bushes, pausing to sit in the sun and listen to the birds, coffee cups dangling from their fingers. 'A day of great gardenings,' begins a typical day in Sylvia's diary. 'We weeded all the

Chaldon, enabled her to move freely among her neighbours, while living openly with another woman. In conversation, 26 November 2018.

front bed, and took out bulbs to dry off; and the currant border, and killed four centipedes; they curl round their tails like scorpions; and did more bottle-edging; and re-arranged the herb-bed.'[167] Like Rebecca's flower patch in *Opus 7*, Sylvia's new garden at Miss Green was becoming an outlet for and a representation of her creativity, an activity as absorbing and inventive as writing poetry.

Gardening agreed with her. She liked the physical exertion and the time spent out of doors, but it also suited her ideal of industriousness. Having a garden (like having a country kitchen) wasn't simply for pleasure, but entailed necessary and hard work. Living in the country, she felt a sense of duty – what she described as her 'responsibility towards [my] half-acre or whatever it may be of tillable ground' – to cultivate and to grow, and to live as self-sufficiently as possible. 'When I began my warfare with weeds I wanted to grow herbs and flowers,' she wrote in 'The Way By Which I Have Come'. 'After a year or so I discovered that it was harder, and more interesting, to grow vegetables. Latterly I have realised that what I most deeply care for is the ground itself, and that a plot of earth, clean, and well dug, and raked fine, and in good heart, is the deepest gratification that gardening affords me.'[168]

It was companionable work, Valentine wearing her broadbrimmed panama and Sylvia her straw hat, both admiring their surroundings and each other as they laboured on. Sylvia recorded the flowers as they came into bloom, the roses – Maiden's Blush, Oeillet Parfait, Coupe d'Hébé, Gloire de Dijon, and Juliet – as well as poppies, cornflowers, sweet williams, Canterbury bells, pinks, lilac, meadowsweet, and Austrian briar. The garden's plenitude, like the crescendo of her private happiness, overwhelmed her. Picking cowslips in the field one afternoon, she thought 'how a year ago I should have been almost embarrassed to be so strewn with pleasures, but now I take them as my right, as a king's daughter would take her needlework, being all glorious within'.[169] She was not ungrateful, but counting her joys, as if to shore up her happiness against the future. In her notebooks, the wavering tables she had drawn to monitor the progress of rose bushes and shrubs from one year to the next – with verdicts such as 'doing well', 'doing fairly' and 'holding on' – showed her attuning to life at Miss Green, for she was also recording her own progress.[170] In London, her gardens had been temporary, and she had sworn not to become 'fast-rooted', saying, 'I am ready, I hope I am able, to move anywhere and remain myself.'[171] Now, as her country garden grew curling around her, she was putting down roots, digging herself in.

During the day, the women worked separately, taking turns to sit in The Sailor's Return, where Florrie Legg's high-spirited interruptions were compensated for by fireside warmth and tankards of ale. Whoever remained at home was liable to visitors: Theo and Violet from Beth Car; Katie or Alyse from Chydyok; or Granny Moxon from the cottage opposite. Sylvia, once so distracted by her neighbour's charming and rustic talk, forgot to cook and light the fire, and so joined Valentine at the pub for a supper of claret and scrambled eggs.

The days at Miss Green were uneventful, a litany of small happenings: work commencing on the woodshed, the water tank empty, a gale, a picnic, William catching a hedgehog, chess after supper. As they worked, the lovers watched one another. 'Sylvia is writing a poem, I think – judging by the sharply-indrawn breath, and her endless cigarettes,' Valentine wrote in her diary. 'She is curled up on the chair by her writing table, elbows on the table and one leg curled under her small buttocks. [. . .] How narrow her hands are – How deeply I love her.'[172] For Sylvia, Valentine's presence was endlessly invigorating: 'So dinner was late, and I rather sadly writing this, when she came down in the new corduroy trousers made in Dorchester; so handsome, so slenderly swaggering, that my life flared up again in admiration.'[173]

~

In *A Radical Romance*, a memoir of her marriage, Alison Light describes her husband – the Marxist historian, Raphael Samuel – subscribing to 'the idea of a political culture which infused every aspect of one's life, including one's pleasures'. Visiting their house at 19 Elder Street in Spitalfields during the 1990s, one would have found an example of 'the good Communist home', a place in which – through its very fabric, its internal processes, and the people and objects gathered there – 'work and love [were] indivisible'.[174] In the writing of Sylvia's life, little attention has been paid to the years she spent at Miss Green, when homemaking with Valentine was her priority. She produced a few articles for left-wing magazines, but was between novels; she didn't publish much. But, to my eyes, this period was one of her most creative and experimental; and, looking to her domestic life, her politics were visible. It was a politics that seemed, domestically at least, to move against the times – in the spurning of bourgeois luxuries like bathtubs in favour of ascetic discomforts, in her preference for old things. In fact, Sylvia was looking to evoke past histories, and align them with her own – of the labourers and rural folk who once lived in her cottage, of the men working the land, while the women washed and cooked and cared. It was a working-class history, specifically a rural one; a 'history from below'.

Sylvia's housewifery was a means of showing devotion, a way of caring for both Valentine and the cottage. But it was also a way for her to set out her thinking. At a moment when many women of her generation were moving away from domesticity and into the world of formalized work, Sylvia appeared to be reclaiming drudge work as a facet of her political life – and one which would liberate her writing, too. In her journalism, including a venture into cookery writing, her domestic life began to represent her broadening ideology, in which everyday tasks were becoming increasingly political gestures. Cooking, gardening, collecting water, washing, disposing of household waste: all became subjects for essays and articles, edging her towards the wider issues of education, labour and community, and towards Party politics as the decade progressed. But, in 1930, Sylvia's emerging ideology was carried out behind closed doors; it was small-scale, private, granular, and lived. Together with Valentine, she was beginning to inhabit a world in which her ideas could be written into everything she did, in which even the smallest daily experiments and interventions seemed worthwhile.

Not unlike the Woolfs' household at Asheham, Miss Green began to resemble a carefully managed economic unit. Routines were followed, and expenditures documented meticulously. The oil stove was supplied by a twelve-gallon drum which was replenished monthly, the grocer's van called once a week, and lettuces were bought from the garden behind the pub.[175] The difference between Sylvia and Virginia – and, perhaps, the majority of her middle-class, intellectual peers – was that Sylvia did the cooking herself. She rose to the challenges of economizing, was canny and contriving; resourcefulness brought out her creativity in the kitchen. Jotted neatly on the verso of her diary, she devised weekly menu plans, demonstrating both inventive and thrifty thinking. There were lean days – toast, tea and marmalade, omelette, milk soup; not-so lean days – toast and honey, ham and green peas, sole, potatoes, braised onions – and the occasional simple but lavish supper: 'Broad beans, unjacketed. The sauce of thick cream, the yolk of an egg, two dashes of champagne, salt and pepper.'[176]

'I love anything to do with cooking,' Sylvia told the journalist Louise Morgan in 1930 during an interview for *Everyman* magazine. 'I'm considered to be quite a successful cook!'[177] In her flat on Inverness Terrace, where she had first learned the habit of living trimly off a small salary, she had recorded recipes in a large cream-coloured canvas notebook; now, in Chaldon, it flourished with country ingredients and additions from new friends. She contrived salads – seakale with tomato, apple and watercress with vinegar cream – and, when Valentine had been handy with her rifle, casseroles – hare with prunes, pickled walnuts and marmite, or pigeon with bacon dripping. She made sandwiches with hard-boiled eggs and combinations of garden herbs, leek and onion pie, vinegar loaf, sweet and sour apples, and Boodle cake. She cooked in rhythm with the seasons, taking pride in her calendar of jams and pickles: marmalade on steaming midwinter mornings; jams from the glut of summer fruits; and, in the autumn, her mother's marrow chutney, gooseberry vinegar and chestnut sauce for the store cupboard. Occasionally, she appended a recipe with a note on what to drink, and in her notebook listed the wines stored at the cottage, which included eighteen half-bottles of Harvey's Margaux, two bottles of Pichon Longueville, six bottles of shooting sherry, and a bottle of sparkling burgundy which she opened to celebrate the publication of *Opus 7*, in March 1931. Even the simplest meals deserved a good drink.

In the kitchen, Sylvia's inclination towards frugality infuriated Valentine, who was prone to treats and over-spending. 'I suppose in time I shall learn not to make this housewifely fuss over small crusts of differences,' Sylvia wrote in her diary after an argument. 'It is just like "my God, I *must* not waste that half tomato—" which is so maddening to her.'[178] Her compulsion to use and reuse was both an effort to save money (a habit learned from living alone in London), but it was also a facet of her increasingly anti-waste ethic. She was an excellent cook, too, and could find a purpose for everything. A Sunday chicken saw its way through the week – boiled with rice on Wednesday, made into a mousse on Friday – and vegetable scraps were thrown into a stout aluminium pot. Wooden spoon in one hand, pen in the other, she was warming to her theme. Soon, she began to write up her domestic experiments in a series of brisk, authoritative articles for *The Countryman*, offering advice on cooking and housekeeping as if she were a country Mrs Beeton. 'With a stockpot I can snap my fingers at tinned soups and meat extracts,' she wrote in one such dispatch. 'At its richest, it gives me a consommé; at its most exhausted, the basis of a mulligatawny.'[179] She advised her reader to be wary of the pot turning sour from steam dripping back into it from the lid, and to flavour the contents using a bouquet of garden herbs. These were essential for the cottage cook. In a bed visible from her own kitchen door, Sylvia had planted sage, mint, marjoram, tansy, chives, parsley, thyme, tarragon, hyssop, basil, savoury, southernwood, rosemary and balm, and now she studied their flavours, recommending the more subtle and unusual. 'Such combinations as chives and nasturtiums, tansy and balm, thyme and southernwood, are as exquisite as the usual mess of dried herbs is dreary,' she counselled.[180]

In 1933, while she was living at Miss Green, Sylvia outlined an idea for a book on cooking. She was writing an article called 'The Kitchen Year' for *Everyman*, in which she playfully compared the art of plain cooking to religion – 'It is not for nothing, surely, that the

Sylvia in the kitchen at 113 Inverness Terrace

chef's cap rises as high as the mitre, that an apron (and we may treat the difference between white linen and black grosgrain as immaterial) girds alike the loins of the cook and the bishop' – and was corresponding once more with Louise Morgan, now the magazine's editor.[181] 'What would please me most would be for you to [. . .] carry on your crusade for cookery as an intellectual thing,' she wrote to Morgan, 'and commission me to do a series of superior Counsels from the Kitchen: say, six, one a month.'[182] Suddenly 'enamoured of this idea', she drew up a list of chapters for the book, which was to be called 'The Devil Sent the Cook':

1. Fish ransomed from the frying-pan.
2. Salads.
3. Unusual Breakfasts.
4. Other herbs than parsley.
5. Sauces and flavours.
6. Traditional and country-side recipes.[183]

Her motivation was partly educational. She had already condemned tinned foods in 'The Kitchen Year' and now took aim at idle and unimaginative modern cooking. 'Think what it would be,' she wrote to Morgan, 'to teach only one per thousand of our population how to make a salad that is a not a green porridge soaked with vinegar and invariably trimmed with tomato and hard-boiled egg.'[184] But, though the book was to be instructive, it would also offer a vision of rural cooking. It would be a celebration of food's pleasures and possibilities, and of the home cook – in starched white linens, a bishop in her own kitchen – as creator and artist. In a handwritten note, Sylvia assured Morgan that 'Each article [would] begin with general principles, essential Don'ts (usually done), and [. . .] go on to original recipes; except the last,' she added ironically, 'and they, I promise, shall be authentic and unheard-of.'[185] The 'authentic' here is knowing: she was wary of rural caricatures. In 'Folk Cookery', a short story published in the *New Yorker* in 1936, Sylvia satirised a village Ladies' Committee dispatched into the community to gather recipes for a book on Old English cookery. Returning from the cottages with handed-down recipes for partridge and port-wine stew, buttery turnips, and quinces baked with Double Gloucester and nutmeg, the Committee is ruffled by the villagers' culinary sophistication, and rules in favour of the humbler bramble-tip cordial, cowslip pie and candied hemlock.[186] But, though the story reveals Sylvia's contempt for the sentimentalizing of rural domestic life, she wasn't immune to the charms of folksy wisdom. Her own cookery book included what she would later describe as 'homely truths', such concoctions as stewed turnip for a tickly cough, or bergamot oil to prevent mildew from ruining books.*

The book on cooking was never written; within months,

---

* So-called in the unfinished sequel to her 1948 novel *The Corner That Held Them*, in which one pilgrim remarks to another that 'a leaf of the traveller's [*sic*] tree, fastened round the heel, cuts every mile to half a mile' and thinks it 'a pity that some clever folks did not learn such homely truths as these'. 'The Unfinished Sequel to *The Corner That Held Them* (Part 1 of 2)', *The Journal of the Sylvia Townsend Warner Society*, Volume 20, Issue 1 (2020), 8–39 (21).

Everyman had closed, and Sylvia was writing to Morgan to express sympathy for its demise. Yet she continued to formulate her ideas about domestic work, steadfast in her belief in the dignity of the kind of housework spurned by her peers on account of its association with women and the working class. In her writing, domesticity as a subject was becoming grounds for both playfulness – as in her essays on cookery – as well as more serious political or educational intent. And whatever principles Sylvia espoused in her journalism, she made sure to integrate into her own life accordingly. At the cottage, she was disdainful of middle-class luxuries which might soften the realities of rural living. When Llewelyn Powys had a bathroom put in at Chydyok at the behest of his wife Alyse, Sylvia raged upstairs to her bedroom and 'spurned the bath-tub' before returning to the sitting room in her French coat and hat, which was 'more culture and civilisation than he cared for'.[187] Once a week, on Saturday evenings, she and Valentine bathed in a copper in the back-kitchen, which they filled with buckets of rainwater and heated by lighting a fire underneath. Sylvia had been taught how to use the copper by Mrs Keates, her London charwoman, who had come to Dorset to visit. The process required patience and slow, graceful movements in order to prevent water from sloshing onto the floor. In 'Bathrooms Remembered', a reminiscence written many years later, Sylvia described the gush of steam on lifting the lid, testing the water's temperature with an elbow, and throwing in the soap. 'Then,' she wrote, 'moving discreetly, you sit down, your toes drawn in, your knees drawn up, your arms embracing your shins, in the posture of ancient British pit burials. And if you have estimated your displacement rightly,' she concluded, 'the suds and the steam will do the rest.'[188] Despite the arduousness of getting the copper ready, and the scruffiness of its kitchen setting, it was no less a treat than her London tub beneath the swaying sycamores.

Sylvia's attitude to domestic labour was not, as it might seem, anti-modern. She was enthusiastic about housework, preferring labour-intensive tasks which demanded carefulness over time. Like Virginia at Asheham, she was teaching herself to pay a different kind of attention to her domestic life. On any given afternoon at Miss Green, the copper bubbled away 'most homelike', but, as well as providing hot water, it also solved that other 'great problem of village living': 'how to dispose of rubbish'.[189] 'To work well, it must be kindled by fire; with sticks, cinders, and enough coal to raise the water almost to boiling point,' she wrote for *The Countryman*. 'After this [. . .] it can be fed with the surprising quantity of papery rubbish which accumulated in any present-day household; [. . .] it will even calcine tins; but it is a waste to feed it with vegetable rubbish, which can be rendered into garden manure.'[190] She liked the copper's ingenuity, its multiplicity of use, but also its connection to the past. Traditionally used for boiling clothes on laundry day or for steaming plum puddings, it suggested a vanishing world of working-class domesticity, calling to mind Dickensian kitchens below-stairs, overseen by women like Mrs Keates. Like the other things in Sylvia's kitchen – the enamel jugs, the tin milk pail, the earthenware dishes, the aluminium stock pot – the copper was made of unpretentious materials and built to last. It accrued meaning through usefulness, and bore the marks of age, a patina of human handling. Sylvia treasured the objects she used every day; over time, they grew in associations, their histories merging with her own. 'An old teapot, used daily, can tell me more of my past than anything I recorded of it,' she wrote.[191]

~

In March 1931, as part of her developing project of documenting every aspect of her new life at Miss Green, Sylvia inventoried all her possessions in the cottage. Taking a notebook (which had begun life as a visitors' book, recording the first visits of Charles Prentice and Mrs Keates to the cottage), she moved slowly from room to room, listing their contents. Starting in the sitting room, she catalogued the papier-mâché chairs and the gilt wall mirror, the silver candlesticks and coal scuttle, and the smaller objects on display: the three lustre jugs on the mantlepiece, one pink and white, one silver, and one gold; the blotter, inkpot and inkstand on the writing table; and the Bible and prayer book on the chest of drawers. Next, she opened the china cupboard, and recorded the numbers of cream-ware fruit and cheese plates, the egg-cups, the liqueur and sherry glasses, and the coloured glass decanter with its stopper. From the wooden chest, she wrote down all the household linen: the blue tablecloth and matching napkins; the pairs of bath towels and the patchwork cushion cover; and her precious linen sheets. Finally, in the kitchen, she listed the soap-tidy and the kitchen pails, her aluminium saucepans, the egg-timer, a Thermos flask, and all her utensils, crockery and cutlery. It was a deliberate process, and would become a habitual one: in the years to come, Sylvia would write packing lists for house moves, lists of Christmas presents, plants for the garden and household repairs. Yet in the first months of 1931, her list-making had a deeper meaning. Walking between the rooms of the cottage, methodically recording their contents, she was stock-taking the life she had built with Valentine. Her list of household objects – from the pudding plates to the fish-kettle – reads like any wedding list of a newly married, middle-class couple in the mid-twentieth century, a collection of acquired belongings which, with additions and subtractions, broadly follows the course of conjugal life. Sylvia was like any young wife, imbuing material things with expectation and hope. In each lengthening list, she was laying out her vision for the future, of the rooms she would inhabit with Valentine, of the bedlinen they would lie in, the meals they would eat off the plates. Her lists were letters to herself, reassurances that her life in 1931 – and so beyond – was happy, and she was well, and living in a household that was efficient, creative, and loving. The tablecloths and lustre jugs, the decanters, dishes and spoons were what gave her faith in the future, and a sense of home. Accounting for her life, object by object, she was taking the measure of her gold, as if to secure her happiness in things.

But a list can also be a brittle thing, an illusion of maintaining order. When Alyse visited from Chydyok, she noticed the way in which Sylvia and Valentine arranged their possessions with care. They have 'built their life much as married people build theirs', she wrote in her diary, 'only it is more sensitively poised – their little love birds, their canary, their vases of spring flowers, V's daggers

Sylvia's inventory

and pistols, the sentiment they attach to the objects about them'.[192] The women's gifts to each other were lovers' tokens, and also ways of communicating their insecurities and fears. In April 1931, when Sylvia returned home from visiting her mother in Devon, she found the cottage filled with flowers – 'lilac and freesias, and flounced pink azalea, and roses and white irises in my bedroom, and the little gallipot of violets and puss willow by my bed' – which spoke to her of Valentine's desolation in her absence: '[I]t almost broke my heart to think how lonely she had been.'[193] In July, she was gone again, and Valentine shopped despondently in Weymouth for gifts for her return. Though she always spent beyond her budget, Valentine had an ability to look out for small, exquisite objects. She listed the gifts for Sylvia in her diary:

a. a very lovely mourning clasp, to wear as a bracelet – sewn on wide black velvet. Date: George II (£6.16.6 & cheap)
b. a picture of Queen Vicky's wedding [sic] (2s)

c. a picture of St Matthew, looking very evil (7.6*d*)
d. a little French contraption, for cutting flowers and such-like – rough, but quite pleasing (9*d*)
e. a bead purse – to be put away, for when she needs a present! (£1.10.0)[194]

There is something fragile and dispiriting about this list; like all lists, it contains omissions. What eventuality, anticipated here, would mean Sylvia needed a cheering present? And who keeps gifts for their lover in reserve, in anticipation not of joy, but need? An unsettled person. Both Sylvia and Valentine wrote lists as ways of defending themselves against unhappiness, and to ward off dangers. During the course of their long relationship, there would be periods of chaos and grief, of household disruption, which would make a mockery of their domestic life. But, in 1931, all future trouble was contained within neat lines. For what lovers embarking on a life together don't feel uncertainty? To make lists, to write things down, is to contain uncertainty, to tether the self to the present, to what is known and good.

In return for the things Valentine bought her, Sylvia made her gifts. She hand-stitched booklets of love poems out of white paper, looping the spines with twine and writing the contents in blue biro; she made cards for Valentine's Day, on which she drew pictures of their cats; and she hid messages in Valentine's typewriter, ready for when she sat down to work. Between them, they exchanged an endless supply of letters. They kept everything: diaries, letters, lists, cookery and gardening notebooks, household memorandum books, visitors' books, scrapbooks, keepsakes, and gifts. The accumulation of these materials was a form of hoarding, but it was also an attempt to keep a written record of their daily lives, which could be glimpsed through a shopping list just as well as a diary or a letter. Every scrap was important, a piece of their private history. And, as with cooking and bathing, there was a political element to this private habit, too. At Miss Green, they were practising forms of record-keeping like the good communists they wished to be, taking up their roles as documentarians of the domestic, archivists of their own experiment in rural living.

~

During their first years living together, as their shared political beliefs began to take a firmer hold, Sylvia and Valentine knew there was one lesson they must continue to teach each other. There must always be room for the flouting of frugality, for frivolity, and sensuality. Where Sylvia could be sulky about bourgeois treats, Valentine taught her occasional extravagance. Once in a while, they drove to Osmington for lobsters, or prepared ceremonial suppers ('Oysters, champagne, truffles cooked gently in cream, and coffee') to be eaten at home.[195] The women celebrated the anniversary of moving into Miss Green, their first night as lovers, and the night of their marriage; all events which made up their private year. For Sylvia, gift-giving and luxury were learned habits, and yet they came to symbolize – like the shrubs and roses she planted in her garden, a practice which came more naturally – a feeling of steadfastness, and her belief in building something for the future, something that would spring up year after year. At Miss Green, she was living out both her political vision, rooting herself in a left-wing, utopian tradition of which she would increasingly become a part; but also a private one. Her domestic life, buttressed by process and principles and lists, was necessarily punctuated with pleasure. Truffles cooked in cream, a lobster cracked open: small eruptions of joy.

In the country with Valentine, Sylvia had chosen a settled life. Like Virginia at Asheham, she treasured the ordinary days, the days on which little happened, but which quietly sang. A Friday, in mid-June:

> Finished and packed The Salutation, my eighth book. Valentine typed some for me, pestered by Mrs Way. Then we soaped the roses, and William. After dinner I walked alone up the Drove, admiring the

sunset, and the smell of the fields, exactly like the smell of cows. Then V. read aloud, The Island of the Pines and some Ford, and I patched. A full happy day.[196]

But the lovers didn't settle for long. The cottage was a place of beginnings. By the spring of 1933, their ideas for writing and living were expanding, and they struggled to contain them within the walls of the small house. What had begun at Miss Green as a series of modest projects – domestic notebooks, essays, articles and poems – now reached beyond itself. Sylvia was hungry for literary experiments on a larger scale. In July, she and Valentine left Chaldon for Norfolk, where they lived for a year in a sixteenth-century manor house. It was here Sylvia began to conceive of her ambitious 1936 novel, a queer love story set in Paris in 1848, called *Summer Will Show*.

Frankfort Manor, near the village of Sloley, was stately, with a Dutch gable and a reed-thatch roof, and pinkish brickwork that glowed through the limewash like 'a ripened pear in the sun'.[197] At £50 a year, its rent was manageable, though Sylvia had to sell her flat on Inverness Terrace and let Miss Green. 'God knows how I am going to support it,' she wrote to Louise Morgan, 'for like other beauties it will need feeding, and its only dower is its apricots, its vine, its orchard, and a ten foot high currant bush trained on a wall. I shall dig with a pen behind either ear, so remember me if there are any jobs going.'[198] Despite its contrast with Miss Green, Frankfort was equally comfortless, and the women worked hard in house and garden. When money was short, they sold potatoes to the local fish-and-chip shop, and at Christmas-time Sylvia advertised her chutneys and jams. But they were still outsiders:

If you arrive to a large house, and have a servant, though you live hard and poor [. . .] you become gentry, and are mistrusted. Equally, if you [. . .] live hard and poor, though you live in a large house and have a servant, you are eccentric, and disliked by people with visiting cards. So we lived in a sort of Mahomet's coffin, mistrusted by the earthy and scorned by the heavenly.[199]

In 1934, they were called back to Dorset by a letter from Llewelyn Powys, with the news that another young woman had run away from the vicarage. Without hesitation, Sylvia and Valentine endorsed a petition – signed by almost forty Chaldon residents – that Miss Stevenson should be investigated by the local council. A financially catastrophic libel claim followed.* With the lease of Frankfort Manor soon up and the prospect of their savings destroyed, they decided to leave Norfolk. They returned to Dorset in August, and, as Miss Green had been let to a labourer and his family, took up residence in a bare, stone-built cottage standing in a field on the road to West Chaldon.

Sylvia and Valentine at Frankfort Manor

* In 1935, Sylvia and Valentine were summoned to appear at the Dorchester Assizes, having been sued for libel by Miss Stevenson. They were two of thirty-six Chaldon residents who had signed a petition naming the tenant of the vicarage. They were fined £50 each in damages and their legal costs surmounted £700, a small financial catastrophe which forced them to leave Frankfort Manor. Harman, *Sylvia Townsend Warner*, 139; Warner, Narrative 5, *I'll Stand by You*, 115.

For the next two years, 24 West Chaldon became the site of fervour and activity. Here, Sylvia and Valentine's record-keeping took on an explicitly political dimension, as they turned their attention from their domestic lives to international politics. At Miss Green, they had been journalists and local historians, documenting their community through fact-gathering and writing about local history, customs, folklore, their own domestic lives and the lives of their neighbours. Now, they began to look beyond Chaldon. In a new scrapbook, they pasted newspaper clippings of events both at home and abroad, building an almost daily record of issues including unemployment, agriculture, children's welfare, armaments, Spain, wages, women and war. Its contents read like a list Sylvia would later give of her long-held aversions – 'Priests in their gowns, anti-Semitism, the white man who is the black man's burden, warmongers' – which, joined with Valentine's increasingly left-wing views, cemented her own. 'I had long been sure of them but, beyond a refusal to give money to people who came collecting for missionary societies, my convictions remained unacted desires. Perhaps this was not enough.'[200] In her scrapbook, Sylvia was gathering material for her novels of the 1930s – two, both of which are explicitly political, and take place in Europe – while establishing a practice of record-keeping which would evolve into one of her finest books, written a decade later in the midst of war, about an enclosed community of women living on English soil.

The scrapbook was a marker of their increasing political awareness. In 1935, both women became members of the Communist Party of Great Britain, taking them to Spain as volunteer medical aides for the Republican forces fighting in Barcelona. But, though their political affiliations would reach an international scale, the roots of their activism were rural and remote. At home in Dorset, Sylvia was invited to become secretary to the Dorset Peace Council and, in Chaldon, she launched a series of campaigns with Valentine. Their schemes included a Women's March, and a Readers and Writers Group, which loaned left-wing books to villagers and later became affiliated with the Left Book Club. At election time, they gallantly drove villagers to and from the local polling station – in Valentine's two-seater MG.

As they settled back into life in Chaldon, they no longer counted themselves among the village intellectuals, who enjoyed the fruits of rural life without engaging with the community. They belonged to 'the more devout', as Valentine had written in 'Country Dealings', 'who do their own housework and cooking', and from their station take up the injustices of the oppressed.[201] For Sylvia, belonging to the Party satisfied a deeply anti-authoritarian streak in her character, a streak which had previously only found expression in her books. 'I became a Communist because I was [against] the Government,' she said in an interview forty years later, when she was eighty-eight. '[B]ut that of course is not a suitable frame of mind for a Communist for very long.' She identified, more seriously, as an anarchist, a state of being that suited her: 'You can go on being an anarchist for the rest of your life.'[202]

The path to Sylvia's freedom went all the way back to Miss Green. She would always think tenderly of the woman who arrived in the village, weary with her own solitude, not yet knowing she was looking for love. But then, a revolution took place in her private life, and in her imaginative life; a romance with a cottage, a woman, politics, place. There were sounds to satisfy her musical ear, and a community of the kind she might have written into one of her books. The country answered her need for lightness and acceptance, small freedoms which found their way into her work, into recipes, inventories, essays and poems. But it was in Valentine that Sylvia found her home. The village of Chaldon, sheltered in the Dorset landscape, had been a place of transformation for them both. There, they established a life on the periphery, and, in doing so, could finally be themselves. 'It is so natural to be hunted, and intuitive,' Sylvia had written on her first day as Valentine's lover as they had lain in the hollow beneath the Marys, listening to the wind. 'Feeling safe and respectable is much more of a strain.'[203]

Sylvia in bed, with Thomas the cat

A dream of winter

'I'm in my cottage at last,' Rosamond Lehmann wrote to Dadie Rylands in early 1942. It was February, an inhospitable time of year to be making a new home in the country. Rosamond didn't yet know her village neighbours; for the first time in her life, she was living alone. Each afternoon, she watched as the garden behind the cottage, and the winter fields beyond, glimmered with the last pale wisps of colour, and were enveloped in darkness. And yet, she wrote, 'I love it, & long to see you here!'[1]

If the letter contained a note of false cheer, it was because Rosamond felt relieved. A year before, her marriage had collapsed, and she had been 'the unhappiest of women', fearing she was 'done for'.[2] 'I thought it had been proved that love was no use, & everything I lived by, and for, a blind alley, a waste and a hideous joke,' she had written. But now, 'it isn't so'. Her new lover, the poet Cecil Day Lewis, had appeared 'like a miracle' and, in loving her, had 'given back my life'. 'I do appreciate it & savour every moment of it,' she told Dadie, '& shall never never get used to it or take it for granted.'[3]

Diamond Cottage, in the Berkshire village of Aldworth, was to be a retreat for lovers, and a refuge from war. It was a simple house, plain and pink-washed, perched on a bend in the road. Along one side, beneath a clipped gable roof, a row of windows looked onto the road; on the other, the view stretched over fields. It had once been inhabited by a blacksmith, and still wore its wrought-iron gate. Inside, there was a sitting room with a brick fireplace, a kitchen with an inglenook and a bread oven, and a study; upstairs, there were four bedrooms. It was spacious enough but without remarkable features: a new kind of living for Rosamond. Would she, in the depths of winter, with her children away at school and a lover in London, trying to write – despite the arduous daily challenges of wartime –, be happy?

Arriving in the village in late 1941, Rosamond was entering a phase of solitude. War had closed over the 1930s, muffling its sounds and shutting the decade with a snap. Her life had contracted, many of her old pleasures taken away. The stability of marriage and the easy gatherings of friends in her large house seemed to belong to another era. She knew she must live differently, and manage by herself. She was an unlikely countrywoman, much used to London; a mother of two, on the cusp of middle age; a willing if inexperienced participant in village life. Yet, as the winter drew on, she took stock of her new surroundings. She had broken with her previous life, and sensed an opportunity to get back to herself, to start again. Summoning her courage, she steeled herself for the months ahead. She could be, she told Dadie, 'perhaps even a better person, and a writer again'.[4]

~

Six years had passed since Rosamond's last novel. During that time, her personal life had fractured, and her inconsistencies – in her working methods, and her character – had bubbled and risen to the surface. She had stopped writing and, after the clamorous political activity of the 1930s, shifted into a new kind of passivity, and a more conservative outlook. Unlike Virginia or Sylvia, whose lives and writing became rooted in the rural world, Rosamond was always caught between places, flitting between London and the country, always deeply preoccupied with a series of relationships that, in the end, wouldn't work. Until 1942, that is. Then, out of the formlessness, new shapes began to emerge. Snatches of time, temporary homes, and personal crises: these, it turned out, were the best conditions for work. Abandoning her usual form, Rosamond produced three introspective, wintry short stories, deeply rooted in her experience of wartime in the country, which would come to be recognized as some of her finest work.

Soon, she was inviting friends to Aldworth to visit. 'I long to shew you the little house,' she wrote to the writer William Plomer, 'which I love dearly now, & in which I hope to spend an old age serene &

bright.'⁵ To Rayner Heppenstall, she gave directions from Reading, where a green Newbury and District bus left three times daily. 'It is a 40 minutes' ride, & a very pretty one,' she told him. 'Take a return ticket to Aldworth, & ask to be put off at Parsonage Green. You will see my house, 1 minute's walk away, just the other side of a smart thatched Golfer's Retreat, when you get off.'⁶

On the bus from Reading, Heppenstall would have followed the path of the Thames as it snaked its way through the Berkshire Downs. The landscape was agricultural and sparsely populated, giving wide views of the surrounding country; then, it seemed as if the bus dipped into narrow lanes, close with foliage, and studded with red-brick cottages and manor houses with white-painted bow windows. The river's presence was palpable, thick and silent behind its screen of trees; at intervals, it lurched into view, a watery snapshot, olive-green and somnolent. Driving through the same country a decade earlier, Virginia Woolf had described it as 'sealed up, silent, remote', scattered with 'little villages' and 'muddy roads'. To her, it was provincial, local: 'solid England'.⁷ Aldworth was surrounded by downland. Nearby, the Ridgeway nudged its way along a line of chalk hills towards Ivinghoe Beacon, north-west of London. In winter, the village had an atmosphere of closeness and quiet. From her cottage, Rosamond could see the square tower of St Mary's Church through the bare trees. To get to the shop, the post office or the village hall, she had to walk down a narrow lane, enclosed on both sides by steep banks; or she could let herself in at the gate opposite, and make her way, with difficulty in snow, directly over the fields.

In some ways, Rosamond hadn't strayed very far at all. For ten years she had lived at Ipsden, a village six miles north of Aldworth across the Oxfordshire border; and her childhood home, Fieldhead, at Bourne End in Buckinghamshire, was less than thirty miles away. All three were situated along the banks of the Thames. One might have walked between them, following the river for a day as it made its way northwards out of London before dipping into the map-green beechwoods and downs towards Oxford. River and city

produced their own rhythms. In childhood, Rosamond had learned
to swim in the Thames, lowered into the water in a harness held by
her father to feel the reeds pulling at her legs; at night, she listened
to the commuter trains bringing home their cargo of city workers.
Later, at Ipsden, she depended upon both: the lush greenery of the
Thames Valley, and its atmosphere of concealed quiet, while maintaining a vital sense of cosmopolitan connection. There was always
a train to catch, an event, dinner, friends; always solitude to return
home to. As for Virginia in Sussex, it was in movement, rhythm and
exchange – the sense that one environment could be relieved and
enlivened by another – that Rosamond discovered the best conditions for writing.

In Berkshire, though the landscape was familiar, Rosamond's circumstances had drastically changed. For most of her life, she had
lived with domestic help. In her memoir, *The Swan in the Evening*,
she recalled a faithful retinue of servants at Fieldhead – cab driver,
maids, gardeners and cooks; a host of local characters – who, with
'perpetual kindliness, willingness to listen, exclaim, explode with
laughter', often took a more meaningful role in the lives of the
Lehmann children than did their parents.[8] Neither, at Ipsden, had
she engaged in the routines and physical demands of rural life.
There was a gardener in his own cottage, Mrs Wickens the cook,
and two parlourmaids – Sindy and her younger sister, who was
employed when she was fifteen and a half. But, in 1942, cottage life
took on a very different flavour. Rosamond couldn't afford household staff (nor were many available), and had with her only Mrs
Wickens, too old for the war effort, to help in the kitchen. An elderly local man was employed for occasional work in the garden.
Rosamond's attitudes to domestic servants reflected the views held
by middle-class women of the time. In their letters, she and her
sister, Beatrix Lehmann, often mimicked working-class people and
domestics, one of their long-running private jokes, and yet Rosamond was avowedly reliant on Mrs Wickens, speaking of her with
exasperation and affection by turns. The frequent appearance of
the cook in her letters suggests a relationship as antagonized and

faithful as Virginia's with her servant Nellie Boxall. Rosamond was amused when her son, Hugo, asked to play dominoes with Mrs Wickens in the kitchen after his tea, and later by the sight of the old woman wrapping her varicosed legs in rags. Yet she always included her in household reckonings of colds and flu. Later, when Mrs Wickens had a heart attack, Rosamond complained of having to nurse her 'one domestic prop', before acknowledging the loss of 'one of the best friends I shall ever have', with whom she had 'weathered much together, these 16 years'.[9]

At Diamond Cottage, the majority of the housework fell to Rosamond. Soon, she was spending 'all day struggling with coke buckets, wood chopper, brooms, pails, scrubbing brushes', an 'exhausted prisoner', as she wrote in tones of mock heroism, of household tasks.[10] And yet she worked gamely, unafraid of getting her hands dirty. She bought six hens – which she fed with gifts of illicit corn from her neighbour, a retired major – and attempted to grow vegetables. The garden at the cottage was south-westerly facing, and one third of an acre. Observed by her neighbour, she planted potatoes and sowed broad beans, wielding a spade with unskilled determination, her grey-blue hair shimmering. Yet Rosamond found satisfaction in her efforts to make the garden plentiful. 'I've only got one flower in my garden,' she wrote proudly to a friend. '[A] thousand thousand Sweet Williams have seeded themselves and come up everywhere. You never saw such a sight.'[11] To another, she signed off: 'I must go and plant lettuces. What a spring, what a spring.'[12]

As she settled in, new friendships began to take root, though Rosamond picked her crowd, at first making literary connections. Diamond Cottage shared a boundary with Rose Cottage, the home of journalists Anne Scott-James, then Women's Editor at *Picture Post*, and Macdonald Hastings. The two women were competitive over mushrooming. One morning, Anne, who was up and afield before Rosamond was awake, was caught returning with her load. Rosamond eyed her brimming basket. 'Are you taking them to market?' she asked drily.[13] A mile away, at Westridge Manor, lived the poet Laurence Binyon, who invited Rosamond to supper. 'I am concerned about the awful mud in our lane,' he wrote on the appointed day. 'I advise you to come in by the garden gate [. . .]. And I expect you will need a torch.'[14]

But Rosamond was also searching for a new kind of belonging. In comparison to the secluded grandeur of Ipsden, Aldworth was a small, provincial place, entailing an altogether different kind of living. Each afternoon, she walked into the village to post her letters – the post office was housed in a wooden lean-to attached to the end of the row of council houses – or queued for food at the village shop. She spoke politely with her neighbours: the Home Guard officer, the retired bank manager, the vicar. Mr McQuhae owned the bakehouse and the shop, and Mr Macaulay ran the pub, The Bell Inn, with its two low-ceilinged rooms, open fires and, over the counter, a hatch with a sliding glass door. While Rosamond waited to cash a cheque, her daughter Sally played with the landlord's daughters outside in the street. Mostly, the villagers were employed as labourers and milkmen at nearby Haw Farm. Several worked for Mr McQuhae who, throughout the war, sent out a fleet of vans delivering newspapers, milk and bread. The villagers were respectful of each other's business, and proud of the place and its history – of the nine effigies of the De La Beche family, medieval knights from Flanders, sleeping in white stone in the parish church, and the well, covered by a red-tiled roof on the green, said to be one of the deepest in England. In wartime, the small community had become closer still. Rosamond did not keep a diary, but she was observing her neighbours and her new surroundings closely; she was taking notes.

At the beginning of her career, Rosamond had achieved a reputation as a frank and perceptive writer of women's private lives. Her early fiction is populated by women who feel cut off from those around them, who drift against the current of everyday life. Take solitary Grace Fairfax in *A Note in Music*, finding solace in her gas fire and toasted buns, or the rootless Olivia Curtis in *The Weather in the Streets*, smoking in her bedsit, daydreaming. Indifferent to world affairs, these women ally themselves to no cause; they do not assert themselves. In their personal relationships, they inhabit ambiguous positions as lovers and mistresses, not quite respectable and always on the outside. But, for all their ambivalence about respectability, they are conflicted, contradictory creatures, needing to be loved. Rosamond was candid about sexual experience and its risks. Her novels captured the mood of the interwar years, when many young women felt adrift between worlds, seizing the opportunity for new sexual freedoms which nevertheless carried the risk of censure and ostracism. *The Weather in the Streets*, published in 1936, described Olivia's abortion (just two years after the first literary representation in Jean Rhys's *Voyage in the Dark*) to the dismay of Rosamond's critics, and yet for her readers exposed an all-too-common truth about the reality of their experience.

Rosamond in the 1930s

Rosamond's ability to write about taboo subjects surprised even herself. She sprang to fame in 1927 at the age of twenty-six with *Dusty Answer*, in which the young Judith Earle becomes fascinated with a group of glamorous siblings, and has an intense, ambiguous friendship with a woman she meets at Cambridge. The novel was an instant success, printed seven times within its first year, selected for the Book of the Month Club in the United States, and translated into French. Yet Rosamond was a reluctant recipient of such intense public interest. With one foot firmly in her Edwardian upbringing, she hadn't intended to tackle social mores, or for the novel, as she told Harold Raymond, her publisher at Chatto & Windus, to be 'taken merely as a study in sexual relationships'.[15] She disliked her readers' assumption that *Dusty Answer* was autobiographical. Though her life story would often appear in 'intricate disguises' in her books – and Judith's sheltered riverside adolescence and time at Girton certainly mirrored her own – Rosamond grew tired of the 'spotters', as she called them, devouring her work for facts about its author. The scrutiny made her feel as if 'I'd exposed myself nude on the platform of the Albert Hall'.[16] For the most part, she later reflected, they were 'more beady-eyed than accurate'.[17]

She responded to fame 'with a sort of anxious shrinking', later rejecting Judith as 'soppy' and 'a revolting character'.[18] With her second novel, she abandoned the voluptuous terrain of the Thames Valley and the romantic preoccupations of its upper-middle-class youth, instead stepping over the threshold of an ordinary suburban house to examine the emotional lives of those within. Little happens in *A Note in Music*, published in 1930, though the textures of Grace Fairfax's interior and domestic worlds are finely drawn. As if in response to the furore caused by her first novel, Rosamond had created an unobtrusive work in a minor key. Virginia Woolf appreciated its subtle tuning – admiring Rosamond's 'clear hard mind, beating up now & then to poetry' – but, like her critics, succumbed to its defeatist air. '[M]uch work for little result,' she noted in her diary, describing the 'flash' of 'clear light here & there; but I suppose no more'.[19]

Next, Rosamond delighted readers with Olivia Curtis, the

heroine of her pair of novels: *Invitation to the Waltz*, published in 1932, and *The Weather in the Streets*, published in 1936. Like Judith and Grace, Olivia is unhappy, a misfit. As a young girl, dressing before a party, she looks at herself in the mirror – unmanicured nails, stockings with cotton tops, vests bulging from beneath her village-made dress – and faces the evening with all the anguish of the outsider.

> Why go? It was unthinkable. Why suffer so much? Wrenched from one's foundations; neglected, ignored, curiously stared at; partnerless, watching Kate move serenely from partner to partner, pretending not to watch [. . .] pretending not to care; slipping off to the ladies' cloakroom, fiddling with unnecessary pins and powder, ears strained for the music to stop [. . .][20]

Unlike her sister, Kate, for whom social gatherings are easy, something in Olivia 'fumbled, felt inharmonious, wanted almost to resist'.[21] Later, Olivia continues to eschew the kinds of behaviour expected of women of her upbringing. Separated from her husband, she works part-time as a photographer's assistant, and lives in her cousin's London flat. When she bumps into Rollo Spencer in a train carriage – handsome, married, carrying *The Times* and a terrier under his arm – her fate is sealed. Sitting across the table from him, she chooses the only identity available to her, that of Rollo's mistress. Then, Olivia enters 'the time [. . .] when there wasn't any time', a period of 'inward double living' of their affair. With Rollo, there is 'No argument, no discussion': 'All was agreeing, answer after answer melting'. And yet, while she is with him, the usual conditions of Olivia's life are suspended. Love shelters her from a squalid existence of buses and cheap cinema seats, for with Rollo there are 'no wet ankles, muddy stockings, blown hair, cold-aching cheeks, fog-smarting eyes, throat, nose [. . .] not my usual bus-taking London winter'. She is protected from the weather, from the city on 'the other side of the glass'. But shelter is only temporary. As she basks in the warmth of restaurants, taxis, small hotels, Olivia accepts – as the women of Rosamond's books often accept – what is only provisional. Bravely, foolishly, she voyages with Rollo, though the 'journey was in the dark'.[22]

Rosamond's novels were studies in alienation, in the uneasy atmospheric shift from one generation to the next. It is no accident Olivia meets Rollo on a train leaving London for the country. Olivia is giving up, for a time, her urban independence for the muffled conservatism of her childhood home, where her father lies ill. Confronted with Rollo, she is caught between her upbringing, her desire and its consequences. When, eventually, she sits on a bench in St James's park, pregnant with Rollo's child, she knows she is paying the price for her choices. Her estrangement, from everyone and everything she knows, is complete. The story resonated with Rosamond's readers. Not straightforwardly romantic, it was a narrative in which they could identify their own longing, but also their loneliness and rejections. Afterwards, Rosamond received hundreds of letters, a chorus of women, clamouring ' "this is my story [. . .] – how did you know?" '[23]

~

Despite her evasiveness about the origins of her books, many of Rosamond's themes came from situations in her own life – from smashed relationships, and periods of despondency. A short, disastrous first marriage to the stern, sober Leslie Runciman – heir to a shipping business, whom she had met at Cambridge – resulted in her own reluctant abortion (Leslie insisted he didn't want children), before she met Wogan Philipps (also heir to a shipping business, and a baronetcy), whom she would also ultimately divorce. But there were periods of happiness. From 1929, Rosamond and Wogan lived at Ipsden in Oxfordshire, an elegant, red-brick Queen Anne manor house from which the green backs of the Berkshire Downs were visible through a screen of trees. Two miles away, the Thames rolled silently through Wallingford and Goring. Here, Rosamond lived according to the principles by which she had been brought up: mildness, tolerance, inward-looking talk. At Ipsden, she had two children: Hugo, born in 1929, and Sally, in 1934.

During the 1930s, Ipsden became a place of gatherings and leisured, long weekends. There were local friends: Carrington and Lytton Strachey lived twenty miles away at Ham Spray, along with Frances Marshall and Ralph Partridge; and Elizabeth Bowen lived in Headington, on the outskirts of Oxford. The poets Stephen Spender and Siegfried Sassoon visited often from London. Rosamond suited her environment. In photographs, she appears at ease with motherhood and the pleasures of country life, reading in a deep armchair, sitting on the lawn in a straw hat, or lounging on the riverbank in a woollen bathing suit and cap.

Rosamond was ripe for teasing by her friends. She was beautiful in an old-fashioned sort of way, like her books, with almond-shaped eyes, smooth, rounded cheeks, and rather sturdy legs. And she dressed elegantly, even demurely, as if to detract from her appearance, her dark hair prematurely threaded with grey. Carrington, so sprightly and bohemian by contrast, made no secret of admiring Rosamond and her clothes. She lived for glimpses of 'R-s-m-on', as she called her breathily in letters, writing in a cloud-like green chiffon dress at teatime, surrounded by her 'little doggies'.[24] (Rosamond's most beloved dog was a Dandie Dinmont called Sheltie.) Despite the frequent visits from Bloomsbury, Rosamond's life and marriage were conventional by Carrington's standards, and she was intrigued, perhaps appalled, by Rosamond's desire to have children. 'It must be a queer feeling to have invented a new character with a new shape,' she wrote to her after Hugo came along.[25]

Some aspects of wifeliness didn't fit. Rosamond was impractical and inefficient, muddling her housekeeping. She resented the 'various footling & infuriating household occupations' which ruptured the leisurely atmosphere of Ipsden and distracted her from work.[26] Her displeasure in domesticity was rooted in inexperience; like Virginia, she had grown up with servants, and didn't know how to cook. 'I am *floundering* in housekeeping problems,' she had written to her mother during her first marriage, before requesting details of servants' wages and recipes to give the cook: 'Ham salad. Eggs à

Rosamond after a swim

l'Aurore. Apple Meringue. Hot apple pudding. Chocolate Sponge. And that new soup with bits of vegetables in it.'[27] Her preference for nursery food persisted. At Ipsden, guests were often given shepherd's pie and milk pudding.

When the Woolfs came to stay in the autumn of 1933, the boiler broke down, and Rosamond fretted. She was apprehensive of Virginia's arrival at Ipsden, of exposing her domestic efforts to someone she admired. In the event, the visit passed off well enough. Virginia described the place as 'stately, arboreous' in her diary, the beech copses on the tops of the downs giving off 'a lovely fox red glow'. She didn't much like the murals in the dining room by the surrealist John Banting, nor the tubular steel chairs – 'I prefer the old to the new,' she commented, 'unless done with more taste' – and thought the house, as Rosamond had dreaded, 'cold'. But she enjoyed the company of her hosts: '[H]ow nice, easy, affectionate, & humane it all was.'[28] The following morning, the two writers went for a walk, the downs enveloped in mist. Rosamond was relieved. She had found the Woolfs 'at their most charming', she reported to her brother, John Lehmann, then assistant at the Woolfs' Hogarth Press. 'What an angel Leonard can be! Also I never realised that V. can be really human – almost cosy to talk to.'[29]

~

Life at Ipsden had had a quality of cosiness; sheltered, shut off from the world. Reflecting on his visits, Stephen Spender later remembered its atmosphere of mildness, in which visitors 'discussed few topics outside literature' and 'gossiped endlessly and entertainingly about their friends'.[30] For much of the decade, Rosamond lived unreflectingly, her life circumscribed by children and guests. She was careful to distance herself from other kinds of country life. Socializing with London visitors rather than her village neighbours, she treated local commitments – such as the meetings of the Women's Institute ('Damn and hell,' she wrote despairingly to Elizabeth Bowen, 'I hate it so') – with disdain.[31] When, in a letter to Beatrix, she described their older sister Helen as living in the 'shires', she meant it with some disparagement.[32] Helen Lehmann, unlike her siblings, had not pursued an intellectual or artistic career, but, like Olivia Curtis's sister, Kate, in *The Weather in the Streets*, had married a country doctor. At Ipsden, local news rarely filtered in. The talk was of literature and art, with modern pictures – of the French school, or a Duncan Grant, perhaps – paired with mahogany and chintz.

The topographies of Rosamond's childhood, and her life at Ipsden, shaped both her writing and her thinking. Her novels of the 1930s, with their apathetic female characters, expressed no interest in international concerns; instead, their terrain was provincial. At first, it might have appeared as though Rosamond was describing rural settings as only the places where drama happened: Judith's sexual encounter on the dusky riverbank; Grace's claim to independence with a solitary excursion to the country. In fact, Rosamond was articulating something more complex about those places she knew best. Riverbanks studded with large houses, sheltered gardens, villages muffled in woodsmoke: the more lusciously described, the more these settings reinforced her characters' insularity, and their closed-mindedness. In *Invitation to the Waltz*, the young Olivia Curtis expresses a learned snobbishness towards the village children (chillingly viewing them as 'rats'); later, after she is disgraced, she is subjected to the condemnation of her own country neighbours.[33] (Rosamond was not as blind to the hypocrisies of her class, and the safety of their country lives, as Stephen Spender thought.) And yet, as if mirroring both her themes and her terrain, she chose to write in a style which has been described as middlebrow, or provincial. She would often be criticized for the insularity of her novels, for their condescension towards working-class characters, and preoccupation with romance; for creating a body of writing which had, especially during the 1930s, failed to expose itself to class and politics, to the issues of the contemporary world.

~

For all its mildness, the period at Ipsden was a creative one, with patches of productivity. With Mrs Wickens to superintend the children, Rosamond produced *A Note in Music* and her two Olivia Curtis books. She was pleased to be published by Chatto, whose list included writers such as the inventive Sylvia Townsend Warner (Rosamond thought Sylvia's third novel, *Mr Fortune's Maggot*, 'an absolutely flawless work').[34] 'When I think of the future, I think mostly of my work, my work, my work,' she wrote energetically to Dadie. 'I do so *long* to be settled at it. I know it could be good if I can manage it.'[35]

Meanwhile, in the dining room, Wogan was beginning to paint, filling the rest of the house with large, byzantine-looking portraits of Rosamond. Under the influence of friends such as Lytton and Stephen, he was becoming enthused by politics. But Wogan was naturally flighty, easily distracted by new ideas and often unable to finish the project in hand. He produced paintings at a terrific rate, though the emphasis was always on the making, not the made. His father, the industrialist Sir Laurence Philipps, disapproved of his new career and his left-wing friends – a 'filthy set, rotten intellectuals', Rosamond reported him saying at Llanstephan, the family's estate in Wales – and periodically cut him off.[36] For long stretches, he and Rosamond relied solely on the money from her books. In 1933, when Rosamond changed publishers, she told Harold Raymond it was 'entirely a question of money'. Collins were offering a good deal more: 'Wogan isn't likely to be able ever to breadwin [. . .] – and there's our family – and this house.'[37]

It was then that she began thinking of a cottage. Financial instabilities, and the responsibility of Ipsden, were starting to weigh heavily. 'Wogan wastes infinite quantities of nervous energy,' she wrote despairingly to Frances Partridge following another 'idiotic exhausting fanatical' row at Llanstephan, after which Wogan's father had threatened to leave them 'without a penny'. She needed a safeguard, a place to bring up the children, preferably in her own name. Briefly, she contemplated leaving Ipsden for a cottage in Wiltshire, '– but I don't know'.[38]

Tensions continued to emerge. Rosamond and Wogan argued, increasingly along political lines. When Wogan insisted Sally be sent to the local school, Rosamond was adamant she attend Westonbirt, a small independent school in Gloucestershire. And, when he left Ipsden to go on painting holidays, he left the children ill, and the telephone bill unpaid. Affairs, first with Julia Strachey and later with Barbara Ker-Seymer, followed. Rosamond felt the fabric of her marriage wearing thin. She knew she was no longer what Wogan wanted, and yet she couldn't follow him. At the house parties he hosted at Ipsden, she retreated into the sensibility which fitted her best, appearing old-fashioned, homely, smartly dressed. She could feel herself failing to live up to the moment. 'I'm a limited character,' she confided in Elizabeth Bowen, '– & now perhaps too fixed in my domestic life to sketch any more.'[39]

Yet, from this period, one sketch remains prominent. *A Letter to a Sister* was to be the third in a new series edited by John Lehmann at the Hogarth Press, in which contemporary writers were asked to reflect, as he later remembered, on 'all the topics of the day'.[40] Rosamond's contribution to the series was pensive, a study in atmosphere. A woman returns from a holiday to her country house in late summer, and meditates on memory and domestic life. In a sequence of 'luscious pen-pictures', she describes picking fruit, watching the baby on his rug, and talking with friends on the lawn beneath the 'ruminative eye' of the two-hundred-year-old house.[41] It is a vision of safety, of a civilized English rural summer. It was as if Rosamond was picking the fruits growing along the garden wall and preserving them for the winter months ahead. She was bottling the feeling of Ipsden, its gentle character and languorous air, the feeling of the house as a protective shield, insulating those within from outside cares.

And yet, in *A Letter*, there lurks an undercurrent of anxiety. The woman is curiously detached. The working machinery of the house – the trunks to unpack, the repairs to inspect, the joint to order; all the domestic arrangements of the place – remains a mystery to her. She is, she confesses, a 'day-dreaming fraud and muddler', for whom there exists a 'great and unbridgeable gulf between the fact and the performance; between being mistress of a house and controlling its internal economy'.[42] Once more, Rosamond was describing a state of disconnection, of uneasy relationship between social position and place. Her speaker is capable only of experiencing her life passively, 'a screen for chaotic images – images assembling, blurring, dissolving', a receptacle for the bits and pieces of other people's lives.[43]

Despite her misgivings, Leonard Woolf was pleased with the piece. 'This is such a relief to me,' she wrote afterwards to John. 'Nothing has ever given me so much trouble! – I mean in proportion to its length.'[44]

~

Sometimes, Rosamond worked well, and quickly; at others, she did very little writing at all. She shrank from deadlines. 'The words "four novels a week" have tolled like a knell through my head,' she wrote to Cyril Connolly in 1936, refusing his offer of a book review

Rosamond at Monk's House

Looking up at the bees

column in the *Daily Telegraph*. She was reluctant, she told him, to feel 'hag-ridden by time'.[45] She blamed domesticity – what she described to John as the 'difficulties of my own life – I mean all the daily things I have to do here' – and yet she needed such fallow periods, idle phases in which she could 'just lie about, walk, & [not] think of anything'.[46] For Rosamond, writing wasn't a discipline, but followed its own rhythms.* Time spent quietly at home, doing nothing, was essential. Homes – Fieldhead, then Ipsden, and later Diamond Cottage – were spaces in which she could think and dream. As a girl, she had had a sluggish, gluttonous nature – 'I would have liked to lie all day in a hot bath, and stay safe in bed eating enormous meals brought to me, lovingly, on trays,' she remembered later – and in adulthood was much the same.[47] At Ipsden during the 1930s, she spent long periods in bed – during pregnancy, or with measles, or propped up on pillows to write. Islanded from the rest of the house, she entered a state of creative idleness, which became the fertile ground where writing took place. In her 1939 short story, 'The Red-Haired Miss Daintreys', Rosamond offered an analysis of this process of literary creation. The speaker of the story – 'a privileged person with considerable leisure' – meditates on the relationship between doing nothing and doing work, between how she uses leisure, and how it uses her. 'When asked how I spend it,' she writes,

> I feel both dubious and embarrassed: for any answer implying some
> degree of activity would be misleading. Perhaps an approximation
> to the truth might be reached by stating that leisure employs me –
> weak aimless unsystematic unresisting instrument – as a kind of
> screen upon which are projected the images of persons – known

---

* Many years later, she reflected on the vicissitudes of her writing life. 'In a way I do wish that I had written more, produced more, regularly, like most of my colleagues,' she said in an interview with Janet Watts in 1988. 'But although I'm tremendously professional about writing, I just can't produce a book a year. [. . .] [A]nd there are so many other things I enjoyed – children, friends, reading, music . . . I always found it very hard to withdraw.' Lehmann, *Writing Lives*, 156.

well, a little, not at all, seen once, or long ago, or every day; or as a kind of preserving jar in which float fragments of people and landscape, snatches of sound.[48]

As in *A Letter to a Sister*, the creative mind exists in a 'detached condition', and yet this shadowy, tranquil region is 'a working-place', abstractedly paying attention, recording images, weaving threads, ready to come to life.[49]

In Rosamond's novels, leisure is a state of mind. Her women cling to it; it defines their attitudes, as well as how they spend their time. In *A Note in Music*, Grace Fairfax turns her back on her marriage and life in the town to indulge in indoor pleasures with a 'cat-like love of comfort'.[50] Her daily life is made up of a series of small rebellions: the stodgy meals she orders for supper (fish pie and chocolate shape); the lists of household tasks she leaves undone.[51] Her greatest enjoyment comes each afternoon, when, in a 'warm sluggish tide of well-being', her housekeeper 'drew the curtains, heaped the fire, and left her with a great cup of coffee and a toasted bun'.[52] Olivia Curtis shares Grace's 'voluptuous, sluggish nature'.[53] As a girl in *Invitation to the Waltz*, she is idle and secretive, sitting in hot baths, reading library novels and craving soft food. She wishes to do 'nothing at all' with her life but 'stay where I am, in my home, and absorb each hour, each day, and be alone'.[54] For both of these women, doing nothing suggests a form of defiance. Soft food becomes a kind of brain food, and what might constitute laziness is, in fact, a practice of passive resistance. Grace is a 'muddler': 'she cooked her housekeeping accounts, she mended neither her stockings nor his socks, she had forgotten for the past two days to ring up the plumber [. . .] but [. . .] she was not weak; no, she was not weak.'[55]

In her novels of the 1930s, Rosamond was attempting to describe ambivalence: the desire for freedom, while fearing and rejecting it at the same time. Grace and Olivia are inconsistent in their desires, neither comfortable with the familiarity of marital domesticity nor with the independence of their urban lives. Instead, both sit on park benches, watching men racing whippets and wasting time. They are among the eccentrics, the out-of-work, the social flotsam of the city. Olivia's instincts are snobbish, and yet she wants to be part of that life. There is empathy in her watchfulness, an emerging compassion for others who are idle and alone. They are all 'atoms', she thinks – the sickly babies, the elderly women on matchstick legs. She and Grace have learned to recognize others like themselves, 'slipshod' characters, a community of outsiders.[56]

~

Rosamond could identify with the outsiderish women of her books. 'I never felt I belonged to any group. I never felt I belonged anywhere,' she said late in her life.[57] By the middle of 1936, the atmosphere at Ipsden was changing. In July, *The Weather in the Streets* was published, heavily publicized by Collins, and civil war broke out in Spain. While Rosamond's reviews poured in, Wogan immersed himself in political activity, in meetings, speeches and fundraising. Soon, Ipsden was filled with left-wing friends, the air charged with energized, political talk. Rosamond felt out of place, overdressed and under-committed among the scruffy communists in her sitting room, smoking and putting their boots on the furniture. After years of 'explosions & reconciliations', her marriage was foundering.[58]

She had been living with Wogan 'in a state of constant anxiety', feeling as if she were 'fighting a defensive battle and being the battle ground at one and the same time'. Her position was tortuous; she felt herself an 'object of hate-love'.[59] The difference between her and Wogan's sensibilities was driving a wedge between them: Rosamond, muddling through her feelings about politics as she muddled through her housework, couldn't subscribe to Wogan's increasingly urgent ideology; he, in turn, felt indignant at her complacency, and misunderstood. 'If I were different or had managed better this wouldn't have happened,' she wrote despondently to Eddy Sackville-West. 'What doesn't seem to count with him, & what I wanted so much, was the gradual growing together of our lives: the *habit* of marriage, so to speak. But he wants endless stimulus. [. . .] Lately he has told me I once gave him all he wanted, that I helped him over his transition period, but that now he has passed on beyond me.'[60] Through Rosamond, Wogan had found a new community of artistic and political friends, and, in political causes, a direction for his otherwise skittish life. In February 1937, he announced he was leaving England for Spain to volunteer as a driver for Spanish Medical Aid.* The outside world had penetrated Ipsden's protective shield and broken in.

Exasperated, Rosamond looked for an escape. The previous September, she had been invited to stay at Elizabeth Bowen's house in County Cork, where she met the left-wing writer Goronwy Rees. On their return to England, she and Goronwy began an affair, much to the displeasure of Elizabeth, who had fallen for Rees first. (Bowen got her own back by portraying Rees as the fickle, slippery Eddie in *The Death of the Heart*.) Rees was eight years younger than Rosamond, yet he shared her love of literature; he was a poet and the author of two novels. Having abandoned a career in academia at Oxford (he was a Fellow of All Souls), he was working at the *Spectator* and living in a rented flat on Ebury Street. Rosamond met him there, though since their affair was conducted openly – Wogan had little ground for disapproval – she was soon bringing him to Ipsden for weekends.

Like Wogan, Rees was politically active. Under his influence, Rosamond's political views sharpened, and with his encouragement she began making them known. Responding to Nancy Cunard's questionnaire 'Authors Take Sides on the Spanish War', published in *Left Review* in November 1937, she wrote from her standpoint as a parent. 'As a mother,' she wrote,

---

* In February 1937, Wogan travelled to Spain and spent several weeks in Barcelona before moving on to Valencia, where he joined the Popular Front Spanish Army as an ambulance driver. At the Battle of Jarama, east of Madrid – at which two-thirds of the British contingent of the International Brigade were killed – he drove the wounded back from the front and assisted in makeshift hospitals. For the first time in his life, he told Rosamond in one of his many letters, he felt useful: 'I seemed at last to have linked myself up to life, to the meaning of history.' On his return, he wrote a moving account of his experiences for *New Writing* titled 'An Ambulance Man in Spain'. Wogan Philips to Rosamond Lehmann, n/d, KCC.

I am convinced that upon the outcome of the struggle in Spain depends the future, the very life of my children. Up till now a pacifist in the fullest sense, I have come to feel that non-resistance can be – in this case, is – a negative, sterile, even a destructive thing [. . .]. Not only as an internationalist, but as an English writer, I must choose to bear my part in the defence of culture against Fascism.[61]

Much as her characters practised a kind of passive resistance, she had always held fast to the view of the non-participating writer; now, with a great change of heart, she urged action and solidarity. She employed similar vocabulary in the *Daily Worker*, when, in 1940, she wrote that she had 'grown to believe it is nonsense to speak of the "inevitable loneliness" of the artist, or to make a virtue of "resisting the temptation" to join a political movement'. The writer, she argued, had an inevitably 'historical position' – part of 'what was, what is, but also as part of the shape of things to come' – and was morally obliged to make use of it for a common cause.[62]

It was as if Rosamond had been brought out of hiding, and out of her country languor into the glare of London political life. A flurry of activism followed. With Wogan in Spain, she was free to go about with Goronwy, and took pleasure in being at his side at public events. On 8 June 1938, she organized 'Writers Declare Against Fascism', a meeting of over fifty writers – including Sylvia Townsend Warner – at the Queen's Hall. Rosamond delivered a speech from the podium, beginning, 'What gives my life my deepest reality is my children'; Cecil Day Lewis was next, cool, nonplussed; and then Goronwy, eyes flashing.[63] Not everyone appreciated Rosamond's efforts. In her diary, Virginia Woolf – who hadn't been invited – disparaged the 'great meeting', which she thought 'foolish'.[64] On the telephone, E. M. Forster agreed. Responding to Rosamond's invitation to speak, Forster prophesied such 'gatherings of worried writers' would prove futile in the face of fascism as it swept across Europe.[65] Wogan, too, downplayed his wife's sudden involvement in politics. 'I can't help being amused at you coming out politically,' he wrote, 'as you aren't exactly a left-wing political writer.'[66] 'Too late!' she quipped, 'I'm off, & can't be stopped.'[67]

She travelled to Paris twice, once in April to speak at a conference organized by the poet Louis Aragon, and again in July, to attend a rally organized for the Popular Front by the International Association of Writers for the Defence of Culture. Wogan was watching from afar. 'Rosie, surely it doesn't need Goronwy to make you believe in what I am doing,' he wrote from Spain. 'Without him explaining to you about Spain would you [. . .] give me the support at all? Have I really got to be thankful to him for that?'[68] She had never been 'deeply honestly interested in politics': 'It needed romance & love to wake you & couple you to them, perhaps.'[69] Rosamond sniped back. 'Wogan is a political commissar,' she wrote to John, 'and his letters (from Barcelona) are chiefly political tracts.'[70] 'You can imagine how useful, popular & altogether indispensable he'll be making himself. It is what he likes best: to live at full pressure in a perpetual state of crisis.'[71] She conceded: 'He is obviously educating himself with enormous enthusiasm, & growing confidence & says his life is very full & exciting.'[72]

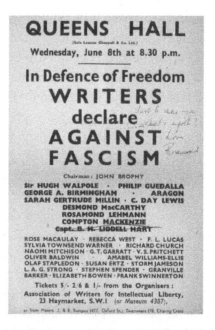

The poster for Rosamond's event at the Queen's Hall, which Sylvia also attended

But radical politics was never Rosamond's style (she had delivered her Queen's Hall speech wearing a silver skirt and purple chiffon blouse), and she moved uneasily among her left-wing friends. Her aversion manifested itself in feelings of discomfort and boredom. When John spent Christmas 1938 at Ipsden, the talk each evening sent her yawning up to bed. And, at London gatherings, she was more pre-occupied with planning her escape. Finding herself in a procession marching down Whitehall in early 1939 as part of a deputation to the prime minister, she was put off by the fervour of her fellow delegates, including a 'prattling' Amabel Williams-Ellis. Shouting a cursory ' "Arms to Spain!" ' outside Number 10, Rosamond dumped her plac-ard, 'jumped into a taxi & came home'.[73] In her letters, she arrived at a kind of flippancy, a useful cover for her embarrassment. 'I've not become a Communist & it's a pretty safe bet that I never shall,' she told Eddy Sackville-West. She was certainly moved by current events – 'these horrors and threats to freedom and culture' – but any activity 'goes hideously against the grain'.[74]

And she was deeply resistant to the idea that art should be political. She disliked literature that was 'too doctrinaire' or contained 'Marxist statements', as she noted of a manuscript sent by John for consid-eration for *New Writing*, the magazine he had founded in 1935. Literature, she felt, should be free of teaching and instead be 'about life as it is to you personally, without any direct propaganda', or it risked becoming 'more valuable *as* propaganda apart from art'.[75] Her own novels treated politics with irony and condescension; there is little by way of public life in the lives of her characters. Instead, she cast sideways looks at the alien fervour of unkempt young men of the sort who put their boots on the furniture at Ipsden – men, like Olivia Curtis's younger brother, who stride about Europe in ill-fitting clothes, look-ing thin and 'midnight-oilish'.[76] Ideology, thinks Olivia, makes them 'bigoted, really'.[77] Observing them, she is both envious and appalled. With only 'a muddled feeling of the importance of intellectual things', Olivia perceives their way of life as one in which she cannot share, a frugal life, 'anti-luxurious, a bit antiseptic, a bit humourless'.[78]

Stephen Spender criticized Rosamond for writing novels not

about 'morals' but about relationships.[79] In the intensifying political atmosphere of the decade, her books were parochial both in subject matter and outlook. But she wasn't alone in rejecting Spender's masculinist assumption of what literature should be. Virginia Woolf used her 'Hogarth Letters' pamphlet, *A Letter to a Young Poet*, to outline the failures of the new generation of 1930s left-wing poets – Auden, Spender and Day-Lewis among them. And, in her 1944 essay 'Panorama of the Novel', Elizabeth Bowen wrote that the compulsion for a politicized art served only to wrest it out of the hands of women.[80] The role of the artist, Rosamond felt, was not to ideologize the contemporary moment, but to absorb it. '[W]riters should stand more patiently at the centre and suffer themselves to be worked upon,' the narrator says in 'The Red-Haired Miss Daintreys', one of her wartime stories. Leisure, for those who can afford it, has its uses; only from that passive process can the writer's art emerge.

Rosamond's flippancy masked a deep ambivalence over where she stood politically. Towards the end of the 1930s, the tension between her bourgeois upbringing and the ideals espoused by left-wing, literary London became increasingly fraught. She was too rooted in the sensibility of her class, and the ease of her cossetted country home, to commit herself convincingly to any cause. Moving between Ipsden and London to spend time with Goronwy, it was as if the transitions between country and city mirrored her political vacillation, establishing a pattern of involvement, resentment and drawing back. She was exhausted with having to explain herself. 'I wish it were summer & we were all sitting in the garden & that we hadn't got to spend nearly all the time making up one's mind about one's political beliefs,' she wrote exasperatedly to John.[81] She was in conflict with herself, aware of her own inconsistencies: that she could be adventurous yet comfort-loving; unconventional in her relationships and yet centred on family life; left-leaning yet traditional; formally more conservative than her peers and yet willing to confront the reality of women's experiences. There were no easy symmetries between art and life, as with Virginia in Sussex, or Sylvia – now at her most politically active, travelling to Spain and writing ardent, allegorical novels – in Dorset.

And yet, could Rosamond find a way to work with asymmetry, to make something of her contradictions? She was hesitating.

In October 1938, she was able to name her distress in a letter to Compton Mackenzie, describing the 'claustrophobic' sensation of not knowing how to behave among her contemporaries. 'I believe this comes from suppressing one's continuity with one's past and traditions,' she explained. 'The fact is I don't see that I really belong in the left wing *actively* – although morally I do.'[82] A few days later, she wrote again: 'My head, what there is of it, is with the Left, my heart is entirely with the people I love, my tastes, traditions, etc. etc. are with the centre-to-leaning Right.' She was trapped, oscillating between the two. 'No wonder I do nothing at all.'[83]

~

The decade marched towards its chaotic conclusion. Wogan returned from Spain 'a true blue, hundred per cent Communist', she remembered, a little mockingly, later. 'I couldn't follow him in that new life he'd found for himself. I couldn't, *couldn't* take it or take to it.'[84] On the question of their marriage, he continued to pre-varicate, suggesting a trial separation – Rosamond to live with Goronwy for a year, and he with Barbara – before, finally, he left (this time for Cristina Casati, a fellow communist he had met in Spain). Worn out and miserable, Rosamond had 'no plans', save the realization that 'I shall have to get rid of this house'.[85] Beatrix urged her to consider her future: 'Why don't you take a tiny house [. . .] and spend several months – and *write*.'[86] Though Rosamond had previously considered buying a cottage in the event of Wogan's dis-inheritance, she now realized the question of where she would live, alone with the children, was critical. During the spring of 1939, she bought a small, pink-washed house in a remote village six miles from Ipsden, sheltered in the Berkshire Downs. But things with Wogan – including a brief, financially motivated attempt at reconciliation – rumbled on. 'The cottage,' she reported to John in the autumn, 'sits empty. Maybe will move there in the spring.'[87] As the months wore on and Rosamond's life unravelled, the house was an assurance, a contingency if Ipsden were suddenly to be let. In her mind, however, living there would be a last resort.

News of the war reached Rosamond as she lay in a nursing home recovering from a miscarriage ('a thing the size of a thrush').[88] As Europe splintered into conflict, she was experiencing her own 'physical & spiritual black-out'.[89] The first winter of the war was incredibly cold. Goronwy gave up his position at the *Spectator* for active service, and, with Wogan in London, Rosamond stayed at home in the country. She was shut off again, absorbed in 'a lot of reading, & solitude'. Outside, the landscape was transformed into a 'spectacle of great fascination & beauty'. A story in the local paper described peacocks frozen to the ground, each encased in a crystal shell of ice. Sally, the cook, and the housemaid both came down with flu, giving Rosamond a brief and unwelcome experience 'of doing or rather skimping all the work of the house'. Nevertheless, the freezing weather was a helpful distraction. 'In a way I think the icy spell got us through the winter,' she wrote to Frances Partridge in February 1940. 'It absorbed one completely & there was very little energy left over to brood about the war.'[90]

Alone at Ipsden, however, Rosamond was becoming anxious. She worried about Hugo at school, wishing he was at home and safely 'under my wing'.[91] And she lived for the rare occasions when she could see Goronwy, saving up petrol to pick him up from Sandhurst for a weekend's leave. Once, he took her and Hugo for a day out at Bristol Zoo. Beneath the shadow of war, and with her lover in uniform, the relationship was becoming increasingly urgent for Rosamond. 'I miss him enormously,' she told Frances, '& often ask myself what horrors will continue to separate us & for how long.'[92] Everyday life took on a precarious, pressing appearance. '[W]hat is going to happen to us?' she wrote to Compton Mackenzie in the early summer of 1940, as German troops advanced through Belgium, the Netherlands and into France.

'This is so TERRIFIC. If only I could do something. What can one do? All day & night I feel as if I were pushing at an overwhelming weight, pushing back the whole German army. [. . .] I wish I could talk to someone. How much longer shall we even be in touch with friends? There's so much to say, to do. Is there time?'[93]

War was creeping steadily across England. At Reading station in May, Rosamond watched trains crowded with British Expeditionary Force soldiers returning from Dunkirk. 'It haunts me day & night,' she told Beatrix. 'Carriage after carriage in total silence, *stacked* with khaki uniforms, their bearded faces utterly serene in the sleep of exhaustion. One could only weep.'[94] Yet she was reluctant to become too involved in the local war effort. Informed she would be receiving a group of evacuees from east London, she prepared Ipsden in a frenzy. 'Oh dear! how little I want them,' she told Compton Mackenzie.

It just makes my last faint hope of preserving a little leisure for writing recede altogether. Were I to say to our local billeting office: 'Lady Low, I am a writer – the fortunes of my family & the upkeep of the house partly depend on my being able to continue to write. My circumstances make it almost impossible to practise my profession: you are now taking away my last hope –' I wonder what the answer would be. A cackle of laughter, I expect – & the grim words: 'It is compulsory.'[95]

In the event, eleven small children were delivered to Ipsden, refusing to sleep anywhere but the floor, wetting their beds, and obviously unhappy. Rosamond noticed two of them had scarlet fever. She called an ambulance, took Sally from the house, and had the place disinfected. So much for writing, she thought a little selfishly. Ipsden, war, her world: all were spiralling rapidly into disorder.

~

In November, Rosamond was reading *The Times* when she came across a notice announcing Goronwy's engagement to someone else. It appeared, in the end, that he felt little inclination for long-term commitment with a twice-married mother of two. Rosamond's grief at being so completely abandoned by both husband and lover was extreme. She had pinned her hopes of a future beyond her marriage on Goronwy, and was distraught. From Ipsden, Beatrix reported 'beating of head, lying senseless on the floor, calling for brandy, screams and cries' a little disbelievingly to their brother John.[96] Rosamond was now faced with the prospect of leaving Ipsden for good. In the end, the house had failed to offer her the tranquillity – in her family life and her writing – she desired. But, though it had become a 'place of painful memories', the alternative was bleaker: 'I dread too much the idea of living alone.'[97] Yet, out of the depths of her despair, she was trying to write. Waiting for Goronwy's final letter, she wrote a story about a woman lying in bed in a country house, watching through a fever as a man removes a swarm of bees from the wall beneath her bedroom window. It is winter and the bees are dying. The woman, having imagined a private supply of sweetness to see her through the war, learns that the honey is spoiled and realizes her self-delusion. She chastises herself bitterly: 'Life doesn't arrange stories with happy endings any more, see?'[98]

In the midst of private crisis and social turmoil, novels were beyond her. Instead, she turned to episodes, and atmosphere. She was beginning some of her most personal work. The story, called 'A Dream of Winter', was the first in a trilogy about a countrywoman living in rural England during wartime. 'I have been struggling with it,' she admitted to John, submitting the piece to *New Writing*, 'only it's seemed like getting one's head & hand out of a swamp to do it, for about an hour a day – then going down again in[to] the foul sticky mud.'[99] But she was encouraged by her friend, the writer Henry Yorke (who published under the pen name Henry Green), who told her it was 'the best I've read of that length since Chekov. [. . .] I really do mean it & hardly ever feel like this [. . .] about some-one else's work.'[100] Though she was living 'in a twilight state', Rosamond was receiving 'more praise than I've had for years'.[101]

~

In late March, as Rosamond – alone – was packing and preparing Ipsden for new tenants, she learned of Virginia Woolf's death. The news was published in *The Times* on 3 April, though it had been circulating among friends for several days. John Lehmann had been among the first to hear. Virginia had sent him the manuscript of her novel, *Between the Acts*, unsettled by the completion of what she felt to be a 'slight and sketchy' book, 'too silly and trivial' for publishing. The following day, on 28 March 1941, fearing another breakdown from which she might never recover, she drowned herself in the River Ouse, about a mile's walk from Monk's House.[102] When her body was found three weeks later, it was drifting downstream near Asheham, where a group of cyclists out from Lewes had stopped for a picnic.

There had been genuine affection between the two women. Introduced by John – who was friends with Virginia's nephew, Julian Bell, from Cambridge – they were separated by a generation, and yet shared a sensibility in writing and living. As a young novelist, Rosamond had looked up to her predecessor, a role Virginia appeared to enjoy. Once, at a dinner party, watching Rosamond talking freely with her male peers, Virginia tapped her on the shoulder and said teasingly: 'Remember, we won this for you!'[103] Later, Virginia treated Rosamond kindly, writing to her when she was ill – 'What a bore being ill is [. . .] except that it's rather nice lying in a garden feeling enormously wise, which I don't do when I'm taking an active part in life' – or to ask about her books.[104] They were both, in many ways, country writers. 'Are you always catching the last train?' Virginia had written. 'That is my impression of you, flying across London to the shades of Oxfordshire – oh how nice!'[105] Privately, Virginia praised Rosamond's writing, expressing admiration for her novels, which displayed 'all the gifts [. . .] that I lack'.[106]

In the weeks following Virginia's death, Rosamond struggled to concentrate and couldn't read. In 'Letter to a Friend', an essay for *New Writing*, she described her search for reassurance in the literature of the past – in the work of Flaubert, Stendhal and 'the great Victorians' – 'but just now the idea of them makes me depressed [. . .] that broad, humanitarian, romantic, expanding scene gives me a nostalgia that has more pain in it than pleasure'.[107] Her world was constricting. During his final visits to Ipsden, John recalled the 'sense of imminent doom and ending' that flavoured the long talks with his sister. Walking in the afternoon, or sitting up late into the evening, the siblings – striking, imperious, now both prematurely grey – tried to imagine the world that would emerge out of the war, what it would do to literature, and what they each hoped to write. 'And day and night the aeroplanes from the Berkshire and Oxfordshire aerodromes roared overhead.'[108]

In early May 1941, Rosamond found herself in one of the small servants' bedrooms on the third floor of her childhood home, surrounded by packing cases. She had finally left Ipsden. But if she was hoping for a moment in which to collect herself, she was to be disappointed. Her mother, Alice Lehmann, was a formidable organizer and member of the county council, and had given the house over to the Air Raid Precaution. Fieldhead was noisy: during the day, ARP wardens and the Red Cross busied themselves in the downstairs rooms; each night, the floors became littered with the drowsy forms of ambulance drivers waiting for the air raid. As soon as the siren sounded, they roused themselves, started the ambulances in the driveway, and set out on their journey into west London.

Rosamond was a spare part in the bustling house. She sensed her mother's displeasure at her arrival, and her disappointment in the daughter who, at forty, was soon to be divorced for the second time. Rosamond's life had broken apart, as if mirroring the chaos around her. After years of arguments and reprieves, the end of her marriage had come quickly. She was, she wrote sadly to her sister, 'baffled and bewildered'.[109] She didn't know how she would get through it this time.

Caught between places, Rosamond considered her options. Should she go to Diamond Cottage, bought during the spring of 1939 as a safeguard against the failure of her marriage, and then dreamed of as a home for her and Goronwy, or London? The cottage was let, and the thought of living there alone depressed her. And yet the city was no place for children. Perhaps she should go to Cambridge, to be nearer Dadie? Her plans hovered in the air.

~

In the early years of the war, John Lehmann, having set up an office in the house, visited Fieldhead frequently from London. Sensing his sister was adrift, he suggested she become a reader for *New Writing*, which was now being published by the Hogarth Press. It was a gesture which proved useful to them both: 'Clear she is going to be an excellent reader-adviser over mss,' he noted in his diary.[110] And, following the success of two earlier stories – 'The Gypsy's Baby' and 'The Red-Haired Miss Daintreys', both written at Ipsden – he asked Rosamond for more of her own contributions to the magazine. Tentatively, she agreed. 'I think I can undertake to do you a bit of prose each month that won't be like other people's. Will that satisfy you?'[111]

With *New Writing* business to attend to, Rosamond escaped Fieldhead for London as often as she could. In early summer, the city was fizzing. There were queues for food and transport, and each evening, as blackout fell, the streets were plunged into darkness. It was the tail-end of the Blitz, and, though sirens continued to wail, nightlife proliferated. The dangers of the city heightened feelings and quickened new attachments; wives and children were evacuated elsewhere. (Elizabeth Bowen, working as an ARP warden near her flat at Regent's Park, distilled the atmosphere of the city, its mood of 'unmarriedness', in *The Heat of the Day*.[112]) For the time being, Rosamond was behaving herself. For two nights a week, she stayed in a flat at Rutland Gate with Henry Yorke, whose novel *Party Going* had come out in in 1939 with the Hogarth Press. He was working night shifts as an auxiliary fireman on Davies Street. She was desperately anxious, planning to be in London, she told John, 'off & on' until Ipsden 'is finally disposed of [. . .] and I make my mind up what to do. It is all very sad bad and hard.'[113] She saw little of Yorke, who entered the house just as she was leaving each morning, his face blackened with smoke. Later, she remembered those weeks in London as like 'an interminable, suffocating, over-crowded tunnel', in which 'from time to time [we] saw one another's faces lit by lurid and scorching flares; and sometimes the tunnel roared and rocked as if it were about to fall down upon and bury us altogether.'[114]

But it wasn't long before she succumbed to London's amorousness. Having recently reviewed two volumes of his poetry in *New Writing*, she received an invitation from Cecil Day Lewis to dinner. They had known each other since meeting at a party hosted by Elizabeth Bowen in 1933. ('[I] rather lost my heart to him,' Rosamond had gushed afterwards to Stephen Spender. 'He's beautiful, isn't he?'[115]) The following year, she had urged Dadie Rylands to read Cecil's manifesto, *A Hope for Poetry*, to his Cambridge undergraduates. As time went on, the two writers maintained a distant flirtatiousness, praising each other's speeches at the event at the Queen's Hall and suggestively reviewing each other's work. Cecil described Rosamond as 'a very talented writer indeed' after *The Weather in the Streets* was published in 1936, praising the novel – about Olivia's affair with a married man – 'for many reasons, not least its power to put any number of ideas into the head of a jaded reviewer'.[116]

Along with Auden, Spender and Louis MacNeice – whom he had met at Oxford – Cecil had become known as one of the 'Thirties Poets', brought to prominence by John Lehmann at the Hogarth Press, most notably in the landmark 1932 anthology, *New Signatures*. With John as editor, the poets ushered in a new mood to suit the decade, one that was highly politicized and left wing. Rejecting the modernism of their forebears, the young poets eschewed Bloomsbury and Eliot to write about the most pressing challenges of the day. But it was Cecil's slim, fervent manifesto which established his reputation. In *A Hope for Poetry*, he argued that poets played a vital role in articulating contemporary issues – from economic recession and unemployment to the war in Spain. His ideas were innovative, and the pamphlet was an immediate success. Even MI5 caught wind of it. Alerted by its rhetoric, an agent was sent to spy on Cecil as he went about in London. But he was disappointed. Off the page, Cecil was rather less charismatic, with all the appearance of his day job as a Devon schoolmaster. The agent was put out that he wasn't wearing a hat.

Rosamond seemed not to mind that Cecil was married. His wife, Mary, lived in the village of Musbury in Devon with their two young sons, and knew little about her husband's London life. Over dinner, hearing about Rosamond's awkward living arrangements between Fieldhead and Rutland Gate, Cecil offered her the use of the service flat below his own at Buckingham Gate. Rosamond accepted, and the progress of the affair was swift. 'I must live with my darling this autumn, this time is so short, every day & minute without her is something lost irretrievably, *nothing* can make up for it,' Cecil wrote to her during the summer.[117] By September 1941, the two had moved into a small rented flat at 31 Gordon Place, off Kensington High Street, where they could enjoy the privacy of makeshift domesticity. When it looked as if Cecil was going to be called up, Rosamond appealed to Harold Nicolson at the Ministry of Information – home to many military-averse artists and writers – who secured Cecil an editorial position in the Publications Department for the duration of the war.

The arrival of Cecil in Rosamond's life was timely. After Goronwy, she had been 'utterly crushed', and ready 'to break with everything'.[118] A short time later, sitting across from the handsome poet in a London restaurant, she felt a future glimmer. She was like Olivia, sitting across from Rollo on the train, about to embark on her journey into the dark. It was about *The Weather in the Streets* that Stephen Spender had written to Rosamond with the accusation that her characters were too hungry for love. Her women, he wrote, were 'gamblers', staking their entire lives on one relationship, so that 'there is nothing else for them at all'. And if the relationship breaks down or goes away, 'one would have asked what are they going to do now? and the answer must be, go through the same set of experiences with someone else – or nothing.'[119] Rosamond was a gambler. Her lack of success seemed not to surprise her – 'I select love-objects who must bring me to disaster,' she had written ruefully after Goronwy – and yet didn't prevent her from making the same mistakes.[120] War, uncertainty, a certain degree of self-delusion – with these, she pursued the affair recklessly. 'Lovers went on looking on the bright side, stitching cosy linings, hopeful of saving and fattening all the private promises,' she would write a year later in one of her darkening wartime stories.[121]

As her relationship with Cecil unfolded, Diamond Cottage lodged itself in her mind. At first, it had been a temporary solution, a contingency while she worked out what she wanted. Having thought she would live there with Goronwy, Rosamond now saw the cottage as a place to be with Cecil. 'I've no doubts now that you & I could make a success of living together,' he wrote to her during those first months.[122] But she also needed a home of her own, somewhere she could be with her children, beyond her mother's disapproval and out of reach of London's bombs. Despite her great need for love, she possessed an instinct for survival. Relationships, she had learned, were unreliable; she knew she must be able to look after herself. Cecil's marriage, his war-work in London, the children and her own determination to write were all factors in the marking-out of their boundaries and routines. It was decided that Rosamond would spend a night or two in London each week, but remain in the

A friend of Barbara Ker Seymer's at Diamond Cottage, 1941

country, and Cecil – when not obliged to go to Devon – would visit at weekends. Along with the pleasures of a new romance, Rosamond's solitude would be preserved. After years of an unhappy and volatile marriage, she allowed herself this arrangement: she would be independent, a countrywoman; at the weekends, a wife.

After several weeks at Gordon Place, Rosamond turned her attention to the country. For most of that year, the cottage had been let to Barbara Ker-Seymer, to whom she felt she owed little. Soon, she had given Barbara notice, packed up her belongings at Field-head and moved in.

Spring 1942, and the chaos of the previous year was dissipating. At Diamond Cottage, Rosamond was reaching a settled feeling. She had been working on a feature programme about George Eliot – a 'sort of play' – for the BBC, and was in the first hard-thinking stages of a new book, 'a long complicated story which I don't yet understand the import of myself'.[123] Save her letters to friends, there is relatively little to document this period of Rosamond's life. A slender volume of short stories would come to stand for this middle period, the quiet years from 1942 until 1946, when she lived at the cottage. Her time in Aldworth would later represent an interval, not much spoken about, in which she had started out as a newly solitary mother before falling into a rehearsal of married life. Later, there would always be the turbulent period before Cecil, and the afterwards. The relationship itself – 'years of tremendous happiness – within difficulties, but great happiness' – became muted, and was allowed to slip through the cracks.[124] Only one side of the lovers' correspondence – Cecil's – survives. And only once in her letters, many years later, did Rosamond refer, not quite wistfully, to 'those far-off Aldworth days'.[125]

But, for the time being, she had found security, and was content. Was this an exercise of pragmatism? It was essential she hold her nerve. Settling into the village required a new kind of courage, the negotiation of her ambiguous social status, and a different way of living. Clouded by war, Rosamond's years in Aldworth were unglamorous years of making do, of seeking refuge, of managing. They would have a different texture to those she had experienced previously in her large house. And yet they would prove quietly sustaining. Making do is still a kind of making. For the first time, Rosamond was living on her own terms, absorbing her own rural hours, like Sylvia had in Dorset, or Virginia at Asheham. Looking to the future, Rosamond knew she must face down the challenges of war and bring up her children as best she could; she must brave the weather, and she must write.

~

The trouble was, she told William Plomer, 'My life is spent in housework, gardening, standing in food queues [. . .] – It might be a very great deal worse, and I realise my luck – but writing is always being squeezed out.'[126] Cecil attempted to encourage her. 'I want you to flower as a writer because of our love,' he wrote from London, 'to have enormous new energy & all sorts of new things to write about, & a stronger impulse than ever before.'[127] Evidently, Rosamond resisted: 'I certainly don't want you to feel that I'm fussing about your writing,' he followed hastily, 'trying to drive you on.'[128]

Instead, Rosamond took pleasure in the children while they were home for the school holidays. Hugo, who was thirteen, was soon to start at Eton (though the battle over his fees continued with Wogan's father, 1st Baron Milford); while Sally, aged eight, was at Westonbirt, having been taken out of the village classes she attended at Ipsden. They were different: the dark-haired and self-composed boy – whom Rosamond would soon describe as 'my uncommunicative son' – and the blonde, pink-cheeked girl, growing like 'a large luxurious dahlia' and 'the only totally unmixed joy in my life'.[129]

Home life was often a matter of contrivance. Along with basic foodstuffs such as sugar, bacon and cheese, petrol, clothes and soap were among the latest goods being strictly rationed. 'I am surveying my orts and greasy relics in the larder & wondering how I can provide Sally with a birthday party tomorrow,' Rosamond wrote to

Plomer. 'The only step forward I've made is to woo Mr McQuhae in the bakehouse last night & wring 2 lbs of icing sugar out of him.'[130] Sally was frightened at the sound of the gunners taking off from the aerodrome at nearby Hampstead Norreys, and slept with her gas mask beside her bed. Yet Rosamond marvelled at the resilience of small children, and dreaded her return, along with Hugo's, to school. As summer drew to a close, their last days at home sped by in 'hectic last-minute washings, mendings, packings & conveyings'. She drove Sally to the train station, and watched as her daughter 'turned pale green as the train drew in, and gave me a smile through pressed lips [. . .]. She will be all right, I know, but I came home rather lacerated.'[131] Without them both, the 'house ached horribly'.[132] But Rosamond was by no means lonely. She still had with her Mrs Wickens, and Cecil at weekends.

With the children away at school, the lovers established a rhythm between London and the country. On Friday evenings, after finishing work at Senate House, Cecil caught a train from Paddington, arriving in the village a few hours later. 'Darling, darling, darling love,' he wrote in one of his many letters from Senate House, 'build yourself up [. . .] – plenty of food, rest & exercise – you'll need all your strength at the weekend – I shall come at you like a tiger, a cloud burst, a toppling mountain, an arrow out of the sun.'[133] He often telephoned Rosamond during Ministry hours, though his director was wont to march in. At the cottage, she would be waiting for him. Her pleasure lay in anticipation, in the weekly ritual of their reunion. Afterwards, they spent their days quietly, reading or walking through the village arm in arm, Rosamond with her shining halo of hair, Cecil conspicuous in his long city coat. At the cottage, he helped Rosamond to chop logs and, in the evenings, entertained her by singing ballads. The most mundane, domestic things pleased her the most. She slipped into wifeliness, telling John she was nursing Cecil through his tenth day of toothache.

In December 1942, Rosamond invited Laurie Lee to stay, having met the poet the previous August in the foyer of the BBC. He was still little known: it would be over ten years before he made his name with his account of his Gloucestershire childhood, *Cider with Rosie*. Walking down Oxford Street together, Rosamond was keen to make his acquaintance. She had read his poems in manuscript – 'beautiful, rich, melancholy' things, she told him – and asked him to visit her at Gordon Place.[134] The next time he was in London, Laurie made his way to Kensington, finding Rosamond in a genteel, cluttered flat. Rosamond put the kettle on and the two talked in the kitchen for a long time, Rosamond telling Laurie about her youth with frankness and simplicity. He was startled by her openness. 'I think perhaps she has this drowsy easy manner because she no longer cares to strike attitudes,' he wrote in his diary the following day. 'From her books she seems tender & sentimental, and in real life she is no different.' When Cecil came in from work, he looked 'thin and brown' but was 'easy & friendly'. Laurie noticed how the couple 'sat together in the same chair'.[135] The evening at Gordon Place was the first of many the three writers spent together. Rosamond and Cecil, older than Laurie by a decade, were drawn to his uncomplicated manner, his unpretentiousness, which was so unlike their other literary friends.

Rosamond wanted Laurie to see her at Diamond Cottage. He was part of her new chapter with Cecil, a friendship untarnished by the conflicts and loyalties of her divorce. He was also, in many ways, similar to Cecil: left-wing, musical, interested in folk songs and rural ways, and not – like the men Rosamond had previously chosen to be in her life – upper class. That December, Laurie met Cecil at Paddington and the two travelled together, stopping for tea and buns at Reading before taking the bus to Aldworth, on which they played pocket draughts. Arriving at the cottage, Rosamond opened the door looking, as Laurie told his diary, 'flowery, handsome'. But he was disappointed with the evening's entertainment. After supper, the trio walked down the lane to a 'weary official Warship Week film show' in the village hall, at which Laurie was introduced to Anne Scott-James ('very Vogue') and Laurence Binyon ('sour & dull & aloof').[136] The next day, however, his spirits improved. He woke early, and walked out into the field where snowdrops were beginning to appear in the hedge. Cecil and Rosamond joined him in the garden, and they took turns taking photographs of each other. After lunch, Laurie went outside to dig while the lovers went for a walk. He was conscious of his presence during their little time together: 'One feels almost guilty to be here, but they shouldn't have asked me.'[137]

The following morning, after Cecil had left for London, Laurie sat with Rosamond in the kitchen in what was shifting into intimacy, she sewing curtains and talking, 'telling me much of her life', of Cecil, '& how & what they meant to each other'.[138] Once again, her openness disconcerted him. He was unsettled by her, as if he couldn't decide whether her freedom from affectation was genuine, or affectation itself.

Laurie's diary of 1942 reveals his mistrustfulness of the Lehmann siblings and their circle. His literary reputation was taking off, but, though his poems had appeared in *Horizon* and his account of fighting in Spain was published in *New Writing*, he had little confidence in his ability to make his way as a writer. Early that year, when he accepted work from the Crown Film Unit – the Ministry of Information's film department, which produced documentaries for the general public – he saw it as a compromise artistically, but an opportunity too lucrative to pass up. John Lehmann, meanwhile, was urging him to continue writing autobiography, suggesting he turn to his childhood in the Cotswolds: 'We are very anxious to have more articles about England and the English countryside [. . .]. The Spanish diary was such a success.'[139] But John intimidated him, as did the other poets he met: Spender, Auden, a swaying Dylan Thomas in the foyer of the BBC. ('[T]hey are sharp and clever, they hypnotise me.'[140]) At parties in John's flat, Laurie drank orangeade and shrank from his host's 'lofty diplomatic smile'.[141] And on the back of one of the first envelopes Rosamond sent him, he drew the Lehmann family tree: the siblings, Helen (whom he had met briefly at the Athenaeum), Rosamond, Beatrix, an actress, and the formidable John; their parents and great-grandparents, one of whom, Robert Chambers, founded the Chambers Dictionary. Laurie had been born in a cottage in the Gloucestershire village of Slad, the youngest of five children. He was trying to make sense of these intellectual, domineering siblings. When he heard from John that

Rosamond liked his poems and wished to meet him, he felt 'almost guilty as if I'm cheating them all'.[142] His personal life was also in turmoil. For five years, he had been in a relationship with Lorna Wishart, the youngest of the bohemian Garman sisters, with whom he secretly had a daughter. But Lorna was married, and would soon leave Laurie to begin a relationship with the painter Lucian Freud.

Neither, when she first met Laurie, did Rosamond have a sure footing. She was shuttling between London and Fieldhead, and searching desperately for things onto which her life could hook and secure itself. Encountering the young poet, she felt a genuine desire for new friendship. And, like her brother John, she believed in supporting emerging writers. She saw in Laurie's poems something worth nurturing. 'Laurie, *please* don't destroy any of your poems unless you yourself are convinced they are of no use,' she wrote. 'It upset me, your saying you had done so because John didn't like them. He is often a sound critic, but by no means always, to my mind. What *one* person is?' Of her own work, she confessed she was struggling. Her new novel was refusing to take shape. 'Every time I try to concentrate on it I feel frightened of it, it seems too complex – and something in me frantically resists,' she wrote.[143] And writing was a challenge logistically. Any serious work was 'difficult to combine with looking after my two extremely energetic children'. She confided in Laurie: 'I've always thought how satisfactory it would be to pull off being a good artist as well as being a successful mother; but time alone will tell if I've done anything of the sort.'[144]

The terms of their relationship were complex. While Laurie enjoyed a simple friendship with Cecil – playing pin-tables after work and discussing poetry over late-night Greek suppers on Percy Street – Rosamond wished to confide in Laurie, and keep him close. He, in turn, eyed her entreaties suspiciously, fearing she could be 'superficial' like her brother.[145] (There was also the matter of Lorna's jealousy: several times, after discovering Rosamond's letters, Lorna had flown into a rage.) Yet, during an unstable period in his life, when both literary success and Lorna seemed beyond his grasp, Laurie found himself at Diamond Cottage. Despite his misgivings, he liked Cecil and Rosamond, and his affection for the couple grew. During his visit that December, Rosamond was 'quieter, kinder' than when he had seen her in London, and the weekend passed easily.[146] Laurie chopped wood and in the afternoon worked through a book of ballads with Cecil, Cecil singing while he played his pipe. Later, Rosamond read Jane Austen aloud. (This was her vision of a perfect sitting-room scene: no political hectoring, no boots on the furniture.) At one point, Laurie admitted he was the father of a little girl. Rosamond was instantly curious. (In 1939, Cecil, too, had fathered a baby with the wife of a Musbury farmer, who had accepted the child as his own.) She asked: 'Were you married then?' And: 'Is the mother married?' Warily, Laurie dodged her questions. That night, struggling to sleep beneath 'insufficient blankets', he felt extremely cold.[147] He was mistrustful again. Was Rosamond's solicitousness sincere? The drama between them hadn't yet played itself out. In the morning, Laurie took a taxi through the dawn to Goring, and caught the first London train.

Cecil and Laurie in the garden at Diamond Cottage

~

As 1942 drew to a close, Rosamond was embedding herself in the country. Her trips to London – to see John on *New Writing* business, or to lunch with Cecil outside his offices at Senate House – were becoming less frequent, and she had grown used to absenting herself from literary parties and events. Diamond Cottage had brought with it contentment and a gradual change in her state of mind. She was retreating into private life. 'I have given up all forms of public living,' she told Rayner Heppenstall. 'They're not my line, and never were.'[148] In the village, her identity as a single woman with a lover had, to all intents and purposes, been accepted. Given her class, she was able – as not all women might have been – to inhabit multiple roles: the solitary, self-supporting writer; the housewife, queuing for provisions; the amorous woman ambling with her lover down the street. She was not unappreciative. 'I am pretty contented and peaceful these days,' she wrote to Henry Yorke, '[and] very much a part of this village community.'[149]

Cecil's letters grew more loving. He teased Rosamond with visions of companionable domestic life, with the image of two lovers reading side by side. The pain of separation intensified when he was in Devon. From Musbury, he wrote to Rosamond of the bright weather, 'but oh the sunshine has a fearful effect on me – it makes me want to take you into a wood over the hill, & undress you & kiss the leaf-shadows moving over your body, & love you till you are quite quite dead'.[150] Most of all, he asked Rosamond to trust him. 'I want to give you back all your confidence, [. . .] & comfort you whenever you feel lost,' he wrote. 'I would like to [. . .] be a land-locked harbour for you.' And: 'you can rely on me'.[151]

Rosamond, for her part, believed him. 'I am so peaceful & happy,' she told John. 'I think I feel confidence for the first time in my life. I never thought it could happen – but he has given me this by the incredible goodness & patience of his love. You've no idea what a true, reliable, grown-up character he is.'[152] As her attachment to Cecil deepened, the proportions of her love for him grew. She wrote to Dadie of her happiness, of her sureness in the relationship: 'I don't see what the future will be – but I don't think it can go wrong through lack of love and trust.'[153] Love was converting itself into creative energy. Finally, after the toneless, barren mood that had trailed in the wake of war, and the interruptions caused by domestic life, she declared, 'I am writing hours every day'.[154]

~

Between 1939 and 1944, Rosamond produced five stories for *New Writing*, later published as *The Gypsy's Baby*. The first two stories in the collection, 'The Gypsy's Baby' and 'The Red-Haired Miss Daintreys', were nostalgic pieces of childhood reminiscence written during the first months of the war, when she was still at Ipsden. The final three – two short, and one very much longer story – formed a series. It was these which would come to stand as the record of Rosamond's wartime experience. Describing episodes in the life of a woman living with her children in the country, Rosamond, inadvertently, created a trilogy, and a small masterpiece. The stories were darker, more sombre than anything she had written before. She struggled with them. 'Here it is, for better or worse,' she wrote to John, sending off the first, the story of the bee man. 'An agony of difficulty & unsatisfactoriness to myself. No time to get it typed. I meant only to be able to think in terms of winter.'[155]

Rosamond set the first two stories of the trilogy in the bitterly cold winter of 1939. It was the period of the 'Phoney War', when England waited uneasily for hostilities to begin. In the stories, war is unsettling and unseen, 'sprawled everywhere inert: like a child too big to get born'. The weather is an almost-welcome distraction. The 'persisting cold, the catastrophes of British plumbing' take precedence 'as everybody's topic and experience. It became the political situation.'[156] And yet weather harbingers danger: animals die; rivers freeze, then flood. Islanded in her large house, the woman protects her young family from the cold. The indoor comforts of their soft beds, the children's hot baths, and the daily miracle of meals are the more reassuring because of the dangers outside. Theirs is a world threatened, poised between catastrophe and survival. Later, we learn the woman is called Margaret Ritchie. She is middle aged, and mostly solitary. Her husband has left her, and her children are lively, matter of fact and always hungry. Yet she manages, despite food shortages and the demands of her neighbours. As war encroaches into daily life, it is the small dramas of home and village life which absorb her.

But Margaret Ritchie is no Mrs Miniver. Neither overly domesticated nor a busybody, she remains abstract and a little aloof. (It was Rosamond's sister, Beatrix Lehmann, who wrote satirical stories about English villages for *New Writing*, with characters such as Mrs Boote-Smith dealing with hordes of incontinent evacuees.) Rather, Margaret is a later version of Rosamond's younger women, of the Olivia Curtis kind. Though she no longer sits in bedsits, smoking and daydreaming, her happiness remains precarious; relationships, we learn, have broken down. She continues to while away hours in idle contemplation, mostly at night, in alternating tides of melancholy and well-being. Her creation was significant for Rosamond. No longer interested in the rootless young women of her early novels, she was beginning to look for different – changed, older – kinds of women; and she was switching urban malaise for rural landscapes. In describing the middle period of a countrywoman's life, she was marking her transition from ambivalence into motherhood and maturity.

The first story of the trilogy, 'When the Waters Came', opens retrospectively – 'Very long ago, during the first winter of the present war' – and leads with a sequence of atmospheric scenes. A great freeze has taken place, transforming the village and the surrounding landscape into an ethereal spectacle. Vegetables come in from the garden mantled in ice; in the street, the women report sheep frozen to the ground, and a peacock found sheathed in a 'crystal case'. The country is luminous, unearthly; it rings with a hollow sound. The story's pacing is unhurried, slow: we are in winter time, rural hours. 'Later she put on nailed shoes and walked with difficulty over the snowy field path to the post office.' That night, in her 'soft bed', the woman listens to the ice shattering. It is 'the end of the world':

She heard the branches in the garden snapping and crashing down with a brittle rasp. It seemed as if the inside of the earth with all its roots and foundations had become separated from the outside by an impenetrable bed of iron; so that everything that grew above the surface must inevitably break off like matchwood, crumble and fall down.

In February, the thaw comes. The snow melts and torrents of water, stained blood-red from the ploughed fields, gush into the village. The farm is submerged and cottages are flooded; ducks cruise beneath the apple trees: 'Wherever you looked, living waters spouted, trickled, leaped with intricate overlapping voices into the dance. Such sound and movement after so many weeks of silence and paralysis made you feel light-headed, dizzy; as if you, too, must be swept off and dissolved.' Warily, the woman walks with her children through the flood, watching as they wade into the distance, becoming smaller, separating, racing sticks, gathering the yellowish foam-whip into piles. ' "Stay together!" '[157]

The next in the series, 'A Dream of Winter', is gloomier. Rosamond had written the story in November 1940, as she waited for Goronwy's final letter. 'It's a queer bit of work,' she told John, '& may not be any good.'[158] But the result, written out of the pain of her desertion and steeped in anxieties about the war, was exceptionally fine. As with 'When the Waters Came', Rosamond had settled on the boundary between safety and danger, exploring a plush interior world which only just manages to fend off the dangers outside. She knew she had hit upon something good. Later, sending the manuscript to Dadie Rylands, she told him to expect 'what I think is my best short story'.[159]

In the story, the same woman lies in bed with influenza, watching as the bee man removes the swarm which has been living in the leads of the balcony roof beneath her bedroom window. It is winter still, and she looks out on a hard, 'mineral landscape'. She has cherished the hope of honey, a 'sweet cheat' to see her through the war, but there is none. As waves of fever beat over her, the woman is engulfed by self-reproach: she was complacent, and shouldn't have waited so long. Yet the dying swarm represents more than her own private failure; it symbolizes another turning, the social changes the war is bringing.

> Just as I thought. Another sentimental illusion. Schemes to produce food by magic strokes of fortune. [. . .] This source of energy whose living voice comforted you at dawn, at dusk, saying: We work for you. Our surplus is yours, there for the taking – vanished! [. . .] It's no use this time, my girl! Supplies are getting scarce for people like you. An end, soon, of getting more than their fair share for dwellers in country houses.

The woman – who, we are told with some irony, 'had had a lot of leisure in her life to look at faces. She had friends with revolutionary ideas, and belonged to the Left Book Club' – senses her world, like the brittle colony, is becoming extinct. But for people of her kind, entitlement wanes slowly, the prospect of a more democratic age greeted less with jubilation than a sense of inevitability.

There are other causes for self-chastisement. Reflecting on her pre-war life, the woman feels ashamed of her previously sluggish existence. 'It seemed to her that her passive, daydreaming, leisured life was nothing, in the last analysis, but a fluid element for receiving and preserving faint paradoxical images and symbols. They were all she ultimately remembered.'[160] She has wasted her life. And she has put her trust too readily into relationships, a gambler on a losing streak. Though the gentle humour of the story nourishes, there is a lingering, bitter taste. In the scouring winter of 1939, as she faced down minor household catastrophes and the collapse of her marriage, Rosamond had felt the threads of her life snapping and wearing thin. For too long she had worn her self-delusion like a protective cloak. *It's no use this time, my girl!* The time for comfort and leisure was over.

Rosamond had begun, more insistently than before, to write directly from life. The children in the stories, John and Jane, were barely disguised portraits of Hugo and Sally; Rosamond was, after all, using their middle names. And the events of the stories had real-life precedents. 'A Dream of Winter', she told her brother, John, was 'founded on the taking of the swarm of bees out of my roof' at Ipsden, while other images reached further into memory.[161] The war had put her in a backward-looking, searching mood, so that images from the past floated to the top. She recollected other misadventures: a boat trip on the Isle of Wight when, as the weather turned, she had feared for the children's lives; a walk in the Scottish Highlands when she lost her way and nearly died in the snow.* In both stories, there is an abiding sense of disaster narrowly averted, and both end with fatalistic, frail intimations of hope. When, in 'When the Waters Came', the little girl falls into the stream and is carried away, the woman feels as if she is watching a disaster about which she has always known, and yet one that both she and her daughter will survive. Later, after her bath, Jane cheerfully recounts her brush with danger.

'I thought I was done for that time,' said Jane complacently.

'It'll take more than that to finish you – worse luck,' said John, without venom. 'We haven't had a moment's peace, any of us, since you were born. Tomorrow I'm going to make a raft and see how far I can get.'

But tomorrow, all will be dry land again. What is it, exactly, that the family has survived? The woman looks out of the window onto an 'exposed' landscape of 'tender greens and browns'. She feels

* In *A Letter to a Sister*, Rosamond recalled walking in a snowstorm in Scotland in December 1925, when she fainted with the pain of cold feet. 'As for my one adventure, [. . .] I mean that one called A Twenty-Mile Tramp in a Snowstorm [. . .] I suppose I didn't really rise up from unconsciousness and float over snowhills and skim down sheer frozen valleys, infinitely powerful and exhilarated, and see the moon riding as full in dark blue deeps of air at half-past three in the afternoon? I know I thought at the time: "This is life indeed"; though I suppose what I should have said was: "This is whisky." ' Lehmann, *A Letter to a Sister*, 22–23.

hope stir in her, like a faint promise. She wonders, 'What will spring bring? Shall we be saved?'[162]

The following year, in late October 1943, when Associated Press correspondent Russell Landstrom asked Rosamond to give her feelings about the war from a writer's perspective, he received an unequivocal response. 'I don't think there is anything a writer of my kind can usefully say just now about the writers' "war effort" and about problems of future peace,' Rosamond wrote from Diamond Cottage.

> I am so tired of pronouncements and prophecies – writers' and politicians' and everybody's – I think of all our declarations before the war, and how infinitely feeble and ineffectual they were. I've retired from the manifesto-making fraternity – & can't see that I can do anything but try to write truthfully within my limits as a novelist, and attempt to preserve some personal values. I don't honestly believe that creative writers, at least of my calibre, have anything more than anybody else of political value to contribute at the moment. Ethical & aesthetic values, yes – but I think they'd better prove this, if they can, in their work – not to talk too much about them.[163]

Rosamond's reply was typical for a writer who had, if only for a time, been politically active before the war. There was much embarrassment among left-wing intellectuals in the admission that the socialist project of the 1930s had failed. In the chastened period of disillusionment which followed, writers were forced to publicly renegotiate their relationship with politics, to acknowledge, according to John Lehmann, 'the spiritual thinness of politics and political slogans' while accepting the 'need for a total reassessment, a new kind of philosophy evolving from artistic [. . .] experience'.[164] Only for Cecil, who was certainly in the minority, had the poetry calling for a classless society, an overhauled economic system in Britain and the principles of social responsibility, any lingering integrity. Unlike many of his contemporaries, including Stephen Spender, he refused to retract his work and would later look back on the 1930s as a visionary 'golden age'.[165] Rosamond, however, was adamant: novelists, she argued, were not spokespeople, and public proclamations were not, nor had ever been, part of the job. 'It was you [. . .] who first made me feel guilty about my lack of political consciousness & persuaded me to read Marx!' she wrote later to John. 'But I shall never be a political animal, could never surrender my conscience to any political party, – & can get no further now than a despairing feeling that every political party betrays the people.'[166] During the early 1940s, she distanced herself from the left, clarifying a position which had been – privately, at least – many years in the making. Throughout her adult life, she had vacillated between political ambiguity and a sort of embarrassed, half-hearted participation, often guided by those around her; now, writing in reply to the Associated Press, she was deliberately unresponsive and aloof. In political pronouncements, it was clear, she would no longer be taking part.

She was focusing her energies on other things: on her home life, on getting through the war, on a new book. A more traditional set of values was surfacing in both her style of living and her work. By 1943, four years safe beneath the impartial Berkshire sky, she was closer to contentment than she had been for a long time. Diamond Cottage had become, in the end, a retreat into a familiar outlook, and a place in which, at last, her inconsistences could flourish. There, she could be both politically aware – given her proximity to Cecil – and conservative, flitting between Berkshire and London. (It was an act of withdrawal both public and private, an elaboration of what, during her own wartime in Sussex, Virginia called 'immunity'.) Rosamond was unapologetic. After the fallout of her marriage to Wogan, she hadn't time for any more experiments in politics or in living, and couldn't afford any more failed attempts. She had arrived at a revised kind of happiness. 'Although my life has completely changed,' she wrote to Rayner Heppenstall, 'I am still in the country, under my own roof, with my children, within reach of my friends, and have privacy, and leisure to write.'[167]

But for all her contentment, Rosamond was living a compromise, and was beginning to feel the strain. She had accepted Cecil with the knowledge of his wife and their two young sons. In Musbury, Mary was getting through the war in her own way. Unaware of her husband's other life with Rosamond, she accepted without question his job at the Ministry, which required him to work most weekends. And when he wrote to her on Ministry-headed notepaper, it was to his office that she sent her newsy replies. The couple had been married for fifteen years. In Berkshire, Rosamond chose not to see Mary as a rival. The two women had, in fact, met in 1936 after Cecil invited Rosamond to address the Cheltenham Literary Society, of which he was chairman. Rosamond was disappointed by the evening. The audience, she told John, consisted of 'dozens and dozens of elderly ladies with iron-grey perms & pince nez', and afterwards, at the Day Lewises' small cottage, her hosts promptly went to bed.[168] In the morning, Cecil left early for school and Rosamond helped Mary make the children's beds. To Rosamond, Mary had seemed pleasant, shy, a dutiful schoolmaster's wife. She scanned her face for signs of her having been pretty. Rosamond, meanwhile, was Cecil's intellectual equal, and the love she was offering more mature, more demanding than Mary's wifely attention. She could take Cecil to parties in London, and introduce him to her wider literary circle. Alongside his job at the Ministry, Cecil began to give lectures and readings, was asked by the BBC to speak on the radio, and to read poetry on programmes such as *And So to Bed*, a weekly compilation put together by Eddy Sackville-West. Cecil's West Country schoolteaching days were behind him. 'You have pushed out the boundaries of my life in so many directions,' he wrote gratefully to Rosamond. 'I feel a new man – really, reborn, like you feel.'[169]

As their lives grew closer together, Rosamond began to hope – gently, at first – for marriage. Surely, Cecil would leave Mary to make a life with her, a life of loving in the country and moving in London literary circles, where he belonged? Cecil reasoned that to break up his home while his sons were young was impossible. On this one point he tried to be clear: marriage was out of the question. So began the couple's longest argument, a bitter rehearsal carried out in letters, or late at night in the kitchen at Diamond Cottage; its aftertaste lingering in the hasty goodbyes in the lane, the morning still dark, trailing Cecil into stuffy train carriages back to London, and turning those unavoidable periods of separation – working weeks, Christmases, school holidays – sour. 'Rosamond, my love, don't get too obsesed by me, will you?' Cecil wrote from his office. '– I mean, I couldn't bear to feel that you hadn't room to move, particularly to write, because I occupied too much of you.'[170] At other times, he fantasized about taking up her space: 'It would be better if we were married or living with each other all the time. But we can't. So we've got to make do with what we have & bear the pain of not having more.' It was all Cecil was able to offer her: 'anything more might be a betrayal all around'.[171]

But soon it was only Rosamond who felt betrayed. In April 1943, Cecil invited Laurie to visit him at Musbury, where he met Mary and the boys. It was 'golden weather', Laurie recorded in his diary, 'we played games & had an easy time'. A few days later, while on fire-watching duty in London, Cecil told Laurie how stressful he was finding 'juggling' his 'two worlds'.[172] He was in love with Rosamond, he confided, but only with Mary at Musbury could he truly relax. Would he be better off with neither? On one thing, both Laurie and Cecil were agreed: 'Marriage [. . .] is death to a poet.'[173] In Aldworth, Rosamond was becoming rattled. The foundations of her life were shaking again. She felt wounded, both by Cecil for asking Laurie into his other life, and by Laurie for agreeing to go. In a long letter, she reprimanded him. 'One of the few things apart from him-and-me that gives me a sense of solidarity & support is the few friends – very few – we are equally fond of, & who accept us as a couple, & whom I can think of as part of our shared life, with no branches back into the unshared past,' she wrote on 23 April. 'You are one of the very few.' But she also revealed the depth of her insecurity, and her extreme vulnerability in hoping to be made Cecil's wife.

The fact is I have taken on something which I can't *always* be equal to [. . .]. In spite of all its joys and beauties there are times when lack of confidence & anxiety about the future overwhelm me. I get terrified that wanting more than I can have will cause [. . .] disaster all round. What I want isn't at all abnormal [. . .]. I want to be with him and look after him [. . .] – in fact what women do want with the person they completely love & trust.

It was Cecil who had the upper hand, who could leave at a moment's notice. In her darkest moments, Rosamond told Laurie,

I get panic, & plunge back into the two bad old times, & feel the rivets in me straining & threatening to give way. I know there is cause for reasonable hope (marriage?) – but equally I know these are [. . .] grounds for alarm & despondency! His determination is to continue to reinforce both his lives, and I'm not at all sure he can do it. Apart from the moral & emotional problems there is the practical difficulty. How is he to divide his time etc? It is not a situation that depends on his wishes and behaviour alone: it is a tripod, & if one leg of it gives way, the whole thing collapses.

Her position was precarious. Like Olivia, her only choice was to accept the position of mistress: insecure, peripheral, demanding, loving in hope. Her arguments with Cecil were getting her nowhere. In the end, she had to accept the terms of their arrangement, though they left her 'even more exposed, & at a disadvantage'.[174]

And so Rosamond continued to take solace in life at the cottage, celebrating her birthday alone with a new issue of *New Writing* and 'hugging' Piper the cat. A neighbour gave her a pheasant, which Mrs Wickens roasted. 'I resisted the temptation to come to London and celebrate,' she wrote to John. 'But I feel a bit lonely!'[175] As her anguish over Laurie's visit to Musbury subsided, she was cheered by the children's arrival for the school holidays. Cecil promised to bring Hugo one or two detective novels from London, signing off his letter with those alluring, alarming words: 'When I come to Aldworth next.'[176] John asked her for another story, but, with the house full, she beat him off: 'Very very very sorry I am incapable of writing any-thing at the moment. In the intervals of washing, sweeping, mending, I am still correcting 3 typescripts.'[177] When he visited, the siblings walked in the woods. As in 1941, they talked about the war, and about their own writing: John's new poems and Rosamond's new book, *The Ballad and the Source.* She was progressing slowly, she told him, 'occasionally floundering, then swimming on a few painful strokes'.[178] A few weeks later, Laurie returned to Aldworth, forgiven, a prodigal son. He visited several times in June and July, spending his twenty-ninth birthday with Rosamond at the cottage. But his rela-tionship with Lorna had been going badly and he was depressed and unwell. Rosamond worried about him, and wrote to John asking if he could give Laurie 'any definite word' about publishing his poems.[179] Despite his health, Laurie delighted Sally with small con-certs on his fiddle. He and Cecil played dominoes, and after dinner Rosamond read aloud from *Invitation to the Waltz.* Once more, the lovers and the young poet formed a trio in the village. Rosamond felt easier: 'I am well, peaceful, generally happy, and very busy.'[180]

~

Rosamond's new novel had begun to take shape the previous spring when she discovered an underground hoard of childhood memories, 'a very queer country full of shadows & echoes'.[181] What started out as a short episode became 'a long, complicated story' and the writing difficult: 'when I get a flash of it I get the trembles, it seems to fright-ening & difficult to drag to the surface'.[182] She was 'moving in a most mysterious way [. . .] & don't know where or how to stop'.[183]

Written at Diamond Cottage between 1942 and 1944, *The Ballad and the Source* is the most enigmatic of Rosamond's books, and home to her most extravagant literary creation: Mrs Jardine. Wrapped in cloaks and jangling with beads, the exotic old woman tells the story of her life to a rapt young girl: a hearty melodrama of divorce, sexual pursuit, mental illness and an abandoned child. It was not entirely a success. Written mostly in dialogue, with key elements of the narrative relayed through reported speech, the reader can be forgiven for stumbling over plot and counter-plot. And, though compelling, the characters are perhaps too broadly drawn. And yet the novel marked an important transition for Rosamond. While she plugged away at her stories, drawing closely from life, she was also, in her longer work, shifting towards increasingly supernatural themes. In *A Letter to a Sister*, she had described a multi-sensory experience, a 'vision'; now, she was attempting to narrate a life in echoes and fragments, and was shifting steadily into a kind of non-chronological time.

By July, after months of 'plugging away', Rosamond was approaching the 'last lap'.[184] She was determined to finish quickly, within the next six months. She turned away visitors to the cottage, and refused trips to London. She felt her literary reputation at stake. 'I don't believe I shall ever do anything better, more concentrated,' she wrote to William Plomer. 'I mean, if it isn't any good, then I really am no good.'[185]

~

In September 1943, the peaceful atmosphere at Diamond Cottage was disturbed once more when Cecil's tenth volume of poetry, *Word Over All*, was published by Jonathan Cape. It was dedicated to Rosamond; Mary was sent a copy in the post. The collection was intensely personal. Cecil had emerged from his political hectoring of the 1930s into a more refined poetic voice, and, for all to see, was writing about his marriage, his mistress and his divided heart. In poems such as 'The Lighted House' and 'The Album', he celebrated the new love in his life; but there was also 'Departure in the Dark', which revealed the burden of responsibility, and the guilt, of living between two families at once.

To Mary, reading the poems in Musbury, all became clear. The following month, Cecil travelled to Devon to talk to her, while Rosamond waited anxiously for news. 'You can be sure that, when I talk to Mary, I shall not attempt to make light of the bond between you & me, any more than when I talk to you I can make light of the bond between her & me,' he wrote from the train, trying to reassure her. 'I do try very hard to be honest; but I can't say it comes natural to me.'[186] In the end, he proposed a compromise, which Mary accepted: he would divide his time between her and Rosamond until the boys left home. To Cecil, it seemed the solution was found by viewing the situation as a question of the proportion of needs. Mary, he told Rosamond, was 'more or less content with what she has got'; she, on the other hand, was demanding more than he felt able to give. He shied away from absolute commitment: 'When you use the word "need" I always feel out of my depth. I just don't know how much I need you – or Mary: how essential you are to me.'[187] And yet, should she accept, he could love her, and need her, enough: 'Good God, Rosamond, do you need convincing, still, after all we have suffered & loved through, that I hold you the most precious blessing of my life?'[188] Finally, he cautioned Rosamond against making him choose. If she did, he would settle down with Mary, which would be the worst outcome for them all. Rosamond, for her part, had little choice. 'I don't really know what is to be done, or what will happen,' she wrote sadly to Laurie, 'but I know we can't let it end.' Like Mary, she was determined to make it work. 'How can I help him not to feel he is falling down on both jobs? I am very good ¾ of the time, & then I am very bad.'[189] It was in her interest to keep the peace.

Laurie was going through a crisis of his own. After six years, he was finally breaking with Lorna and, fearing he was on the verge of breakdown, Rosamond offered him Hugo's bedsitting-room on the ground floor of the cottage for as long as he should need it. '[Y]ou would be perfectly independent – & needn't come sit with me in the evenings unless you choose to,' she wrote. 'Nothing would please me more than to look after you [. . .] – and as for Mrs Wickens, she'd burst with maternal love for you. There'd be a pile of wood to saw!'[190] She made two further requests: could he bring his fiddle, and a 1lb tin of Lyons coffee?

~

Laurie arrived in Aldworth on 7 October, and stayed for six weeks. He was 'pretty rocky', as Rosamond told John, 'broken & in need of friends & help', but 'I think being here will get him through a very bad patch.'[191] The atmosphere at Diamond Cottage was pleasant and productive. While Laurie worked on his book about farming (he had given up his scriptwriting job with the Crown Film Unit, and had been commissioned to write a short book on agriculture for the Ministry of Information Publications Division, edited by Cecil), Rosamond was, as usual, struggling to balance both domestic and working life. 'The days go by without my ever finding time to write,' she told John. 'I keep 10 a.m. to 11 a.m. for correspondence – but then, how to fit in the washing? the ironing? the chopping? as well as make a hole in the piling drifting heap of correspondence? How to make a parcel of Sally's Holy Bible, shampoo, savings book, Teddy bear & brown velvet rabbit?'[192] Laurie, she reported, was 'definitely on the up-grade' and, alongside his agriculture book, was writing 'some electrifying poems'.[193]

When Laurie returned to London on 25 November, he found Putney devastated. A bomb meant for Putney Bridge had missed, falling instead on the dance hall, and killing an appalling eighty-one people. Life in London took on a very different tone. Yet Rosamond continued to send him updates from the country: Mrs Wickens had a cough; she had bought a new saw and received a brace of pheasants from her neighbour; and she had found Laurie's pyjamas, shirt and fiddle, which would be sent with Cecil to London. She missed his company during kitchen hours, her afternoon walks and the crossword. It had been, she reflected, 'a strange and happy interlude': 'I shall never forget it. Nothing quite like it has ever happened to me, and I have never in my life felt such perfect ease, affection, lack of friction with any member of the opposite sex. You are my brother, and I love you.'[194] Laurie, in turn, was grateful for the kindness she had shown during such a dark time. 'What a lovely person you are, really,' he wrote on 26 November, '– two months ago I just couldn't picture myself living reasonably or sanely with anyone in the world. But I was really soothed and ridiculously content with you.'[195]

Rosamond was only too happy to repay the debt she felt owing for Laurie's support through her own 'nasty crisis' in April.[196] She had grown to depend on his friendship, and felt his absence in the cottage. But in the interval between his leaving and the children's return

for the Christmas holidays, she was absorbed in a new literary enterprise, and her first collaboration with Cecil. In the spirit of wartime
creativeness, she and Cecil decided to launch a magazine – *Orion* –
dedicated to new writing. Her motivations were mixed. In her
determined blindness about their relationship, she was willing to
accept crumbs, and yet *Orion* was also a way of overcoming their difficulties, working side by side. She was demonstrating a remarkable
ability to lurch from disaster to domestic calm. But there was also
the fact that, after years of reading manuscripts for John, Rosamond
was eager to set up on her own. 'I want to do it very much – I've
always wanted to try myself out at editing,' she wrote to him, perhaps a little modestly. Her contribution to *New Writing* had been
crucial: throughout the war, the siblings kept up – distinct from their
personal letters – a stream of magazine-related correspondence.
Rosamond read with care and offered detailed, sincere responses to
the material John sent her. And she continued to read for the Hogarth Press, of which she had become an advisory board member in
1938, after John had taken Virginia's share.

With her own periodical, she would finally be able to publish the
writing that interested her most (John's being a little too doctrinaire
for her tastes). Her chief worry was offending her competitive and
temperamental brother. In several letters that winter, she attempted to
assuage John, who feared *Orion* would rival *New Writing*. 'It won't
"compete with" [*New Writing*] any more than *Horizon* does or the *Corn-
hill* will,' she wrote on 7 December. 'When I contemplate the hunger of
the public for good reading matter I feel there is room for another
dozen productions of similar character.'[197] A few weeks later, she
wrote again to reassure him. 'Not only needn't we overlap & destroy
each other, but we very much hope that you will be a contributor –
just as I hope to continue writing for you.'[198] John continued to
discourage her partnership with the other proposed editors – the poet
and critic Edwin Muir, and Denys Kilham Roberts from the Society of
Authors ('I wonder who you would approve of my associating with!').
But Rosamond was determined. Plus, 'The pay is not princely, but will
make a most necessary addition to my income.'[199]

When the first issue eventually appeared two years later, in 1945, it reflected Rosamond's tastes, wavering somewhere between the innovative and the old-fashioned. In their opening letter, the editors wrote that they would steer clear of politics – *Orion* was 'attached to no group or movement' – and dedicate themselves to literary culture. Finally, they – or, more likely, Rosamond, with John in mind – acknowledged 'the debt they, and all who love letters, owe to the magazines that have kept our literary standard high throughout these hard years, and refused to despair of reason or imagination'.[200] In the issue, there was prose and memoir by Rose Macaulay, Leonard Woolf and Edith Sitwell, and poems from Walter de la Mare and Stephen Spender. In a show of magnanimity, John congratulated his sister on the result. But something had gone awry at the printers, and Rosamond was furious: 'I can scarcely speak about Orion, & nor can Cecil. After all our efforts & rages & frustrations what should those f—ing publishers dare to do but produce it on filthy shiny paper with a revolting paper cover instead of the binding we had chosen – price 5/- for what looks like an inferior pocket magazine.'[201] Nevertheless, working on the magazine was a satisfying process, putting her skills to the test. She enjoyed leaving the country for editorial meetings at the magazine's offices on Manchester Square, where she wrote to her wide network of literary friends and acquaintances on pale-grey headed paper. She deferred to Cecil's judgment, while he took prospective writers out to lunch. Two nights a week, she stayed at the small house on Hasker Street which Cecil rented, and where Laurie, now working at the Ministry of Information, also lived. His presence acted as a chaperone, giving credence to Rosamond's status as a divorcing woman living with another man. But none of that mattered. At last, she and Cecil were collaborating as a couple.

~

As 1943 drew to a close, Rosamond surveyed her endeavours. Her country years had been quietly productive. The war had galvanized her, while her life at Diamond Cottage had given her new kinds of experience, and a new style of country living about which to write. Cecil increased her confidence. Towards Christmas, Hugo and Sally arrived for the school holidays, and the cottage was filled once more with noise and their village friends. In the mild weather, Rosamond took her children into the ploughed fields where they pulled a horse and trap through the furrows. There were occasional stings. A box of cakes arrived at the cottage for Cecil, baked by Mary. And on 22 December, fruitlessly it now seemed, her divorce from Wogan was finalized, and her income from Wogan's father, Lord Milford, ceased. Soon, Cecil departed for Christmas at Musbury. 'We got through the difficult last evening which always weighs on us with flags flying,' she told Laurie resiliently. A postscript: 'Still no eggs!'[202]

In 1944, Rosamond was settling back into the rhythms of country life. She had been at Diamond Cottage for nearly two years. Though she continued to travel to London, her trips were infrequent, and the grain of daily life was at the cottage. In letters to friends, she described the weeks passing in a litany of household events: her gardener had grown old, as had Mrs Wickens; she had run out of corn for her hens, and so was unable to collect more than one or two eggs. She continued to make many small requests of Laurie, which reached out from her letters like supplicatory arms, unsettling yet familiar. Would he find a replacement for Hugo's threadbare jacket? Would he take Hugo to a film? And come to Aldworth to play the fiddle for Sally? 'You know how my children dote on you, but I don't want them to suck your blood.'[203] But it was her own insecurity which intermittently broke the surface.

In the early autumn, she began writing 'Wonderful Holidays', the last and longest of her wartime trilogy of stories. Despite John's efforts to hurry his sister along, it took her several weeks. ('This instalment [. . .] will be finished in a couple of days – (cross my heart!),' she promised in late September.[204]) In the end, the

Hugo and Sally in the fields during wartime, and Sally with her rabbit

story grew to almost a novella in length, and was serialized in four issues of *New Writing* over the course of the following year. It was to be based on events in the spring, when she had helped the village women organize an evening's entertainment for 'Salute the Soldier' week, just as, in the story, the woman – whom we are now told is called Margaret Ritchie – will do. The revue was to take place in Aldworth on 22 April. When the children returned for the Easter holidays, the house became filled with their noisy rehearsals, but Sally's school trunk was lost and Rosamond was unable to get hold of a film as 'the van that serves the district has been removed for "special duties"'.[205] She asked Laurie to play his fiddle: 'I have booked you for 30 minutes of divine music, & you don't know how passionately we count on you. The whole village is clamouring for your return. The programme I leave to you: you know exactly what they like.'[206] As the day approached, she wrote again: 'I shall never be able to show my face again if I don't produce you. All the children beg &

implore you to come: you are the king pin of this entertainment. Really and truly.'[207] After the revue, Rosamond battled feelings of flatness. The children had 'enjoyed it madly, & both now fancy the stage as a profession'; but, she told William Plomer, 'I am a wreck'.[208] To Laurie, she was more confiding. 'I'm feeling rather grey this morning, owing [. . .] to the fact that I won't see Cecil for another 3 weeks at least, owing to Easter, then beastly Musbury, then fire-watching.'[209] In 'Wonderful Holidays', Margaret isn't given the mixed blessing of a lover who arrives from London. The textures of her life – in the country, under her own roof, and with her children – remain hers alone.

Yet the story captures Margaret's newfound ease among her neighbours, and her willingness to become involved in the village community. Gone is the lonely, luxuriant atmosphere of the earlier stories; briskness replaces lethargy. Margaret's large house in isolated, open country has been replaced by a smaller dwelling on a village street, and her days are filled with bustle and chatter. The children, now older, are rehearsing their skits for a revue in the village hall, and spend most of their time with the young Carmichaels, who live down the lane. As they thunder in and out of the house, Margaret goes about the day's tasks: ordering meals and talking with Mrs Plumley, the cook; placating the vicar on the telephone; cycling to the station to see about Jane's missing school trunk. She even grills her neighbour's chop for his lunch. In this series of everyday encounters Margaret is indispensable, depended upon by others, and very much a part of the village community. Her solitariness has given way to a new kind of belonging.

The change in tone and tempo had much to do with the war. During the spring of 1944, Britons waited daily for news of D-Day, doom was receding, spirits were up, and the war was expected to be won. In the story, rumours of the impending invasion produce barely suppressed hysteria among the uninformed villagers. ' "[T]here's a lot of funny things occurring on the lines just now," ' the station-master tells Margaret when she goes to look for Jane's trunk. ' "Heavy traffic. Priority. If you get my meaning." "I do." She charged her voice with significant reserve.' But, despite the prospect of victory, war continues to occupy every aspect of daily life. Margaret is busy providing food for the children: cereal loaf, tins of minced beef, the occasional fried egg. Endlessly, she mends their outgrown and threadbare clothes. Nonetheless, it's an affectionate portrait of wartime and family life. Mostly, the villagers pull together. Making a note to thank the baker, Mr MacBean, for tolerating the midnight raid of his dough-cakes by John and the Carmichael boys, Margaret meditates on the man who delivers the milk before breakfast, runs the stores, and makes loaves late into the night. She considers the quiet arcs of ordinary, country lives: 'The birth-beds, the death-beds; and in between the schooling, the church, the chapel; the start in life, the rise, the stumble, the downfall: all followed the same banal yet portentous pattern.' And she values her own part in the design. Offering to help Captain Moffat, a damaged veteran of the previous war, with his chop, she reflects: ' "That's one good thing that's come out of the war – at least for me. I mean, people like us really being neighbours. Knowing we can call on one another in a tight spot." ' Momentarily, Margaret is swept along in the tide of her own goodness. Leaving the Captain's, she imagines the ways in which she can improve his life – bringing cheer to his wife, even encouraging the couple to have children – before realizing the preposterousness of her reverie. She checks herself: ' "Really, you're revolting." '

> Still this sickening, self-indulgent daydreaming, this perpetual wash of emotional flotsam, blocking the channels of the clear flow of reason. No ideas, no intellectual progress, none. No wonder, perhaps, that Charles her husband had left her years ago, transferring his suitcases, his typewriter, his notes for a book on Marxist aesthetics and his affections to a clear-browed female research student in physics.

Despite the increasing contentment of Margaret's life, the bitter, self-chastizing woman is still there; occasionally, she breaks through the calm exterior, making her presence known.

The story crescendos towards the evening when the revue is to be staged in the village hall. The entertainment marks the beginning of 'Salute the Soldier', a local fundraising scheme typical of the war years in which, at the behest of the National Savings Committee, civilians were encouraged to raise money for government deficits. ('Suppose these damned official brutes can't find anything better to do than pester us with their tomfoolery,' moans the vicar. 'We can't call our souls our own.') In the show, Margaret and Mrs Carmichael perform a skit wearing floppy Edwardian hats. A comedy sketch follows, in which the Carmichael boys disgrace their father by wearing skirts. The laughter is uproarious, the audience on the brink of anarchy. Only Roger Wickham, house guest of the Carmichaels – and modelled on Laurie: clear-eyed, cool, distant – can quell the unruly crowd with his fiddle. He plays tunes for young and old alike and, gradually, the villagers begin to sing. Margaret watches as, across the hall, the voices join together, gathering in strength and volume: 'Husky, unpractised, droning and wailing voices, they all sang *Annie Laurie*.' Slipping into an empty seat, she takes in this rare moment of togetherness, the entire community crooning in unison beneath the pitched roof. Is this what the war will achieve, the emergence of a looser, more egalitarian society? Not quite. Class differences are what have given the evening its flavour. The sight of Mrs Ritchie and Mrs Carmichael, gentry housewives, on their hands and knees, has proved too much for their neighbours. And Margaret, swaying between Mrs Plumley and Mrs Fuller, can't help noticing the 'adenoidal' infants, the loose dentures, the mountainous forms and 'complex odours of the unventilated crowd'. As ever, she is full of contradictions: she wishes to be part of the community, and yet its members appear alien to her. Later, discussing the politicized arena of village committees, she and Mrs Carmichael bemoan their status, which begs aloofness and involvement at the same time. It seems they can't get it right: ' "If we butt in they think we're patronising and if we retire they think we're snobbish. Both ways they're resentful." ' War has only masked inequalities. In the wobbling darkness of the hall, the fraternizing is momentary; the lines separating villagers and gentry will remain firmly drawn.

And yet, for the time being, Margaret takes pleasure in the familiarity of the village. Talking to shopkeepers and stationmasters, cycling to committee meetings or to buy fish, she thinks contentedly of herself as an 'obscure countrywoman, parent and housewife'; an Everywoman, playing her small but essential part. In many ways, 'Wonderful Holidays' offers a confirmation, albeit a conservative one, of home and community, with all the humour, warmth and upbeat Englishness John Lehmann was looking for when he commissioned the story for *New Writing*. But, though Rosamond was striking the note of 1944, she was also venturing into the darker truths of the lives of ordinary women, exploring their roles as mothers and mainstays. Lending herself to others, Margaret's identity is obliterated. '*Forget yourself –*' she tells herself onstage. Later, when John telephones to say he won't be coming home, she sees the moment repeating itself, watching her own image in the hallway 'glide out before her into the future in multiple projection [. . .], over and over again lifting the instrument to her ear to receive similar announcements'. Mothering in wartime is a solitary experience. Darning socks late into the night, Margaret listens to the bombers taking off on their night-time raids, and, as on so many evenings, sits with her fears alone.

> Bomb, bomb, bomb, bomb. Burn, burn, burn, burn. Fuller, fuller, fainter, fainter. A strong force of our aircraft passing overhead. Impersonally exulting and lamenting, deadly, mild, soothing in its husky reiterated burden as a familiar lullaby. Four years safe beneath this portion of the impartial sky, Jane, who had called out on the first night of the war: 'Do they make special small bombs for children?'[210]

There are dark corners of her existence still. At the story's close, Margaret walks out into the night with Jane at her side. The

Carmichaels' party has ended, and, left behind by the others, mother and daughter pick their way home. The scene is a fitting one to describe Rosamond's wartime years in Aldworth when, stepping back from politics and retreating into a quieter outlook, she was also choosing the quieter roles of mother and villager – the obscure countrywoman of her story. She was, perhaps, willing a kind of obscurity for herself – a loss of self, and of identity (as would Virginia during wartime in Sussex). For, as Margaret and Jane journey alone together, their forms merge with the darkness. Their walk is the final act of the evening, an image both of intimacy and total effacement.

~

As Rosamond was writing 'Wonderful Holidays', *The Ballad and the Source* was published and, to celebrate, Cecil arrived from London for the evening with a half-bottle of wine. Rosamond waited anxiously for reviews, aware she had created an extravagant melodrama that didn't quite fit the times. In fact, some critics expressed their admiration for such an intricate, escapist tale offering respite from the dreary wartime palette – the 'dingy interiors and cabbage-water smells', as the *New Statesman* put it – of so many other contemporary novels.[211] Mrs Jardine was refreshing, deliciously fraudulent, uninhibited. She was, Rosamond admitted to William Plomer, her most fully ' "realised" ' character, 'by far the most complex piece of invention I have ever undertaken'.[212] But others were less encouraging, dismissing the novel as high-flown Edwardian nostalgia and Jamesian pastiche, and suggesting that its writer's powers – so potent in the 1930s – were on the wane. In truth, the novel had taken what was best about her writing – her ear for naturalistic dialogue, her acute sensitivity to atmosphere and place, her depictions of children, and her ability to write about women's lives – and tipped them into excess, as if the jug had slipped and the contents poured forth unchecked. When she had written to William Plomer that the novel would decide her literary capabilities, she was acknowledging the risk she had taken with the book. In her mind, the success of her writing was tied up with the success of Diamond Cottage: as if, after the smash of her divorce, she had to prove her ability to make a new life for herself, and to work. But it was possible to be oversensitive, perhaps, to people, to atmosphere, and place. She had produced a saga, written during her saga with Cecil, which now seemed destined to fail. Like her life at the cottage, she could make a go of it, it seemed, though reality came biting at her heels.

Yet there was virtuosity elsewhere. At the same time as writing *The Ballad and the Source*, Rosamond had produced 'When the Waters Came', 'A Dream of Winter' and 'Wonderful Holidays'. Elizabeth Bowen thought the stories 'the loveliest' of all her work.[213] Diamond Cottage, then, was suited to certain kinds of writing. Out of Rosamond's experience of village life during wartime had emerged an entirely new form. For a writer who had only ever managed her life in fits and starts, running a household and a complicated life, it was oddly fitting that her best work from this fractured period should be a set of short stories. Writing about her children and her immediate surroundings, she touched on brilliance; only in the realm of fantasy and pure fiction did she lose her way. All of this tallied with her inconsistencies, that she could produce such different versions of her work, and of herself.

Rosamond's wartime endeavours didn't quite add up. But then, life at Diamond Cottage had that mixed quality, of everyday triumphs mingled with disappointment and regret. She received short, ardent letters of appreciation for her stories, and turned away from the worst of the reviews for *The Ballad and the Source*. In the aftermath of publication, she clung to the most heartening responses, which were closest to home. 'Hugo has been lying flat on his bed reading it for 2 days & has just finished it & flung it down (10.30 p.m.) with quite enthusiastic appreciation,' she wrote.[214]

Soon afterwards, in the kitchen at Diamond Cottage, Cecil sat writing on a small sheet of paper. With a careless, satisfied smile, he tossed it across the table to Rosamond. On it was written the poem 'Is It Far to Go?', which encapsulated the impossibility of their relationship. It was a poem about arriving and leaving at the same time, about absence, in which questions are left unanswered, and hang forever suspended in the air.

~

Winter – the last of the war – descended on the cottage. Rosamond was entering a fallow period. She hadn't enjoyed the last lap of the year, when she had brooded, 'inert & apathetic', unable to pick up her pen.[215] The children were back at school, and Cecil had been unwell, staying in Devon for weeks on end on doctor's orders. 'It's such a hand to mouth existence here alone,' she wrote to William Plomer, though 'I suppose I ought to think myself lucky to be safe under my own roof in the country.'[216] No matter; she was 'dreadfully, dreadfully depressed'.[217] It felt as if she hadn't moved very far at all. With Cecil being cossetted by Mary in Devon, the prospect of his leaving the marriage seemed more distant than ever, and now that Rosamond was divorced, she was all too aware of her status as a single woman, financially precarious until her settlement with Wogan came through. Each time a cheque arrived from *New Writing* for 'Wonderful Holidays' – fifteen guineas for each instalment – she wrote gratefully to John.

She was fretting, too, that Laurie was withdrawing from her. Speaking at length about his private life came unnaturally to him, and he was embarrassed by his confessions the previous autumn. At Diamond Cottage, he wrote in answer to her letter, 'the weight of my misery and your very dear understanding, both together, opened floodgates of confidences such as could not have occurred at any other time, or could again'. He hadn't been wishing to avoid her, but 'took for granted that nothing more would be said'.[218] Rosamond was stung by his rebuff. She craved intimacy, and was alarmed that their friendship had shifted so drastically onto new ground. Laurie, working at the Ministry and living with Cecil on Hasker Street, had moved on, and no longer needed weekends of respite – doing crosswords and being read Jane Austen – in the country. And her love with Cecil had changed. There were fissures, fights and silences, boundaries that could never now be crossed. Rosamond was bitterly disappointed. 'It isn't enough to know I'll always be loved, needed – and missed,' she wrote.[219] Yet they were still capable of happiness. She clung to the prospect of his arrival in the village, where they would read and walk, begin work on a new issue of *Orion*, and continue to socialize as a couple. She had invested too much in their relationship. After three years of loving Cecil, she was content to wait a bit longer.

The winter went on tirelessly and was bitterly cold, punctuated by a series of household disasters. On a night in February 1945, part of the ceiling in Rosamond's bedroom fell in, '& now the wind hums & whistles down on me through a cavern of broken lathes & plaster'. And when the pipe to the cistern froze, she was forced to stand on a ladder in the loft, waving a flame beneath it in an attempt to thaw the ice. 'How right you are,' she wrote to John, '– any breakage now becomes a symbol of irreparable destruction.'[220] She was running out of wood and coal, and the lorry with supplies couldn't get up the hill in the snow. 'Oh, the cold, I mind it so,' she wrote to her friend Grizel Hartley. 'I don't keep warm day or night.' Meanwhile, Cecil was still in Devon: 'I must be patient & not allow my morale to collapse.'[221]

Wartime in the country had taught Rosamond a lesson in resilience. Following the breakdown of her marriage, she had left behind a lethargic, hassling decade, and entered a new phase of solitude, but also belonging. She had gained in confidence, and self-acceptance. And out of broken time, fits and starts, she had learned to settle, and to be patient. Winter, she knew now, was a waiting game. She was grateful for indoor comforts, for her soft bed. From her cottage, she looked out over 'this iron landscape, this mineral sky', waiting for spring to pierce the cold earth.[222]

Rosamond at her cottage

PART TWO

Afterlives

An England of waifs & strays

'Again, back from London. But its here that the events take place,' Virginia Woolf wrote in her diary on 4 July 1940.[1] She had been gone from Sussex for three days, and reported everything that had happened while she was away: Louie, her cook-housekeeper, had been chased in from fruit-picking by the 'pop pop pop' of a German bomber flying low over the marshes; a train at Newhaven had been bombed, the driver killed; and another plane – British – shot down near the village of Southease. All Lewes had been pinned to the radio, listening to Churchill's speech about the French fleet; Mr Uridge, who sold the butter, said he thought it the beginning of the fighting proper.

The Second World War shattered the quiet of country life. Stationed at Monk's House, Virginia sensed a different atmosphere in the village. The place was on edge, jittery; the talk of bombs and invasion. Since 1919, when she had taken a house in the village, she had grown used to relying on Rodmell as the place she could go to recover, to shrug off the frenetic energy of London and absorb herself in work. Now, as war got under way, it was blighted by gossip, meetings, a host of new noises. Was that a headache she felt, a twinge of anxiety? Her health was beginning to suffer again.

And yet the country would always have its consolations. 'The truth is,' she wrote in her diary, 'we've not seen spring in the country since I was ill at Asheham – 1914 – & that had its holiness in spite of the depression.' Despite the war, arriving in Sussex in 1940 was still to enter 'a state of peace & sensation feeling' – though 'not idea feeling'. Perhaps, after all, this wasn't the time for serious work. Did it matter? She flipped through her notebooks, looked elsewhere for small, domestic comforts. The freedoms of the garden, of living without servants, even doing a little cooking, were unexpectedly appealing. 'I think I'll also dream a poet-prose book,' she wrote, 'perhaps make a cake now & then.'[2]

One hundred miles away along the south coast, in the Dorset village of Maiden Newton, Sylvia Townsend Warner was also turning stoically to her larder, having received the last of the plum cakes from the baker. She, too, felt international events trickling down to her local high street, sensed a world on the brink of change. But she was weary after the political failures of the 1930s, and in the midst of crisis in her private life. Valentine was in love with another woman, and the future of their relationship – Sylvia's bedrock – was uncertain.

As both women were to realize, country places aren't immune to change; even in the most secluded corners, it is impossible to escape history. Reflecting on their earlier experiments at Asheham and Miss Green, both Virginia and Sylvia felt something coming to an end. Nothing so idyllic could last indefinitely, though there were lessons and strategies – Virginia's belief in the natural world, for example, or Sylvia's in communism – that could be drawn upon in times of need. Hadn't Virginia survived illness and war once before, at Asheham, in 1914? And yet, she knew, there were things – like war, like depression – that were beyond her control, however powerful her personal philosophies might be. For Sylvia, nothing could be more disappointing than her lover's change of heart, except perhaps the failure of her own idealism.

Yet, as war took hold, they discovered – as Rosamond Lehmann had – reservoirs of determination. Country life, as once before, could still yield new possibilities for experience and creativity. After her flat at 37 Mecklenburgh Square was bombed in October 1940, Virginia lived exclusively at Monk's House: not since Asheham had she spent such a sustained period in the country. In her diary, country news was already taking precedence; from the very beginning, her experience of war was a rural one. She adjusted her vision, tuned her ear to a local frequency; as at Asheham in 1917, she immersed herself in her surroundings.

For Sylvia, war brought down barriers, and ushered in a different style of village living. Gone were the periods of private, uninterrupted work. A new mode of participation was called for. History was arriving in her quiet village, and she stepped up to meet it, joining the local branch of the Women's Voluntary Service, and learning to shoot. She charted the changes being wrought on her surroundings with a mixture of awe and scepticism, observed warily the frenzy of her neighbours. And, like Virginia, she adopted a style of reportage, documenting her daily life and the lives of others in her diary and letters.

Their landscapes were being transformed: lorries trundled along the roads; great whorls of wire were installed on the Downs and along the coast. For these women, for many years, fiction writing had arisen from the aesthetic of the artist isolated in her landscape, places of solitude and self-acceptance, of love and recovery. Now, these backdrops were peopled, and questions of history and class were becoming increasingly urgent and necessary. But even in the midst of war, creative aspiration would not be defeated easily. Hastily, the women took stock, assessing the time available to them. In Sussex and Dorset, war was demanding; their rural hours were compressed, changing. And yet, perhaps, after all, something could be made of shifting their attention, of describing the texture of events taking place around them. How best to work efficiently? And so, for Virginia and Sylvia, a different kind of literature began to take shape in wartime: in the form of diaries, short stories, and two remarkable late novels about landscape and Englishness, about the making of art and the making of history, each sounding with the many voices – both real and imagined – of community. These fictions were departures, though they were not entirely new. Both writers were returning to old habits. The gifts of attention and independence bestowed by Asheham and Miss Green continued to give, and to shape their writing.

Following the declaration of war in September 1939 – when she had been at Monk's House, sewing blackout curtains, sleeveless in the late-summer heat – Virginia spent six uninterrupted weeks in

Sussex, breaking the rhythm of her London and country life. Her immediate concerns were domestic. She began hoarding paper, sugar and matches, and calculated that a fallen tree would 'see us through 2 winters. They say the war will last 3 years.' The days began a perceptible, remembered shrinking. 'Theres no petrol today,' she wrote in her diary, 'so we are back again with our bicycles at Asheham 1915.'[3] Increasingly, London seemed out of the question. When she travelled to Mecklenburgh Square to unpack the Hogarth Press in its new home on the ground floor, and her belongings in the flat upstairs, she was 'harassed & distracted' and complained of 'the extreme jadedness of London'. Her health was failing again. The city seemed remote and unfamiliar. The Tube was closed, sandbags littered the pavements, and workers rushed about 'humped' with gas masks. Only in the dark was London agreeable. At night, the streets reverted to empty, primeval darkness, 'so verdurous & gloomy that one expects a badger or a fox to prowl along the pavement. A reversion to the middle ages with all the space & the silence of the country set in this forest of black houses.' She needed silence, and space. Driving back to Sussex with Leonard, she watched as the world rose 'out of dark squalor' into 'divine natural peace'. Days of solitude beckoned. She could feel her brain 'smoothing'.[4]

The prospect of spending wartime in the country was not unpleasant. 'Queer the contraction of life to the village radius,' she wrote at teatime at Monk's House on 12 October 1940.[5] Life had constricted, but pleasurably so. Since the publication of her biography of Roger Fry in June, she had turned her attention to a new novel, a 'medley', and was cooling her mind with scraps of autobiography.[6] It was enjoyable, fertile ground. From the window in her writing lodge in the garden, she watched the marsh 'fading & freshening' as she moved from one 'pleasant' thing to another: 'breakfast, writing, walking, tea, bowls, reading, sweets, bed'. Was it 'treasonable' to admit to such pleasures, she wondered? Leonard was gathering apples in the garden, while she worked on her rug: 'its all so heavenly free & easy – L. & I alone.'[7] Weeks later, and a hard frost prevented travel to London. Virginia imagined her friends and family – Nessa and Duncan at Charleston, Angelica and Bunny at Claverham – all similarly isolated over winter fires. Out on her walks, she marvelled at the marsh, muffled by winter: 'All silent, as if offered from another world. No birds, no carts, men shooting. This specimen against the war. This heartless & perfect beauty.'[8] She was cut off from the old rhythm, marooned in a frozen land-scape. 'Settled in for another 2 weeks, & only village meetings & books,' she noted in January 1940.[9] 'This life here has now become the rule; t'other the exception.'[10]

War had brought about a new kind of privacy. Unable to travel and cut off from friends, Virginia was entering into a 'curious sub-life'; for the most part, 'rather leisured, & secluded & content'.[11] Domesticity was reassuring. Having long desired greater independence in her own home, she dismissed her servant, Mabel, and attempted to manage wartime housekeeping alone. 'Now we go to our last Cook cooked meal for I don't know how long,' she wrote on the eve of Mabel's departure, on 15 September. 'Could it be the end of resident servants for ever?' She looked forward to her own 'merry kitchen harum scarum ways': she had learned to make bread, casseroles and pies, and took pleasure in preparing supper, turning the sausages in their glass dish – Leonard had donated all their aluminium saucepans to Mrs Ebbs for the making of aeroplanes – with her penholder.[12] In the event, the cooking became a little erratic – 'Fish forgotten, I must invent a dinner' – and Virginia gave up on her plan to prepare all their meals.[13] Louie Everest, a local woman from Southease who had been with the Woolfs since 1934 (and continued to clean Monk's House), pitched in to help. Yet Virginia continued to note the events and victories of the kitchen: the hanging of a great hare ('odd that we shall eat it'), bottling honey from the bees in the garden, preserving eggs.[14] Louie picked currants and gooseberries, and showed Virginia how to make butter (she took the pat in to show Leonard in 'a moment of great household triumph').[15] Every now and then, she took stock of domestic shortages, conducting a household reckoning in her diary:

margarine rationed, meat scarce; no pudding save milk pudding; very little petrol; no possibility of buying new clothes. What had begun as excitement was now making her weary. 'These are inconveniences rather than hardships. We don't go hungry or cold. But luxury is nipped off,' she wrote in December 1940.[16] She grumbled at the pettiness of domestic life. When Desmond McCarthy ate more than his share of sugar and cream, she complained, 'the housekeeper in me rises into being, in this miserable life of detail & bombast'.[17] Yet rationing could also be a stimulus for invention: 'How one enjoys food now: I make up imaginary meals.'[18]

At last, Virginia was mistress of her own hours. She fell into routine. In the afternoons, she put on an old coat and woollen helmet to 'flounder' over the marsh with Leonard's spaniel, Sally ('Rubber boots help').[19] Her long, solitary walks were as absorbing as ever: 'Making up again. So that I couldnt remember, coming home, if I'd come by the mushroom path or the field.'[20] The Downs showed an 'incredible loveliness' in winter, 'breaking their wave' over a landscape of pale barns and stacks; in the spring, she listened to 'my Asheham rooks dropping their husky caws' and watched the 'passages of colour, over Asheham, like the green backgrounds in Vermeer'.[21] When, in November 1940, a bomb exploded on the riverbank and the Ouse flooded, water covered the marsh and the landscape appeared transformed, as if reverted to its primeval appearance: 'no bungalows; as it was in the beginning,' she wrote; 'Medieval in the mist.'[22] Walking, she noticed 'the ancient bits' of Sussex: old farm waggons and ploughs, the roads made by the earliest carts.[23] At a moment of mounting international crisis, her country corner was anchorage and history. 'How England consoles & warms one,' she wrote, 'in these deep hollows, where the past stands almost stagnant.'[24]

At first, war produced an eerie, reverberating quiet. Up on the Downs, or on the marsh, Virginia could hear her ears ringing. On one of the last nights of peace, she had gone up onto the Downs and lain 'under a cornstack & looked at the empty land' and heard 'Not a sound.'[25] The following January, walking out into the frozen landscape, she listened to 'the silence, the pure disembodied silence'.

Only the workmen in the road discussing war were audible, and the men with their guns waiting for widgeon. With the sun in her eyes, she felt the landscape's emptiness, its sudden quiet, 'correspond to my own vacancy'; in her mind, 'No thoughts populated.'[26] For, though she was experiencing a state of private, domestic pleasure, Virginia also feared she was facing a public death.[27] In the weeks following the publication of her biography of Roger Fry, she was stung to have received so few letters from friends. 'Complete silence surrounds that book. It might have sailed into the blue & been lost,' she wrote in her diary. ' "One of our books did not return" as the BBC puts it.'[28] It was a reminder of 1915 at Asheham, when the emergence of her first novel, *The Voyage Out*, passed by unnoticed. Now, in 1940, she described a similarly 'curious feeling' of insubstantiality.[29] The 'writing "I" has vanished,' she wrote. 'There's no standard to write for: no public to echo back.'[30]

The Downs in winter

She had mixed feelings about the silence into which war had cata-
pulted her. Partly, it was longed for. Following her political essay
Three Guineas in 1938, in part a defence of pacifism, Virginia had, she
told herself, fulfilled her obligation to contribute to the debates of
the 1930s, and now desired privacy, to step back from scrutiny into a
place of artistic freedom and integrity. 'No longer famous, no longer
on a pedestal; no longer hawked in by societies,' she had written
triumphantly in her diary after its publication; 'on my own, forever.
That's my feeling: sense of expansion, like putting on slippers.'[31]
She was reaching 'immunity', her word – scattered throughout her
diaries and essays – to describe the fleeting yet pleasurable state of
detachment from the world and its demands. She reached it best in
Sussex, where, islanded at Monk's House, she could slough off politics
and public life, and retreat into herself, just as Rosamond Lehmann
was choosing to do during her own wartime interlude at Diamond
Cottage in Berkshire. At first, for Virginia, the word had private res-
onance. 'To be immune,' she had written in a 1932 diary entry,
'means to exist apart from rubs, shocks, suffering; to be beyond the
range of darts; to have enough to live on without courting flattery,
success; not to need to accept invitations; not to mind other people
being praised [. . .] Immunity is an exalted calm desirable state, &
one I could reach much oftener than I do.'[32] It was useful as a form
of reassurance, a way of writing herself, in her diary, beyond the
petty jealousies and conflicts which caused her pain. And yet, as the
decade progressed, the word took on political meaning. As Hermione Lee has written, Virginia's desire for immunity represented a
complicated form of resistance: inaction, but not passivity.[33] 'To be
passive is to be active,' she had written in *Three Guineas*, arguing that
there were many forms of political resistance – usually carried out
by women – that were not to be discounted for their lack of visibil-
ity in the public sphere.[34] And yet what could those forms consist of,
exactly? It was a great interior debate she carried on into the war.
'I'm terrified of passive acquiescence,' she told her diary; and to her
nephew, Julian Bell: 'What can I do but write?'[35] Later, she would
famously declare 'Thinking is my fighting', convinced that she

could – at least, in the way she felt able – 'catch Hitler', 'if only with even the end of an inky old pen'.[36]

Being in Rodmell exacerbated Virginia's conflict between her desire for both privacy and exposure, for a form of passivity that didn't constitute submission. During the long, continuous stretches of country life, she felt 'no longer in the movement'; there was 'No audience. No echo. Thats part of one's death.'[37] And yet literal death was becoming an all-too-real possibility. During the summer of 1940, the Battle of Britain was being fought in the air above Virginia's head. Rodmell, less than five miles from the coast at Newhaven, was poised for Hitler's invasion. Out walking, she noticed preparations being made – lorries thundering along the lanes and men digging guns into the riverbank – and the planes appearing with a 'cadaverous twanging in the sky'.[38] 'A haystack was handy,' she noted glibly, forced to dive for cover in the fields.[39] 'So, the Germans are nibbling at my afternoon walks.'[40] At Monk's House, she and Leonard lay 'flat on our faces' beneath the apple tree as a plane circled overhead; another was shot down over Lewes as they were at tea ('a scuffle; a swerve: then a plunge; & a burst of thick black smoke'); and a bomb caused the pen to jump from Virginia's hand.[41] After speaking on the telephone to Vita Sackville-West, the bombs falling around Sissinghurst in Kent, Virginia was 'too jaded to give the feeling – of talking to someone who might be killed any moment'.[42] Each day brought with it a feeling of finality and flatness: 'This, I thought [. . .] may be my last walk.'[43] Coolly, she and Leonard discussed suicide. 'We pour to the edge of a precipice [. . .] & then?' she wrote on 27 June 1940. 'I cant conceive that there will be a 27th June 1941.'[44]

And yet, despite the mounting horror, Virginia was determined to stave off paralysis, to make something of the circumstances in which she found herself. At the age of fifty-eight, she was entering one of the most generative, creative phases of her writing life. The war, though 'the worst of all my life's experiences', was also extraordinary, and she needed to absorb its intensity.[45] 'In London, now, or 2 years ago, I'd be owling through the streets,' she wrote in her diary, acknowledging her rapacious nature, her desire to record and observe. 'More pack & thrill than here. So I must supply that – how?'[46] She answered herself: 'I must tuck myself in with work [. . .] in fact, these are the moments for compacting; for living; unless one's to blow out; which I entirely refuse to do.'[47] She considered her plans, for a new novel – 'Pointz Hall', her provisional title for *Between the Acts* – and a book of English literary history, described jauntily in her diary as 'my trip thro' English lit', for which she was reading Dante, the Elizabethans and Coleridge, 'like swinging from bough to bough'.[48] It was a time for notebooks. Virginia's ideas, for both her novel and her history book, were developing in tandem; she was nosing her way ('The idea is, accumulate notes'), her head filling with fragments of poetry and plays.[49] Though she would inevitably worry that the project was futile ('This little pitter patter of ideas is my whiff of shot in the cause of freedom'), she was nonetheless managing, in the silence, to consolidate her ideas.[50] Writing was giving shape to formlessness. Looking out over the flooded landscape, pristine in winter, she was listening for an echo.

She had first conceived of 'Reading at Random', as the book was to be called, while out blackberrying in September 1940. And, though she would write only an introductory chapter, 'Anon', and a second, titled 'The Reader', before her death, her notes reveal her acute sense of its texture and shape. In 'Anon', Virginia set out on a history of English literature and culture, by tracing literature to its origins. She imagined England's earliest poets moving over the landscape – from the 'untamed forest' to 'the Manor, from the Manor to the Church' – in possession of song.[51] The book was to describe a predominately oral tradition, from which a shared cultural heritage emerged. In time, this was to be cut short by the arrival of the printing press, at which point the audience were to become readers, and Anon – who was he, exactly? – would be absorbed into print. (The printing press, Virginia was to argue, signalled the death of a shared artistic tradition. From then on, hierarchies would emerge. 'I would venture to guess that Anon, who wrote so many poems without signing them,' she had mused in *A Room of One's Own*, 'was often a woman.'[52]) It was an expansive, adventurous project, to follow her previous critical works – *The Common Reader* books of 1925 and 1932 – and yet 'Reading at Random' was to break from that pattern. Form was important; Virginia was searching for a 'new critical method – something swifter and lighter and more colloquial', as she wrote in her diary.[53] Her methodology was to 'range at will', to weave the fabric of the book – and of cultural history – intuitively, 'in & out, round & round', as if she were 'thread[ing] a necklace through English life & lit'.[54]

As Alexandra Harris has written, 'Reading at Random' was, at its heart, 'a book about place'.[55] Virginia wished, she wrote in her notebook, to explore the 'effect of country upon writers', traversing her own corner of rural Sussex in order to imagine the landscapes and weathers from which English literature took shape.[56] She was looking, she wrote in her preparatory notes, for the origin of the creative impulse – 'the germ of creation' – which, before society was built up around it, had its seed in old England, in its woods and byways, the voices rising up in the lanes.[57] This impulse was a 'universality', she wrote: the book was, too, a celebration of community (Anon, 'lifting a song or a story from other peoples [*sic*] lips, and letting the audience join in the chorus'), and the idea of a cultural heritage which could be pooled, and shared.[58] The poet Anon was to be wandering, ordinary and unassuming (perhaps, even a woman); his words, like birdsong, released freely into the folk.

And yet, in looking to England's past, Virginia was, in fact, thinking about the future. Resisting the staleness of scholarly conventions, 'Anon' both outlined and embodied a literature available to all. There were to be no specialists, no exclusions. 'I like outsiders better,' she wrote in her diary. 'Insiders write a colourless English . . . They do a great service like Roman roads. But they avoid the forests & the will o the wisps.'[59] She was reaching towards a more democratic form, tramping the footpaths and the field margins of Sussex in search of what she called – in her lecture 'The Leaning Tower', delivered to the Workers' Educational Association at Brighton in April that year – literature's 'common ground'.[60] For common ground is the most fertile ground, the ground from which emerges creativity, community, art; and, in a time of war, hope.

~

As at Asheham in 1917, the country and its inhabitants were Virginia's window onto the war; and, as during her many years in the country, she had an instinct to set down local history. 'Now let me become the annalist of Rodmell,' she had written in her diary in 1927. ('Thirty five years ago, there were 160 families living here . . .'[61]) But, though at Asheham she had first practised her 'concise, historic style', now, in Rodmell in 1940, her project grew in scope and form.[62] With greater confidence, she adopted the role of public historian, observing her surroundings closely, and listening to her neighbours. In detail, she set down their descriptions, and collected their stories, as part of her project to make a record of her corner of Sussex at war. For, in the country, the silence Virginia heard reverberating in her ears was never absolute. The empty landscape was populated by village- and townsfolk, the quiet broken by voices. Chatter circulated in the village hall or floated up in the lanes, and she adjusted her ear to its frequency, listening in. She recorded what she heard in her diary – snippets of conversation, gossip and rumour (just as she had collected specimens at Asheham) – in a direct, purposeful shorthand; her entries becoming bulletins, local reports of the war.

She described the baker at Newhaven 'boasting' of an evening's twenty-five bombs; of Mr Hanna, captain of the Rodmell Defence Volunteers, tipped off about invasion and 'standing by' half the night; of Mrs Ebbs, watching a plane go down at Seaford, the tea-cups rattling in her hand.[63] Other news was gathered second- or third-hand. Virginia gleaned as much as she could from her servant, Louie, who moved with greater ease among the villagers of Rodmell and Southease. From Major Westmacott's gardener, Louie was given an account of the fighting at Boulogne; and from Audrey Hubbard, a story of a German pilot in the pea field being given first aid. Virginia snatched at details. After a plane was shot down at Tarring Neville, killing four Germans, Louie told her 'the country people' had '"stomped"' on their heads.[64] And when Louie's brother, Harry West, returned from Dunkirk, Virginia wrote his story rapidly – 'hadnt boots off for 3 days; [. . .] – the bombers as low as trees – the bullets like moth holes in his coat' – as if to preserve the momentum of Louie's telling, which had interrupted a game of bowls.[65] She was interested in the ways these stories were told: the 'self-consequence' of the baker at Newhaven; Louie all 'agog'.[66] Until September 1940, when Hitler's invasion was called off, her rural community was lying in wait. Rumours circulated with abandon. Virginia noted hearing of clergymen in parachutes, of 'the Nun in the bus who pays her fare with a mans hand'.[67] Percy, the Woolfs' gardener, told her the streets would be machine-gunned, that villagers were arming themselves with pitchforks. 'Rumour, via Percy,' she wrote a little warily; 'I see the imagination – that should have turned a wheel.'[68] (Yet even she, while out walking, saw cavalry on the Downs instead of cows.) As she listened, stories shifted in the telling; passed from villager to villager, narratives loosened and facts changed. Human history, she was suggesting, was taking place not only on the battlefields but also in shops, village halls and country lanes; and its protagonists were local – a Mrs Ebbs, or a Harry West.

But Virginia's descriptions of her neighbours weren't straightfor-wardly dedicatory: she knew better than to sentimentalize. She was resistant to jingoism, especially the 'dreary false cheery hero-making' kind put about by wartime propaganda.[69] 'Is Harry the real animal behind the brave, laughing heroic boy panoply which the BBC spreads before us nightly?' she asked on 22 June 1940, the day after his return from Dunkirk. To her, he seemed 'a natural human being, not made for shooting men, but for planting pota-toes'.* For, though she could be deeply compassionate about her

---

* Woolf, 22 June 1940, *Diary*, V, 298. But Virginia doesn't stop here. She goes on to describe Harry West as 'a frightened timid simple rustic, who cant resist a jewel-lers shop, nor think for himself'. Finally: 'All his valiancy oozes as soon as its pricked.' Cut from the original edition of the *Diary* by Anne Olivier Bell on

neighbours, she could also be snobbish, such condescending descriptions revealing her mixed feelings about communal life. The war meant immunity disturbed – 'we hear Hitler's voice as we sit at home of an evening,' she said in her lecture 'The Leaning Tower' – and she found herself rubbing shoulders with the people she described in her diary more than she would have liked.[70] While Leonard hosted Labour Party meetings at Monk's House and travelled into Brighton to lecture to the Workers' Educational Association, Virginia became a reluctant if increasingly active participant in the Rodmell Women's Institute. The branch met in the village hall, a draughty building approached through nettles. As she sat through first-aid demonstrations and lectures, Virginia observed the women keenly and without reserve: Mrs Chavasse, a doctor's widow from Birmingham, who presided over the meetings; Diana Gardner, an artist and her neighbour; Mrs Thompsett, the carter's wife; Mrs Ebbs, of the saucepans; the spinsters Miss Green and Miss Emery, who bred dogs; and a number of labourers' and bailiffs' wives. She noted the subtle differences between the 'tweed wearing sterling dull women' and Mrs Chavasse's 'tight dress'.[71] (Mrs Chavasse might have been a model for 'wild child' Mrs Manresa in *Between the Acts*.[72]) And she raised an eyebrow at the 'red lipped' woman who, without irony, asked if Aga pans were made of aluminium.[73]

On the whole, it was a friendly affair, and she was pleased when, in her honour, Mrs Chavasse organized a 'Book tea'.[74] But she detested the performative patriotism of the gatherings, and the parochial outlook of the women. 'I dont like any of the feelings war breeds: patriotism, communal &c, all sentimental & emotional parodies of real feelings,' she wrote in her diary after a lecture on bomb damage, in which Miss Green, in blue trousers, demonstrated

---

account of members of the West family still living, and now republished by Granta, the description reveals Woolf at her most disdainful towards her country neighbours, a gauge of – in this instance – her severe disillusionment with war feeling. My thanks to Matthew Holliday for the notes to the new editions.

shimmying down from a window.[75] She reserved her bitterest feelings for the WI plays, two of which were written by village women and rehearsed at Monk's House. 'My contribution to the war is the sacrifice of pleasure,' she wrote on 29 May, the day after a rehearsal. 'I'm bored: bored & appalled by the readymade commonplaces of these plays: which they cant act unless we help.'[76] She was frustrated with the class striations of the WI, and the 'simper' with which the poorer members deferred to 'the gentry' – women like her, or Mrs Chavasse.[77] Such uneasy intimacy between classes brought out Virginia's prejudices – as it did Rosamond's during the village festivities in Berkshire – and yet she respected these women. During the performance of a play at the summer fête, the sirens sounded. 'All the mothers sat stolid,' she wrote. 'I [. . .] admired that very much.'[78]

Her relationship with Rodmell had always been one of half-in, half-out. Soon after arriving from Asheham in 1919, she had described her pleasure at the intimacy and synchronicity of the place: 'One of the charms of Rodmell is the human life, everyone does the same thing at the same hour. What I mean is that we are a community.'[79] And yet, during her years in the village, she was careful to keep herself apart, observing her fellows from a distance. (Later, in wartime, her outsiderliness would become necessary when, in her diary, she adopted the role of local historian, taking down events and stories with the comfort of one at a remove.) She liked inhabiting the 'lower village world', where Monk's House bordered the cottages (bought by the Woolfs to house Percy and Louie and their families), the water meadows and the school; proudly, she wrote, 'the gentry dont call'.[80] In wartime, the sense of synchronicity she had once cherished bred new feelings of discomfort: she was quietly appalled by the tides of 'community feeling' that washed over her neighbours, and the sense, more broadly, of 'all England thinking the same thing – [. . .] at the same moment'.[81] Though she had often been pleased to be part of village life, it seemed to her more important than ever to remain on the outside, impervious to rhetoric and hysteria, looking in.

And yet she felt deeply about the village and the surrounding landscape, reserving a particular kind of patriotism for the England that felt her own. 'Of course I'm "patriotic",' she had written defensively to Ethel Smyth in 1938, before clarifying her attachments: 'that is English, the language, farms, dogs, people'.[82] Though her ambivalence would periodically resurface – 'My old dislike of the village bites at me. I envy houses alone in the fields,' she wrote in December 1940 – after twenty-one years, Rodmell had become 'familiar & even friendly'.[83] Besides, marooned in the country, the small community was all that was available to her. She noted dryly: 'If one lives in a village, one had better snatch its offerings.'[84]

~

In Rodmell in 1940, Virginia was feeling the tension between her public and private lives. With the sitting room at Monk's House filled with village players, and the upstairs sitting room shared with Leonard, she complained of having 'No room of my own'.[85] She had meetings to attend, and yet she wanted desperately to write. She seized on the feeling of scrappiness. 'This diary shorthand comes in useful,' she wrote in November, as she worked at her novel, 'Pointz Hall'.[86]

She was piecing it together, working in short, energetic bursts. It was a pleasurable experience, an antidote to the 'steep grind' of writing biography, and a 'relief after a long pressure of Fry facts'.[87] Outlining her plans for the novel in her diary, she was determined to devise a new narrative method, something 'random & tentative', and which – taking its cue from her research for 'Reading at Random' – could include 'anything that comes into my head'.[88] The result was a novel composed of 'Scraps, orts & fragments', echoing a refrain from the book: verses of poetry, plays, scenes from English history.[89] But it also contained pieces of her diary, and of her own experience, as she presented a version of English rural life and a community on the brink of war.

The novel takes place over the course of a summer's day. Pointz Hall – a 'whitish house' with a 'wing thrown out at right angles, lying unfortunately low on the meadow', very much like

Asheham – is home to the Oliver family, who sit reading the papers beneath portraits of their ancestors (some genuine, some not), and order fish for lunch.⁹⁰ Their conversation, about the weather for the village pageant, which will take place on the lawn that afternoon, chimes with the inevitable consistency of a peal of bells. But, in the newspaper, Europe is 'bristling with guns, poised with planes', and there are traces of other, older battles, lingering in the watch preserved under glass, its motion frozen by a bullet at Waterloo; and in the surrounding landscape, pockmarked with scars 'made by the Britons; by the Romans; by the Elizabethan manor house; and by the plough, when they ploughed the hill to grow wheat in the Napoleonic wars.'⁹¹ But it is the present war which is fraying nerves: Bartholomew jumps out at his grandson, and makes the little boy cry; Giles, impotent with rage, stamps on a snake and bloodies his tennis shoes; and his unhappy wife, Isa, thinks there are only two emotions, 'Love and hate'.⁹² Human history is repeating itself, the novel suggests; another chapter of toil and conflict embedding itself in the landscape like the furrows made by the first carts.

In the garden, villagers are dressing in the bushes, the pageant's director, Miss La Trobe, standing anxiously by. The pageant is her great work, both a dramatic outline of England's history – the villagers dressed as Elizabethans and Victorians in bedspreads and sixpenny dishcloths – and an attempt to describe a vision of unity. (Like Rosamond, Virginia had turned to the play as a device for thinking about rural community; 'a complete whole: thats my idea', as she had written in her diary.⁹³) Miss La Trobe wishes to bring her audience out of discord and into harmony, to 'see the hidden, join the broken'.⁹⁴ Her vision of history shows only England at peace. Her plot skips over wars, battlefields and the lives of great men (' "Why leave out the British Army? What's history without the Army, eh?" ' complains Colonel Mayhew), and lights instead upon female monarchs, maids-of-all-work, pilgrims and lovers.⁹⁵ The Victorians are shown gossiping and picnicking. (' "Oh but it was beautiful," ' the elderly women in the audience croon.⁹⁶) Finally, in the last act, the players face the audience, holding up an assortment of mirrors. What Miss La Trobe wishes to show the villagers is themselves, faces bobbing and bewildered, a ramshackle community. ' "[W]e are members one of another. Each is part of the whole," ' interprets the reverend, addressing the crowd before asking for donations towards the installation of electric lights in the church.[97] His voice is drowned out by the sound of aeroplanes passing in formation overhead. Harmony is essential, Miss La Trobe is trying to tell her audience; by looking to England's shared past, the villagers might better understand their collective role in securing future peace.

In the event, the pageant is a failure. Miss La Trobe watches from behind a tree as cotton-wool moustaches come loose, words are whisked away by the wind, and a rain shower engulfs the second act. At the interval, her audience breaks apart and scatters over the lawn, the emotion of the play 'spilt'.[98] Her meaning has evaded the villagers, her vision of England destroyed by parochial-mindedness and premonitions of war. (' "[I]f one spirit animates the whole, what about the aeroplanes?" ' someone asks.[99]) And yet the novel does, in fact, offer a vision of unity, one revealed in the everyday, informal moments that interrupt the drama, in the snippets of conversation that take place between the acts. At the pageant's close, the villagers begin to leave and the day diffuses into comfortable, absent-minded chatter. Old women begin 'stooping, peering, fumbling' for gloves and sticks lost beneath the seats; Mr Cobbet hurries home to water his plants.[100] These are village hall-type characters of the kind Virginia encountered in Rodmell, and there is something quietly ennobling about their dispersal, ambling in small groups to cars and bicycles, talking disjointedly about the pageant and the war; making plans, offering lifts. Miss La Trobe's pageant has held the villagers together only momentarily, perhaps, but there are myriad threads – woven into the landscape in which they live, and their shared history – which will continue to connect them once the drama is done.

Pilgrims looping through the trees, swallows darting, a cow bellowing for her calf. Throughout the pageant, the view of the landscape beyond offers the villagers another form of community. In the moments when Miss La Trobe's drama fails, it is the natural world which brings the villagers together: the trees, the darting swallows, and the rooks join with the landscape in folding the audience in a 'triple melody'.[101] In the fields, the bellowing cows pick up and continue the emotion of the drama where the players leave off. The reverend understands. ' "I thought I perceived that nature takes her part. Dare we, I asked myself, limit life to ourselves?" ' he asks.[102]

Boundaries between the human and natural worlds become porous. As the villagers dress among the brambles, their brightly coloured costumes attract butterflies, 'flitting and tasting'; in the barn, as Mrs Sands distributes tea, the structure is teeming with life – 'nibbling' mice, 'busy' swallows, a stray bitch with her puppies.[103] In the 'Barn scene', as Virginia referred to it in her diary, she was back with her magnifying glass, practising her microscopic vision in order to describe insect and animal life. It took several attempts to get right. An earlier typescript of the novel shows her debating whether or not to anthropomorphize the insects, to show ecstasy in the butterfly sunning its wings, or simply to leave them to their darkened corners, an unseen mass of 'expanding and narrowing' eyes.[104] In the end, she left the creatures to their own devices. Only Mrs Swithin notices the swallows flitting among the rafters and between the trees, moving not to any human music, but 'to the unheard rhythm of their own wild hearts'.[105]

The novel was a continuation of the thinking she had begun at Asheham, when she had conducted her enquiry into the natural world. Then, she had sat for long periods on the Downs watching for beetles and butterflies, imagining insects and humans as belonging to a connective tissue, a shared biotic community; she had lain and watched the hare, thinking 'This is "Earth life" '.[106]

~

Connection, and the place of human life within the scheme entire, were thoughts which became more urgent as the world was splintering into war. The early typescript of the novel reveals something else, a passage describing a 'nameless spirit', a 'being' – 'not "we" nor "I", nor the novelist either' – unconcerned with human drama, but present in the barn and in the trees, uniting swallows and players, cows and villagers, as if by innumerable, invisible threads.[107] The novel simulates the thinking of her earlier book, *The Waves*, that 'abstract mystical eyeless book', as she had described it in her diary, in which life would be represented as a 'continuous stream, not solely of human thought . . . all flowing together'.[108] It was Virginia's abiding idea, a theory of presence and connection she had been developing throughout her writing life. It was, she explained in the memoir she was writing in 1940, 'what I might call a philosophy; at any rate it is a constant idea of mine; that behind the cotton wool is a hidden pattern; that we – I mean, all human beings – are connected with this; that the whole world is a work of art; that we are parts of the work of art.'[109] *Between the Acts* is made up of such concealed patterns, patterns visible only to an all-seeing eye: the audience assembling and dispersing; the swallows flitting; the aeroplanes passing. Planning the book, she had written that there must be 'an order evident', the reader made 'aware that we are spectators and also passive participants in a pageant' – a pageant which is 'all life, all art'.[110] It was a searching, unifying impulse, an attempt to ward off disorder and chaos. For otherwise, there is only darkness, like the darkness that engulfs the final scene of the novel, suspending Isa and Giles in the dreadful pause before conversation starts, or the night that falls in 'The Moment', her preparatory sketch. That darkness is a primordial darkness, in which there is no sequence, no movement, no shelter; a darkness through which voices cannot pass.

In late 1940, Virginia's health was growing worse. She struggled to sleep, became agitated and terribly thin. Her old demons were returning. Leonard appointed a doctor in Brighton. And yet Virginia continued to think about her private creed. Isolated in the country, she reminded herself that this was the time to test whether 'the belief in something existing independently of myself will hold good'.[111] She had always written of her sense of a spirit, a life-force, moving through the physical world. She felt it most strongly in Sussex where, as she had written before, she came close to 'what I call "reality": a thing I see before me, something abstract; but residing in the downs or sky;

beside which nothing matters; in which I shall rest & continue to exist'.[112] It was a vital, immaterial, earthy thing, belonging to the particular enchantment of the Sussex landscape, which had been her mainstay and her greatest consolation. In one of her last essays, she described it as an 'energy' connecting the rooks with the ploughmen and the wave-like Downs, inspiring even the last jagged movements of the dying moth on her windowpane.[113]

News of Britain's declaration of war on Germany on 9 September 1939 reached Sylvia Townsend Warner in rural Connecticut, where she was staying with Valentine Ackland and Valentine's lover, the American writer Elizabeth Wade White. The three women had travelled together to America from Dorset, so that Sylvia could attend the Third American Writers' Conference in New York, which convened to consider the failure of democracy in Europe; afterwards, at Elizabeth's suggestion, they rented a farmhouse in Warren, Litchfield County, for the rest of the summer. They were negotiating an uneasy intimacy. 'I shall be sharing a house [. . .] with two other petticoats (both of them, of course, wearing trousers),' Sylvia had written to her friend, the composer Paul Nordoff, whom she had met in New York.[114] But the situation was far from idyllic. The weather was hot, the news from Europe bleak, and Sylvia had little choice but to stand by unhappily as Valentine conducted her affair. At night, she listened to the lovers' voices rising and falling in the room they shared together, while she slept alone. She longed to return to England. When the news reached her of the sinking of the *Courageous*, with the loss of five hundred lives, Sylvia felt a sense of duty to be among her countrymen – while sensing an opportunity to get away from Elizabeth for good. Her editor at the *New Yorker*, William Maxwell, urged her to stay. 'I have the profoundest doubts about this war,' she wrote to him. 'I don't feel that it is being fought against Nazidom, and while Chamberlain is around I doubt if it will be. And I can't suppose that going back will better it or me. But for all that, I feel that my responsibilities are there, not here.'[115]

But there was little consolation to be found in Dorset when she arrived in late October, having sailed with Valentine alone. Their house, Frome Vauchurch, on the riverbank near the village of Maiden Newton – where the couple had lived since 1937, after leaving West Chaldon – smelled of mutton fat, having sheltered Sylvia's old charlady who had decamped from London for several weeks. Sylvia's first act was to throw open the windows, which looked out along one side of the house onto the River Frome. Usually, the river was her 'incessant pleasure', where she watched moorhens and fat young water-rats learning to swim.[116] Now, the water curled and curdled beneath her. The war had brought with it other, private disasters. In her life with Valentine, and her domestic life, nothing felt familiar, nothing would ever be the same.

The summer with Elizabeth had left Sylvia feeling 'as hollow as a hemlock stalk'.[117] As they were crossing the Atlantic, Valentine tried to reassure her their relationship would recover, but a muddle with telegrams from America soon revealed the affair – at least, emotionally – wasn't over. Valentine loved two women at once, she would later explain in her memoir, *For Sylvia*, a public apology of sorts. Elizabeth had arrived at a difficult moment in her life, when money worries, her drinking and a lack of recognition for her poetry depressed her. (Since 1936, Sylvia's stories had been published in the *New Yorker*; she was still the more successful.*) Like others, the affair had begun with Sylvia's encouragement. In fact, Sylvia had met Elizabeth first, at a party in New York in 1929, when she was working as a guest critic for the *Herald Tribune*; she kept up a correspondence until, in 1937, Elizabeth wrote to say she would be in Paris, and Sylvia invited her to Dorset to stay. Well-educated, left-wing and wealthy

---

* Following the publication of her first story in 1936, Sylvia developed a lasting relationship with the *New Yorker* and its fiction editor, William Maxwell. Over a thirty-year period, she published nearly 150 stories in the magazine, to which she referred fondly as 'my gentleman friend' on account of its making her financially secure for the rest of her life. Harman, *Sylvia Townsend Warner*, 145.

(she contributed generously to Sylvia's campaign for Spanish Medical Aid), Elizabeth stayed at Frome Vauchurch for four months. Sylvia, believing herself to be 'behaving correctly in a quite usual situation', moved into the spare room.[118] Condoning Valentine's infatuations was, she felt, a way of confronting the seemingly increasing distance between their ages. In 1937, when the affair with Elizabeth first began, Sylvia was in her middle forties while Valentine was thirty-one. But it was also to exercise the principles she lived by. She refused to curtail Valentine's personal freedoms: there would be no rehearsals of wifeliness, no expressions of disappointment; Valentine must act as she pleased. Sylvia had strength of character enough to witness – even to be amused by – Valentine's other loves.

But Elizabeth was different, and the affair was wild and deep. All through the summer of 1939, Sylvia looked on as Valentine became moody and unusually quiet. After they had returned home, she answered the telephone to hear the cable operator query the wording of a message Valentine had intended for her lover. Slamming down the receiver, she hid in the bathroom, 'Embarrassed and sick at heart'.[119] Her unhappiness was 'now almost inattentive', she wrote in her diary, 'so natural does it seem to me to get such cuffs as this morning's'.[120] Elizabeth, she realized, was 'my doing'.[121] Yet, she continued to have faith in the relationship begun nearly a decade earlier at Miss Green's cottage; its foundations, she believed, were still strong. 'I am glad we did not part, that we were neither of us unfaithful to our love, and our belief in each other,' she wrote to Valentine in April 1940 in one of their daily domestic letters from her writing room in Rat's Barn.[122] Each was trying to give the other courage. Little did Sylvia know Elizabeth would muddy the water for another ten years.

The disappointment of Sylvia's homecoming was compounded by the realization that she had arrived in a country already fully preoccupied with being at war. Though the fighting wouldn't arrive in England for another six months, she and Valentine were issued with gas masks – making them unrecognizable to each other, their voices 'spectral and distorted' – and were faced with immediate disruptions to domestic life.[123] The worst of these was the necessity, given the price of petrol, to sell Valentine's beloved car. But it wasn't long before they bought two motorized bicycles, and took to zooming along the country lanes. Sylvia's other great affliction was the blackout. '[H]ow hunted one feels,' she wrote, echoing the language of their first days in Chaldon, when they had lain among the gorse, 'as every evening one has to [. . .] go round letting down blinds, drawing curtains, putting up screens, all the maddening expedients for turning a room into a shoebox.'[124] In the spring, the women looked to the garden to supplement their diet. They extended the vegetable beds, and began to keep table rabbits, a buck and doe called Joseph and Rhoda. (Their rabbits were rarely eaten, but were sold off to good homes.) There were few eggs, and so Valentine fished the river, along with several young soldiers, who took to sitting in the garden with rabbits in their laps or along the opposite bank. (They were much relieved when Valentine offered to kill their catches with a small mallet she possessed for the purpose.) Soon, the garden was flourishing. 'We have eleven rabbits,' Sylvia wrote to Paul Nordoff, 'and six rows of peas, and five rows of broad beans, and as many of French beans, and a stand of sweet corn, and a vegetable marrow bed which is positively alarming, and a fine crop of onions and a crop, not so fine I'm afraid, of potatoes, [. . .] and millions of raspberries [. . .] and a lot of globe artichokes, and vast quantities of greens for the winter; and I have been up to my elbows in canning and preserving and conserving, and drying of herbs.'[125] Keeping busy, Sylvia could ward off the despondencies of war. And she seized at moments of unexpected beauty. When searchlights were installed along the riverbank, she and Valentine stood in the dark watching as the long, bright beams rolled over the trees. 'What a pity that they are not just turned on for glory and delight,' she mused, 'like the fountains at Versailles.'[126]

Still, she was disappointed, let down by the political failures of the previous decade, particularly the British government's failure to intervene in the Spanish Civil War. As Paris capitulated to Germany in June 1940, she meditated sadly on Europe's slide towards fascism, and the numbers who would be killed without purpose. In Sylvia's mind, the USSR remained the only example of decisive resistance to oppression. 'For war – this sort of war – is no way to attack fascism,' she wrote in her diary. 'And I am fretted to think how every day my chances of seeing other methods tried out are diminished. I feel like a scientist who has to wait in a queue to get to the laboratory – while both the laboratory and he are under bombardment.'[127] So much political energy had been wasted. Tidying her study, she sorted through piles of papers to be thrown away. 'So much about Spain. Thinking how vainly I worked, I wish I had worked a hundred times harder. Strange how there was room for one in that war: and in this – none. This war has not issued a single call for the help of intellectuals. It is just – your money and/or your life.'[128] Her disappointment was intensified by the feeling that, in Maiden Newton, she and Valentine would never truly feel at home. Unlike Chaldon, the place was pre-dominantly a working village (not an enclave for artists), and she feared that her neighbours, uninterested in communism and regard-ing her and Valentine as the odd couple with 'dangerous' and 'uncongenial' views, would surely now confuse them with Black-shirts. 'What more likely?' she remarked in her diary. 'We were anti-fascists long before the war [. . .] [They] will now remember their impression rather than our views.'[129]

Instinctively, she was seeing the war historically, through the lens of Spain. When she visited London during the bombing, she com-pared the rubble-strewn streets to Madrid. (And eerily she echoed Virginia Woolf's imagery of the blackout, the city 'abandoning itself to darkness, as though it were any country landscape', the entrances to the Tube lit by 'a few modest mediaeval little lanterns'.[130]) The war had damaged her capacity for utopian thinking, and a new strain of melancholy set in. Her hope for economic advancement in Britain, which had driven her writings about rural poverty in East Chaldon in the early 1930s, shrank to gloomy pronouncements about the long-term effects of war – 'hunger, poverty, famine, slow ruin'.[131] Her diary dwindled to almost nothing: a single entry for 1939 described Valentine's cable to Elizabeth. In her relationship with herself, with the world, and with her own idealism, her passion was gone.

And yet, Sylvia wrote, 'Counterpointing the war is the loveliest summer I have ever known.'[132] She and Valentine slept out beneath the apple tree, listening to the nightingale and waking to the scent of pinks. 'For all its violence, war is papery-thin compared to a garden with apple trees and cabbages in it,' she wrote. 'Even when it's forced down one's throat one can't swallow it. Whereas one goes out and eats great mouthfuls of cabbage and appletree and moonlight.'[133] The women went on fire-watching duty together, walking along the dusky country lanes, poised to blow whistles in the event of incendiary bombs. It was 'a most pastoral and contemplative pursuit', Sylvia wrote to Paul Nordoff. 'Valentine's whistle is just a whole tone lower than mine, and the same interval exists between the male and female owl, and we might have such lovely conversations.' ('It always seems to me that owls are very happy in their married lives, perhaps because they never speak during the day,' she added.)[134] Resuming their routines at Frome Vauchurch, the women were beginning to recover. But, in July 1940, as rumours of an invasion of the east coast grew, they travelled to Norfolk to help Valentine's mother, Ruth. The Hill House, Valentine's childhood home, had been requisitioned for an anti-aircraft battery, and Ruth was to move into a cottage in the village. Clearing the house was a considerable task, and Sylvia and Valentine stayed for almost six months. In Winterton, the streets were full of soldiers, and the dunes and beach were mined, cutting Sylvia off from the consoling sea. Walking inland, where there had been flooding two years previously, she saw in the barren landscape a reflection of her own sorrow. Valentine was returned to her, they had survived the deluge, but there was little life in their soil. 'We had lost confidence,' she wrote later, 'not in each other but in our own capacities to nourish and support.'[135]

~

Sylvia returned to Maiden Newton in the spring of 1941 to 'a buzz of compulsive activity', and an incendiary bomb through the spare room roof.[136] Like Virginia, she felt the local war effort to be a little ridiculous – inefficient, bordering on hysterical. New wartime labour laws required unmarried women to work and Valentine, being of the right age, was assigned as a clerk to the Territorial Army. Sylvia railed against the new regulations, which, when they were updated in 1943, also required her to work part-time. 'Being kept by a husband is of national importance enough,' she wrote angrily to Nancy Cunard, having received her summons from the Labour Exchange. 'But to be femme sole, and self-supporting, that hands you over, no more claim to consideration than a biscuit.'[137] Valentine travelled daily to the TA's headquarters in Dorchester, where she was set to work in an atmosphere of grave secrecy. She copied out various formulae assiduously, believing them to be code, until a mistake with the paper led the head clerk to reveal the dispatches – 'K.2, p.2, slp 1, K.2 tog.' – were, in fact, knitting patterns.[138]

'It is my belief,' Sylvia wrote to Paul Nordoff, 'that if our local villages were invaded, nobody would have time to notice the enemy, they would all be too busy taking sides over Mrs Tomkins and Mrs Bumkin.' Ruth Ackland was a case in point. 'In her ardour for service she has undertaken the charge of so many things that as far as I can reckon she will be essential in five different places at once,' Sylvia continued,

> and as she attains terrific velocity, fells whatever stands in her path, and is permanently fitted with a screaming device like a German bomb, she will create incalculable havoc amid both defenders and attackers, besides spraining her ankle and getting very much out of breath. I often think that Mrs Ackland is the real reason why Hitler has not yet tried a landing on the East Coast. She thinks so, too.[139]

Sylvia could make fun of her neighbours, but she was also growing weary. Shopping for bread in Maiden Newton, the baker's sister, telling her about the 'government loaf' scheme, stood 'beaming with patriotism'; Miss Harrison, organizing an inspection of Valentine's car for their YMCA round – on which they delivered cigarettes and sweets to troops billeted along the coast – was 'rosy with self-importance'.[140] When the baker warned there would be no more plum cakes, the factory in Bristol having burned down, Sylvia admired his attempt to make the villagers realize what war would mean for their daily lives, and yet imparting realism to the people of Maiden Newton was to work in 'the stiffest clay'.[141] 'England is not nice,' she wrote in early 1940. 'This kind of war is an essentially middle-aged pursuit; its aims, its ideals, its methods, are all middle-aged.'[142]

In her letters, she described the absurdity of a Red Cross demonstration on how to undress a wounded man: ' "First of all," said the lecturer boldly, "you remove the trousers." Cries from the audience, matrons and virgins' voices mingled. "No you don't! You take off his shoes." "Yes, yes. Of course. You take off his shoes. The next step is to pull down his trousers." Renewed cries. "You've forgotten his braces".' And an ARP air-raid rehearsal in Maiden Newton, which had the air of a 'knock-about farce film done in slow motion': 'at intervals some member of the local gentry pipes up to say, "Well, let's hope it will never be needed", or "We can't really get on with it without Mr Thompson", or "has it started yet, do you know?" '[143] Sylvia couldn't tolerate ineptitude, and reserved special disdain for flapping local gentry. Yet it struck her as strangely unfair that death could arrive at any time. 'It is very odd to look at all these poor consequential idiots and remember that war might at any moment make real mincemeat of them,' she wrote to Nordoff. 'Even under the shadow of death man walketh in a vain shadow.'[144]

As for Virginia, war for Sylvia meant the 'the horror of boredom' and the frustration of 'being compelled to attend things that don't interest one'.[145] She was willing to work, but was less enthusiastic about spending her time with the women who managed the local war effort. Nevertheless, she made herself available to the Dorchester branch of the Women's Voluntary Service and spent two days a week at its headquarters in Colliton House. Despite her displeasure, she was resourceful and efficient, and was soon appointed secretary, working closely with the section leader, Mrs Egerton, an admiral's wife. The organization appealed to Sylvia. In notes about the WVS written later, she described its pyramidal structure: at the top, Mrs Egerton was in charge; beneath her, every village in the district had a representative; and each representative her team of workers.[146] All the women were voluntary (with other domestic responsibilities that prevented them from full-time war work), all were local, most were middle-aged. There was much squabbling and petty feuding (especially during election time), but there was also gossip and good cheer. It was with this community of women, engaged in collective work, that Sylvia would see out the war.

With Mrs Egerton, Sylvia toured the county to inspect sites for 'Rest Centres', which were being set up in the larger villages to temporarily house bombed-out evacuees. Equipped (often poorly) by the Rural District Council, they were run by the WVS but, as Sylvia later reflected, the scheme had mixed success. Often, the centres lay dormant for months at a time, before the women received notice that up to fifty evacuees would arrive the following day. They cleaned and swept, prepared hot meals, shook out moth-eaten blankets and replenished stores of mice-infested dry food. But the arriving evacuees were mistrustful of their new surroundings, alarmed by the rural quiet and unhappy in their rickety beds. To the WVS helpers, they appeared ungrateful, and ill-feeling bred on both sides. When the centres were busy, Sylvia felt herself to be pacifying evacuees and volunteers alike,

saying words of comfort such as soap flakes can be made out of solid soap by means of a cheese-grater, nobody need be ashamed of lice nowadays, salads will not be appreciated without vinegar, Londoners seldom like porridge, pubs open at six, nettle stings are not the same as nettle-rash, fish and chips will come out in a van, lost prams shall be traced, those are *our* planes, Londoners can't be expected to go to bed before eleven, the old lady will probably leave off crying if you can get her to take her shoes off, cows don't bite, have you put up a washing-line, nursing mothers must have early morning tea, buses run on Wednesdays and Saturdays, etc . . .[147]

Yet she enjoyed her part in the scheme, which was to drive through rural Dorset inspecting disused schoolrooms and dusty church halls. The work reminded her of her *Tudor Church Music* days, and she noticed faces of the dead from the previous war peering out at her from photographs with sombre recognition, 'as if we might once have exchanged a few words at a promenade concert in 1913'.[148] At Langton Herring, she was shown around by a schoolmistress with a First Aid qualification and no supplies; at Tincleton, by a farmer's wife with 'a head of some heart-of-oak, rum-drinking, man-flogging Admiral of Nelson's day'; at Abbotsbury, by a 'lemon-coloured old lady' who boasted of cousins bombed in Liverpool; and at Winterbourne Abbas, by two Mrs Biggses.[149] It was old-world Dorset – 'beautiful [. . .] and still for ever new' – and yet Sylvia resisted its charms.[150] She roved the dilapidated buildings as she had at Chaldon, appalled by the leaks, the outdoor privvies and the contaminated wells. On the coldest days, she noted in her diary, the children in the schoolrooms shivered and wrote in their gloves.

In Dorchester, she threw herself into her WVS work with some of the gusto she had shown to Spain, organizing small campaigns and corralling goods. Recalling her 'Soap for Spain' initiative (to which Rosamond Lehmann had donated five pounds) and her Chaldon book-lending scheme, she fulfilled an order from the local Home Guard for three hundred tin hats, and implemented a programme of sending books to billeted soldiers. In this particular enterprise she was extremely successful. In the basement of the new WVS offices on High West Street was the Salvage Depot, where books were brought in from the surrounding villages for pulping. With Valentine (then working in the same building for Civil Defence), Sylvia trawled through the stores, rescuing anything she thought soldiers might find useful or enjoy. A steady trickle was sent to Army Welfare, including technical training manuals and a consignment of books in Italian for prisoners of war. A further thirteen crates were sent to Exeter as part of the Blitzed Libraries Scheme. Sylvia was satisfied with her quietly rebellious campaign, which cut through the housewifery of her day-to-day WVS work.

She was pleased to have found an outlet which quenched her old desire to promote intellectual causes, advocate for the disadvantaged, and bring about a measure of practical good. But her political energies had shifted. When the Communist Party printing press took over the *Dorset Country Chronicle* in 1942, moving into offices in Dorchester, she declined to get involved. Her fervour was of a lower pitch. At most, she continued fundraising sporadically for Soviet Aid, and took pleasure in telling Mrs Egerton 'All about Communism'.[151] One gets a sense of her stubbornness and her dry, dark humour in the fact that she enjoyed the reactions of visitors to her office in Colliton House where, above her desk, she had installed a photograph of 'Uncle Joe', as she referred to him in her diary. But her belief in the USSR had developed into a quieter, more private creed. In her diary, she thought back to the horror of the declaration of war, and her feelings were unchanged. 'I knew the defence of USSR was the defence of my deepest concerns; and I know it still.'[152]

~

Just as Virginia wrote about the war by writing about her village neighbours, so Sylvia became increasingly engaged in her own kind of rural reporting. At the WVS, volunteers were required to fill in 'day books' with daily updates on the district unit's progress in the war effort. It was an activity absolutely suited to Sylvia. Of the various hands discernible in the notebooks, hers is the most prominent (she slipped into dating her entries as she dated her diaries). She recorded the Dorchester WVS's activities with the utmost efficiency. Heading opposing pages 'In' and 'Out', she kept up a brisk inventory of gas masks, stationery, saucepans, hot-water bottles, wool, mittens, blankets and quilts. She recorded the commencement of the 'sock repair scheme', of visitors (Mrs Ratclyffe resigning from her post, Mrs Shepherd bringing knitting), requests from evacuees (a book of wild flowers), all correspondence sent and received. There were typically economizing notes about donations, of 'an old riding-habit, which could be cut into several suits'.[153] She was enjoying contributing to the day books, a collective chronicling of historical events through material goods. And she threw herself into paperwork, preparing statistics, filling in forms. 'I hope to go on wrapping my paper insulation round me,' she wrote from her office, 'while high-bred passions rage.'[154]

The atmosphere of provincial life became Sylvia's principal subject matter in wartime, during which she continued to publish stories in the *New Yorker*. She drew upon people and events in Dorchester – thinly disguised as the market town of 'Dumbridge' – to turn her observations of the local war effort into a comedy of English parochialism for American readers. In one story, a woman returns from a long absence to find her home destroyed by a series of unwelcome guests, including billeted soldiers and a batch of evacuees; in another, a women's shooting class descends into chaos; while another deals with a group of women struggling with an influx of bombed-out Londoners, including a Mrs Leopard, who ruthlessly takes advantage of their rather insipid kindness.[155] As in her letters, Sylvia was often unsparing in her depictions of her working-class neighbours, a surprising lack of generosity for a communist who had spent a decade writing in their defence. But she had never tolerated small-mindedness or incompetence, as demonstrated by her forthright essays of the 1930s and her first stories for the *New Yorker*, which sent up farmers' wives and gentry, city-dwellers and rural folk alike.

And yet, she was uncomfortable seeing her fellows up close. The war pierced solitude and let the real-life stuff of neighbourliness and cross-class intimacy come flooding in, just as Virginia had experienced in Sussex. She found that the local war effort in Dorchester, compared to her work for Spain, felt feeble. 'Why do I write about old people when I write about war?' she wrote in her diary after finishing another story, 'because it seems, down here, so much an old persons' war.'[156] Sylvia was disenchanted, but still internationalist in outlook. In presenting Englishness without sentimentality to an American audience, she was refusing to participate in the rhetoric which called for national insularity in a time of crisis and was intent, as in her earlier writings, on dispelling myths of national identity. The stories were critical examinations of all that patriotic war feeling. In 'English Climate', a young solider returns to Dumbridge on leave from his barracks to discover 'a dingy caterpillar' of books laid end-to-end down the middle of the street, a recreation of Dorchester's own 'book mile' as part of national salvage week.[157] Sylvia and Valentine had been so appalled at the willingness of the townsfolk to commit such an act of vandalism they retreated to Valentine's office 'glittering with fury'.[158] In the story, the soldier soon discovers his own copy of the poems of Edward Thomas on the ground, donated by his fanatical mother.

The stories show the war taking its toll. 'Poor Mary', published in 1945, depicts a marriage barely surviving, a portrait of Sylvia's own unhappy domestic life. In the story, a woman arrives at a cottage to see her husband after a long absence. She has been in the army, while he has been a conscientious objector, living in the country and working with pigs. She smells of metal, he of dung. Their bodies have changed, and each is aware of the other's lack of desire. Weathering the war has meant weathering a marriage, a partnership both intimate and inarticulate, brokered over increasing distances, and gradually becoming chaste.

~

Throughout 1942, domestic life rumbled on, of a more sombre character than before. In the spring, Valentine started to dig a trench in the garden, and Sylvia planted onions. Spitfires somersaulted overhead, occasionally fitted with screamers. The hawthorn hedge was spattered with cement from the laying of tank traps, and Home Guard officers whistled in the lane. On fire-watching duty, Sylvia observed German planes on their way to Bristol, Plymouth and Yeovil; and there was bombing in Bath and Exeter, and gunfire in Poole. She thought of the fragility of the human body against the destructiveness of metal and machinery. In the lanes, the soldiers looked like *'objets de luxe'*, and she stared 'at the craftsmanship of their eyelashes and fingernails, their eyelids like flower-petals'.[159] Being so near the coast, Maiden Newton became a 'Restricted Area', and she and Valentine were informed that in the event of invasion, Frome Vauchurch would be used as a machine-gun post. They packed up their most valued possessions and put them into storage, and attended classes in shooting rifles and throwing grenades under the tutelage of the local Home Guard. Sylvia admired Valentine's graceful arm, while noting that she was surpassed by the quiet young woman from the grocer's shop. It was useful and disconcerting to possess such a skill.

By now, war was interwoven with daily domestic life. On Valentine's Day, she and Valentine exchanged a humble selection of their usual gifts: an enamel box, snowdrops and daffodils and 'a very industrious exceedingly handmade regrettably tubular Fair Isle scarf', which Sylvia had been working on all the winter.[160] Their daily walks became pinecone-gathering expeditions, as they needed fuel; the doctor's daughter brought eggs, and Mr Gould brought paraffin, which was often filched. A muntjac ate the broccoli. Sylvia was growing weary of 'the everlasting problem of finding something new to cook or some new way of cooking the old. Supplies are very mingy and monotonous.'[161] Now, housekeeping – one of her oldest and greatest pleasures – seemed 'child's play'. 'I don't at all object to being simplified,' she wrote. 'I feel domesticity just slipping off me.'[162] Coming back from Weymouth, her way was blocked by a herd of cows in the road, and she guided them into a field; on a train from Dorchester, she listened to a woman telling how she had lost her husband in the last war, and now both her sons. Sylvia felt melancholy, and was becoming thin. But she was determined to keep busy. There was the WVS contribution to Warship Week to organize, and a washing-day march around Dorchester ('just as we were due to start everyone had sudden doubts as to whether gas-masks were worn to the right or to the left. Like swords, I said').[163] Slices of pleasure broke through. Turning on the wireless, she caught Beethoven's Symphony No. 9, though 'the chorus singers had the tone of people who had spent a lean winter, and coughed oft'; and Pergolesi's *Stabat Mater*, which she liked for being 'so noble and unassuming and humane'.[164] She continued to monitor the events of the war closely. In May, on hearing the news that British bombers had been sent to Cologne, she was 'almost on my knees in thankfulness for the news we had done something. But oh the poor bloody army: which is assuming a female role of sheltered domesticity and retirement, broken by bouts of such frightful activity as only women are expected to undertake.'[165] ('It's not patriotism, and it's not obtuseness,' she had written about the necessity of violence in an otherwise unnecessary war. 'It's realism.'[166])

~

Sylvia was making sense of the war by thinking about history. In early 1942, she threw herself into public speaking, first to the Educational Workers' Association (to whom Virginia and Leonard Woolf had lectured in Brighton), then the Labour Party, and finally the forces. She walked to a women's secretarial college near Bridport, arriving 'as blouzed as Lizzy Bennet', where she talked about Queen Elizabeth.[167] In Weymouth, a group of Labour women 'restrained their coughs and listened nicely' as she discussed the role of women in the Renaissance, the reformation martyrs (countering Anne Askew with Margaret Clitheroe), and the nineteenth century, including the poem 'The Song of the Shirt', about an impoverished seamstress.[168] Like Virginia, Sylvia's first lectures uncovered a common ground of history – a history of those often incidental to main events, and of the everyday. When she spoke to troops at Toller Porcorum, she adapted her message, covering the twentieth century from the New Deal ('I spoke too fast, as usual'), to modern Germany and housing.[169] To the Royal Army Service Corps at Charminster, she dipped back into English antiquity with Christopher Wren, before the soldiers requested lectures on the USSR and the emergence of fascism in Europe. '[Y]ou would never believe what a lot of subjects I can talk about,' she wrote energetically to Harold Raymond at Chatto & Windus. 'I haven't repeated myself yet, though we are getting wilder and wilder. Next time I discourse to them it will be on How Bugles Blow; and I still have theology up my sleeve.'[170] She enjoyed her spirited discussions with the young soldiers, which often reached good-humoured agreement ('General feeling that we are waiting for the end of the war to see what happens next.').[171] 'I myself think I teach history very well,' she wrote, 'going on the principal that one can't make it too much like the Chamber of Horrors and the Musée Grevin.'[172]

It suited Sylvia to roam freely, lighting upon subjects which interested her and sharing the expertise she had acquired over the course of her reading and writing life. She was, in a sense, following in the footsteps of her father, both in her lecturing, and also in her plans for a book on domestic history which she briefly discussed with his publisher, Blackie's. But, just as before – when she had written about her community at Chaldon in the 1930s – she was developing her own style, one that moved away from the broader scope of large events to examine their impact on ordinary communities and everyday lives, particularly the lives of women. George Townsend Warner had laid out his theory of historical method. History writing was a matter of 'selection and arrangement', he wrote in *Tillage, Trade and Invention*, his history of British industrialism published in 1912; the historian's task being to 'trace out the main threads' while 'omitting small and unfruitful details'.[173] Thirty years later, Sylvia revised the process. 'After you have gathered your material,' she said in a lecture on the historical novel in 1939, 'use a fruit-press. It's the juices you want.'[174] She was setting out on a new novel, set in the Middle Ages, and was relishing the pleasures of period detail, of recreating a fleshly, full-blooded past. While she was turning to historical sources – to accounts of medieval nunneries and memoirs of the court at Versailles ('The society is so limited, the passions are so parochial and so parochially intense'[175]) – the novel also arose out of her own historical moment, which lent itself to comparisons with a more distant past. Listening to the wireless 'had something of the quality of news of a pestilence', she had written in her diary in 1940, likening the German army to the Black Death. 'It has made it, in a fashion, an atmospheric rather than a territorial phenomenon.'[176] Yet, she assured Nordoff, her new novel was 'not in any way a historical novel, it hasn't any thesis, and so far I'm contentedly vague about the plot'. But she was 'interested to find out how much I know' about the characters who were presenting themselves to her, who were all 'professionally religious, nuns, or parsons, or bishops'.[177] One afternoon, after sending a priest out hawking, she noted: 'Sometimes my book seems to walk around the room alive.'[178]

Sylvia began the novel, which would become *The Corner That Held Them*, on a bitter day in February 1942, starting with a scene about a nun weeding shallots in the shadow of a gleaming spire, the building of which has almost brought her convent to ruin. 'Our pipes freeze,' she wrote in her diary that evening, 'and I begin to write a story about a medieval nunnery: to be entirely taken up with their money difficulties.'[179] Like Virginia, she was wary of imposing a framework on her ideas, which provided an escape from the grim realities of war. Sitting in the sun-parlour at Frome Vauchurch, she worked almost guiltily: 'shame on me for a gadabout'.[180] Sylvia dispensed with the usual conventions of structure and plot, and drew on her experience of wartime Dorchester to unfurl a diffuse and detailed chronicle of daily life for an enclosed community of women. The novel covers thirty years in the life of Oby, a ramshackle convent on an East Anglian fen, and shifts between innumerable points of view with dazzling rapidity. Time is measured by the succession of one prioress to another (Prioress Isabella chokes on a plum stone, so Dame Alicia takes over), novices becoming nuns, a visit from the bishop, and the building of the spire, which crumbles and is rebuilt. Beyond the reed fence of Oby, the Black Death rages through the nation, and, later, discontented peasants march across the landscape. News of the outside world reaches the nuns via serfs and pedlars, and through open windows, yet such events are significant only insofar as they affect the convent's account books and store cupboard. National life has little bearing on the lives of the nuns, who are more intrigued by a sister breaking her vows or attempting to fly, or by the drowning of a corrodian in the fish pond.

Topography is important; the novel is a novel of flatlands and fens. In her subsequent notes on writing *The Corner That Held Them*, Sylvia recalled how it originally took place in Somerset, with the river running through Sedgemoor. Her decision to move the nuns to Norfolk took into consideration climate, architecture and her developing sense of how to depict the progression of history. A flat landscape would better capture, she noted, 'the feeling of how [. . .] Ely must have looked [. . .] how intimidatingly, tyrannically large, to the 12th century peasant, coming out of his smoking hovel to stare over the fen'.[181] Landscape is history, and that history – the history of nationhood and ecclesiastical power – is not for him; his lies at his feet, a note of little consequence, as incidental and muddy as the Waxle Stream, which doggedly cuts and recuts its pathway through the fen. Ultimately, Sylvia overlaid this Norfolk scene with Dorset; in it lived her wartime neighbours, reimagined as a group of wholly unholy sisters, their quotidian lives destined for obscurity, their features shaped from the same dough.

'A good convent,' Sylvia writes near the beginning of the novel, 'should have no history. Its life is hid with Christ who is above. History is of the world, costly and deadly.'[182] The nuns of Oby, isolated in flat, marshy fen country, are reconciled to leading a humdrum life.[183] The minutiae of their daily lives – going into the chapter, darning holes, making marzipan – is not the stuff of the annals, the written records of a religious institution which describe, year by year, 'usually deplorable' events – a flood, a fire, a baby.[184] They know they will leave no mark on history. Instead, they must live quietly and devoutly, no more conspicuous than their sisters, for in a convent there is 'no place for aberrations of individuality'.[185] Looking at their faces, Prioress Alicia thinks they are like 'a tray of buns':

> In some the leaven has worked more than in others, some are a little under-baked, some a little scorched, in others the spice has clotted and shows like a brown stain; but one can see that they all come out of the same oven and that one hand pulled them apart from the same lump of dough. A tray of buns, a tray of nuns . . .[186]

Yet, far from behaving like 'a flock ascending to a heavenly pasture', the nuns of Oby are a 'flock of magpies' – bickering and comfort-loving.[187] When the bishop visits, he is distressed to hear not religious music but 'the yelpings of little dogs and the clattering of egg-whisks'. He sees the nuns talking at meals, eating sweets in the dormitories, using little combs, sitting on soft cushions and decking themselves out in scented mantles 'better befitting harlots than the brides of Christ'. And he is appalled at the state of the convent's account books, defaced with entries such as *'things bought at Waxelby'* or, inexplicably, *'Rabbit'*.[188] '[A] household of nuns might be forgiven their careless stewardship (the more so since women are ordained the weaker vessel and have no business sense),' he rebukes the prioress afterwards by letter, 'if those same nuns neglected the goods of the world by reason of their devotion to heaven.' But at Oby, concludes the bishop, there is little by way of piety; instead the house is 'full of pride, sloth, greed, falsehoods, worldliness, pet animals and private property'.[189]

Yet Sylvia's medieval world is a world beset by problems – pestilence, draughty buildings, fluctuating supplies of foodstuffs and dry goods – and the nuns have little time for spirituality. (This is probably a good thing, muses Prioress Alicia, 'since they would then be able to give an undivided attention to the mortifying tranquillity of their lives'.[190]) Though the nuns live within a religious framework, their days plotted according to its calendar, they are worldly creatures, pragmatic and secular by nature. The novel was begun 'on the purest Marxian principles', Sylvia said later, adding that 'if you were going to give an accurate picture of the monastic life, you'd have to put in all their finances'.[191] She had spent the war years in Dorchester contributing to the WVS day books, a continuous, handwritten inventory of moth-eaten blankets, saucepans, second-hand clothes and books, which, many years later, reads like a history of the war in miniature, its advances and abeyances, the availability of goods, the atmosphere of gloom or good cheer. In *The Corner That Held Them*, the convent's account book functions similarly. Moments of crisis mean economic reckoning, lists of everyday items, deaths totted up on fingers, dowries accounted for. The novel's abundance of material detail indicates poverty or prosperity: the buildings require upkeep, there are lice in the bedding, a shard of eggshell is found in a pancake. Ultimately, a nun's life is a life of work, worry and domestic economy. Prioress Alicia has become weary of steering her sinking ship. Her life has been administrative, unremarkable; her faith has been mislaid along the way. 'Beef and mutton, clothing and firing, that is the life-work for a prioress,' she thinks. 'Not souls. Not even spires.'[192]

Sylvia felt the truest title for the novel was an early one – 'People Growing Old'. It was to the melancholy music of ageing and infirmity that she worked the story. Many is the nun who looks up at the clouds scudding across the Oby sky and realizes she has spent her life between its walls. As the older nuns resign their posts and prepare to live out their days in obscurity, arthritic and forgetful, the younger ones push up beneath them. Sylvia was drawing out her own private weariness. In the midst of her crisis with Valentine, in which she felt secondary to Elizabeth, she was like Prioress Alicia, a woman preoccupied with evaluating her life's work, finding its architecture unstable and her faith lost. '[H]ere am I,' thinks the prioress, 'fixed in the religious life like a candle on a spike. I consume, I burn away, always lighting the same corner, always beleaguered by the same shadows; and in the end I shall burn out and another candle will be fixed in my stead.'[193]

In the end, though Prioress Alicia is disappointed in her spire – which from a distance appears to be sinking into the formless landscape, her history submerged – *The Corner That Held Them* celebrates other moments of art-making and achievement. Following the bishop's damning report, the nuns of Oby begin an altar-hanging in a bid to raise the convent's status. Through two cold winters they sit together, their many fingers plying satin with pearls and gold thread. At first, the altar-hanging becomes 'an instrument' in the entrenched familial factions of the convent – 'a de Retteville banner waved against de Stapledons' – yet, as the winters wear on, it fosters communal feeling. As they work, the women's voices rise and fall, individual threads weaving into a collective tissue of sound. With a shared interest and purpose, they become knitted together, for 'Something was being made, they had a reason for living together, the blue satin roofed them like a tabernacle.'[194] In her sixth novel, Sylvia was returning to images of collective labour which had pre-occupied her throughout her writing life. On a walk in Long Melford in 1927, she had come upon a factory where women were employed weaving horsehair on handlooms. She had been transfixed by the sight of 'the women's heads and shoulders moving to and fro above the fixed hands, the lights flaring'.[195] The sight of the concentrating, silent women, an image of social harmony, sent her down a rabbithole of story-making. And yet she remained alert to the material conditions of the workplace. As in her first published article, in which she criticized conditions in the women-only munitions factory where she worked during the First World War, Sylvia noted the discomforts of the Long Melford women – the noise, the unshaded gas-jets – and in *The Corner That Held Them* described the fires lighted to keep the nuns' chilblained fingers warm. Only Dame Lovisa stands apart from the group, her skin too rough for sewing, a reminder of poverty and loneliness, of the wolf never far from the door.

At the novel's close, the altar-hanging is stolen from Oby by a novice and a peasant woman from the wicket. Its loss is beyond measure to the nuns, though, in the wider scheme, it is also just an accident of history. Instead, its enduringness lies in its making, which forms an indelible contribution to early-English culture. Elsewhere the novel describes other emergent art forms – the singing of the new *Ars nova*, the writing of vernacular poetry – which suffer similar fates. Spires fall, a manuscript is lost. But destruction can be regenerative: cultural artefacts perish, only for their forms to resurface anew. Sylvia was still interested in magic. In *The Corner That Held Them*, there are moments of transcendence in the everyday. Singing the *triste loysir*, the monks' voices, like the voices of the nuns, enkindle each other so that the music, a pure, paradisal sound, is 'continually renewed'.[196] Art is always in the making, springing up like nettles from the folk. It is a part of human history, which, like the Waxle Stream threading through the Oby landscape, is an ongoing process, 'full of loops and turnings, and constantly revising its course'.[197] All through the war, the novel itself had 'persisted in getting written through an endless series of interruptions, distractions, and destructions, [. . .] as persistent as a damp patch in a house wall', Sylvia had written.[198] Human endeavour suffers setbacks; like the corner of the altar-hanging left unfinished, nothing is ever completed.

And no one has the final word. In this long, multi-perspectival story, there is no ending as such. Almost arbitrarily, the narrative stops, a thread left to hang loose. The novice Adela, travelling to the coast, is abandoned on a boat with the stolen embroidery in her lap. In leaving the convent, and taking the nuns' work with her, she has opened Oby up to the outside world, which seeps in as though through a crack. The geography of the novel has expanded, its action moving into territory beyond the quiet corner of the East Anglian fen. History, for the time being, at least, will forget the nuns, leaving their stories to be reclaimed and retold at some future date.

In her 1971 notes to the day books, Sylvia described the disbanding of the Dorchester WVS, another sturdy, determined unit of local women, as the war was won. Its stores were dismantled, the bolts of black-market material sent to France to make pinafores for schoolchildren; the vitamins, sent by America to boost the volunteers' energy, to the Netherlands. Victory flags were bought to decorate the shop. History was chomping at the bit, restless and eager to move on. 'By the beginning of May 1945, when the last Day Book runs out, we were less important in a roomier world,' Sylvia wrote. '*Unarm, Eros; the long day's task is done* . . . There was not much left to do, except to tidy things up.'[199]

With *The Corner That Held Them*, Sylvia was rejecting the individual to explore the intimate workings of a community, searching for the

indomitable spirit of the group. She was writing her way into a
pioneering new tradition of economically focused women's histories, following in the footsteps of historians like Eileen Power. 'This
book is chiefly concerned with the kitchens of history,' Power had
written in her bestselling book *Medieval People* (though it was her
1922 *Medieval English Nunneries* that Sylvia borrowed from the
London Library).[200] In her research, Power looked at sources,
including nuns' account books and ecclesiastical registers, to piece
together their material lives. But, while Sylvia certainly drew on
Power's methodology in her creation of Oby, she also had her own
living source to hand. Her convent revealed itself to her in time
with the creation of the WVS day books, with their wealth of
material detail, the work of many hands. She was developing her
own kind of historical realism, if not concerned with kitchens, then
with a regional office peopled by women, less interested in battle-
fronts than in repairing socks and salvaging books. Sylvia's nuns,
cracking almonds, bickering over elections, taking up their posts as
treasuress, cellaress and infirmaress, owed much to the women of
Dorchester – the Miss Clarks, Mrs Shepherds and Mrs Ratclyffes –
who worked tirelessly at canteens and rest centres, received evacuees
(not unlike the nuns at the wicket), and rounded up donations from
their village neighbours; their contributions unacknowledged, their
stories untold until after the war.

And yet the best stories are those which happen at the margins.
In the Restoration comedy couched in the pageant in the middle of
Virginia's *Between the Acts*, a servant abandons her tyrannical mistress to join 'the raggle-taggle gipsies'.[201] (There, she might meet
the wandering poet Anon, 'the common voice' singing 'at the back
door'.[202]) A play within a play, and an English folk song. Virginia,
too, was thinking about anonymous lives. She was picking up a
strand of her thinking in *A Room of One's Own*, her lecture delivered
to the women-only colleges of Cambridge in 1928, in which she
imagines her narrator wandering through London's streets at dusk,
and sensing – at street corners, in kitchens and doorways – the
untold presences of everyday women, a vast 'accumulation of

unrecorded life'.[203] Now, in her diary, she looked for rural snap-shots. The girl who kept elk hounds out walking on the Downs. The woman in the baker's shop, pregnant, lounging in a beam of sun. And, in her novel, she noticed myriad women. The servants who believe the myth about a ghost by the lily pond. The cook who, in all her fifty years, has never been over the hill. Secretive, queer women like Miss La Trobe. These are the women, as Laura laments in Sylvia's first novel, *Lolly Willowes*, who populate rural landscapes, 'living and growing old, as common as blackberries, and as unre-garded'.[204] They were the same as Sylvia tried to make vivid in her lectures, when she had spoken to women-only audiences in the early years of the war. 'All these infinitely obscure lives remain to be recorded,' Virginia had written ten years previously.[205] In their wartime writing, both she and Sylvia looked to their own experiences – not the stuff of history books, but a humbler sequence of undistinguished, populated rural hours – in their search for ways to collect such lives, tell stories out of fragments, and so narrate an alternative version of English history; one peopled by country folk and women, by pilgrims, peasants, servants and schoolmistresses, by all those Virginia called 'waifs & strays'.[206]

Between the Acts and *The Corner That Held Them* were both war novels, and oddly similar responses to national crisis. Both emerged from broad, unwavering philosophies for life. Sylvia's, a mellowing belief in communism; Virginia's, a desire for a metaphysics of con-nection. At the centre of each novel is a work of art – a tapestry, a pageant – which tries to embody that vision: a community, or a col-lective; and an alternative to the way history and culture are usually made. The pageant is a disaster, and the tapestry is stolen; both, in their own ways, fail. And yet, in failing, each work of art dramatizes something of its writer's ambivalence towards history and English-ness, to what it means to belong. Had Sylvia made sense of it all? Privately, she raged against governments, while into her novel she put the hysteria and pettiness she encountered in everyday life. There were no heroes; war made a mockery of everyone. (Like Virginia, she would always have a contradictory relationship with class.) And yet, both writers had refused to lose heart. Because, is failure ever absolute? Miss La Trobe's play germinates the seed for its sequel; the tapestry, the work of so many hands, is absorbed into the folk. And in wartime, amid the more private disasters of illness, heartache and upheaval, these extraordinary novels were conceived, and written against all odds. Art, as Virginia wrote in 'Anon', is the first note sounded into silence, mutating, resurgent, enduring; a note of hope.

~

Virginia finished the draft of *Between the Acts* in the middle of November 1940, and was pleased. 'I am a little triumphant about the book,' she wrote in her diary. 'I think its an interesting attempt in a new method. I think its more quintessential than the others. More milk skimmed off.' – (Louie had just shown her how to make butter) – 'A richer pat.'[207] In December, she began to revise the manuscript, but left off to turn her mind to other things – her memoir, several short pieces, and 'Anon' – until the new year. But, over the following months, her health declined. She became elegiac about the Sussex landscape, lost confidence in her work, and was increasingly unable to write. *Between the Acts* was, to her mind, 'trivial' (as she wrote to John Lehmann) and 'a completely worthless book'.[208] She looked to the landscape, her ballast, for consolation. In January 1941, frost crept over the marsh, and, from her lodge, she couldn't 'help even now turning to look at Asheham down, red, purple, dove blue grey [. . .]. What is the phrase I always remember – or forget. Look your last on all things lovely.'[209]

But her unifying vision was fading. She was struggling to keep on at her wartime project of recording, of weaving the multiple threads of other people's lives. 'Endless local stories,' she had written in September following a night of raids, when planes had zoomed over her in the garden and bomb casings were found in the field. 'No – its no good trying to capture the feeling of England being in a battle.'[210] Her diary was inadequate, verbose. Following another day of rumour and fearful speculation, she wrote, 'And so this page is perhaps unnecessarily filled.'[211] Rather than strengthening her

Sally the spaniel, napping

resolve, the solitude of the country was biting at her. 'There is no echo in Rodmell,' she wrote in February 1941, a month before her death; 'only waste air'.[212]

In 1915, during the long phase of her recovery from illness, Virginia had often been sustained by domestic routine, had had enough pleasure for kitchen life, games of bowls, dahlias, apples. ('Happiness is to have a little string onto which things will attach themselves,' she had later written in her diary.[213]) Material things tethered her to the simplest and most manageable version of living. 'Occupation is essential,' she wrote on 8 March, as she suggested possible plans to herself ('Suppose, I bought a ticket at the Museum; biked in daily & read history. Suppose I selected one dominant figure in every age & wrote round & about'). To keep busy, to think of the endless continuity of history, and to hold fast to nearby things. 'Haddock & sausage meat,' she wrote, before leaving her diary to cook dinner. 'I think it is true that one gains a certain hold on sausage & haddock by writing them down.'[214] But her tetherings were breaking loose. Three weeks later, on 28 March 1941, she left Monk's House and walked along the track through the water-meadows to the river where, a few hours later, her walking stick was found on the bank. She had waded into the Ouse, and let herself be drowned. She left a letter for Leonard, in which she wrote gratefully of the care she had received during their marriage, and of her contentment at living and working beside him. The letter recalled a diary entry of 1925, thirteen years into their marriage, in which she had mused on the quiet joys of their private life. Like the couple in 'A Haunted House', her story about Asheham, the 'immense success' of their life was, she felt, 'that our treasure is hid away; or rather in such common things that nothing can touch it. That is, if one enjoys [. . .] sitting down after dinner, side by side, & saying "Are you in your stall, brother?" – well, what can trouble this happiness?'[215] Leonard is the final word in her diary, 'doing the rhododendrons' in the garden in the pale spring sun.[216]

~

The following year, when the librarian at Boots pressed *Between the Acts* into Sylvia's hands, she 'received an extraordinary impression how light it was, how small, and frail'. The novel, published four months after Virginia's death, seemed to her like a 'premature-born child, and motherless, and literally, the last light handful remaining of that tall and abundant woman'.* A last light handful, like the swallows flitting between the trees in the garden at Pointz Hall. If Sylvia thought Virginia's novel lacked substance of a kind, Rosamond Lehmann did, too. Reviewing *Between the Acts* in the *New Statesman*, she described a lyrical if jagged book, a series of dreamlike scenes collected from notebooks, linked by 'extraordinary fragments of doggerel'. 'One longs for a concrete foothold,' Rosamond wrote.[217] Experiments fail; or, the artist's vision – for the

* Warner, 26 January 1942, *Diaries*, 113. Yet Sylvia had much enjoyed Virginia's biography of Roger Fry, commending it to Paul Nordoff as a life 'as free and rapscallionly and outrageously honest as any man might be, sitting on benches in dusty cheap parks talking to burglars, and laying down the law with all the bravura of the lawless. Such a nice comforting story.' 5 September 1941, *Letters*, 73.

unity of all things – is impossible to achieve. It is made of too fine a stuff; airy, capacious, as Virginia had originally conceived. The version that reaches the audience is a worldly, material thing, like Miss La Trobe's play, with villagers bedecked in teacloths, mouthing words into the wind. Virginia had attempted to lay down a pattern, but, in the months leading up to her death, they were perhaps patterns only she could see. Rosamond wasn't dismissing her last book, or being cruel. She was reeling, writing into the silence that follows death. Virginia had left a void, Sylvia wrote, a feeling which 'haunted me all day'.[218]

~

Sylvia's own experiments in living were suffering as a result of war. In May 1944, as she was midway through her own wartime novel ('yes, it will be a longish one; longer than me, I sometimes think in moments of despondency'), she received the news that a German Messerschmitt, aiming for the military base at Lulworth, had dropped a bomb on East Chaldon, destroying Miss Green.[219] She and Valentine absorbed the news in silence. 'Our little house is gone,' she wrote later to Nancy Cunard, 'the little stocky grey house that sat there looking so mittened and imperturbable.' The tenants escaped unhurt, but she was angry at the loss of 'the only decent cottage in that village', while, in a return to old scores, 'the hovels belonging to the Weld estate, God damn it, are untouched in all their filth, scarcely a bug shaken out of them'.[220]

Sylvia didn't visit Miss Green until several years after the war. On a July morning in 1949, she drove to East Chaldon with Valentine and, getting out of the car, stood quietly in the road looking at the wreckage of the small house. It was early and cool. A wind was blowing over the chalk downs from the sea and, in the soft grey light, the hedges looked brilliantly green. From the rubble, she could make out the shell of the sitting room. There was the brick hearth and the step leading into the garden, which was now overrun with weeds. She watched as Valentine picked her way through the long grass to where the kitchen had been. There was buddleia growing, and the water butt – once attached to the back of the house like a swallow's nest – now lay crumpled 'like a concertinaed hat'. It had been a plain little house, so unassuming, Sylvia had always thought, that it might have been missed from the road. Yet it had been their home. When Valentine drew their initials in the loop of a sickle, Sylvia carved them into the trunk of a hawthorn tree. They had been happy on the outskirts of the village, invigorated by possibility, living fervently and free.

Like the couple in 'Poor Mary', Sylvia and Valentine were damaged, but by more than war. That July morning, they were awaiting the arrival of Elizabeth, with whom Valentine had resumed her affair. It had been agreed that, with Elizabeth staying at Frome Vauchurch, Sylvia would move temporarily into a hotel in Yeovil. Looking at the ruined cottage, Sylvia saw the crisis in her own relationship. She stood to lose everything. Around her, the village had changed, the roads newly surfaced and the electricity cables looping and crackling overhead. Her friends were no longer there. In the years she had been away, it seemed, the village had begun its inevitable creep towards modernity. But the wind in the ash trees sounded the same, and the weather was overcast and sticky from the sea: 'a Chaldon morning'.

Valentine made her way back to Sylvia carrying sprigs of the tansy they had planted years before. Silently, they drove away, taking the lane that leads away from the coast to the Marys. At the opening to the steep, gorse-covered path, Sylvia saw their familiar blackthorn bush, and was overcome with emotion. 'I cried, and she halted the car, and embraced me,' she wrote in her diary. Afterwards, 'we sat on the heath, drinking tea and eating seed-cake. We said very little. Perhaps one day, to rebuild, if we could do it decently.'[221]

Hauntings

On the evening of 8 May 1945, after victory was declared in Europe, Rosamond took Sally up onto the downs to see the bonfires glittering on the hilltops, lighting paths across the south of England, the same fires 'that were lit during the Spanish Armada time, & in the Napoleonic wars. One felt part of history; & all the people who came over the downs & gathered round the beacon might have come out of the Dynasts. I shall never forget it.'[1] Her wartime chapter closed with an image of connection and continuity, a celebration, solemn, watchful, timeless, among the people with whom she had lived out the war. Afterwards, she and Sally – like Margaret Ritchie and Jane in 'Wonderful Holidays' – walked home to Diamond Cottage in the dark, an image of intimate, abstracted figures in an ancient landscape.

She had sold the film rights to her novel, *The Ballad and the Source*, to an American producer for a considerable sum, and with the proceeds bought an elegant Queen Anne house in Little Wittenham, a village on the Berkshire–Oxfordshire border, beneath the Wittenham Clumps. After the modest proportions of the cottage, the Manor House promised a life like the one she had lived at Ipsden, stately, arboreous. She furnished it handsomely. She would, she intended, live there with Cecil for many years after the war. The following spring, in April 1946, she left Diamond Cottage. After years of frugal living, of contrasts – food shortages and pinching cold, the impenetrable shelter of love – the cottage became simply an interval in her life about which little more was said.

But Rosamond's plans didn't come to bear. Cecil, ill at ease at Little Wittenham and with Rosamond, continued his double marriage until, in the winter of 1949, he met a young woman and, the following January, left both Rosamond and Mary. Both women were humiliated, though Rosamond had more people to tell.[2] For nine years, she had loved, hoped, raged; believed in – and been complicit in – an affair that had now clearly, inevitably failed.

She sold the new house, and put her possessions into an auction on Friar Street in Reading. A pair of fawn velvet curtains, three damask tablecloths, two bedspreads, a bundle of towels, sundry kitchen crockery, a pair of bronze candlesticks, six silver coffee spoons, a dog basket and its contents, a patterned carpet (worn).[3] The dismantling of a life, an inventory in reverse.

For the first time, she moved permanently to London, into a small flat on Eaton Square. Later, she reflected, 'I remember two years of absolute despair, and not writing anything at all.'[4]

~

In fact, Rosamond did write a novel, a chastened, bitter book called *The Echoing Grove*, published in 1953. In it, love is thwarted, no longer an ideal. The novel begins at the end of the story. Two sisters, Madeleine and Dinah, meet after an interval of fifteen years. The last time they saw each other was at the deathbed of Rickie, Madeleine's husband, a charming, inscrutable, slippery man, who had loved and betrayed them both.

The sisters are of different worlds: Madeleine, stolidly conventional, frigid despite her marriage and children; Dinah, bohemian, socially dislocated, worn out after years of drinking in bedsits with left-wing friends. (Later, Rosamond said, 'The two sisters are partly aspects of myself, I suppose.'[5]) At Madeleine's cottage, where their meeting takes place, conversation is cautious, rivalrous, barbed.

'Are you a gardener?'
[. . .]
'I do garden.'
'You find it soothing?'
'I find it a job of hard work . . . But I've taken to it. Had to.'
'Vegetables and all?'
'Of course. I don't potter about in embroidered hessian with a dainty trowel and a raffia basket, if that's what you mean.'[6]

Recriminations, telephone calls, leave-taking. The narrative unfurls in episodes, moving backwards and forwards in time. Few dates add up. Madeleine and Dinah survey the past as if from a great distance, aged by war, love, betrayal, death. In fact, both women are in their middle forties. John Lehmann challenged Rosamond's failure of temporality. And yet, in her writing, Rosamond, was shifting into another kind of time, non-linear, perspectival: psychological time (to borrow Gillian Tindall's phrase).[7] (The novel's temporality owes much, in fact, to the quietly experimental passages of *The Weather in the Streets* in which Olivia recounts her affair with Rollo. Then, Olivia thinks, 'there was no sequence, no development', only darkness and formlessness; a 'vacuum' when he was not there.[8]) Towards the end of writing, Diamond Cottage had already slipped into the oblivion of discretion. '[T]hose far-off Aldworth days,' was all Rosamond would comment, from a distance of twelve years, though the rupture seemed infinitely greater.[9]

Observing her sister, Dinah thinks, incredulously, 'Could Madeleine really have retired in her prime, become a country woman on her own, her days plotted by the seasons, evenings alone with books and wireless, or writing letters to her children; a friend occasionally for week-ends perhaps?'[10] Madeleine sees the shortcomings of her own existence, fantasizes two versions of her lonely heart.

Refined educated lady of good appearance (early forties) cheerful disposition artistic tastes, widow (one child, girl, school holidays), thoroughly domesticated, country lover, fond animals, experienced cook gardener washerwoman, able drive car, undertake all household duties, rough (coals, boots, wood-chopping, scrubbing, etc.) not objected to . . .

and

Emotionally frustrated unadaptable class-conscious matron victim circumstances upbringing personal tragedies, exploited rejected (grounds age, moral intellectual maladjustment) by lover renovating sexual requirements, unwilling to accept suggestions re courage pride eventual resignation, unable to

*contemplate living a) alone b) for others i.e. family friends community spirit-
ual values or any other form abhorrent vacuum, seeks instantaneous return
status quo, failing which immediate euthanasia . . .*[11]

The advertisements are caustic, and amazingly revealing. Was
Rosamond confronting the different parts of herself, both versions
approximations of the truth? After Cecil left, her feelings towards
country life changed. In *The Echoing Grove*, Madeleine's rural existence seems one of disappointment and solitude, a widowhood, her
expensive clothes unsuited to the grittiness of gardening and daily
tasks. Rosamond was up to her old tricks. As with Grace Fairfax in
her first novel, *A Note in Music*, her character was acting as a warning to herself, and an exhalation of relief; a last, long look at a life
from which she had narrowly escaped.

~

Four years after the publication of *The Echoing Grove*, on midsummer's night in 1958, Rosamond's daughter, Sally, died of polio in
Djakarta, where she was living with her husband, the poet P. J.
Kavanagh. She was twenty-four. Rosamond recounted her grief in
an autobiography, *The Swan in the Evening*. In the immediate aftermath of Sally's death, her experience of the world shifted. Staying
with friends in the country, she began to see in shimmering, incan-
descent colour. Trees appeared larger and brighter than before, a
secret hidden in the blackbird's song. She beheld a 'visionary world',
was held aloft in a 'cosmic' dimension.[12] Chronological time, 'earth
time', slipped.[13] Now, there was only the time before Sally's death
and the afterwards, a time of 'deepest listening'.[14]

She bought tarot cards, and a large, spiral-bound notebook in
which to record her encounters with Sally: dreams and conversations, visions, presences – an archive of 'parallel experiences'.[15] She
attended spiritualist meetings, and described her investigations
in the psychic journal, *Light*. Friends tolerated her need for solace;
to her wider circle, she appeared laughable, mad with grief.
She persisted, 'lonely, secretly consoled, troubled, disorganised,

intellectually engrossed, aggressively on the defensive'.[16] She had already learned – at Diamond Cottage, and afterwards – how to retreat. In the years following Sally's death, her world contracted.

For the two surviving women in this book, withdrawal from the realities of the world was an essential form of self-protection. They counted their losses, the losses of lovers and daughters, of those interludes of quiet living in the country, the safe passage of rural hours. But, in mourning, they were also remembering. The past could be kept alive, they each discovered, even if it could only live on privately, in the mind. Skinning a rabbit at the sink in May 1972 ('hard work, but the smell and the feeling brought back the old knack'), Sylvia was taken suddenly to Chaldon. Memories of the 1930s 'closed round me'. She saw the slope of High Chaldon as if she were standing beneath it, heard the wind from the sea. She recalled Miss Green's cottage, and later 24 West Chaldon, where Valentine had written *Country Conditions* and she had written *Summer Will Show*. She remembered driving over the downs at Bovington, secreting anti-war leaflets into army tanks. Painting, distempering, gardening, sewing; 'Our contrivance against our poverty, our amazing industry'.[17] Looking back, Chaldon 'seemed so rich, so richly pastoral, though it is poor country, thistles and flints'. There, she had known 'amplitude of days, richness of feeling'.[18] 'All this,' she wrote, 'because I skinned a rabbit, and was back again in being so passionately loved, so passionately loving, with my slender strong arms & my black hair, in my bright boiling summer.'[19]

Following Valentine's death on 9 November 1969, Sylvia had taken to inhabiting the past as much as the present. Time became a discontinuous, shifting thing. Reading their letters, she was 'swept back' to the early years of their relationship, to the feeling of Valentine's young body, the sun through the windows of Miss Green.[20] What can a letter hold for almost forty years? Out springs sensation, smell, desire, like the snail's shell her lover sent to her in 1931, doused with scent. 'One preserves a time so completely intact,' she had written in 1960, while translating Proust, 'that one feels like an airtight jar when it comes out again.'[21] Letters were tripwires, a dangerous, delicious path through grief. Chaldon emerged from the pages almost claustrophobically, like listening with instant recognition to a strain of music. It was comfort, and happiness. The past was, she wrote in her diary, an 'amazing euphoric reality'.[22] And: '[T]his is immortality. *It was. It is.*'[23]

The days passed, and Sylvia began to feel Valentine's presence, 'not remembered, not evoked, not a sense of presence. *Actual.*'[24] A feather, a single cresting wave were signs. She went through Valentine's pockets, finding pencils, interesting pebbles, elegant small combs. She rearranged Valentine's room, guiltily ransacked after death, to look inhabited. As the months drew on, she continued to intuit her impressive height in doorways, to feel her on the stairs. 'Her love is everywhere,' she wrote to friends.[25] And in her diary 'she followed me out of my room, watched me do the evening routine, followed me to bed (but was already there, waiting for me)'.[26] Consolation as strategy: 'This is the practice of the presence of Valentine.'[27]

Skinning a rabbit. Sylvia remembered with her hands. In the course of her life with Valentine, domestic tasks – sewing, gardening, cooking – were celebration, reassurance, relief. Needlework, like a diary, is continuous, making sense of itself, moving over breaks and patches. And, like a diary, it can document a life. The quilt Sylvia made in the midsummer heat of 1930, which adorned her bed at Miss Green. A tuxedo jacket, lovingly stitched from silk, velveteen, cordur- oy and taffeta patches – a 'coat of many colours' to gild her slender form.[28] The roller-towels embroidered with her own initials, put away silently, muffled, in anticipation of Elizabeth's visit. The linen sheets, bought with her first wages in 1918, laid on the bed at Miss Green, darned and mended in 1957 – '*Credo in linium* was part of my protestant upbringing' – and later put on Valentine's death-bed.[29] ('I unmake the death-bed I remake the marriage bed,' she wrote afterwards. 'And as I lay thinking of all the beds we had lain in, she came and pulled aside the sheets & leaped in bedside me.'[30]) Finally, a dress, sewn from a piece of Paisley cloth, assembled, ingeniously, without a pattern.[31] ('[Do] something you wouldn't do normally, which will tax your wits without involving your heart,' she had urged her friend Alyse Gregory, as they were growing old. 'I would often have been lost without such little tricks.')[32] She was still thrifty, emotionally cunning. Over the years, sewing had been her salvation in moments of doubt and discord, a way for her and Valentine to broker distances, to 're-knit together'; a private history of repair and renewal.[33]

As she organized Valentine's letters, Sylvia chastised herself bitterly for past mistakes. The catastrophe of 1949, when she had gone to live in a hotel in Yeovil, now seemed like a drastic failure of nerve. She thought she had been acting rightly, would witness Valentine's replenishment through love. Instead, she had tramped Sedgemoor alone, writing daily letters to Valentine, stealing clandestine meetings, as if she were the mistress, the outside party in an unhappy affair.

But she had left only a small part of herself on Sedgemoor, a wedge of grief. Everything that was important remained, in her mind's eye, at Miss Green. Her love for Valentine had been the greatest event of her life. Thinking of their vows, made solemnly in the cottage on 12 October 1930, she knew their marriage-night was 'real and abiding: far beyond any reality of today. It is still there. We are still lying on the Maries in sun and wind.'[34]

~

In 1971, Sylvia wrote a faerie story, set in a minutely realized fantasy kingdom. She was drawing on her knowledge of myth and English folklore, while continuing to write about history and material culture. There is nothing whimsical about her faeries: the inhabitants of Elfindom are cool, dispassionate winged creatures, as shrewd and pragmatic as the nuns of Oby. Fifteen more stories followed, all published in the *New Yorker*. She knew she was breaking, perhaps

irrevocably, from her previous work. She was seized by adventur-
ousness, pleased to realize 'that *something entirely different* is still
possible for me, that I can still pull an unexpected ace out of my
sleeve'.[35] But the stories had also arisen out of weariness, the feeling
of being burdened by the weight of her grief. 'Bother the human
heart,' she remarked in an interview. 'I'm tired of the human
heart.'[36]

In the stories, the faeries take to the air swiftly, like hawks.
(Descending, they fold their wings, a single, rapid movement. She
was borrowing imagery from her 1967 biography of T. H. White.)
Sylvia found relief in the weightlessness of imagination, in moments
of suspension. She had been 'in flight from my sad self without Valentine', she told Rosamond; she had 'sheltered in a non-human
world where I have been ever since'.[37]

In 1975, the two writers exchanged a series of letters. Rosamond
was searching, perhaps, for reassurance: increasingly friendless,
she remained immersed in a spiritual world, had written about it in
her next – and what would be her final – novel. Sylvia's responses
were measured – 'the trouble will be that if one uses the word
supernatural it falls on misunderstanding ears' – but deeply sympathetic. The world she was creating in her own stories was pure
fantasy, but she did, she told Rosamond, believe in ghosts. 'It has
been a great solace to inhabit another world, from which I can look
back at the oddities of this one – a dear world, too, if we didn't
bedevil it so much,' she wrote. She encouraged Rosamond: 'I am
glad you are writing another novel, and about what you have at
heart. A hopeless task, you say. I can't think so. You know your
subject, that is the essential.'[38] Two years later, Rosamond's *The
Sea-Grape Tree* was published as Sylvia's collected *Kingdoms of Elfin*
came out. Sylvia remarked on the uncanniness of dates: their first
novels, *Dusty Answer* and *Lolly Willowes*, both published by Chatto
& Windus, had appeared in 1926. 'We recur in our courses like
comets,' she wrote.[39]

~

In one of Sylvia's late stories, a mortal falls in love with a faerie. He will age and die, while she remains earthbound, forever young. Love is their consolation, for

> Love was in the present: in the sharp taste of the rowanberries he plucked for her, in the winter night when a gale got up and whipped them to the shelter of a farm where he kindled a fire and roasted turnips on a stick, in their midnight mushroomings, in the long summer evenings when they lay on their backs too happy to move or speak, in their March-hare curvettings and cuffings. For love-gifts, he gave her acorns, birds' eggs, a rosegall because it is called the fairies' pincushion, a yellow snail shell.[40]

~

Non-human worlds, spiritual states, other dimensions: all are connected with place. Asheham, Miss Green and Diamond Cottage haunted their occupants long after they had left. They reverberated in diaries, novels and letters, a shared history of country living, of rural hours spent.

Some literary houses survive to welcome visitors of the future, beckoned into immaculate kitchens and restored gardens, fresh flowers in vases, a dried teasel on a chair. Some are lived in, as Diamond Cottage is lived in, a surly woman – and a CCTV camera – eyeing me suspiciously from the gate. Others perish. A smart bungalow has been built where Miss Green once stood. Chaldon hasn't much changed: an out-of-the-way feeling; the sign of The Sailor's Return creaking in the wind.

Others are destroyed, despite efforts to save them. In March 1932, Virginia noticed the appearance of 'vast elephant grey sheds' at Asheham, signs of the impending Blue Circle Cement Company.[41] A cement works existed next to the house – damp, lived in sporadically – until 1992, when plans were made public to demolish it for landfill. A campaign followed, in which Quentin and Anne Olivier Bell petitioned East Sussex County Council to preserve the literary heritage of that quiet corner by the Ouse. The house was pulled down. Fireplaces were salvaged, and a donation from Blue Circle was made to the hostel at Southease, for walkers of the South Downs Way, to Charleston, Monk's House, and a literary endowment fund. The woods were cleared.

Nothing of Asheham now remains, save an impression of where it stood, a scent on the air. There is the basin-shaped hollow scooped out of the hillside, the footpath winding up and over the Down, the cries of the rooks.

Virginia with Sally in the garden at Monk's House

Illustrations

Sylvia Townsend Warner walking Vicky the goat at Frankfort Manor, c.1933. Material in this work that is the copyright of Dorset History Centre is published with the permission of Dorset History Centre.

Rosamond Lehmann wrestling a goat, from Barbara Ker-Seymer, photograph album, 1 April 1934–30 August 1935. Tate. Reproduced courtesy of The Estate of Barbara Ker-Seymer.

Virginia Stephen, photographer unknown. This was the photograph Virginia enclosed with her letter to Leonard Woolf in May 1912. The Keep, Sussex. Reproduced courtesy of The Charleston Trust.

Vanessa Bell, *Asheham House*, 1912. Oil on board, 47 x 53.5 cm, Private Collection. © The Estate of Vanessa Bell. Reproduced courtesy of Matthew Hollow.

Vanessa Bell, *Landscape with Haystack, Asheham*, 1912. Oil on canvas, board: 60.32 x 65.72 cm, Smith College Museum of Art, Northampton, Massachusetts. © The Estate of Vanessa Bell, courtesy of Henrietta Garnett. Reproduced courtesy of The Charleston Trust.

Leonard Woolf, Roger Eliot Fry and Virginia Woolf sitting outdoors, 1912. Virginia Woolf Monk's House Photographs, circa 1867–1967, MS Thr 557. Harvard Theatre Collection, Houghton Library, Harvard University.

Leonard Woolf and Vanessa Bell sitting outdoors; Virginia Woolf standing nearby, 1912. Virginia Woolf Monk's House Photographs, circa 1867–1967 MS Thr 557. Harvard Theatre Collection, Houghton Library, Harvard University.

Virginia Stephen and Leonard Woolf at Dalingridge Place: photographic postcard by George Duckworth, 1912. Virginia Woolf Monk's House Photographs, circa 1867–1967 MS Thr 564 (58). Harvard Theatre Collection, Houghton Library, Harvard University.

Annie and Lily picking apples, undated. Virginia Woolf Monk's House Photographs, circa 1867–1967, MS Thr 559. Harvard Theatre Collection, Houghton Library, Harvard University.

Annie and Lily sitting on haystacks, undated. Virginia Woolf Monk's House Photographs, circa 1867–1967 MS Thr 559. Harvard Theatre Collection, Houghton Library, Harvard University.

Virginia Woolf sitting outdoors and petting a dog. Cornwall, 1916. Virginia Woolf Monk's House Photographs, circa 1867–1967 MS Thr 559. Harvard Theatre Collection, Houghton Library, Harvard University. (Author's note: I suggest this photograph is mislabelled, the pavilion of Asheham being clearly visible in the background.)

Vanessa Bell, *Virginia Woolf*, c.1912. Oil on board, 40 x 34 cm. © National Portrait Gallery, London.

Virginia Woolf's laundry list. Reel 1: D7–1917, [Diary] Holograph notebook, unsigned. Aug. 3, 1917–Oct. 6, 1918. Berg Collection, New York Public Library.

Vanessa Bell, *A Conversation*, 1913–16. © Estate of Vanessa Bell.

Virginia Woolf's Asheham diary, 31 July 1918. Reel 1: D7–1917, [Diary] Holograph notebook, unsigned. Aug. 3, 1917–Oct. 6, 1918. Berg Collection, New York Public Library.

Sylvia Townsend Warner by Cecil Beaton, 1930. National Portrait Gallery. © Cecil Beaton Archive / Condé Nast.

Miss Green's cottage, East Chaldon. Material in this work that is the copyright of Dorset History Centre is published with the permission of Dorset History Centre.

Sylvia Townsend Warner, with William the dog. Inscription on reverse reads: 'MINE – V. Ackland'. Material in this work that is the copyright of Dorset History Centre is published with the permission of Dorset History Centre.

Valentine Ackland in 1936. Material in this work that is the copyright of Dorset History Centre is published with the permission of Dorset History Centre.

Sylvia Townsend Warner in bed at Miss Green, a patchwork quilt hanging in the background. Material in this work that is the copyright of Dorset History Centre is published with the permission of Dorset History Centre.

Sylvia Townsend Warner in the kitchen at 113 Inverness Terrace, in Louise Morgan's 'Sylvia Townsend Warner: A Writer Who Follows None of the Rules', *Everyman*, New Series 4 (1930). British Library.

Pages from Sylvia Townsend Warner's 'Visitors' Book, The Late Miss Green's Cottage, Chaldon Hering [sic], Oct. 1930–'. Material in this work that is the copyright of Dorset History Centre is published with the permission of Dorset History Centre.

Sylvia Townsend Warner and Valentine Ackland at Frankfort Manor, 1933–4. Material in this work that is the copyright of Dorset History Centre is published with the permission of Dorset History Centre.

Rosamond Nina Lehmann by Howard Coster. Nitrate negative, 1930s, 111 mm x 73 mm. Given by the estate of Howard Coster, 1959. © National Portrait Gallery, London.

Rosamond Lehmann at Ham Spray. © Frances Partridge. Reproduced by permission of the Partridge Estate.

Rosamond Lehmann sitting in an armchair, undated. Virginia Woolf Monk's House Photographs, circa 1867–1967, MS Thr 560. Harvard Theatre Collection, Houghton Library, Harvard University.

Rosamond Lehmann looking up at a swarm of bees, Ipsden, Oxfordshire. Rosamond Lehmann's photograph album, courtesy of Roland Philipps.

Poster for 'Writers Declare Against Fascism', the Queen's Hall, 8 June 1938, organized by Rosamond Lehmann. King's College, Cambridge.

Diamond Cottage in 1941, from Barbara Ker-Seymer, photograph album, 1938–December 1941. Tate. Reproduced courtesy of The Estate of Barbara Ker-Seymer.

Cecil Day Lewis and Laurie Lee in the garden at Diamond Cottage, Aldworth. Rosamond Lehmann's photograph album, courtesy of Roland Philipps.

Hugo and Sally in the fields during wartime, and Sally with her rabbit. Photographs from Rosamond Lehmann's photograph album, courtesy of Roland Philipps.

Rosamond Lehmann lying on a patchwork quilt at Diamond Cottage, 1940s. Photograph from Laurie Lee's album, courtesy of Jessy Lee.

Scenic view of countryside in winter. Possibly Monk's House (Rodmell, England), undated. Virginia Woolf Monk's House Photographs, circa 1867–1967, MS Thr 561. Harvard Theatre Collection, Houghton Library, Harvard University.

Sally the dog napping in an armchair, undated. Virginia Woolf Monk's House Photographs, circa 1867–1967, MS Thr 561. Harvard Theatre Collection, Houghton Library, Harvard University.

Virginia Woolf walking a dog on a leash in front of Monk's House (Rodmell, England): black-and-white photograph, undated. Virginia Woolf Monk's House Photographs, circa 1867–1967, MS Thr 564. Harvard Theatre Collection, Houghton Library, Harvard University.

Notes

In the country

1 Sylvia Townsend Warner, 'The Essex Marshes', *With the Hunted: Selected Writings of Sylvia Townsend Warner*, ed. Peter Tolhurst (Black Dog Books, 2012), 29–32.

2 For another reading of Warner's use of the word 'socketted', see David Trotter, 'The Ultimate Socket', *London Review of Books*, Volume 44, Number 12 (23 June 2022), 3–8 (3).

3 Sylvia Townsend Warner to Rosamond Lehmann, 25 February 1975, King's College, Cambridge (KCC hereafter).

4 Virginia Woolf, 'Heard on the Downs: The Genesis of Myth' (August, 1916), *The Essays of Virginia Woolf*, ed. Andrew McNeillie and Stuart N. Clarke, 5 volumes (The Hogarth Press, 1986–2011), II, 40.

5 Warner, 'The Way By Which I Have Come' (July 1939), *With the Hunted*, 18.

6 Rosamond Lehmann, 'Wonderful Holidays', *The Gypsy's Baby* (1946; Virago, 1982), 120.

7 Virginia Woolf to Rosamond Lehmann, 2 July (1928?), KCC.

8 Woolf, 'Some of the Smaller Manor Houses of Sussex', *Essays*, IV, 315.

9 Virginia Woolf, 11 July 1927, *The Diary of Virginia Woolf*, eds. Anne Olivier Bell and Andrew McNeillie, 5 volumes (The Hogarth Press, 1977–1984), III, 147.

10 Woolf, 21 August 1927, *Diary*, III, 153.

11 Woolf, 10 September 1921, *Diary*, II, 134.

12 Stanley Baldwin, 'On England' (1926), *On England and Other Addresses* (Philip Allan, 1933), 7.

13 Woolf, 9 May 1926, *Diary*, III, 81.

14 Virginia Woolf to Lady Simon, 25 January 1941, *The Letters of Virginia Woolf*, ed. Nigel Nicolson, assisted by Joanne Trautmann, 6 volumes (The Hogarth Press, 1975–1980), VI, 464.

15 Virginia Woolf to Rosamond Lehmann, 28 July 1928, KCC.

16 Sylvia Townsend Warner, 23 November 1961, *The Diaries of Sylvia Townsend Warner*, ed. Claire Harman (Chatto & Windus, 1994), 277.

17 Warner, 'The Way By Which I Have Come', *With the Hunted*, 15.

18 Virginia Woolf to Margaret Llewelyn Davies, 9 September 1917, *Letters*, I, 178.

19 Warner, 'The Way By Which I Have Come', *With the Hunted*, 15.

20 Sylvia Townsend Warner, *Lolly Willowes or: The Loving Huntsman* (1926: Virago Press, 2012), 90–94.

21 Rosamond Lehmann to Edward Sackville-West, 13 May 1938, in Selina Hastings, *Rosamond Lehmann: A Life* (Chatto & Windus, 2002), 195.

22 Rosamond Lehmann, *Invitation to the Waltz* (1932; Virago Press, 1981), 9.

23 Rosamond Lehmann, *The Echoing Grove* (1953; Collins, 1984), 159.

24 Woolf, 22 August 1929, *Diary*, III, 248.

25 Woolf, 21 April 1918, *Diary*, I, 143.

Part One: Experiments

Beetles & the price of eggs

1 Virginia Woolf, 3 January 1897, *A Passionate Apprentice: The Early Journals, 1897–1909* (Harcourt Brace Jovanovich, 1990), 5.

2 Daniel Ferrer, *Virginia Woolf and the Madness of Language* (Routledge, 1990), 6.

3 Anne Olivier Bell, *Diary*, I, 179, n5; Anne Olivier Bell, *Editing Virginia Woolf's Diary* (The Perpetua Press, 1989), 25. In June 2023, Woolf's Asheham diary was published in its entirety as part of Granta's reissue of *The Diary of Virginia Woolf*. In the new editions, Olivier's volume divisions, notes and indexes remain intact; the diary for 1918 at Asheham can be found at the end of the first volume, beneath the title

'Appendix 3'. See my essay, 'Virginia Woolf's Forgotten Diary', *Paris Review*, https://www.theparisreview.org/blog/2023/06/21/virginia-woolfs-forgotten-diary/, accessed 21 June 2023; also *The Diary of Virginia Woolf*, 5 volumes (Granta Books, 2023).

4 Virginia Stephen to Leonard Woolf, 21 October 1911, *Letters*, I, 479.

5 Virginia Stephen to Leonard Woolf, 14 September 1911, *Letters*, I, 478.

6 Frances Spalding notes that Vanessa Bell may have first heard about Asheham through the sculptor Eric Gill, who in 1910 proposed to build a modern Stonehenge in the six acres of land surrounding it. Frances Spalding, *Vanessa Bell* (Weidenfeld and Nicolson, 1983), 104. David Garnett describes the appearance of Asheham in *The Flowers of the Forest* (Chatto & Windus, 1953), 102. For histories of the house, see Carol Hansen, *The Life and Death of Asham: Leonard and Virginia Woolf's Haunted House* (Cecil Woolf, 2000); and Richard Shone, 'Asheham House: An Outline History', *The Charleston Magazine*, Issue 9, Spring/Summer 1994.

7 Virginia Stephen to Leonard Woolf, 13 January 1912, *Letters*, I, 488.

8 Virginia Stephen to Lady Ottoline Morrell, 13 November 1911, *Letters*, I, 480; 9 November 1911, *Letters*, I, 480.

9 Virginia Stephen to Molly MacCarthy, March 1912, *Letters*, I, 492.

10 Woolf, 28 November 1928, *Diary*, III, 208.

11 Virginia Stephen to Katherine Cox, 7 February 1912, *Letters*, I, 488; Virginia Stephen to Molly MacCarthy, March 1912, *Letters*, I, 493.

12 Virginia Stephen to Leonard Woolf, 5 March 1912, *Letters*, I, 491.

13 Virginia Stephen to Molly MacCarthy, March 1912, *Letters*, I, 492.

14 Virginia Stephen to Leonard Woolf, 1 May 1912, *Letters*, I, 496–497.

15 Vanessa Bell to Roger Fry, 11 September 1912, in Shone, 'Asheham House: An Outline History', 37.

16 Vanessa Bell to Virginia Woolf, 6 February 1913, *The Selected Letters of Vanessa Bell*, ed. Regina Marler (Bloomsbury, 1993), 137.

17 Vanessa Bell to Roger Fry, 5 June 1912, *Selected Letters*, 119.

18 Vanessa Bell to Roger Fry, 24 August 1914, *Selected Letters*, 169; to Leonard Woolf, 21 September 1912, *Selected Letters*, 128.

19 Dora Carrington to Lytton Strachey, 4 February 1917, *Carrington: Letters and Extracts from Her Diaries*, ed. David Garnett (Jonathan Cape, 1970), 56, 57.

20 Virginia Woolf to Violet Dickinson, 24 June 1912, *Letters*, I, 505.

21 Virginia Woolf to Molly MacCarthy, early April 1914, *Letters*, II, 47.

22 Woolf, 22 January 1915, *Diary*, I, 25.

23 Woolf, 3 January 1915, *Diary*, I, 5.

24 Woolf, 5 January 1915, *Diary*, I, 7.

25 Woolf, 13 February 1915, *Diary*, I, 33.

26 Woolf, 9 January 1915, *Diary*, I, 13; 19 January 1915, *Diary*, I, 22.

27 Virginia Woolf to Leonard Woolf, (27?) March 1941, *Letters*, VI, 481.

28 Virginia Stephen to Violet Dickinson, January 1912, *Letters*, I, 488.

29 Sara Crangle, 'Out of the Archive: Woolfian Domestic Economies', *Modernism/modernity*, Volume 23, Issue 1 (2016), 141–176 (148).

30 Vanessa Bell to Leonard Woolf, 14 January 1912, *Selected Letters*, 113.

31 Virginia Woolf to Leonard Woolf, 1 August 1913, *Letters*, II, 33.

32 Virginia Woolf to Leonard Woolf, 3 August 1913, *Letters*, II, 33.

33 Virginia Woolf to Leonard Woolf, 4 August 1913, *Letters*, II, 34.

34 Virginia Woolf to Leonard Woolf, (December?) 1913, *Letters*, II, 35.

35 Virginia Stephen to Violet Dickinson, 4 June 1912, *Letters*, I, 500.

36 Virginia Woolf to Violet Dickinson, 24 June 1912, *Letters*, I, 505.

37 Virginia Stephen to Madge Vaughan, June 1912, *Letters*, I, 503.

38 Virginia Stephen to Violet Dickinson, 4 June 1912, *Letters*, I, 500.

39 Virginia Woolf, 'Sketch of the Past', *Moments of Being: Autobiographical Writings* (Pimlico, 2002), 79.

40 Virginia Stephen to Leonard Woolf, 1 May 1912, *Letters*, I, 496; Virginia Stephen to Violet Dickinson, June 1912, *Letters*, I, 502.

41 Virginia Stephen to Duncan Grant, 8 August 1912, *Letters*, I, 508.

42 Virginia Woolf to Ethel Smyth, 2 August 1930, *Letters*, IV, 195.

43 Woolf, 28 May 1931, *Diary*, IV, 27.

44 Woolf, 22 November 1938, *Diary*, V, 188.

45 Virginia Woolf, 'Lappin and Lapinova', *Selected Short Stories* (Penguin, 1993), 100.

46 Virginia Woolf to Margaret Llewelyn Davies, 30 September 1915, *Letters*, II, 65; Virginia Woolf to Lady Robert Cecil, 13 September 1915, *Letters*, II, 63.

47 Virginia Woolf to Lady Robert Cecil, 13 September 1915, *Letters*, II, 64.

48 Virginia Woolf to Violet Dickinson, 24 January 1911, *Letters*, I, 451.

49 Virginia Woolf to Molly MacCarthy, April 1911, *Letters*, I, 456; Virginia Woolf to Leonard Woolf, 31 August 1911, *Letters*, I, 476.

50 Woolf, 10 September 1928, *Diary*, III, 196.

51 Woolf, 14 August 1928, *Diary*, III, 192.

52 Virginia Woolf to Lady Robert Cecil, 29 September 1915, *Letters*, II, 64.

53 Virginia Woolf to Margaret Llewelyn Davies, 30 September 1915, *Letters*, II, 65.

54 Virginia Woolf to Lytton Strachey, 22 October 1915, *Letters*, II, 67.

55 Virginia Woolf to Jacques Raverat, 10 December 1922, *Letters*, II, 592.

56 Virginia Woolf to Lady Robert Cecil, 29 September 1915, *Letters*, II, 64.

57 Virginia Woolf to Lady Robert Cecil, 14 October 1915, *Letters*, II, 66.

58 Virginia Woolf to Katherine Cox, 12 February 1916, *Letters*, II, 77.

59 Virginia Woolf to Duncan Grant, 15 November 1915, *Letters*, II, 71.

60 Virginia Woolf to Molly MacCarthy, 28 May 1913, *Letters*, II, 29.

61 Virginia Woolf to Molly MacCarthy, 15 December 1914, *Letters*, II, 56.

62 Virginia Woolf to Lytton Strachey, 28 February 1916, *Letters*, II, 82.

63 Virginia Woolf to Margaret Llewelyn Davies, 27 March 1916, *Letters*, II, 85.

64 Woolf, 23 October 1917, *Diary*, I, 65. Though she was intimidated by Margaret Llewelyn Davies, Virginia had, in fact, known her for many years, Margaret being the daughter of a prominent Christian Socialist clergyman who had taught Leslie Stephen at Cambridge. Clara Jones, *Virginia Woolf: Ambivalent Activist* (Edinburgh University Press, 2016), 109–110.

65 Virginia Woolf to Katherine Cox, 19 March 1916, *Letters*, II, 83.

66 Virginia Woolf to Vanessa Bell, 14 May 1916, *Letters*, II, 95; Virginia Woolf to Vanessa Bell, 5 April 1916, *Letters*, II, 88.

67 Virginia Woolf to Katherine Cox, 25 June 1916, *Letters*, II, 102.

68 Dora Carrington to Lytton Strachey, 4 February 1917, *Carrington: Letters and Extracts*, 57.

69 Virginia Woolf to Vanessa Bell, 30 July 1916, *Letters*, II, 109.

70 Richard Shone, *The Art of Bloomsbury* (Tate Publishing, 1999), 86–89. And I very much like Lauren Elkin's writing on Vanessa's 1912 series of portraits of Virginia, which 'deal with the instability of identity'. With these paintings, Elkin argues, Vanessa was grappling with the

greatest questions: 'How to be an artist, or a writer, how to live up to the challenge, how to embody it.' Lauren Elkin, *Art Monsters: Unruly Bodies in Feminist Art* (Chatto & Windus, 2023), 266–267.

71 For a full description of the mechanics of the press, and who did what, see Hermione Lee, *Virginia Woolf* (Chatto & Windus, 1999), 363–364.

72 Virginia Woolf to Vanessa Bell, 26 April 1917, *Letters*, II, 150.

73 Virginia Woolf to Violet Dickinson, 21 July 1917, *Letters*, II, 165.

74 Virginia Woolf to Margaret Llewelyn Davies, 2 May 1917, *Letters*, II, 151.

75 Virginia Woolf to Lady Ottoline Morrell, 5 June 1917, *Letters*, II, 158.

76 Virginia Woolf to Leonard Woolf, 29 October 1917, *Letters*, II, 191; 31 October 1917, *Letters*, II, 194.

77 Alison Light, *Mrs Woolf and the Servants* (Penguin, 2007), 128–131; also Frances Spalding, Editorial, *Charleston Magazine*, Issue 9, Spring/Summer (1994), 3–27.

78 Virginia Woolf to Vanessa Bell, 16 August 1916, *Letters*, II, 109.

79 Virginia Woolf to Vanessa Bell, 26 April 1917, *Letters*, II, 150.

80 Virginia Woolf to Leonard Woolf, 11 March 1914, *Letters*, II, 43.

81 Light, *Mrs Woolf and the Servants*, 136.

82 Virginia Woolf to Leonard Woolf, 4 December 1913, *Letters*, II, 35.

83 Virginia Woolf to Saxon Sydney-Turner, 16 January 1917, *Letters*, II, 135; to Dora Carrington, 11 August 1918, *Letters*, II, 266.

84 Virginia Woolf, 'A Haunted House', *Selected Short Stories*, 3–4.

85 Virginia Woolf to Lady Robert Cecil, 14 April 1917, *Letters*, II, 148.

86 Virginia Woolf to Violet Dickinson, 10 April 1917, *Letters*, II, 148.

87 Virginia Woolf, '"Past and Present" at the English Lakes', *Essays*, II, 32.

88 Michèle Barrett writes that Woolf was 'a meticulous, even slightly pedantic scholar', whose use of bibliographic referencing and scholarly footnoting conventions suggest that she 'was perhaps enjoying her work'. For a detailed account of Woolf's research for *Empire and Commerce in Africa*, see Barrett, 'Virginia Woolf's Research for *Empire and Commerce in Africa* (Leonard Woolf, 1920)', *Woolf Studies Annual*, Volume 19, 83–122. My thanks to Michèle for suggesting a connection between paragraphs and index cards.

89 Virginia Woolf to Leonard Woolf, 29 October 1917, *Letters*, II, 191.

90 Virginia Woolf to Saxon Sydney-Turner, 31 December 1916, *Letters*, II, 133.

91 Woolf, 12 October 1918, *Diary*, I, 199.

92 Woolf, 15 October 1932, *Diary*, II, 270.

93 Woolf, 5 January 1915, *Diary*, I, 7.

94 Virginia Woolf to Leonard Woolf, 30 October 1917, *Letters*, II, 192.

95 Virginia Woolf to Lady Robert Cecil, 14 April 1917, *Letters*, II, 149.

96 Virginia Woolf to Violet Dickinson, 10 April 1917, *Letters*, II, 147.

97 Virginia Woolf to Vanessa Bell, (19?) October 1916, *Letters*, II, 123.

98 Virginia Woolf to Saxon Sydney-Turner, 3 February 1917, *Letters*, II, 140.

99 Virginia Woolf, 'Thoreau', *Essays*, II, 133–135.

100 Virginia Stephen, 6 August 1899, *Passionate Apprentice*, 137.

101 Virginia Woolf, 'Dorothy Wordsworth', *Essays*, V, 482; Frances Wilson, *The Ballad of Dorothy Wordsworth* (Faber, 2008), 4. Wilson's detailed analysis of Dorothy's journals, and her imaginative piecing-together of daily life through her subject's compressed style, illnesses and ellipses, encouraged my thinking about Virginia at Asheham, and the diary she kept there.

102 Woolf, 'Dorothy Wordsworth', *Essays*, V, 482, 479.

103 Woolf, 'Dorothy Wordsworth', *Essays*, V, 479.

104 Virginia Woolf to Vita Sackville-West, 18 August 1929, *Letters*, IV, 79–80.

105 Virginia Woolf to Vita Sackville-West, 15 August 1929, *Letters*, IV, 78. This image is from Vita Sackville-West's book-length poem, 'The Land', a Georgic celebration of the Kentish rural landscape, which was published in 1926 and awarded the Hawthornden Prize for Literature. See *Essays*, V, 485, n1.

106 Virginia Stephen, 12 March 1897, *Passionate Apprentice*, 53.

107 Virginia Stephen to Thoby Stephen, 14 May 1897, *Letters*, I, 7; (?) May 1902, *Letters*, I, 52.

108 Virginia Stephen, 13 August 1899, *Passionate Apprentice*, 145.

109 Virginia Stephen, 13 August 1899, *Passionate Apprentice*, 145.

110 Virginia Woolf, 'A Scribbling Dame', *Essays*, II, 22.

111 Virginia Woolf, 'Reading', *Essays*, III, 150–151.

112 Virginia Woolf, 'Butterflies and Moths: Insects in September', *Essays*, VI, 382.

113 Woolf, 3 August 1918, *Diary*, I, 177.

114 Woolf, 7 August 1918, *Diary*, I, 179.

115 Gillian Beer, *Virginia Woolf: The Common Ground* (Edinburgh University Press, 1996), 19, 17. Beer continues: 'There is no need to assert the prevalence of evolutionary theory during Virginia Woolf's lifetime and we know that Darwin's writings had had direct effects upon her early family circumstances', 7.

116 Woolf, 20 October 1940, *Diary*, V, 331.

117 Darwin concludes *On the Origin of Species* (1855) with a description of 'an entangled bank, clothed with many plants of many kinds, with birds singing on the bushes, with various insects flitting about, and with worms crawling through the damp earth'. Quoting his lines in full, Beer notes, 'The emphasis in these final affirmative pages is on the delicate richness and variety of life, on complex interdependency, ecological interpretation, weaving together an aesthetic fullness.' Gillian Beer, *Darwin's Plots: Evolutionary Narrative in Darwin, George Eliot and Nineteenth-Century Fiction* (Cambridge University Press, 1983), 159.

118 Virginia Woolf, 'Kew Gardens', *Selected Short Stories*, 46.

119 Woolf, 12 August 1928, *Diary*, III, 191.

120 Woolf, 'Butterflies and Moths: Insects in September', *Essays*, VI, 382.

121 Virginia Woolf to Vita Sackville-West, 15 September 1933, *Letters*, V, 226.

122 Virginia Woolf to Duncan Grant, 6 March 1917, *Letters*, II, 144.

123 Woolf, 2 March 1918, *Diary*, I, 119.

124 Woolf, 'Reading', *Essays*, III, 152–153.

125 Woolf, 8 September 1918, *Diary*, I, 190.

126 Virginia Woolf to Dora Carrington, 13 July 1917, *Letters*, II, 162.

127 Virginia Woolf to Vanessa Bell, 14 September 1917, *Letters*, II, 179.

128 Virginia Woolf to Dora Carrington, 13 July 1917, *Letters*, II, 163; to Roger Fry, 22 July 1917, *Letters*, II, 166.

129 Virginia Woolf to Vanessa Bell, 1 July 1918, *Letters*, II, 257.

130 Vanessa Bell to Virginia Woolf, 3 July 1918, *Selected Letters*, 214.

131 Woolf, 'Kew Gardens', 50.

132 Virginia Woolf to Vanessa Bell, 15 July 1918, *Letters*, II, 259.

133 Virginia Woolf to Vanessa Bell, 7 November 1918, *Letters*, II, 289.

134 Woolf, 9 June 1919, *Diary*, I, 278.

135 Virginia Woolf to David Garnett, 26 July 1917, *Letters*, II, 167.

136 Virginia Woolf to Vanessa Bell, 1 July 1918, *Letters*, II, 257.

137 Frances Spalding, *Roger Fry: Art and Life* (Granada, 1980), 159–165.

138 Woolf, 18 April 1918, *Diary*, I, 141, n29; Virginia Woolf to Nicholas Bagenal, 15 April 1918, *Letters*, II, 230.

139 Virginia Woolf to Nicholas Bagenal, 15 April 1918, *Letters*, II, 230.

140 Woolf, 22 November 1917, *Diary*, I, 80.

141 Virginia Woolf to Katherine Cox, 12 February 1916, *Letters*, II, 78.

142 Woolf, 7 December 1918, *Diary*, I, 225; Virginia Woolf to Vanessa Bell, 15 July 1918, *Letters*, II, 259.

143 Virginia Woolf to Vanessa Bell, 1 July 1918, *Letters*, II, 257.

144 Virginia Woolf to Vanessa Bell, 15 July 1918, *Letters*, II, 259.

145 Virginia Woolf to Vanessa Bell, 25 June 1918, *Letters*, II, 255.

146 Virginia Woolf, 'The Mark on the Wall', *Selected Short Stories*, 53–54.

147 Virginia Woolf, 'Monday or Tuesday', *Selected Short Stories*, 22.

148 Virginia Woolf, 'Walter Sickert: A Conversation', *Essays*, VI, 37.

149 Katherine Mansfield to Virginia Woolf, 23 August 1917, *The Edinburgh Edition of the Collected Letters of Katherine Mansfield*, Volume 2, eds. Claire Davison and Gerri Kimber (Edinburgh University Press, 2022), 748.

150 Virginia Woolf to Lytton Strachey, 25 July 1916, *Letters*, II, 107.

151 Virginia Woolf to Vanessa Bell, 26 April 1917, *Letters*, II, 150.

152 Virginia Woolf to Vanessa Bell, 27 June 1917, *Letters*, II, 159; to Clive Bell, 16 July 1918, *Letters*, II, 262.

153 Virginia Woolf to Clive Bell, 17 September 1917, *Letters*, II, 179, n2.

154 Virginia Woolf to Vanessa Bell, 11 February 1917, *Letters*, II, 144.

155 Virginia Woolf to Janet Case, 20 March 1922, *Letters*, II, 514.

156 Virginia Woolf to Katherine Mansfield, 19 December 1920, *Letters*, II, 449; Woolf, 19 December 1920, *Diary*, II, 80.

157 Virginia Woolf to Janet Case, 20 March 1922, *Letters*, II, 515; Woolf, 25 January 1921, *Diary*, II, 87.

158 Virginia Woolf to Roger Fry, 1 August 1920, *Letters*, II, 438.

159 Woolf, 12 December 1920, *Diary*, II, 79.

160 Katherine Mansfield to Ottoline Morrell, 15 August 1917, *Collected Letters*, Volume 2, 208–209. For a wonderful reading of Katherine Mansfield's *Prelude* against her life, and discussion of Katherine as influence on Virginia, see Claire Harman, *All Sorts of Lives: Katherine Mansfield and the Art of Risking Everything* (Chatto & Windus, 2023), 181–207.

161 Virginia Woolf to Ottoline Morrell, 15 August 1917, *Letters*, II, 174.

162 Katherine Mansfield to Virginia Woolf, 23 August 1917, *Collected Letters*, 748.

163 Woolf, 31 May 1920, *Diary*, II, 43.

164 Woolf, 31 May 1920, *Diary*, II, 43.

165 Woolf, 22 March 1919, *Diary*, I, 257.

166 Woolf, 5 June 1920, *Diary*, II, 45.

167 Katherine Mansfield to Virginia Woolf, 23 August 1917, *Collected Letters*, 748.

168 Woolf, 28 January 1923, *Diary*, II, 228; 16 January 1923, *Diary*, II, 226.

169 John Lehmann, *Thrown to the Woolfs* (Weidenfeld and Nicolson, 1978), 10.

170 John Lehmann, *Thrown to the Woolfs*, 11.

171 Virginia Woolf to Ethel Smythe, 16 October 1930, *Letters*, IV, 231.

172 Woolf, 26 January 1920, *Diary*, II, 13.

173 Virginia Woolf to Katherine Cox, 27 February 1917, *Letters*, II, 222.

174 Woolf, 17 December 1918, *Diary*, I, 228.

175 Virginia Woolf to Molly MacCarthy, 7 June 1918, *Letters*, II, 247.

176 Woolf, 3 September 1918, *Diary*, I, 188.

177 Woolf, 29 January 1915, *Diary*, I, 30.

178 Woolf, 3 August 1918, *Diary*, I, 177.

179 Woolf, 7 May 1919, *Diary*, I, 269.

180 Woolf, 31 July 1918, *Diary*, I, 176.

181 Woolf, 3 August 1918, *Diary*, I, 177.

182 Woolf, 8 August 1918, *Diary*, I, 180.

183 Woolf, 5 August 1918, *Diary*, I, 178. (This date is incorrectly noted as 4 August in the *Diary*.)

184 Woolf, 24 August 1918, *Diary*, I, 185.

185 Woolf, 7 August 1918, *Diary*, I, 179; 3 August 1918, *Diary*, I, 177.

186 Woolf, 20 April 1919, *Diary*, I, 265.

187 Woolf, 28 May 1918, *Diary*, I, 149.

188 Woolf, 13 September 1926, *Diary*, III, 110.

189 Woolf, 22 August 1929, *Diary*, III, 248.

190 Virginia Woolf to Katherine Arnold-Forster, 5 February 1919, *Letters*, II, 326.

191 Virginia Woolf to Katherine Arnold-Forster, 12 August 1919, *Letters*, II, 382.

192 Woolf, 24 January 1919, *Diary*, I, 235.

Miss Green

1 Warner, 21 April 1930, *Diaries*, 59–60.

2 Warner, 21 April 1930, *Diaries*, 60.

3 Woolf, 1 June 1925, *Diary*, III, 26.

4 Warner, in Claire Harman, *Sylvia Townsend Warner: A Biography* (Chatto & Windus, 1989), 66.

5 Warner, 28 August 1930, *Diaries*, 66.

6 Warner, 5 March 1920, *Diaries*, 56.

7 Warner, 22 May 1930, *Diaries*, 60.

8 Warner, 22 May 1930, *Diaries*, 60.

9 Warner, 19 April 1930, *Diaries*, 58.

10 Sylvia Townsend Warner to Valentine Ackland, 20 June 1930, Dorset.

11 Sylvia Townsend Warner, 'Bathrooms Remembered' (January 1964), *With the Hunted*, 40.

12 Sylvia Townsend Warner to Valentine Ackland, 22 June 1930, Dorset. Sylvia is here referring to a sale held by the Weld family in 1929 of a series of estate cottages in the villages of Wool, Winfrith Newburgh and Chaldon Herring, as documented in 'Particulars of Sale (with 3 maps) of Portions of Weld Estate, 1929', Dorset History Centre. See also Judith Stinton, *Chaldon Herring: The Powys Circle in a Dorset Village* (The Boydell Press, 1988), 25.

13 Sylvia Townsend Warner to Valentine Ackland, 22 June 1930, Dorset.

14 Sylvia Townsend Warner to Valentine Ackland, 5 July 1930, Dorset.

15 Sylvia Townsend Warner to Valentine Ackland, 22 June 1930, Dorset.

16 Sylvia Townsend Warner to Valentine Ackland, 22 August 1930, Dorset.

17 Sylvia Townsend Warner to Valentine Ackland, 5 July 1930, Dorset.

18 Sylvia Townsend Warner to Valentine Ackland, 9 September 1930, Dorset.

19 Sylvia Townsend Warner to Valentine Ackland, 5 July 1930, Dorset.

20 Sylvia Townsend Warner to Valentine Ackland, 9 September 1930, Dorset.

21 Warner, 4 July 1930, manuscript diary, Dorset.

22 Sylvia Townsend Warner to Valentine Ackland, 5 July 1930, Dorset.

23 Sylvia Townsend Warner to Valentine Ackland, 9 September 1930, Dorset.

24 Sylvia Townsend Warner to Valentine Ackland, 5 July 1930, Dorset.

25 Sylvia Townsend Warner to Valentine Ackland, 9 September 1930, Dorset; 5 July 1930, Dorset.

26 Sylvia Townsend Warner to Valentine Ackland, 20 June 1930, Dorset.

27 Sylvia Townsend Warner to Valentine Ackland, 22 June 1930, Dorset.

28 Sylvia Townsend Warner to Valentine Ackland, 5 July 1930, Dorset.

29 Sylvia Townsend Warner to Valentine Ackland, 9 July 1930, Dorset.

30 Warner, 25 July 1930, Dorset.

31 Sylvia Townsend Warner to Valentine Ackland, 9 July 1930, Dorset.

32 Sylvia Townsend Warner to Valentine Ackland, 26 August 1930, Dorset; 9 September 1930, Dorset.

33 Sylvia Townsend Warner to Valentine Ackland, 20 June 1930, Dorset.

34 Sylvia Townsend Warner to Valentine Ackland, 22 June 1930, Dorset.

35 Valentine Ackland to Sylvia Townsend Warner, 21 August 1930, Dorset.

36 Sylvia Townsend Warner to Valentine Ackland, 21 August 1930, Dorset.

37 Sylvia Townsend Warner to Valentine Ackland, 27 March 1931, *I'll Stand by You: The Letters of Sylvia Townsend Warner and Valentine Ackland*, ed. Susanna Pinney (Pimlico, 1998), 62.

38 Warner, 23 September 1930, *Diaries*, 67.

39 Warner, 25 September 1930, in Harman, *Sylvia Townsend Warner*, 98.

40 Warner, 4 October 1930, *Diaries*, 68; Warner, Narrative 1, *I'll Stand By You*, 13.

41 Warner, 30 September 1930, *Diaries*, 68.

42 Warner, Narrative 1, *I'll Stand by You*, 13.

43 Valentine Ackland to Sylvia Townsend Warner, 21 August 1930, Dorset.

44 Warner, 25 April 1930, *Diaries*, 60.

45 Warner, 9 January 1928, *Diaries*, 10.

46 Warner, 22 December 1928, *Diaries*, 29.

47 Warner, Narrative 1, *I'll Stand by You*, 14.

48 Warner, Narrative 1, *I'll Stand by You*, 13.

49 Peter Swaab, 'Sylvia Townsend Warner and the Possibilities of Freedom: The Sylvia Townsend Warner Society Lecture 2019', *The Journal of the Sylvia Townsend Warner Society*, Volume 20, Issue 1, 63–88 (66).

50 Warner, *Lolly Willowes*, 9.

51 Warner, 1 December 1963, in Harman, *Sylvia Townsend Warner*, 59–60.

52 Sylvia Townsend Warner to Charles Prentice, 25 February 1925, *The Letters of Sylvia Townsend Warner*, ed. William Maxwell (Chatto & Windus, 1982), 5.

53 Warner, *Lolly Willowes*, 193–194.

54 Warner, *Lolly Willowes*, 196.

55 Warner, *Lolly Willowes*, 203.

56 Warner, *Lolly Willowes*, 72.

57 Warner, *Lolly Willowes*, 90.

58 Sylvia Townsend Warner to David Garnett, 11 November 1925, *Sylvia & David: The Townsend Warner/Garnett Letters*, ed. Richard Garnett (Sinclair-Stevenson, 1994), 26.

59 Warner, *Lolly Willowes*, 106.

60 Warner, *Lolly Willowes*, 196.

61 Warner, in Harman, *Sylvia Townsend Warner*, 59.

62 Warner, *Lolly Willowes*, 202.

63 Warner, *Lolly Willowes*, 99.

64 Warner, Narrative 1, *I'll Stand by You*, 13.

65 Harman, *Sylvia Townsend Warner*, 20.

66 Sylvia Townsend Warner to William Maxwell, 9 April 1971, *Letters*, 251.

67 Established in 1913 by the Scottish-American philanthropist Andrew Carnegie, the Carnegie UK Trust funded a number of high-profile projects in the arts in the 1920s and 30s. The ten-volume *Tudor Church Music* – published between 1922 and 1929 on behalf of the Carnegie UK Trust by Oxford University Press – aimed to edit and restore an extensive collection of English sacred music, predominantly choral music in English and Latin, from the Tudor and Jacobean periods. Alongside Sylvia Townsend Warner, the editorial committee included Sir Percy Buck, Edmund H. Fellowes and R. R. Terry, and was guided by the general editorship of John Milsom. See https://london.ac.uk/senate-house-library/our-collections/special-collections/printed-special-collections/tudor-church-music-collection, accessed 12 May 2020; also, in Harman, *Sylvia Townsend Warner*, 38–39.

68 Sylvia Townsend Warner, 'The Way By Which I Have Come', *With the Hunted*, 15.

69 Sylvia Townsend Warner, 'Being a Lily', *Scenes of Childhood* (Viking, 1982), 142.

70 Warner, 17 September 1930, *Diaries*, 66.

71 Warner, 'Being a Lily', *Scenes of Childhood*, 141–142.

72 Warner, 26 July 1931, *Diaries*, 86.

73 Warner, 'Bathrooms Remembered', *With the Hunted*, 40–41.

74 Warner, 20 January 1928, *Diaries*, 12.

75 Warner, 15 May 1929, manuscript diary, Dorset.

76 Warner, 5 December 1927, *Diaries*, 5.

77 Sylvia Townsend Warner to Charles Prentice, 15 February 1926, in Harman, *Sylvia Townsend Warner*, 65.

78 Warner, 20 February 1930, *Diaries*, 55.

79 Warner, Narrative 1, *I'll Stand by You*, 6.

80 Valentine Ackland, *Journey from Winter: Selected Poems*, ed. Frances Bingham (London: Carcanet, 2008), 19.

81 David Garnett described Sylvia as 'dripping with tassels [. . .] with jingling ear-rings, swinging fox-tails, black silk acorn hanging from umbrella, black tasselled gloves, dog chains, [and] key rings', Harman, *Sylvia Townsend Warner*, 51.

82 Warner, Narrative 1, *I'll Stand by You*, 6.

83 Valentine Ackland, *For Sylvia: An Honest Account* (Chatto & Windus, 1985), 99–100.

84 Ackland, *For Sylvia*, 86.

85 Ackland, *For Sylvia*, 108, 106.

86 Ackland, *For Sylvia*, 115.

87 In her Introduction to *For Sylvia*, Bea Howe wrote: 'In an odd way, Valentine's dressing of herself was a kind of protective clothing such as Nature gives to disguise an animal living in the wild. [. . .] She was like a very handsome boy, which her high-bred and somewhat haughty features, her close-cropped nut-brown hair, and the look of a real dandy: for she chose, whenever suitable, to cover her long, slender legs in well-cut and well-pressed trousers, and her trim shirts and sports jackets, even in the country, were *comme il faut*', Ackland, *For Sylvia*, 9.

88 Ackland, *For Sylvia*, 139.

89 Ackland, *For Sylvia*, 134.

90 Ackland, *For Sylvia*, 133.

91 Stephen Tomlin to Sylvia Townsend Warner, in Stinton, *The Powys Circle*, 39.

92 T. F. Powys to John Cowper Powys, in Stinton, *The Powys Circle*, 42.

93 Sylvia Townsend Warner to T. F. Powys, in Stinton, *The Powys Circle*, 53.

94 T. F. Powys to Sylvia Townsend Warner, in Stinton, *Writers in a Dorset Landscape* (Black Dog Books, 2004), 55.

95 Sylvia Townsend Warner to T. F. Powys, in J. Lawrence Mitchell, *T. F. Powys: Aspects of a Life* (The Brynmill Press, 2005), 128. Sylvia thought Powys 'not a writer for everybody, but I am sure that he is a writer for posterity: indeed, of living authors I consider him the most notable, both as a thinker and a stylist.' Sylvia Townsend Warner to David Garnett, 15 June 1928, *Selected Letters*, 71.

96 T. F. Powys, *This Is Thyself*, *The Powys Review*, Number Twenty (1987), 15–17.

97 Warner, in Mitchell, *T. F. Powys*, 128.

98 Dora Carrington, in Judith Stinton, *Chaldon Herring: The Powys Circle in a Dorset Village* (Black Dog Books, 2004), 42.

99   Warner, 1 October 1929, *Diaries*, 45.

100 Warner, in Harman, *Sylvia Townsend Warner*, 83.

101 Warner, 20 November 1929, *Diaries*, 49.

102 Sylvia Townsend Warner to Paul Nordoff, 13 August 1958, *Letters*, 168.

103 Warner, 23 October 1929, *Diaries*, 46.

104 Warner, 20 January 1928, *Diaries*, 12.

105 Warner, 22 December 1928, *Diaries*, 29.

106 Sylvia Townsend Warner, *Opus 7* (Chatto & Windus, 1931), 30.

107 Warner, *Opus 7*, 32, 34, 9.

108 Warner, *Opus 7*, 45.

109 Sylvia Townsend Warner to Paul Nordoff, 18 July 1954, *Letters*, 150.

110 Sylvia Townsend Warner to Paul Nordoff, 18 July 1954, *Letters*, 150. I owe many of these ideas to discussions with Peter Swaab, and his marvellous lecture on Sylvia's commitment to personal freedom, delivered to The Sylvia Townsend Warner Society in 2019 and reprinted as 'Sylvia Townsend Warner and the Possibilities of Freedom'.

111 Warner, 'The Way By Which I Have Come', *With the Hunted*, 17. Janet Montefiore notes the 'small rural world' of the poem 'represents issues beyond itself'. For the ways in which *Opus 7* is a political poem, see Montefiore, *Men and Women Writers of the 1930s: The Dangerous Flood of History* (Routledge, 1996), 134; Martin Seymour-Smith, 'Notes of Sylvia Townsend Warner's Poetry', *PN Review*, 8:3, Jan 1, 1981, 57–61; and Gay Wachman, *Lesbian Empire, Radical Crosswriting in the Twenties* (Rutgers University Press, 2001), 32.

112 Warner, *Opus 7*, 27, 32.

113 Warner, 23 July 1930, *Diaries*, 63.

114 Sylvia Townsend Warner to Valentine Ackland, 19 July 1930, Dorset.

115 Warner, 'The Way By Which I Have Come', *With the Hunted*, 16.

116 Warner, 5 September 1958, *Diaries*, 250.

117 Warner, 10 July 1930, *Diaries*, 61, 62.

118 Warner, 22 May 1930, *Diaries*, 61.

119 Warner, 21 June 1930, *Diaries*, 62.

120 Warner, 26 June 1930, *Diaries*, 62.

121 Warner, 5 October 1930, *Diaries*, 69.

122 Warner, 11 October 1930, *Diaries*, 69.

123 Warner, Narrative 1, *I'll Stand by You*, 16.

124 Warner, 12 October 1930, *Diaries*, 70.

125 Sylvia Townsend Warner to Valentine Ackland, 14 October 1930, *I'll Stand by You*, 18; Warner, 16 October 1930, *Diaries*, 71.

126 Warner, 16 October 1930, *Diaries*, 71.

127 Warner, 13 October 1930, *Diaries*, 70.

128 Sylvia Townsend Warner to Valentine Ackland, 14 October 1930, *I'll Stand by You*, 18.

129 Sylvia Townsend Warner to Valentine Ackland, 16 October 1930, *I'll Stand by You*, 23.

130 Warner, Narrative 2, *I'll Stand by You*, 24.

131 Warner, Narrative 2, *I'll Stand by You*, 24; Warner, 19 October 1930, *Diaries*, 72.

132 Warner, Narrative 2, *I'll Stand by You*, 24.

133 Warner, 31 October 1930, *Diaries*, 73.

134 Warner, 17 November 1930, *Diaries*, 75.

135 Warner, 12 November 1930, *Diaries*, 74.

136 Warner, Narrative 2, *I'll Stand by You*, 24.

137 Warner, 14 June 1931, *Diaries*, 83.

138 Warner, 19 November 1930, *Diaries*, 75.

139 Warner, 11 November 1930, *Diaries*, 74.

140 Ackland, *For Sylvia*, 136.

141 Warner, 13 October 1930, *Diaries*, 71.

142 Warner, in Harman, *Sylvia Townsend Warner*, 122.

143 Bea Howe, in Ackland, *For Sylvia*, 20.

144 Alison Light, *A Radical Romance* (Fig Tree, 2019), 127.

145 Warner, 19 January 1931, *Diaries*, 77.

146 Warner, Narrative 1, *I'll Stand by You*, 16.

147 Warner, 12 January 1931, *Diaries*, 77.

148 Warner, Narrative 3, *I'll Stand by You*, 48.

149 Ackland, *For Sylvia*, 145.

150 Warner, 'The Way By Which I Have Come', *With the Hunted*, 19.

151 Warner, 'The Way By Which I Have Come', *With the Hunted*, 13.

152 Warner, 'The Essex Marshes', *With the Hunted*, 32.

153 Warner, 'The Essex Marshes', *With the Hunted*, 32.

154 Warner, 'The Way By Which I Have Come', *With the Hunted*, 16.

155 Warner, 'The Way By Which I Have Come', *With the Hunted*, 16.

156 J.W. Robertson Scott, *England's Green and Pleasant Land* (Jonathan Cape, 1925), 255.

157 Robertson Scott, *England's Green and Pleasant Land*, 247.

158 Warner, 'The Way By Which I Have Come', *With the Hunted*,16–17.

159 Warner, 'The Way By Which I Have Come', *With the Hunted*, 17.

160 Warner, 'Love Green', *With the Hunted*, 302–309.

161 Warner, 'The Way By Which I Have Come', *With the Hunted*, 17. As Judith Stinton notes, housing quality in the area had long been poor. In 'The Commission on the Employment of Children, Young Persons and Women in Agriculture', published in 1867, cottages in Winfrith – belonging to the Weld estate – were described as 'Miserable. Most of them belong to one owner, some few being still out on lease. Almost all are wretched. [. . .] In some cases the flooring is so bad that the water stands in it in rainy weather. The greater number have no privies.' Stinton, *The Powys Circle*, 60.

162 Warner, 'The Way By Which I Have Come', *With the Hunted*, 18.

163 Sylvia Townsend Warner to Nancy Cunard, 9 June 1944, *Letters*, 85.

164 Jean Starr Untermeyer, *Private Collection* (Alfred A. Knopf, 1965), 144–145.

165 Untermeyer, *Private Collection*, 145.

166 Warner, 4 April 1931, *Diaries*, 81.

167 Warner, 31 July 1931, manuscript diary, Dorset.

168 Warner, 'The Way By Which I Have Come', *With the Hunted*, 19.

169 Warner, 14 April 1931, *Diaries*, 81.

170 Warner, manuscript notebook inscribed 'Visitors' Book, The Late Miss Green's Cottage, Chaldon Hering [*sic*], Oct. 1930–', Dorset.

171 Warner, 'The Way By Which I Have Come', *With the Hunted*, 19.

172 Ackland, 23 July 1931, in Harman, *Sylvia Townsend Warner*, 122.

173 Warner, 18 June 1932, *Diaries*, 91.

174 Light, *A Radical Romance*, 19, Preface.

175 Untermeyer, *Private Collection*, 146.

176 Warner, 28 July 1932, manuscript diary, Dorset.

177 Louise Morgan, 'Sylvia Townsend Warner: A Writer Who Follows None of the Rules', *Everyman New Series* 4 (1930), 229–230.

178 Warner, 10–12 February 1931, *Diaries*, 78.

179 Warner, 'I Cook on Oil', *With the Hunted*, 34. Originally published as ninth in the series 'Concerning Authors' Cottages', in Robertson Scott's *The Countryman Book* (Odhams Press Limited, 1948), 136–138.

180 Warner, 'I Cook on Oil', *With the Hunted*, 34.

181 Sylvia Townsend Warner, 'The Kitchen Year', *Everyman*, 29 July 1933, 145.

182 Sylvia Townsend Warner to Louise Morgan, 24 June 1933, Beinecke Rare Book and Manuscript Library.

183 Sylvia Townsend Warner to Louise Morgan, 24 June 1933, Beinecke.

184 Sylvia Townsend Warner to Louise Morgan, 24 June 1933, Beinecke.

185 Sylvia Townsend Warner to Louise Morgan, 24 June 1933, Beinecke.

186 Sylvia Townsend Warner, 'Folk Cookery', *Scenes of Childhood*, 165.

187 Warner, 15 June 1932, manuscript diary, Dorset.

188 Warner, 'Bathrooms Remembered', *With the Hunted*, 42.

189 Warner, 19 March 1931, manuscript diary, Dorset; 'I Cook on Oil', 33.

190 Warner, 'I Cook on Oil', *With the Hunted*, 33.

191 Sylvia Townsend Warner to Alyse Gregory, 26 May 1953, *Letters*, 140. Sylvia's teapot makes me think of Raphael Samuel's glass bottles and his dented milk jug, those 'humble objects which were far less likely to survive in museums than the household goods of the more affluent sort', but which were, writes Alison Light, 'part of an argument or an interpretation of history'; 'a way of thinking about the past', Light, *A Radical Romance*, 81.

192 Alyse Gregory's journal for 26 February 1933, in Harman, *Sylvia Townsend Warner*, 127.

193 Warner, 3 April 1931, *Diaries*, 81.

194 Valentine Ackland's diary for 14 July 1931, in Harman, *Sylvia Townsend Warner*, 119.

195 Warner, n/d, manuscript diary, Dorset.

196 Warner, 17 June 1932, *Diaries*, 91.

197 Warner, 'The Way By Which I Have Come', *With the Hunted*, 18.

198 Warner to Louise Morgan, 24 June 1933, Beinecke.

199 Warner, 'The Way By Which I Have Come', *With the Hunted*, 18.

200 Warner, Narrative 6, *I'll Stand by You*, 123.

201 Valentine Ackland, 'Country Dealings' (III), *Left Review*, September 1935; a version of which was later published as *Country Conditions* (Lawrence & Wishart, 1936).

202 Warner, 'Sylvia Townsend Warner in Conversation', *PN Review 23*, Volume 8, Issue 3 (1981), 35–37.

203 Warner, 12 October 1930, *Diaries*, 70.

A dream of winter

1 Rosamond Lehmann to George Rylands, 4 February 1942, KCC.

2 Rosamond Lehmann to George Rylands, 4 February 1942, KCC; to John Lehmann, 17 October 1942, KCC.

3 Rosamond Lehmann to George Rylands, 4 February 1942, KCC.

4 Rosamond Lehmann to George Rylands, n/d (1940), KCC.

5 Rosamond Lehmann to William Plomer, 7 July 1942, Durham University Library (DUL hereafter).

6 Rosamond Lehmann to Rayner Heppenstall, n/d, Harry Ransom Humanities Research Centre (HRHRC hereafter).

7 Woolf, 18 January 1932, *Diary*, IV, 64.

8 Rosamond Lehmann, *The Swan in the Evening* (1967; Virago, 1982), 21.

9 Rosamond Lehmann to Laurie Lee, 11 January 1947, British Library (BL hereafter); to William Plomer, 22 May 1946, DUL.

10 Rosamond Lehmann to Herman Ould, 25 February 1943, University of Tulsa.

11 Rosamond Lehmann to William Plomer, 7 July 1942, DUL.

12 Rosamond Lehmann to Rayner Heppenstall, 13 April 1945, HRHRC.

13 Anne Scott-James, *Sketches from a Life* (London: Michael Joseph, 1993), 102.

14 Laurence Binyon to Rosamond Lehmann, n/d, KCC.

15 Rosamond Lehmann to Harold Raymond, 9 May 1927, in Wendy Pollard, *Rosamond Lehmann and Her Critics* (Routledge, 2004), 35.

16 Lehmann, *The Swan in the Evening*, 65, 66; Rosamond Lehmann interviewed by Janet Watts, *Writing Lives: Conversations between Women Writers*, ed. Mary Chamberlain (Virago, 1988), 154.

17 Lehmann, *The Swan in the Evening*, 66.

18 Lehmann, *The Swan in the Evening*, 69; *Writing Lives*, 153.

19 Woolf, *Diary*, III, 315, n315.

20 Rosamond Lehmann, *Invitation to the Waltz* (1932; Virago, 1981), 127.

21 Lehmann, *Invitation to the Waltz*, 126.

22 Rosamond Lehmann, *The Weather in the Streets* (1936; Virago, 1981), 144–145.

23 Lehmann, *The Weather in the Streets*, Introduction.

24 Dora Carrington to Julia Strachey, August 1927, *Carrington's Letters: Her Art, Her Loves, Her Friendships*, ed. Anne Chisholm (Chatto & Windus, 2017), 321; to Julia Strachey, March/April 1929, *Carrington's Letters*, 356.

25 Dora Carrington to Rosamond Lehmann, 6 September 1929, *Carrington's Letters*, 363.

26 Rosamond Lehmann to John Lehmann, n/d (1930), Princeton University Library (PUL hereafter).

27 Rosamond Lehmann to Alice Lehmann, 12 January 1924, KCC.

28 Woolf, 12 November 1933, *Diary*, IV, 188.

29 Rosamond Lehmann to John Lehmann, 25 November 1933, PUL.

30 Stephen Spender, *World within World* (Faber and Faber, 1951), 144.

31 Rosamond Lehmann to Elizabeth Bowen, 10 June (1935?), HRHRC.

32 Rosamond Lehmann to Beatrix Lehmann, n/d, KCC.

33 Lehmann, *Invitation to the Waltz*, 75.

34 Rosamond Lehmann to Harold Raymond, 4 May 1927, in Pollard, *Rosamond Lehmann and Her Critics*, 154.

35 Rosamond Lehmann to George Rylands, 2 August 1929, KCC.

36 Rosamond Lehmann to Frances Partridge, n/d (August 1932), KCC.

37 Rosamond Lehmann to Harold Raymond, 23 November 1933, in Pollard, *Rosamond Lehmann and Her Critics*, 85.

38 Rosamond Lehmann to Frances Partridge, n/d (August 1932), KCC.

39 Rosamond Lehmann to Elizabeth Bowen, n/d (8 July), HRHRC.

40 John Lehmann, in Hermione Lee's Introduction to *The Hogarth Letters* (Chatto & Windus, 1985).

41 Rosamond Lehmann, *A Letter to a Sister*, *The Hogarth Letters*, No. 3 (The Hogarth Press, 1931), 13.

42 Lehmann, *A Letter to a Sister*, 7–8.

43 Lehmann, *A Letter to a Sister*, 15.

44 Rosamond Lehmann to John Lehmann, 29 July 1931, KCC.

45 Rosamond Lehmann to Cyril Connolly, in Pollard, *Rosamond Lehmann and Her Critics*, 156.

46 Rosamond Lehmann to John Lehmann, 11 August 1936, PUL; to Beatrix Lehmann, n/d, KCC.

47 Rosamond Lehmann, typescript memoir, KCC.

48 Rosamond Lehmann, 'The Red-Haired Miss Daintreys', *The Gypsy's Baby*, 57.

49 Lehmann, 'The Red-Haired Miss Daintreys', *The Gypsy's Baby*, 57.

50 Rosamond Lehmann, *A Note in Music* (1930; Virago, 1982), 279.

51 Lehmann, *A Note in Music*, 21.

52 Lehmann, *A Note in Music*, 7.

53 Lehmann, *Invitation to the Waltz*, 7.

54 Lehmann, *Invitation to the Waltz*, 67.

55 Lehmann, *A Note in Music*, 4–5.

56 Lehmann, *A Note in Music*, 3.

57 Lehmann, *Writing Lives*, 155.

58 Rosamond Lehmann to Laurie Lee, 30 April 1943, BL.

59 Rosamond Lehmann to Laurie Lee, 30 April 1943, BL.

60 Rosamond Lehmann to Eddy Sackville-West, n/d, in Hastings, *Rosamond Lehmann*, 171.

61 Rosamond Lehmann, in 'Authors Take Sides on the Spanish War', *Left Review*, November 1937.

62 Rosamond Lehmann, *Daily Worker*, 29 October 1940.

63 Rosamond Lehmann, speech for 'Writers Declare Against Fascism' (1938), KCC.

64 Woolf, 24 May 1938, *Diary*, V, 142.

65 E. M. Forster to Rosamond Lehmann, 27 April 1938, KCC.

66 Wogan Philipps to Rosamond Lehmann, 25 May 1937, KCC.

67 Rosamond Lehmann to John Lehmann, 18 November 1937, PUL.

68 Wogan Philipps to Rosamond Lehmann, 10 May 1937, KCC.

69 Wogan Philipps to Rosamond Lehmann, 25 May 1937, KCC.

70 Rosamond Lehmann to John Lehmann, 18 November 1937, PUL.

71 Rosamond Lehmann to John Lehmann, 30 April 1937, PUL.

72 Rosamond Lehmann to John Lehmann, 18 November 1937, PUL.

73 Rosamond Lehmann to John Lehmann, 25 January 1939, PUL.

74 Rosamond Lehmann to Edward Sackville-West, 13 May 1938, in Hastings, *Rosamond Lehmann*, 195.

75 Rosamond Lehmann to John Lehmann, 16 September 1935, PUL.

76 Lehmann, *The Weather in the Streets*, 270, 228.

77 Lehmann, *The Weather in the Streets*, 227.

78 Lehmann, *Invitation to the Waltz*, 66; *The Weather in the Streets*, 228.

79 Stephen Spender to Rosamond Lehmann, 26 July (1935/6), KCC.

80 Elizabeth Bowen, 'Panorama of the Novel', *Listening In: Broadcasts, Speeches and Interviews*, ed. Allan Hepburn (Edinburgh University Press, 2010), 135–144.

81 Rosamond Lehmann to John Lehmann, 22 January 1937, KCC.

82 Rosamond Lehmann to Compton Mackenzie, 23 October 1938, HRHRC.

83 Rosamond Lehmann to Compton Mackenzie, 30 October 1938, HRHRC.

84 Rosamond Lehmann, BBC *Bookmark*, unedited typescript, November 1984, KCC.

85 Rosamond Lehmann to Beatrix Lehmann, 10 April 1938, KCC.

86 Beatrix Lehmann to Rosamond Lehmann, n/d (August 1938), KCC.

87 Rosamond Lehmann to John Lehmann, 21 November 1939, KCC.

88 Remembered by Barbara Ker-Seymer, in Hastings, *Rosamond Lehmann*, 200.

89 Rosamond Lehmann to Marthe L'Évêque, 8 October 1939, in Hastings, *Rosamond Lehmann*, 200.

90 Rosamond Lehmann to Frances Partridge, 28 February 1940, KCC.

91 Rosamond Lehmann to Compton Mackenzie, 22 May 1940, HRHRC.

92 Rosamond Lehmann to Frances Partridge, 28 February 1940, KCC.

93 Rosamond Lehmann to Compton Mackenzie, 22 May 1940, HRHRC.

94 Rosamond Lehmann to Beatrix Lehmann, 3 June 1940, KCC.

95 Rosamond Lehmann to Compton Mackenzie, n/d (1940), HRHRC.

96 Beatrix Lehmann to John Lehmann, 29 November 1940, PUL.

97 Rosamond Lehmann to George Rylands, n/d, KCC; Rosamond Lehmann to George Rylands, n/d, KCC.

98 Rosamond Lehmann, 'A Dream of Winter', *The Gypsy's Baby*, 106.

99 Rosamond Lehmann to John Lehmann, 19 November 1940, PUL.

100 Henry Yorke to Rosamond Lehmann, 9 January 1941, KCC.

101 Rosamond Lehmann to Beatrix Lehmann, 6 February 1940, KCC; Rosamond Lehmann to Beatrix Lehmann, n/d, KCC.

102 Virginia Woolf to John Lehmann, 20 March 1941, *Letters*, VI, 482; (27?) March 1941, *Letters*, VI, 486; to Octavia Wilberforce, 31 Dec 1940, *Letters*, VI, 456.

103 Rosamond Lehmann, *Rosamond Lehmann's Album* (Chatto & Windus, 1987), 53.

104 Virginia Woolf to Rosamond Lehmann, 2 July 1928, KCC.

105 Virginia Woolf to Rosamond Lehmann, n/d (1932 or 1933), KCC.

106 Woolf, 28 August 1930, *Diary*, III, 315.

107 Rosamond Lehmann, 'Letter to a Friend', *Penguin New Writing*, Volume 5, April 1941, 80.

108 John Lehmann, *I Am My Brother* (Longmans, 1960), 36.

109 Rosamond Lehmann to Beatrix Lehmann, n/d, KCC.

110 John Lehmann, 2 March 1941, manuscript diary, PUL.

111 Rosamond Lehmann to John Lehmann, 19 November 1940, PUL.

112 Elizabeth Bowen, *The Heat of the Day* (1949; Vintage, 1998), 125.

113 John Lehmann, n/d, KCC.

114 Rosamond Lehmann, *Britain Today*, No. 122, June 1946.

115 Rosamond Lehmann to Stephen Spender, n/d, KCC.

116 Cecil Day Lewis, *Daily Telegraph*, 11 July 1936.

117 Cecil Day Lewis to Rosamond Lehmann, n/d, KCC.

118 Rosamond Lehmann to George Rylands, n/d, KCC.

119 Stephen Spender to Rosamond Lehmann, 28 July 1936, KCC.

120 Rosamond Lehmann to George Rylands, 7 January 1941, KCC.

121 Lehmann, 'A Dream of Winter', *The Gypsy's Baby*, 93.

122 Cecil Day Lewis to Rosamond Lehmann, n/d, KCC.

123 Rosamond Lehmann to William Plomer, 7 July 1942, DUL.

124 Lehmann, *Writing Lives*, 155.

125 Rosamond Lehmann to Rayner Heppenstall, 27 September 1958, HRHRC.

126 Rosamond Lehmann to William Plomer, 7 July 1942, DUL.

127 Cecil Day Lewis to Rosamond Lehmann, n/d, KCC.

128 Cecil Day Lewis to Rosamond Lehmann, n/d, KCC.

129 Rosamond Lehmann to John Lehmann, 26 July 1943, KCC; to William Plomer, 15 September 1945; to Compton Mackenzie, n/d (1940), HRHRC.

130 Rosamond Lehmann to William Plomer, 12 January 1946, DUL.

131 Rosamond Lehmann to Rayner Heppenstall, 18 September 1943, HRHRC.

132 Rosamond Lehmann to Laurie Lee, n/d, BL.

133 Cecil Day Lewis to Rosamond Lehmann, n/d, KCC.

134 Rosamond Lehmann to Laurie Lee, 3 March 1942, BL.

135 Laurie Lee, 13 October 1941, manuscript diary, BL.

136 Lee, 14 March 1942, manuscript diary, BL.

137 Lee, 15 March 1942, manuscript diary, BL.

138 Lee, 16 March 1942, manuscript diary, BL.

139 John Lehmann, in Valerie Grove, *Laurie Lee: The Well-Loved Stranger* (Penguin, 2000), 151.

140 Lee, 31 December 1941, manuscript diary, BL.

141 Lee, 13 March 1942, manuscript diary, BL.

142 Lee, 15 August 1941, manuscript diary, BL.

143 Rosamond Lehmann to Laurie Lee, 3 March 1942, BL.

144 Rosamond Lehmann to Laurie Lee, 16 September 1941, BL.

145 Lee, 14 March 1942, manuscript diary, BL.

146 Lee, 11 December 1942, manuscript diary, BL.

147 Lee, 12 December 1942, manuscript diary, BL.

148 Rosamond Lehmann to Rayner Heppenstall, 18 September 1943, HRHRC.

149 Rosamond Lehmann to Henry Yorke, 19 June 1943, in Hastings, *Rosamond Lehmann*, 228.

150 Cecil Day Lewis to Rosamond Lehmann, n/d, KCC.

151 Cecil Day Lewis to Rosamond Lehmann, n/d, KCC.
152 Rosamond Lehmann to John Lehmann, 17 October 1942, KCC.
153 Rosamond Lehmann to George Rylands, 4 February 1942, KCC.
154 Rosamond Lehmann to John Lehmann, 17 October 1942, KCC.
155 Rosamond Lehmann to John Lehmann, n/d, KCC.
156 Rosamond Lehmann, 'When the Waters Came', *The Gypsy's Baby*, 93.
157 Lehmann, 'When the Waters Came', *The Gypsy's Baby*, 93–95.
158 Rosamond Lehmann to John Lehmann, 19 November 1940, PUL.
159 Rosamond Lehmann to George Rylands, 26 May 1942.
160 Lehmann, 'A Dream of Winter', *The Gypsy's Baby*, 101–110.
161 Rosamond Lehmann to John Lehmann, 19 November 1940, PUL.
162 Lehmann, 'When the Waters Came', *The Gypsy's Baby*, 98.
163 Rosamond Lehmann to Russell Landstrom, 4 November 1943, HRHRC.
164 John Lehmann, *I Am My Brother*, 88–89.
165 Cecil Day Lewis to George Rylands, 23 February 1949, KCC.
166 Rosamond Lehmann to John Lehmann, 16 October 1946, PUL.
167 Rosamond Lehmann to Rayner Heppenstall, 6 September 1943, HRHRC.
168 Rosamond Lehmann to John Lehmann, 20 October 1936, HRHRC.
169 Cecil Day Lewis to Rosamond Lehmann, n/d, KCC.
170 Cecil Day Lewis to Rosamond Lehmann, n/d, KCC.
171 Cecil Day Lewis to Rosamond Lehmann, n/d, KCC.
172 Lee, 13 April 1943, manuscript diary, BL.
173 Lee, 7 April 1942, manuscript diary, BL.
174 Rosamond Lehmann to Laurie Lee, 23 April 1943, BL.
175 Rosamond Lehmann to John Lehmann, 3 February 1943, PUL.
176 Cecil Day Lewis to Rosamond Lehmann, n/d, KCC.
177 Rosamond Lehmann to John Lehmann, 16 April 1944, PUL.
178 Rosamond Lehmann to John Lehmann, 30 June 1942, PUL.
179 Rosamond Lehmann to John Lehmann, 26 July 1943, HRHRC.
180 Rosamond Lehmann to William Plomer, 27 July 1943, DUL.
181 Rosamond Lehmann to George Rylands, 26 May 1942, KCC.
182 Rosamond Lehmann to William Plomer, 7 July 1942, DUL.

183 Rosamond Lehmann to John Lehmann, 30 June 1942, PUL.

184 Rosamond Lehmann to George Rylands, 26 May 1942, KCC; to John Lehmann, 24 June 1943, PUL.

185 Rosamond Lehmann to William Plomer, 27 July 1943, DUL.

186 Cecil Day Lewis to Rosamond Lehmann, n/d, KCC.

187 Cecil Day Lewis to Rosamond Lehmann, n/d, KCC.

188 Cecil Day Lewis to Rosamond Lehmann, n/d, KCC.

189 Rosamond Lehmann to Laurie Lee, 23 April 1943, BL.

190 Rosamond Lehmann to Laurie Lee, 2 September 1943, BL.

191 Rosamond Lehmann to John Lehmann, 8 October 1943; 5 November 1943, PUL.

192 Rosamond Lehmann to John Lehmann, 18 October 1943, PUL.

193 Rosamond Lehmann to John Lehmann, 8 October 1943; 18 October 1943, PUL.

194 Rosamond Lehmann to Laurie Lee, 1 December 1943, BL.

195 Laurie Lee to Rosamond Lehmann, 26 November 1943, BL.

196 Rosamond Lehmann to Laurie Lee, 1 December 1943, BL.

197 Rosamond Lehmann to John Lehmann, 7 December 1943, PUL.

198 Rosamond Lehmann to John Lehmann, n/d, HRHRC.

199 Rosamond Lehmann to John Lehmann, 7 December 1943, PUL.

200 Editors' letter, *Orion: A Miscellany*, eds. Rosamond Lehmann, D. Kilham Roberts, C. Day Lewis and Edwin Muir, Volume 1 (Nicholson & Watson, 1945).

201 Rosamond Lehmann to John Lehmann, n/d, PUL.

202 Rosamond Lehmann to Laurie Lee, 22 December 1943, BL.

203 Rosamond Lehmann to Laurie Lee, n/d (Easter Sunday, 1944), BL.

204 Rosamond Lehmann to John Lehmann, 25 September 1944, PUL.

205 Rosamond Lehmann to Laurie Lee, n/d, BL.

206 Rosamond Lehmann to Laurie Lee, 3 April 1944, BL.

207 Rosamond Lehmann to Laurie Lee, n/d, BL.

208 Rosamond Lehmann to William Plomer, 1 May 1944, DUL.

209 Rosamond Lehmann to Laurie Lee, 3 April 1944, BL.

210 Lehmann, 'Wonderful Holidays', *With the Hunted*, 115–180.

211 *New Statesman & Nation*, 30 September 1944.

212 Rosamond Lehmann to William Plomer, 31 July 1944, DUL.

213 Elizabeth Bowen's review of *The Gypsy's Baby* in *The Tatler*, 17 April 1946, KCC.

214 Rosamond Lehmann to William Plomer, 31 July 1944, DUL.

215 Rosamond Lehmann to William Plomer, 15 September 1945, DUL.

216 Rosamond Lehmann to William Plomer, 31 July 1944, DUL.

217 Rosamond Lehmann to William Plomer, 22 December 1944, DUL.

218 Laurie Lee to Rosamond Lehmann, 27 November 1944, BL.

219 Rosamond Lehmann to Laurie Lee, 23 April 1943, BL.

220 Rosamond Lehmann to John Lehmann, 4 February 1945, PUL.

221 Rosamond Lehmann to Grizel Hartley, n/d, KCC.

222 Rosamond Lehmann to Grizel Hartley, n/d, KCC.

Part Two: Afterlives

An England of waifs and strays

1 Woolf, 4 July 1940, *Diary*, V, 299.

2 Woolf, 29 March 1940, *Diary*, V, 276.

3 Woolf, 23 September 1939, *Diary*, V, 237.

4 Woolf, 22 October 1939, *Diary*, V, 242.

5 Woolf, 12 October 1940, *Diary*, V, 328.

6 Woolf, 19 December 1938, *Diary*, V, 193.

7 Woolf, 12 October 1940, *Diary*, V, 328.

8 Woolf, 20 January 1940, *Diary*, V, 259.

9 Woolf, 31 January 1940, *Diary*, V, 262.

10 Woolf, 2 December 1939, *Diary*, V, 249.

11 Woolf, 24 March 1940, *Diary*, V, 273.

12 Woolf, 15 September 1940, *Diary*, V, 321.

13 Woolf, 12 October 1940, *Diary*, V, 328.

14 Woolf, 9 December 1939, *Diary*, V, 250.

15 Woolf, 23 November 1940, *Diary*, V, 340.

16 Woolf, 19 December 1940, *Diary*, V, 344.

17 Woolf, 20 May 1940, *Diary*, V, 286.

18 Woolf, 29 December 1940, *Diary*, V, 347.

19 Woolf, 30 November 1939, *Diary*, V, 248.

20 Woolf, 31 May 1940, *Diary*, V, 291.

21 Woolf, 24 December 1940, *Diary*, V, 346; 24 March 1940, *Diary*, V, 274; 12 July 1940, *Diary*, V, 301.

22 Woolf, 3 November 1940, *Diary*, V, 336.

23 Woolf, 23 November 1940, *Diary*, V, 341.

24 Woolf, 24 December 1940, *Diary*, V, 346.

25 Woolf, 28 August 1939, *Diary*, V, 231.

26 Woolf, 20 January 1940, *Diary*, V, 259.

27 In her chapter, 'Anon', Hermione Lee writes that Woolf's late diary entries reveal an increasing desire for total effacement and submersion. The watery imagery of the flooded Ouse Valley, Woolf's elegiac feelings about landscape beauty, and her interest in prehistory all ultimately point towards loss of self. Lee, *Virginia Woolf*, 745–756.

28 Woolf, 2 August 1940, *Diary*, V, 308.

29 Woolf, 9 June 1940, *Diary*, V, 293.

30 Woolf, 9 June 1940, *Diary*, V, 293; 24 July 1940, *Diary*, V, 304.

31 Woolf, 28 April 1938, *Diary*, V, 137.

32 Woolf, 14 July 1932, *Diary*, IV, 117.

33 Lee, *Virginia Woolf*, 694.

34 Virginia Woolf, *A Room of One's Own* and *Three Guineas* (Oxford World's Classics, 2015), 245.

35 Woolf, 12 October 1940, *Diary*, V, 329; Virginia Woolf to Julian Bell, 28 June 1936, in Lee, *Virginia Woolf*, 694.

36 Woolf, 15 May 1940, *Diary*, V, 285; Virginia Woolf to Judith Stephen, 2 December 1939, *Letters*, VI, 372.

37 Woolf, 7 February 1940, *Diary*, V, 263; 9 June 1940, *Diary*, V, 293.

38 Woolf, 2 October 1940, *Diary*, V, 326.

39 Woolf, 16 August 1940, *Diary*, V, 311.

40 Woolf, 4 July 1940, *Diary*, V, 300.

41 Woolf, 16 August 1940, *Diary*, V, 311; 11 September 1940, *Diary*, V, 318; 29 September 1940, *Diary*, V, 325.

42 Woolf, 31 August 1940, *Diary*, V, 314.

43 Woolf, 22 June 1940, *Diary*, V, 298.

44 Woolf, 27 June 1940, *Diary*, V, 299.

45 Woolf, 6 September 1939, *Diary*, V, 234.

46 Woolf, 12 October 1940, *Diary*, V, 328.

47 Woolf, 20 January 1940, *Diary*, V, 260.

48 Woolf, 12 October 1940, *Diary*, V, 329; 29 March 1940, *Diary*, V, 276.

49 Woolf, 17 October 1940, *Diary*, V, 330.

50 Woolf, 6 September 1939, *Diary*, V, 234.

51 Virginia Woolf, 'Anon', in Brenda R. Silver, '"Anon" and "The Reader": Virginia Woolf's Last Essays', *Twentieth Century Literature*, Autumn/Winter (1979), Volume 25, Number 3/4, 356–366 (382–383).

52 Woolf, *A Room of One's Own* and *Three Guineas*, 63.

53 Woolf, 22 June 1940, *Diary*, V, 298.

54 Woolf, 12 September 1940, *Diary*, V, 318; 6 October 1940, *Diary*, V, 327.

55 Alexandra Harris, *Romantic Moderns: English Writers, Artists and the Imagination from Virginia Woolf to John Piper* (London: Thames & Hudson, 2010), 155–158.

56 Woolf, 'Notes for Reading at Random', 18 September 1940, in Silver, '"Anon" and "The Reader"', 373.

57 Woolf, 'Notes for Reading at Random', in Silver, '"Anon" and "The Reader"', 376.

58 Woolf, 'Notes for Reading at Random', in Silver, '"Anon" and "The Reader"', 376, 382.

59 Woolf, 26 October 1940, *Diary*, V, 333.

60 Virginia Woolf, 'The Leaning Tower', *Essays*, VI, 259–278.

61 Woolf, 25 September 1927, *Diary*, III, 158.

62 Woolf, 5 January 1918, *Diary*, I, 100.

63 Woolf, 29 October 1940, *Diary*, V, 334; 31 May 1940, *Diary*, V, 290.

64 Woolf, 23 November 1940, *Diary*, V, 341.

65 Woolf, 20 June 1940, *Diary*, V, 297.

66 Woolf, 29 October 1940, *Diary*, V, 334; 20 June 1940, *Diary*, V, 297.

67 Woolf, 25 May 1940, *Diary*, V, 288.

68 Woolf, 31 May 1940, *Diary*, V, 290; 5 July 1940, *Diary*, V, 301.

69 Woolf, 3 June 1940, *Diary*, V, 292.

70 Woolf, 'The Leaning Tower', *Essays*, 259–278.

71 Virginia Woolf to Ethel Smythe, 25 September 1940, *Letters*, VI, 434; 24 July 1940, *Diary*, V, 303.

72 Virginia Woolf, *Between the Acts* (Oxford World's Classics, 1992), 41.

73 Woolf, 12 July 1940, *Diary*, V, 301.

74 Woolf, 24 July 1940, *Diary*, V, 303.

75 Woolf, 12 July 1940, *Diary*, V, 301.

76 Woolf, 29 May 1940, *Diary*, V, 288.

77 Woolf, 29 May 1940, *Diary*, V, 288. Also Jones, *Virginia Woolf: Ambivalent Activist*, 154–207.

78 Virginia Woolf to Ethel Smythe, 11 September 1940, *Letters*, VI, 430.

79 Woolf, 1 October 1920, *Diary*, II, 71.

80 Virginia Woolf to Lady Simon, 25 January 1941, *Letters*, VI, 464.

81 Woolf, 15 April 1939, *Diary*, V, 215.

82 Virginia Woolf to Ethel Smythe, 7 June 1938, *Letters*, VI, 235.

83 Woolf, 16 December 1940, *Diary*, V, 343; 23 November 1940, *Diary*, V, 340.

84 Woolf, 1 November 1940, *Diary*, V, 334.

85 Woolf, 24 July 1940, *Diary*, V, 303.

86 Woolf, 5 November 1940, *Diary*, V, 336.

87 Woolf, 6 September 1939, *Diary*, V, 234; 19 December 1938, *Diary*, V, 193.

88 Woolf, 26 April 1938, *Diary*, V, 135.

89 Woolf, 31 May 1940, *Diary*, V, 290.

90 Woolf, *Between the Acts*, 6.

91 Woolf, *Between the Acts*, 49, 3–4.

92 Woolf, *Between the Acts*, 194.

93 Woolf, 12 April 1938, *Diary*, V, 133.

94 Woolf, *Between the Acts*, 108.

95 Woolf, *Between the Acts*, 141.

96 Woolf, *Between the Acts*, 155.

97 Woolf, *Between the Acts*, 172.

98 Woolf, *Between the Acts*, 85.

99 Woolf, *Between the Acts*, 178.

100 Woolf, *Between the Acts*, 177.

101 Woolf, *Between the Acts*, 121.

102 Woolf, *Between the Acts*, 173.

103 Woolf, *Between the Acts*, 63, 100.

104 Woolf, *Between the Acts*, 90.

105 Woolf, *Between the Acts*, 60.

106 Woolf, 8 September 1918, *Diary*, I, 190.

107 Woolf, as quoted in Mark Hussey, *The Singing of the Real World: The Philosophy of Virginia Woolf's Fiction* (Ohio State University Press, 1986), 153; and Maud Ellmann, 'Everyday War: Sylvia Townsend Warner and Virginia Woolf in World War II', *Novel*, Volume 50, Issue 1 (2017), 77–96 (91).

108 Woolf, 7 November 1928, *Diary*, III, 203; 18 June 1927, *Diary*, III, 139.

109 Woolf, 'Sketch of the Past', *Moments of Being*, 85.

110 Woolf, 'The Moment: Summer's Night', *Essays*, VI, 510; 26 April 1938, *Diary*, V, 135.

111 Woolf, 7 February 1940, *Diary*, V, 263.

112 Woolf, 10 September 1928, *Diary*, III, 195.

113 Woolf, 'The Death of the Moth', *Essays*, VI, 442.

114 Sylvia Townsend Warner to Paul Nordoff, 14 July 1939, *Letters*, 54.

115 Sylvia Townsend Warner to William Maxwell, 30 September 1939, *Letters*, 55.

116 Sylvia Townsend Warner to Steven Clark, 11 May 1938, *Letters*, 51.

117 Sylvia Townsend Warner to William Maxwell, 22 April 1972, *Letters*, 258.

118 Warner, Narrative 8, *I'll Stand by You*, 164.

119 Warner, 25 October 1939, manuscript diary, Dorset.

120 Warner, 25 October 1939, manuscript diary, Dorset.

121 Warner, Narrative 8, *I'll Stand by You*, 163.

122 Sylvia Townsend Warner to Valentine Ackland, (April) 1940, *I'll Stand by You*, 183.

123 Warner, Narrative 9, *I'll Stand by You*, 185.

124 Sylvia Townsend Warner to Paul Nordoff, 17 October 1940, *Letters*, 66.

125 Sylvia Townsend Warner to Paul Nordoff, 28 July 1941, *Letters*, 72.

126 Sylvia Townsend Warner to Paul Nordoff, 28 July 1941, *Letters*, 72.

127 Warner, 17 June 1940, *Diaries*, 105.

128 Warner, 20 June 1940, *Diaries*, 106.

129 Warner, 15 June 1940, *Diaries*, 104.

130 Sylvia Townsend Warner to Paul Nordoff, 16 March 1940, *Letters*, 61.

131 Warner, 14 June 1940, *Diaries*, 104.

132 Warner, 18 June 1940, *Diaries*, 105.

133 Sylvia Townsend Warner to Paul Nordoff, 17 November 1940, *Letters*, 68.

134 Sylvia Townsend Warner to Paul Nordoff, 27 February 1941, *Letters*, 70.

135 Warner, Narrative 9, *I'll Stand by You*, 186.

136 Warner, Narrative 9, *I'll Stand by You*, 186.

137 Sylvia Townsend Warner to Nancy Cunard, 28 April 1944, *Letters*, 84.

138 Warner, Narrative 9, *I'll Stand by You*, 186.

139 Sylvia Townsend Warner to Paul Nordoff, 9 April 1942, *Letters*, 80.

140 Warner, 22 March 1941, *Diaries*, 108.

141 Warner, 10 December 1940, *Diaries*, 106.

142 Sylvia Townsend Warner to Steven Clark, 3 February 1940, *Letters*, 59.

143 Sylvia Townsend Warner to Paul Nordoff, 5 September 1941, *Letters*, 74; 30 May 1940, *Letters*, 62.

144 Sylvia Townsend Warner to Paul Nordoff, 9 April 1942, *Letters*, 80.

145 Sylvia Townsend Warner to Paul Nordoff, 17 November 1940, *Letters*, 68.

146 Sylvia Townsend Warner, notes accompanying 'Three Day Books, Dorchester Rural District W.V.S.', 1973, Dorset.

147 Sylvia Townsend Warner to Nancy Cunard, 26 June 1944, *Letters*, 86.

148 Warner, 10 February 1942, *Diaries*, 115.

149 Warner, 10 February 1942, *Diaries*, 115; 24 February 1942, *Diaries*, 117.

150 Warner, 22 January 1942, *Diaries*, 113.

151 Warner, 22 January 1942, *Diaries*, 113.

152 Warner, 23 January 1942, *Diaries*, 113.

153 Warner, entry dated 25 April 1945, 'Three Day Books, Dorchester Rural District W.V.S.', Dorset.

154 Sylvia Townsend Warner to Bea Howe, 4 December 1941, *Letters*, 75.

155 As they appeared in *The New Yorker*: 'Rainbow Villa', 18 October 1941; 'England, Home and Beauty', 10 October 1942; 'It's What We're Here For', 20 February 1943. In her detailed account of Warner's wartime short stories, particularly those published in *A Garland of Straw*

(1943) and *The Museum of Cheats* (1947), Judith Stinton details the extent of Warner's involvement with the community of Maiden Newton, and uncovers the real-life precedents for people and places. Stinton, 'At War: Sylvia Townsend Warner and Maiden Newton', *The Journal of the Sylvia Townsend Warner Society*, Volume 19, Issue 1–2 (2020), 77–89.

156 Warner, 12 March 1942, *Diaries*, 119.

157 Sylvia Townsend Warner, 'English Climate', *Museum of Cheats* (Chatto & Windus, 1947), 56.

158 Warner, Narrative 9, *I'll Stand by You*, 187.

159 Warner, Narrative 9, *I'll Stand by You*, 189.

160 Warner, 14 February 1942, *Diaries*, 116.

161 Sylvia Townsend Warner to Bea Howe, 4 December 1941, *Letters*, 74.

162 Sylvia Townsend Warner to Paul Nordoff, 9 April 1942, *Letters*, 78.

163 Warner, 11 March 1942, *Diaries*, 119.

164 Warner, 29 March 1942, *Diaries*, 120; 31 March 1942, *Diaries*, 121.

165 Warner, 31 May 1942, *Diaries*, 124.

166 Sylvia Townsend Warner to Paul Nordoff, 1 June 1940, *Letters*, 63.

167 Sylvia Townsend Warner to Bea Howe, 4 December 1941, *Letters*, 75.

168 Warner, 20 January 1942, *Diaries*, 112; 17 February 1942, *Diaries*, 116.

169 Warner, 15 April 1942, *Diaries*, 121.

170 Sylvia Townsend Warner to Harold Raymond, 14 November 1942, *Letters*, 81.

171 Warner, 1 July 1942, *Diaries*, 125.

172 Sylvia Townsend Warner to Elling Aanestad, 14 February 1942, in Harman, *Sylvia Townsend Warner*, 193.

173 Warner, in Rosemary Sykes, ' "This was a Lesson in History": Sylvia Townsend Warner, George Townsend Warner and the Matter of History', *Critical Essays on Sylvia Townsend Warner: English Novelist 1893–1978*, eds. Gill Davies, David Malcolm and John Simons (Edwin Mellen Press, 2006), 105–112 (105).

174 Warner, in Donald Ogden Stewart, *Fighting Words* (Harcourt Brace, 1940), 53.

175 Sylvia Townsend Warner to Steven Clark, 3 February 1940, *Letters*, 60.

176 Warner, 14 June 1940, *Diaries*, 104.

177 Sylvia Townsend Warner to Paul Nordoff, 9 April 1942, *Letters*, 79.

178 Warner, 28 March 1942, *Diaries*, 120.

179 Warner, 21 February 1942, *Diaries*, 117.

180 Warner, 21 February 1942, *Diaries*, 117.

181 Sylvia Townsend Warner, 'Notes on *The Corner That Held Them*, 1977', Dorset.

182 Sylvia Townsend Warner, *The Corner That Held Them* (1946; Virago, 1988), 7.

183 Warner, *The Corner That Held Them*, 32.

184 Warner, *The Corner That Held Them*, 7.

185 Warner, *The Corner That Held Them*, 91.

186 Warner, *The Corner That Held Them*, 34.

187 Warner, *The Corner That Held Them*, 5.

188 Warner, *The Corner That Held Them*, 183.

189 Warner, *The Corner That Held Them*, 184, 183.

190 Warner, *The Corner That Held Them*, 8.

191 'Sylvia Townsend Warner in Conversation', *PN Review* 23, Volume 8, Issue 3, 36.

192 Warner, *The Corner That Held Them*, 95.

193 Warner, *The Corner That Held Them*, 80.

194 Warner, *The Corner That Held Them*, 245.

195 Warner, 9 December 1927, *Diaries*, 6.

196 Warner, *The Corner That Held Them*, 204. Also Ellmann, 'Everyday War', 88.

197 Warner, *The Corner That Held Them*, 6.

198 Sylvia Townsend Warner to Paul Nordoff, 5 January 1946, *Letters*, 91.

199 Warner, notes accompanying 'Three Day Books, Dorchester Rural District W.V.S.', Dorset.

200 Eileen Power, *Medieval People* (Methuen, 1963), 19. Also Light, *Mrs Woolf and the Servants*, 199; and Francesca Wade, 'A Good Convent Should Have No History', *Paris Review*, 6 February 2020, https://www.theparisreview.org/blog/2020/02/06/a-good-convent-should-have-no-history/, accessed 20 October 2022.

201 Woolf, *Between the Acts*, 132.

202 Woolf, 'Anon', in Silver, ' "Anon" and "The Reader" ', 382–383.

203 Woolf, *A Room of One's Own* and *Three Guineas*, 117.

204 Warner, *Lolly Willowes*, 193–194.

205 Woolf, *A Room of One's Own* and *Three Guineas*, 116.

206 Woolf, 26 April 1938, *Diary*, V, 135.

207 Woolf, 23 November 1940, *Diary*, V, 340.

208 Virginia Woolf to John Lehmann, (27?) March 1941, *Letters*, VI, 486; to Octavia Wilberforce, 31 Dec 1940, *Letters*, VI, 456.

209 Woolf, 9 January 1941, *Diary*, V, 351.

210 Woolf, 31 August 1940, *Diary*, V, 314.

211 Woolf, 2 September 1940, *Diary*, V, 315.

212 Woolf, 26 February 1941, *Diary*, V, 357.

213 Woolf, 20 April 1925, *Diary*, III, 11.

214 Woolf, 8 March 1941, *Diary*, V, 358.

215 Woolf, 14 June 1925, *Diary*, III, 29.

216 Woolf, 8 March 1941, *Diary*, V, 358.

217 Rosamond Lehmann reviewing *Between the Acts* in *The New Statesman and Nation*, 3 March 1945, BL.

218 Warner, 26 January 1942, *Diaries*, 113.

219 Sylvia Townsend Warner to Ben Huebsch, 21 December 1944, *Letters*, 88.

220 Sylvia Townsend Warner to Nancy Cunard, 9 June 1944, *Letters*, 85.

221 Sylvia Townsend Warner, 31 July 1949, manuscript exercise book, Dorset History Centre.

Hauntings

1 Rosamond Lehmann to John Lehmann, 16 May 1945, HRHRC.

2 On the event of Cecil's death in 1972, Rosamond argued with Elizabeth Jane Howard, who, in writing Cecil's obituary for the *Sunday Times*, relegated Rosamond to a footnote – an ' "emotional involvement" ' – in his life story. 'He broke our vows and laid waste my life,' Rosamond hit back defensively. 'I am no longer able to be proud, as once I was, of being "the great love of his life"; but I know what I know; and, apart from my private and personal records, which will not yet be published – I mean, not in my life time – it is reflected

in his poetry.' Rosamond Lehmann to Elizabeth Jane Howard, as reported to Laurie Lee, n/d (1972), BL.

3 Items listed in catalogue for auction, 'Sale of High-Class Furnishings, Carpets, China Etc.', Merchants Place, Friar Street, Reading, 5 August 1954, KCC. ('More and more I hate possessions,' Rosamond wrote to her brother, John. 'When their sentimental point has gone they can only be burdens on the spirit, and remind me of hopes and schemes that now must for ever be discarded.' Rosamond Lehmann to John Lehmann, n/d, HRHRC.)

4 Lehmann, *Writing Lives*, 156.

5 Lehmann, *Writing Lives*, 156.

6 Rosamond Lehmann, *The Echoing Grove* (1953; Collins, 1984), 14.

7 'We are dealing here, I would suggest, with chronological and psychological time which do not entirely coincide.' Gillian Tindall, *Rosamond Lehmann: An Appreciation* (Chatto & Windus, 1985), 164.

8 Lehmann, *The Weather in the Streets*, 144.

9 Rosamond Lehmann to Rayner Heppenstall, 27 September 1958, HRHRC.

10 Lehmann, *The Echoing Grove*, 16.

11 Lehmann, *The Echoing Grove*, 306–307.

12 Lehmann, *The Swan in the Evening*, 114, 115.

13 Lehmann, *The Swan in the Evening*, 94.

14 Lehmann, *The Swan in the Evening*, 95.

15 Lehmann, *The Swan in the Evening*, 87.

16 Lehmann, *The Swan in the Evening*, 129.

17 Sylvia Townsend Warner, manuscript notebook, 'Garden 1969', Dorset.

18 Warner, 3 July 1961, *Diaries*, 273.

19 Warner, 'Garden 1969', manuscript notebook, Dorset.

20 Warner, 17 November 1969, *Diaries*, 331.

21 Warner, 23 July 1960, *Diaries*, 265.

22 Warner, 9 January 1970, *Diaries*, 336.

23 Warner, 9 December 1969, *Diaries*, 334.

24 Sylvia Townsend Warner, 24 September 1972, manuscript diary, Dorset.

25 Sylvia Townsend Warner to Marchette and Joy Chute, 27 November 1969, *Letters*, 244.

26 Warner, 9 January 1970, *Diaries*, 336.

27 Warner, 22 May 1970, *Diaries*, 345.

28 Warner, 'Garden 1969', manuscript notebook, Dorset.

29 Sylvia Townsend Warner, 4 June 1957, manuscript diary, Dorset. With thanks to Ailsa Granne for the quotation.

30 Warner, 20 November 1969, *Diaries*, 331.

31 With thanks to Claire Harman for showing me her 'Warner clobber', including the Paisley dress, her chest, 'Mrs Johnson' the prayer book, and her gardening hat.

32 Sylvia Townsend Warner to Alyse Gregory, n/d, in Harman, *Sylvia Townsend Warner*, 268.

33 Warner, 31 December 1951, *Diaries*, 184.

34 Warner, 12 October 1970, *Diaries*, 349.

35 Sylvia Townsend Warner to William Maxwell, *The Element of Lavishness: Letters of Sylvia Townsend Warner and William Maxwell, 1938–1978*, ed. Michael Steinman (Counterpoint, 2004), 216.

36 Sylvia Townsend Warner in conversation with Val Warner and Michael Schmidt in 1975, *With the Hunted*, 399–406 (402–403).

37 Sylvia Townsend Warner to Rosamond Lehmann, 29 January 1975, KCC.

38 Sylvia Townsend Warner to Rosamond Lehmann, 25 February 1975, KCC.

39 Sylvia Townsend Warner to Rosamond Lehmann, 12 January 1977, KCC.

40 Sylvia Townsend Warner, 'The Five Black Swans', *Kingdoms of Elfin* (1977; Handheld Press, 2018), 23.

41 Woolf, 24 March 1932, *Diary*, IV, 85.

Select Bibliography

Ackland, Valentine, *Country Conditions* (Lawrence & Wishart, 1936).

— *For Sylvia: An Honest Account* (Chatto & Windus, 1985).

— *Journey from Winter: Selected Poems*, ed. Frances Bingham (Carcanet, 2008).

Alexander, Neal, and James Moran, eds., *Regional Modernisms* (Edinburgh University Press, 2013).

Alt, Christina, *Virginia Woolf and the Study of Nature* (Cambridge University Press, 2010).

Baldwin, Stanley, *On England and Other Addresses* (Philip Allan, 1926).

Barrett, Michèle, *Virginia Woolf: On Women and Writing* (The Women's Press, 1979).

Barrett, Michèle, 'Virginia Woolf's Research for *Empire and Commerce in Africa* (Leonard Woolf, 1920)', *Woolf Studies Annual*, Volume 19 (2013), 83–122.

Beaton, Cecil, *Air of Glory: A Wartime Scrapbook* (His Majesty's Stationery Office, 1941).

Beer, Gillian, *Darwin's Plots: Evolutionary Narrative in Darwin, George Eliot and Nineteenth-Century Fiction* (Cambridge University Press, 1983).

— *Virginia Woolf: The Common Ground* (Edinburgh University Press, 1996).

Bell, Anne Olivier, *Editing Virginia Woolf's Diary* (The Perpetua Press, 1989).

Bluemel, Kristin and Michael McClusky, eds., *Rural Modernity in Britain: A Critical Intervention* (Edinburgh University Press, 2018).

Blythe, Ian, 'Woolf, Rooks, and Rural England', *Woolfian Boundaries, Selected Papers from the Sixteenth Annual Conference on Virginia Woolf*, eds. Anna Burrells, Steve Ellis, Deborah Parsons and Kathryn Simpson (Clemson University Digital Press, 2006), 80–85.

Bowen, Elizabeth, *Listening In: Broadcasts, Speeches and Interviews*, ed. Allan Hepburn (Edinburgh University Press, 2010).

— *The Heat of the Day* (1949; Vintage, 1998).

— *Pictures and Conversations* (Allen Lane, 1975).

Bowlby, Rachel, *Everyday Stories* (Oxford University Press, 2016).

Brassley, Paul, Jeremy Burchardt and Lynne Thompson, eds., *The English Countryside Between the Wars: Regeneration or Decline?* (The Boydell Press, 2006).

Briggs, Julia, *Virginia Woolf: An Inner Life* (Allen Lane, 2005).

Brooks-Motl, Hannah, ' "From the Middle Distance": Sylvia Townsend Warner's War Pastorals', *Modernism/modernity*, Volume 26, Number 2 (April 2019), 289–308.

Burchardt, Jeremy, *Paradise Lost: Rural Idyll and Social Change Since 1800* (I. B. Tauris, 2002).

Carrington, Dora, *Carrington: Letters and Extracts from her Diaries*, ed. David Garnett (Jonathan Cape, 1970).

— *Carrington's Letters: Her Art, Her Loves, Her Friendships*, ed. Anne Chisholm (Chatto & Windus, 2017).

Castle, Terry, *The Apparitional Lesbian: Female Homosexuality and Modern Culture* (Colombia University Press, 1993).

Chamberlain, Mary, ed., *Writing Lives: Conversations between Women Writers* (Virago, 1988).

Connolly, Cyril, *The Missing Diplomats* (Queen Anne Press, 1952).

Crangle, Sara, 'Out of the Archive: Woolfian Domestic Economies', *Modernism/modernity*, Volume 23, Number 1 (January 2016), 141–176.

Davies, Gill, David Malcolm and John Simons, eds., *Critical Essays on Sylvia Townsend Warner, English Novelist 1893–1978* (Edwin Mellen Press, 2006).

Doan, Laura, *Old Maids to Radical Spinsters: Unmarried Women in the Twentieth-Century Novel* (University of Illinois Press, 1991).

Doan, Laura and Jane Garrity, eds., *Sapphic Modernities: Sexuality, Woman and the National Culture* (Palgrave Macmillan, 2006).

Ellis, William, *England and the Octopus* (Council for the Protection of Rural England, 1928).

Ellmann, Maud, 'Everyday War: Sylvia Townsend Warner and Virginia Woolf in World War II', *Novel*, Volume 50, Issue 1 (2017), 77–96.

Esty, Jed, *A Shrinking Island: Modernism and National Culture in England* (Princeton University Press, 2004).

Feigel, Lara, *The Love-Charm of Bombs: Restless Lives in the Second World War* (Bloomsbury, 2013).

Felski, Rita, *Doing Time: Feminist Theory and Postmodern Culture* (New York University Press, 2000).

Ferrer, Daniel, *Virginia Woolf and the Madness of Language* (Routledge, 1990).

Froula, Christine, *Virginia Woolf and the Bloomsbury Avant-Garde: War, Civilization, Modernity* (Columbia University Press, 2005).

Garnett, David, *The Flowers of the Forest* (Chatto & Windus, 1953).

Garrity, Jane, *Step-Daughters of England: British Women Modernists and the National Imaginary* (Manchester University Press, 2012).

Gindin, James, *British Fiction in the 1930s: The Dispiriting Decade* (Macmillan, 1992).

Greenwood, Jeremy, *Omega Cuts: Woodcuts and Linocuts by Artists Associated with the Omega Workshops and the Hogarth Press* (Wood Lea Press, 1998).

Gregory, Alyse, *The Cry of a Gull: Journals 1923–48* (The Ark Press, 1973).

Grove, Valerie, *Laurie Lee: The Well-Loved Stranger* (Penguin, 2000).

Hansen, Carol, *The Life and Death of Asham: Leonard and Virginia Woolf's Haunted House* (Cecil Woolf, 2000).

Harman, Claire, *Sylvia Townsend Warner: A Biography* (Penguin, 2015).

— ed., *PN Review*, Volume 8, Number 3 (1 January 1981).

Harris, Alexandra, *Romantic Moderns: English Writers, Artists and the Imagination from Virginia Woolf to John Piper* (Thames & Hudson, 2010).

— *Virginia Woolf* (Thames & Hudson, 2011).

— *Woolf in Winter* (Virginia Woolf Society of Great Britain, 2015).

Hastings, Selina, *Rosamond Lehmann: A Life* (Chatto & Windus, 2002).

Holtby, Winifred, *Women and a Changing Civilization* (John Lane, 1934).

Howkins, Alun, *The Death of Rural England: A Social History of the Countryside since 1900* (Routledge, 2003).

Humble, Nicola, *The Feminine Middlebrow Novel, 1920s to 1950s: Class, Domesticity and Bohemianism* (Oxford University Press, 2001).

Hussey, Mark, *The Singing of the Real World: The Philosophy of Virginia Woolf's Fiction* (Ohio State University Press, 1986).

— 'I'd Make It Penal': The Rural Preservation Movement in Virginia Woolf's Between the Acts (Cecil Woolf, 2011).

Isherwood, Christopher, *Christopher and his Kind* (1976; Vintage Classics, 2012).

James, David, 'Localizing Late Modernism: Interwar Regionalism and the Genesis of the "Micro Novel"', *Journal of Modern Literature*, Volume 32, Number 4 (Summer 2009), 43–64.

Joannou, Maroula, ed., *The History of British Women's Writing, 1920–1945* (Palgrave Macmillan, 2013).

— *Women Writers of the 1930s* (Edinburgh University Press, 1999).

Jones, Clara, 'Bloomsbury's Rural Cross-Class Encounters', *The Handbook to the Bloomsbury Group* (Bloomsbury Academic, 2018).

— *Virginia Woolf: Ambivalent Activist* (Edinburgh University Press, 2016).

Knoll, Bruce, ' "An Existence Doled Out": Passive Resistance as Dead End in Sylvia Townsend Warner's *Lolly Willowes*', *Twentieth Century Literature*, Volume 39, Number 3 (Autumn, 1993), 344–363.

Kumar, Krishan, *The Making of English National Identity* (Cambridge University Press, 2003).

Lee, Hermione and Kate Kennedy, *The Lives of Houses* (Princeton University Press, 2020).

Lee, Hermione, *Virginia Woolf* (Vintage, 1997).

— ed., *The Hogarth Letters* (Chatto & Windus, 1985).

Lee, Laurie, *Land at War: The Official Story of British Farming, 1939–1944* (H.M.S.O: Ministry of Information, 1946).

Lehmann, John, *Thrown to the Woolfs* (Weidenfeld and Nicolson, 1978).

— *I Am My Brother* (Longmans, 1960).

Lehmann, Rosamond, *A Letter to a Sister*, The Hogarth Letters, No. 3 (The Hogarth Press, 1931).

— *Invitation to the Waltz* (1932; Virago, 1981).

— *A Note in Music* (1930; Virago, 1982).

— *The Weather in the Streets* (1936; Virago, 1981).

— *The Gypsy's Baby* (1946; Virago, 1982).

— *The Swan in the Evening* (1967; Virago, 1982).

— *Rosamond Lehmann's Album* (Chatto & Windus, 1987).

Lehmann, Rosamond, D. Kilham Roberts, C. Day Lewis and Edwin Muir, eds., *Orion: A Miscellany*, Volume 1 (Nicholson & Watson, 1945).

Lewis, Cecil Day, *Word over All* (Jonathan Cape, 1943).

— *The Buried Day: An Autobiography* (Chatto & Windus, 1960).

— *The Complete Poems* (Sinclair-Stevenson, 1992).

Light, Alison, *A Radical Romance* (Fig Tree, 2019).

— *Forever England, Femininity and Literature* (Routledge, 1991).

— *Composing One's Self: Virginia Woolf's Diaries and Memoirs* (Joshua Horgan, 2007, for The Virginia Woolf Society of Great Britain).

— *Mrs Woolf and the Servants* (Penguin, 2007).

Lounsberry, Barbara, *Becoming Virginia Woolf: Her Early Diaries and the Diaries She Read* (University Press of Florida, 2014).

Love, Heather, *Feeling Backward: Loss and the Politics of Queer History* (Harvard University Press, 2009).

MacNeice, Louis, *The Strings Are False* (Faber and Faber, 1965).

Mansfield, Katherine, *The Edinburgh Edition of the Collected Letters of Katherine Mansfield: Volume 2*, eds. Claire Davison and Gerri Kimber (Edinburgh University Press, 2022).

Marcus, Jane, 'A Wilderness of One's Own: Feminist Fantasy Novels of the Twenties: Rebecca West and Sylvia Townsend Warner', *Women Writers and the City*, ed. Susan Merrill Squier (The University of Tennessee Press, 1984).

Matless, David, *Landscape and Englishness* (Reaktion Books, 1998).

Micir, Melanie, ' "Living in two tenses": The Intimate Archives of Sylvia Townsend Warner', *Journal of Modern Literature*, Volume 36, Number 1 (Fall 2012), 119–131.

Mitchell, J. Lawrence, *T. F. Powys: Aspects of a Life* (The Brynmill Press, 2005).

Montefiore, Janet, *Men and Women Writers of the 1930s: The Dangerous Flood of History* (Routledge, 1996).

— 'Englands Ancient and Modern: Sylvia Townsend Warner, T. H. White and the Fictions of Medieval Englishness', *Intermodernism:*

Literary Culture in Mid-Twentieth-Century Britain, ed. Kristen Bluemel (Edinburgh University Press, 2009), 38–55.

— 'Sylvia Townsend Warner Scholarship 1978–2013: An Annotated Bibliography with Introduction', *Literature Compass*, Volume 11, Number 12 (2014), 786–811.

Morgan, Louise, 'Sylvia Townsend Warner: A Writer Who Follows None of the Rules', *Everyman New Series 4* (1930).

— *Writers at Work* (Chatto & Windus, 1931).

Morton, H. V., *In Search of England* (Methuen, 1944).

Mulford, Wendy, *This Narrow Place: Sylvia Townsend Warner and Valentine Ackland: Life, Letters and Politics, 1930–1951* (Pandora Press, 1988).

Mullholland, Terri, *British Boarding Houses in Interwar Women's Literature: Alternative Domestic Spaces* (Routledge, 2017).

Munton, Alan, 'Rural Radical', *The Cambridge Quarterly*, Volume 28, Number 2 (1999), 171–174.

Mutti, Lynne, 'Music, Death-in-life and Paradise in Sylvia Townsend Warner's *The Corner That Held Them*', *Postgraduate English*, Issue 29 (September 2014), 2–20.

Nesbitt, Jennifer Poulos, 'Footsteps of Red Ink: Body and Landscape in *Lolly Willowes*', *Twentieth-Century Literature*, 49 (2003), 449–471.

Neve, Christopher, *Unquiet Landscape: Places and Ideas in 20th-Century British Painting* (Thames & Hudson, 2020).

Olson, Liesl, *Modernism and the Ordinary* (Oxford University Press, 2009).

Partridge, Frances, *Everything to Lose: Diaries, 1945–1960* (Gollancz, 1985).

Philip, Neil, 'Robertson Scott and *The Countryman*', *The Journal of the Sylvia Townsend Warner Society*, Volume 9, Number 1 (2008), 24–35.

Pinney, Susannah, 'Sylvia, A Memoir', *The Journal of the Sylvia Townsend Warner Society*, Volume 18, Issue 1 (2018), 1–10.

Podnieks, Elizabeth, *Daily Modernism: The Literary Dairies of Virginia Woolf, Antonia White, Elizabeth Smart, and Anaïs Nin* (McGill-Queen's University Press, 2000).

Pollard, Wendy, *Rosamond Lehmann and Her Critics* (Routledge, 2004).

Powys, T.F., *This Is Thyself, The Powys Review*, Number Twenty (1987).

Power, Eileen, *Medieval People* (Methuen, 1963).

Randall, Bryony, *Modernism, Daily Time and Everyday Life* (Cambridge University Press, 2007).

Reed, Christopher, *Bloomsbury Rooms: Modernism, Subculture, and Domesticity* (Yale University Press, 2004).

Roach, Rebecca, ' "How Writers Work": Interviewing the Author in *Everyman*', *Textual Practice*, Volume 30, Number 4 (2016), 645–667.

Sackville-West, Vita, *The Land* (William Heinemann, 1934).

Scott, Bonnie Kime, *In the Hollow of the Wave, Virginia Woolf and Modernist Uses of Nature* (University of Virginia Press, 2012).

Scott, J.W. Robertson, *England's Green and Pleasant Land* (Jonathan Cape, 1925).

Scott-James, Anne, *Sketches from a Life* (Michael Joseph, 1993).

Shone, Richard, 'Asheham House: An Outline History', *The Charleston Magazine*, Issue 9 (Spring/Summer 1994).

— *The Art of Bloomsbury* (Tate Publishing, 1999).

Simons, Judy, *Rosamond Lehmann* (Northcote, 2011).

Silver, Brenda R., ' "Anon" and "The Reader": Virginia Woolf's Last Essays', *Twentieth Century Literature*, Volume 25, Number 3/4, Virginia Woolf Issue (Autumn–Winter, 1979), 356–441.

Snaith, Anna, *Virginia Woolf: Public and Private Negotiations* (Palgrave, 2000).

Solnit, Rebecca, *Orwell's Roses* (Granta Books, 2021).

— *Wanderlust: A History of Walking* (Granta Books, 2002).

Spalding, Frances, *Vanessa Bell* (Weidenfeld and Nicolson, 1983).

— *Roger Fry: Art and Life* (Granada, 1980).

Spender, Stephen, *World Within World: The Autobiography of Stephen Spender* (Faber, 1977).

Stinton, Judith, *Chaldon Herring: The Powys Circle in a Dorset Village* (The Boydell Press, 1988).

— *Chaldon Herring: Writers in a Dorset Landscape* (Black Dog Books, 2004).

— 'At War: Sylvia Townsend Warner and Maiden Newton', *The Journal of the Sylvia Townsend Warner Society*, Volume 19, Issue 1–2 (2020), 77–89.

Swaab, Peter, 'The Queerness of *Lolly Willowes*', *The Journal of the Sylvia Townsend Warner Society*, Volume 11, Number 1 (2010), 35–37.

— 'Sylvia's Similes: A Stylistic Approach to Sylvia Townsend Warner', *Literature Compass*, Volume 11, Number 12 (2014), 767–775.

— 'Sylvia Townsend Warner and the Possibilities of Freedom: The Sylvia Townsend Warner Society Lecture 2019', *The Journal of the Sylvia Townsend Warner Society*, Volume 20, Number 1 (2020), 63–88.

Tindall, Gillian, *Rosamond Lehmann: An Appreciation* (Chatto & Windus, 1985).

Tolhurst, Peter, *Virginia Woolf's English Hours* (Black Dog Books, 2015).

Trotter, David, '"My Usual Despicable Hold on Life": The View from Sylvia Townsend Warner's Diaries (The Sylvia Townsend Warner Society Lecture 2021)', *The Journal of the Sylvia Townsend Warner Society*, Volume 21, Number 2 (June 2022), 97–123.

— 'The Ultimate Socket', *London Review of Books*, Volume 44, Number 12 (23 June 2022), 3–8.

Untermeyer, Jean Starr, *Private Collection* (Alfred A. Knopf, 1965).

Wade, Francesca, 'A Good Convent Should Have No History', *Paris Review*, 6 February 2020, <https://www.theparisreview.org/blog/2020/02/06/a-good-convent-should-have-no-history/.

— *Square Haunting: Five Women, Freedom and London between the Wars* (Faber and Faber, 2020).

Warner, Sylvia Townsend, *I'll Stand by You: The Letters of Sylvia Townsend Warner & Valentine Ackland*, ed. Susanna Pinney (Pimlico, 1998).

— *Lolly Willowes* (1926; Virago, 2012).

— *The True Heart* (1929; Virago, 1978).

— *Opus 7* (Chatto & Windus, 1931).

— *Summer Will Show* (1936; Virago, 1987).

— 'The Historical Novel' (1939), in Donald Ogden Stewart, *Fighting Words* (Harcourt, Brace and Company, 1940).

— *The Corner That Held Them* (1946; Virago, 1988).

— *Scenes of Childhood* (Viking, 1982).

— *The Letters of Sylvia Townsend Warner*, ed. William Maxwell (Chatto & Windus, 1982).

— *The Diaries of Sylvia Townsend Warner*, ed. Claire Harman (Chatto & Windus, 1994).

— *With the Hunted, Selected Writings*, ed. Peter Tolhurst (Black Dog Books, 2012).

— 'The Unfinished Sequel to *The Corner That Held Them* (Part 1 of 2)', *The Journal of the Sylvia Townsend Warner Society*, Volume 20, Issue 1 (2020), 8–39.

Westling, Louise, 'Virginia Woolf and the Flesh of the World', *New Literary History*, Volume 30, Number 4 (Autumn 1999), 855–875.

Williams, Raymond, *The City and the Country* (Oxford University Press, 1975).

Wilson, Frances, *The Ballad of Dorothy Wordsworth* (Faber and Faber, 2008).

Woolf, Leonard, *Growing: An Autobiography of the Years 1904–1911* (The Hogarth Press, 1961).

— *Beginning Again: An Autobiography of the Years 1911–1918* (The Hogarth Press, 1964).

Woolf, L. & V., *New Signatures* (The Hogarth Press, 1934).

Woolf, Virginia, *A Passionate Apprentice: The Early Journals, 1897–1909*, ed. Mitchell A. Leaska (Chatto & Windus, 1990).

— *The Voyage Out* (1915; Oxford World's Classics, 2009).

— *Night and Day* (1919; Oxford World's Classics, 2009).

— *Walter Sickert: A Conversation* (The Hogarth Press, 1934).

— *A Room of One's Own and Three Guineas* (Penguin Classics, 2019).

— *Between the Acts*, ed. Mark Hussey (1941; Cambridge University Press, 2011).

— *Moments of Being: Autobiographical Writings*, ed. Jeanne Schulkind (Pimlico, 2002).

— *A Haunted House: The Complete Shorter Fiction*, ed. Susan Dick (Vintage Classics, 2003).

— *The Diary of Virginia Woolf*, eds. Anne Olivier Bell and Andrew McNeillie, 5 volumes (The Hogarth Press, 1977–1984; Granta, 2023).

— *The Letters of Virginia Woolf*, ed. Nigel Nicholson, assisted by Joanne Trautmann, 6 volumes (The Hogarth Press, 1975–1980).

— *The Essays of Virginia Woolf*, eds. Andrew McNeillie and Stuart N. Clarke, 5 volumes (The Hogarth Press, 1986–2011).

Acknowledgements

I owe the greatest thanks to my agent, Harriet Moore, without whom this book would not have come into existence. To Chloe Currens, my editor at Penguin, for showing such an early interest in the project, and for her subsequent wisdom and understanding. To Thea Tuck, and the rest of the team at Penguin, for their invaluable help with everything else.

Thanks to Ariane Bankes and all at The Biographers' Club, and to readers Alex Clark, Lindsay Duguid and Edmund Gordon, for awarding me the 2018 Tony Lothian Prize. The award set the book in motion.

Thanks to archivists at the Dorset History Centre, the Beinecke Rare Book & Manuscript Library at Yale University, The Keep at the University of Sussex, the Berg Collection at the New York Public Library, the Harry Ransom Center at the University of Texas, Durham University Library, the British Library, Princeton University Library, the University of Reading, and the Archive Centre at King's College, Cambridge.

To Alison Light, who helped shape my thinking about Virginia Woolf through both her friendship and her books. To Michèle Barrett, Richard Shone and Virginia Nicholson, for their generosity and expertise. To SW, for helping me to see the entangled bank, and so much more. To the Paul Mellon Centre, for supporting my research in New York.

To Clara Jones, who led me to Sylvia Townsend Warner. To Claire Harman, Susannah Pinney, Janet Montefiore and Peter Swaab, whose enthusiasm for her writing is infectious. To all at the Sylvia Townsend Warner Society, for such brilliant discussions.

To Roland Phillips, Selina Hastings, Gillian Tindall and the late Carmen Callil, who all knew Rosamond Lehmann and gave me insight into her character and her life. To Kate Miller, who showed me around Ipsden House, and to Heather Macaulay, former landlady at The Bell Inn, for village gossip.

To Scott McCracken and Suzanne Hobson, for their patience as I doggedly wrote a book rather than a PhD. To Brian Dillon and Alexandra Harris, for reading the manuscript and appreciating what it was I was trying to do.

To my parents, Oliver and Charlotte, my siblings, Toby and Amy, and my parents-in-law, David and Christine, for endless encouragement and support. To Harriet Moore, who belongs here, too, for sharing art-making and motherhood with me. Lastly, to Mike, for our talk, our books, and our baby; and all the daily, hidden treasure which makes a life.

Index